Eve Arden

ALSO BY DAVID C. TUCKER
AND FROM McFARLAND

*Lost Laughs of '50s and '60s Television:
Thirty Sitcoms That Faded Off Screen* (2010)

Shirley Booth: A Biography and Career Record (2008)

*The Women Who Made Television Funny:
Ten Stars of 1950s Sitcoms* (2007)

Eve Arden

*A Chronicle of All Film,
Television, Radio and
Stage Performances*

DAVID C. TUCKER

McFarland & Company, Inc., Publishers
Jefferson, North Carolina, and London

LIBRARY OF CONGRESS CATALOGUING-IN-PUBLICATION DATA

Tucker, David C., 1962–
Eve Arden : a chronicle of all film, television,
radio and stage performances / David C. Tucker.
p. cm.
Includes bibliographical references and index.

ISBN 978-0-7864-6131-8
softcover : 50# alkaline paper ∞

1. Arden, Eve, 1912–1990.
2. Actors—United States—Biography.
I. Title.
PN2287.A684T83 2012   792.02'8092—dc23   [B]   2011037851

BRITISH LIBRARY CATALOGUING DATA ARE AVAILABLE

© 2012 David C. Tucker. All rights reserved

*No part of this book may be reproduced or transmitted in any form
or by any means, electronic or mechanical, including photocopying
or recording, or by any information storage and retrieval system,
without permission in writing from the publisher.*

On the cover: Eve Arden, © 2012 Photofest/National Broadcasting
Company (NBC); background image © 2012 Shutterstock

Manufactured in the United States of America

*McFarland & Company, Inc., Publishers
Box 611, Jefferson, North Carolina 28640
www.mcfarlandpub.com*

To my friend Lynn Kear,
exactly the sort of smart, accomplished,
and witty woman that Eve so often played.

Acknowledgments

I'm indebted to several people who made valuable contributions to this project. Film historian Richard Barrios generously provided information on Eve's film debut, *The Song of Love*. Fredrick Tucker shared several photos from his own collection, and assisted with compiling credits for guest players on *Our Miss Brooks*. As always, Ken McCullers was a top-flight proofreader. The staff and collections at the University of Georgia Libraries were invaluable, as they have been on my previous books.

Special thanks to my mother, Louise Tucker, and to many good friends and family members whose support and encouragement I appreciate. I'm grateful for my friends and colleagues at the DeKalb County Public Library as well, who have been so supportive of my goals as a writer.

Table of Contents

Acknowledgments — vi
Preface — 1

I. Biography — 3
II. Filmography — 39
III. Television Performances — 139
   Our Miss Brooks — 139
   The Eve Arden Show — 156
   The Mothers-in-Law — 158
   Guest Appearances — 167
IV. Broadway Performances — 185

Bibliography — 187
Index — 191

Preface

Eve Arden had a face, and certainly a voice, that was completely distinctive and instantly recognizable to audiences. Some know her best as Connie Brooks, the warm-hearted but wisecracking schoolteacher on the long-running radio and TV comedy *Our Miss Brooks*. Others remember her as the Oscar-nominated character actress who appeared in more than 60 motion pictures from 1929 to 1982, notably as the loyal but plain-spoken best friend to Joan Crawford in *Mildred Pierce*. And a later generation may think of her first and foremost as the hapless school principal Miss McGee in *Grease*. Eve herself was particularly fond of working in the theater, and took pride in her stage work on Broadway, in summer stock, and wherever else interesting roles presented themselves.

For many, her most distinctive trait was her ability to snap out a witty, sardonic line with impeccable timing. Even today, when a movie or television show features a smart, slightly caustic, stylish woman, reviewers are likely to call that character an Eve Arden type. Said Leonard Maltin, profiling her in *Leonard Maltin's Movie Encyclopedia*, "If this tall, attractive blonde didn't exactly invent the character of the leading lady's sardonic, wisecracking, and usually dateless best friend, she certainly set the standard for all the others."

I first wrote about the marvelous Eve Arden, one of my favorite actresses, in *The Women Who Made Television Funny: Ten Stars of 1950s Sitcoms* (McFarland, 2007). Her chapter in that book focused primarily on her starring role in *Our Miss Brooks*, placing her context alongside her fellow female sitcom stars of early television, such as Lucille Ball, Joan Davis, and Donna Reed. Now, with the luxury of devoting a full-length book to her work, I have been able to delve more deeply into a career that is truly impressive not only in its length but its variety.

This book begins with an overview of her career, which lasted for some 60 years and was noteworthy for her mastery of virtually every entertainment medium. Part one provides information about her radio career, as well as her many stage performances. Part two provides a detailed filmography of 62 feature films, covering a period from 1929 to 1982. Each entry provides a brief synopsis of the film, and of Eve's role within it, as well as critical commentary. Excerpts from published reviews are provided as well.

Part three covers the actress's extensive career in television. Included are episode guides not only for *Our Miss Brooks* but also her two later sitcoms, *The Eve Arden Show* (1957–1958) and *The Mothers-in-Law* (1967–1969). In addition, the book documents more than 70 one-time appearances in television dramatic, variety, and talk shows, as well as the unsold series pilots that aired as TV specials.

Eve herself said on more than one occasion that she became typecast in films, and wasn't permitted to display the full range of her talents. "I wanted to play the kind of comedy parts offered to Irene Dunne and Rosalind Russell," she told journalist Jim Bawden in an interview for the *Toronto Star* (February 2, 1991). "Instead, Mr. [Jack] Warner used me as what he called his back door insurance. I was always in the back of the picture and whenever it got boring I'd come forward with a few wisecracks."

While this was a valid complaint, especially during her seven years as a Warner Bros. contract player (from 1944 to 1951), a review of her entire film output shows clearly that she not only could, but did, play a variety of types. Those who know her film work for little more than her roles in *Mildred Pierce* and *Grease* might be surprised to see that she also played the ruthless leader of an Old West gang (*Last of the Duanes*), a husband-stealing chorus girl (*The Song of Love*), a small-town lawyer (*She Couldn't Say No*), a world-weary clip joint hostess (*Manpower*), a glamorous French music-hall singer (*Night and Day*), and even an unhappily married bigot (*The Dark at the Top of the Stairs*). Contrary to the popular view that she played only frustrated career women who couldn't land a man, she in fact plays married women in *My Reputation*, *Let's Face It*, *Three Husbands*, *The Lady Wants Mink*, *Under the Rainbow*, and (despite the title) *We're Not Married!* Perhaps the only type of woman Eve seldom, if ever, played, was a stupid one. Even if her characters lacked formal education, her keen intelligence was nearly always evident in any performance.

After years of best-friending notable leading ladies of the movies, among them Joan Crawford, Doris Day, Barbara Stanwyck, Jane Wyman, and Lizabeth Scott, Eve herself became the top-billed star when she took the title role in *Our Miss Brooks*. She achieved perhaps her greatest fame (not to mention an Emmy Award) with this popular series, which lasted eight years on radio and television, and continued to be a staple in syndicated reruns long beyond that. The role of Constance Brooks, everyone's favorite English teacher, set Eve apart. As Jefferson Graham would write for a memorial tribute that appeared in *USA Today*, "Virtually every other woman on early TV was a homemaker and a mother. But Miss Brooks was a single working woman, the model for future TV women like Rhoda, Mary Richards and Murphy Brown" (November 13, 1990).

As indicated by the title, the focus here is on Miss Arden's professional career, which in itself handily fills a book. While the basics of her personal life—an unsuccessful first marriage, followed by a long-lasting one with actor/artist Brooks West, as well as mothering four children—are covered here, her autobiography, *Three Phases of Eve*, published in 1985, is enthusiastically recommended to those wanting to know more about her private life.

Having spent many pleasurable hours watching Eve Arden at work, I can only concur with critic Gerald Nachman's assessment in the *San Francisco Chronicle*, published shortly after her death in 1990: "Arden had a long, beloved, relaxed, much too undervalued career. There was never nearly enough of Eve Arden to go around. Let's name a high school after her" (December 23, 1990). Until that worthy goal is attained, this book will have to suffice as a tribute to one of Hollywood's most memorable, hard-working, and talented actresses.

I

Biography

I don't believe in looking at the past. I was born in Newark, New Jersey. Every time I go through on a train, I pull down the shade.
— Eve, as "Woody" in *Goodbye, My Fancy*

The future Eve Arden was born Eunice M. Quedens on April 30, 1908, in Mill Valley, California, daughter of Charles Peter Quedens and Lucille Frank Quedens. Due to Mr. Quedens's gambling habit, the couple was divorced while their only child was still a toddler, leaving young Eunice to be raised by her mother. Mother and daughter left Mill Valley for nearby San Francisco, occupying an apartment on the top floor of the house owned by Eunice's maternal grandmother, Louisa Frank.

The ex–Mrs. Quedens, who had herself worked briefly as an actress, supported herself and her daughter by opening a hat shop. The business venture was a successful one, but required Mrs. Quedens to work long hours and allowed her limited time to spend with Eunice. Left to her own devices for several hours each day, young Eunice indulged her imagination and her creativity to keep herself entertained.

By the age of seven, Eunice had learned that she enjoyed the spotlight. In a November 1957 article for the syndicated *Parade* magazine, Eve recalled the day she was called upon by her second-grade teacher to recite a poem. A shy child, she reluctantly made her way to the front of the classroom, where she launched into a bit of doggerel called "No Kicka My Dog," about an immigrant and the lowly mutt that befriends him.

> As the emotion of the poem built up, a strange thing happened. A chubby little girl with long yellow pigtails suddenly burst into heart-rending sobs. My recital had filled her with loud, overflowing compassion for the poor immigrant and his brave dog. Those sobs were music to my ears ... for the first time in my life I felt that intangible reward which every performer hopes for—the sense of having fully captured an audience's heart.

Another recitation won her a gold medal in a competition staged by the Women's Christian Temperance Union. Having been introduced to the world of the theater by her mother, Eunice often staged plays for children in the neighborhood, the attic of her grandmother's San Francisco house serving as her performance space.

After two years attending a convent school, she moved back to suburban Mill Valley, California, where she lived with her aunt while continuing her education. In high school, she began to appear in school plays, snagging the lead in Tamalpais High's production of

Dulcy, the early 1920s George S. Kaufman/Marc Connelly comedy. She graduated from Tamalpais High School in 1926, uncertain as to what lay ahead for her. Though her most famous character, radio and TV's *Our Miss Brooks*, would embody the value of higher education, Eunice's own formal education ended with her graduation from the 12th grade.

Some family friends who had noted her interest, and acumen, for performing invited her to dinner, and then dropped her off unexpectedly at the stage door of the San Francisco Theater where Henry Duffy's stock company was performing. The teenager was told to go inside and get herself a job. Duffy was an established professional, and Eunice was intimidated by the notion of approaching him, but finally decided it was better than waiting outside in the cold for her friends to return.

As the *New York Times*'s Helen Colton would later comment in her profile, "All About Eve," "For some reason no one can figure out, the usually irascible Duffy did not send her packing with a well-aimed insult. Even after she told him her sole acting credit had been as 'Dulcy' in her Tamalpais High School senior play, he still said he might call her in a month. And he did" (February 4, 1951). First cast in a minor role, she soon proved her abilities, and graduated to featured characters. Her salary of $35 a week seemed munificent to the young lady from Mill Valley, and she loved the work. With her mother's permission, Eunice stayed with the Duffy company even after it left Frisco for other engagements.

By 1927, the *Los Angeles Times* reported that the Henry Duffy Players, Inc. had active companies in L.A., San Francisco, Seattle, and Portland. That fall, Eunice Quedens was among the featured players supporting Duffy and co-star Dale Winter (Mrs. Duffy) in *The Patsy*, at Los Angeles's El Capitan Theater. Also in the cast were Alice Buchanan, Florence Roberts, and Kenneth Daigneau. In the summer of 1928, the Duffy Players were staging the comedy *Lombardi, Ltd.* at the Hollywood Playhouse; it then moved on to an engagement in Oakland. That show starred Leo Carrillo, recreating his Broadway role described by the *Oakland Tribune* as "Tito, the youthful, excitable, credulous and romantic Italian proprietor of a fashionable dressmaking establishment." Eunice was cast as one of the "mannequins" modeling Tito's creations.

Her stage work brought Eunice to the attention of Columbia Pictures, where she made her film debut in 1929's *The Song of Love*. Although her featured performance as a *femme fatale* home-wrecker was well-received, it did not lead to other motion picture assignments, and the young actress's film career would be dormant until 1933.

Like many other Americans, actors found it difficult to make a living during the Great Depression of the early 1930s. Ticket sales at most entertainment venues were down, and it was an inauspicious time for a young hopeful to be finding a foothold in the theater. Eunice found work with a traveling company of players called the Bandbox Repertory Theatre.

Of her work with the Bandbox Theatre, Eve would recall to *Cosmopolitan*'s Hyman Goldberg, in a June 1953 article, "We scooted all over California in a Model-A Ford, with our scenery and props in a beat-up old trailer we dragged behind us, and we acted our heads off in barns, in hotel lobbies, in private homes, and sometimes on the street." Managing the troupe was Catherine Turney, later a notable screenwriter (who worked on *Mildred Pierce*, among others). The *Los Angeles Times*'s Katherine T. von Blon caught what was billed as a dress rehearsal of the troupe's show *The Marriage of Kitty* held in the patio and garden of a private home, prior to its opening at a hotel in Long Beach. She was enthusiastic about the show's prospects when it debuted, and noted in her August 9, 1931, *Times* review, "Eunice Quedens, a recruit from the Duffy Players in San Francisco, proved a thoroughly engaging Kitty quite capable of winning a recalcitrant husband. She has vivid personal magnetism and a deft comedy sense."

Eunice was featured in *The Passion Flower* at L.A.'s Teatro Leo Carrillo in the spring of 1932. The leading lady in this production of Jacinto Benavente's historical Spanish drama was Nance O'Neil, remembered today for having had a friendship with the infamous Lizzie Borden. The *Times'* critic Edwin Schallert reviewed the production on May 19, 1932, and noted, "In it, Nance O'Neil re-enacts with power one of her finest emotional roles, and a company that numbers interesting and surprisingly effective members supports her."

In the summer of 1933, Eunice was cast in *Low and Behold* at the Pasadena Playhouse. This revue was one of the earliest production credits for Leonard Sillman, who would go on to become the well-known impresario responsible for the *New Faces* showcases of the 1950s. Sillman, who considered his misspelled title quite witty at the time, built his show around talented newcomers he discovered, among them Tyrone Power (supposedly then employed as Sillman's chauffeur), Kay Thompson, and future MGM choreographer and director Charles Walters. Ultimately he signed 27 players, including Eunice, to perform a staggering 75 numbers, resulting in a much-too-long show that, on opening night, ran well past midnight.

Aiming for what he considered sophisticated material, Sillman ran afoul of some hidebound members of the Pasadena Playhouse, who found his sketches and songs too radical for their taste. Among the controversial elements was a Eunice Quedens-Tyrone Power skit called "Cupid and Psyche." Sillman explained in his 1959 autobiography, *Here Lies Leonard Sillman: Straightened Out at Last*, "It consisted of two statues coming to life in the park and complaining to one another about the people scratching matches on them and the dreadful things the birds had done to them over the years and what a bore it was for Cupid to hold Psyche in that Godawful position for such a long time." Playhouse founder Gilmor Brown interceded on Sillman's behalf, allowing the material to remain intact.

The show's run at the Pasadena Playhouse was extended from one week to three and marked by favorable notices. The *Arcadia Tribune* reported, "Mirthful, tuneful, saucy, satirical … this musical show is entertaining capacity audiences at the Playhouse every night" (May 26, 1933). Flushed with success, Sillman decided to mount a Los Angeles production of his revue, and with financing from his father, opened it at the Hollywood Music Box Theatre in July. Unable to pay standard Actors' Equity salaries, he convinced his cast to work for a percentage of the show's proceeds. Eunice's take consisted of half of one percent, more than Sillman paid Tyrone Power, whose role was less significant.

During the show's run, Eunice's role was gradually enlarged. "The movies kept hiring people out of the show," she explained in a 1953 *Cosmopolitan* interview, "and every time someone left, I got another part. Pretty soon I was in every skit." (She, too, drew at least a bit of attention from the movies, hired to play a small role that summer in MGM's *Dancing Lady*, her first picture since 1929's *The Song of Love*.) *Low and Behold* producer Sillman, whose *New Faces* revues would become a staple of New York theater, later told the *Los Angeles Times*'s Philip K. Scheuer of his propensity for finding talented newcomers, "I find 'em and others cash in. I should have been an agent instead of an idealist! But there is great satisfaction in proving that you are right about someone you've discovered" (May 1, 1943). The show finally posted its closing notice in August, with the Los Angeles engagement to be followed by a run in San Francisco.

Her stage success in California brought her to the attention of New York producers. She accepted an offer from impresario Lee Shubert to play a featured role in the *Ziegfeld Follies*, at a salary of $100 per week. While Florenz Ziegfeld himself had passed away in 1932, his widow, actress Billie Burke, contracted with the Shubert organization for a new show done in his signature style and bearing her imprimatur of approval. For her New York debut, Eunice was asked to assume a new professional name, as her employers didn't think her given name was the kind that lit up a marquee. By combining names she found on a jar of Elizabeth Arden cosmetics, and the heroine of the book she was then reading, Eve Arden was officially born. Only later did she learn that there was in fact another Eve Arden in show business, one who earned her keep disrobing in a Boston burlesque show.

The star attractions of the 1934 *Follies* were Fanny Brice and comedians Willie and Eugene Howard. Others in the cast were Buddy Ebsen (doing dance routines with his sister Vilma) and singer Jane Froman. In one sketch, Eve played the mother to a bratty child who is told the story of George Washington in an unsuccessful attempt to curb her propensity for lying. Fanny Brice had played a similar character previously, but it was here that she adopted the name Baby Snooks, the character that would bring her such enduring radio success. Eve also volunteered to serve as Brice's understudy, though it was well known that the star rarely, if ever, missed a performance. The 1934 edition of the *Follies* opened in early January and ran successfully through early summer. A cross-country tour followed, concluding with a brief Los Angeles engagement in early 1935.

After the *Follies* closed, Eve looked for more work on the New York stage. Still under contract to the Shuberts, Eve was limited in the roles she could play, but was allowed to join the cast of a Theatre Guild production, *Parade*. Billed as "a socially conscious musical revue," *Parade*, which gave star billing to a now nearly-forgotten comedian named Jimmy Savo, enjoyed only a brief run, and represented a substantial loss for the Theatre Guild.

Though many of the Guild's most loyal patrons were politically conservative, *Parade* was largely assembled by talent that leaned to the left. Author Eric A. Gordon (*Mark the Music: The Life and Work of Marc Blitzstein*) described Eve's best scene in the show, the musical number "Send for the Militia," written by Blitzstein.

> Attired in a society matron's flowered dress, wearing a lorgnette and a closely cropped coiffure, she enacted the hostess of a women's tea and discussion club, which has the topic of socialism on the agenda of its afternoon meeting. The song has four stanzas and a chorus, in which the hostess bemoans the dreadfulness of war, discusses the longshoremen's strike in San Francisco, and gives a beggar a dime for dinner. With each insult or threat to her own security, however, or to her banker husband's profits, she calls for the militia, the army, and the navy to put down the rebellion.

Don O'Malley, in his nationally syndicated "New York Inside and Out" column, described *Parade* as "a satirical revue which has fun with the depression, industrialists, cops, government agencies, workers and almost everything else you've been reading about in the papers these past few years" (June 10, 1935). O'Malley noted the presence of Eve, calling her "an up-and-coming comic actress who will bear watching in the future." Prominent critic Burns Mantle thought the show "doesn't mean much as a protest because it is mostly dull and silly," though he did enjoy "Send for the Militia." The show closed in late June after only 40 performances.

After *Parade*, Eve returned for a second edition of the *Ziegfeld Follies*, once again headlined by Fanny Brice. They were joined this time by Bob Hope, Josephine Baker, and singer Gertrude Niesen, as well as comedienne Judy Canova. Eve and Bob Hope teamed for a routine, "I Can't Get Started with You," described thusly by Raymond Strait in *Bob Hope: A Tribute*: "The scene featured Miss Arden, in a curve-caressing evening gown by Balenciaga, and Hope in a tux, attempting to seduce her on a street corner. In the beginning, Arden is cool to his advances but by the end of the skit she succumbs as the stage goes to black." In other sketches, she played mother (again) to Fanny Brice in "Baby Snooks Goes Hollywood," and played both kazoo and cymbals as one of the auditioning hopefuls in "Amateur Night."

Catching the show during previews at the Boston Opera House prior to its New York

Eve takes center stage in this shot from the *Ziegfeld Follies of 1936*.

opening, "L.A.S." of the *Christian Science Monitor* noted that several changes had been effected during the tour, mostly for the better. "Eve Arden," he noted, "struggles with partial success against some remarkably uninteresting material" (January 9, 1936).

By the time the show reached Broadway, however, the kinks had mostly been worked out. The *New York Times*'s Brooks Atkinson (January 31, 1936) liked what he saw. "Without being devastatingly funny," he noted, "the sketches are neatly written and they are acted in the highest good humor." Eve he credited with "an alert sense of humor." Again serving as Brice's understudy, Eve suffered through one nerve-wracking evening when the star was too sick to go on, managing to complete a performance successfully nonetheless. The show enjoyed a brief run brought to a close by Brice's illness. It reopened later that year once Brice had recovered, but by then Eve had moved on to other projects.

Rapidly building a reputation with New York audiences and producers as a gifted comic actress, Eve found that her stage credentials opened the door to radio work. As early as 1935, she turned up as a guest star on Rudy Vallee's popular show. In the spring of 1936, Eve joined the cast of Ken Murray's CBS radio show, *Laugh with Ken Murray*. Her function in this show was not unlike much of what would comprise her pre–*Our Miss Brooks* radio career—the sharp-tongued female who cut the male star down to size with caustic one-liners. Footage of Eve rehearsing her dialogue with Murray appeared in Paramount's short *Broadway Highlights* ("intimate news of the Great White Way"). Tenor Phil Regan was heard regularly on the broadcast, as was the Russ Morgan orchestra. *Laugh with Ken Murray* had its first broadcast on March 24, 1936, under the sponsorship of Rinso soap.

According to the *Sheboygan Press* "Pickin' the Programs" column of March 24, 1936, "In his initial performance tonight, Murray will be introduced by Rudy Vallee as 'Dr. Slipshod,' in which Ken promises to 'out Boris' Karloff as the sinister creator of a modern monster. Aiding and abetting Murray in this spine-chilling 'drayma' are the two 'Frankenstein' stooges, Eve Arden and 'Sassafras,' who will be around to pester and heckle their boss as only stooges extraordinary can do." Of this series opener, *Variety* opined, "Ken Murray's half-hour of comedy did not develop on its first time out as a sockeroo humor session. But it was easy to take and it did suggest that the way is clear for a stronger wallop on subsequent broadcasts.... Miss Arden ... handles her lines exceptionally well" (April 1, 1936).

A running gag in the show involved the star's purported search for a woman to marry. In response, the *Oakland Tribune*'s K.L. Ecksan printed a photo of Eve and said, "Why should Ken have to look all over the country for a wife, with a titian-haired Eve like Miss Arden in his garden?" (June 9, 1936). Eve also sang from time to time on the show, as noted in a listing for a late May broadcast: "Lovely Eve Arden presents a new 'blues' number in the manner she made famous." Despite the talent involved, the show was not a hit. Writing his autobiography, *Life on a Pogo Stick*, some years later, star Ken Murray remembered that his mother had liked the show, and that he'd received fan letters from two friends, W.C. Fields and Bing Crosby. With that evidence in hand, Murray titled the chapter about *Laugh with Ken Murray*, "At Least We Had Three Fans on Radio."

Near the end of her run in the second *Follies*, Eve's mother fell ill with cancer. Intending to give up her *Follies* role and be at her mother's side, she was persuaded not to do so, and knew her mother would have felt she should complete her professional obligation. After Mrs. Quedens's death, however, Eve returned to the West Coast to resolve her mother's affairs, and decided to stay for a while. Unexpectedly, she found better prospects than before for film work. Her movie career began in earnest in 1937, when she was signed to play a featured villainous role in the comedy *Oh, Doctor*, starring Edward Everett Horton. That picture came and went without attracting much attention, but *Stage Door*, released by RKO that October, was quite a different matter. Director Gregory La Cava worked closely with the young actresses cast as residents of a theatrical boardinghouse, using elements from their own personalities and even snippets of their own speech to flesh out the charac-

Eve's first role in a radio series found her supporting comedian Ken Murray in his short-lived CBS show, *Laugh with Ken Murray.*

ters they played. Intrigued by Eve's style, he enlarged her part, enabling her to stand out among a stellar cast that included Katharine Hepburn, Ginger Rogers, Lucille Ball, and Ann Miller.

Rapidly carving out a viable career as a film actress, Eve accepted a marriage proposal from a young insurance agent, Edward (Ned) Bergen. Having just worked opposite ventriloquist Edgar Bergen in *Letter of Introduction,* the similarity in names caused some fans to think that he and Eve had married. The new Mr. and Mrs. Bergen settled into daily life in Hollywood, building a home for themselves that allowed Eve to indulge her flair for interior design and love for antiques.

By the late 1930s, having received good notices for her supporting performances in *Stage Door, Having Wonderful Time,* and others, Eve was a movie character actress in demand. More than one studio made overtures to her about a long-term, exclusive contract, but she declined all such offers. Although free-lance employment was chancier, it also gave her the freedom to choose her own roles, as well as entertain the offers she might receive from Broadway producers, as her love for stage work was undiminished.

As her movie career picked up steam, Eve began to be heard occasionally on CBS's popular *Lux Radio Theatre,* hosted by Cecil B. DeMille. This long-running show presented slightly condensed versions of Hollywood movies in a radio format, often with one or more of the original stars. The prestigious show, which originated first from the Music Box Theatre on Hollywood Boulevard and later from the Vine Street Playhouse, broadcast live to a studio audience, and tickets to the performances were highly sought after by movie fans. Performers were expected to take part in extensive rehearsals that took up much of the week prior to the Monday night broadcast.

Eve was first heard on the broadcast of February 20, 1939, in an adaptation of her 1937 film *Stage Door.* Interestingly, this program cast her not in her original movie role of Eve, the young lady with the cat, but in the larger featured role of Linda Shaw, originated by Gail Patrick. Ginger Rogers reprised her character of Jean Maitland, but Rosalind Russell took Hepburn's movie role of Terry Randall. Radio historians Connie Billips and Arthur Pierce, in their book *Lux Presents Hollywood: A Show-by-Show History of the* Lux Radio Theatre *and the* Lux Video Theatre, *1934–1957,* rated this broadcast "a reasonably good rendering of the picture, though it does not entirely succeed in creating the film's atmosphere of the second-rate boarding house. To a large extent, this is caused by the elimination of much of the banter among the girls of the Footlights Club, which was understandably excised due to time limitations."

Despite her Hollywood success, Eve never lost her affinity for live theater, and she was delighted to be offered a prestigious Broadway gig in 1939. Eve's return to the stage placed her in the company of some of its brightest lights. She accepted a featured role in Jerome Kern and Oscar Hammerstein II's musical comedy *Very Warm for May,* their first collaboration to open on the Great White Way since *Music in the Air* seven years earlier. Producing the new show was Max Gordon, whose many successful shows included *The Women.*

Originally, *Very Warm for May* was the story of an aspiring actress, May Graham (Grace McDonald), on the run from gangsters, who hides out in a third-rate summer stock company in Connecticut. Ogdon Quiler's Progressive Playshop Theatre Guild, Inc. operates under the flamboyant and overwrought direction of Quiler (Hiram Sherman). Eve played a featured role as Winnie Spofford, a well-heeled matron who hosts the Quiler company on her estate, and looks on as her son and daughter seek fame and fortune. Having observed her 30th birthday not long before, Eve was somewhat oddly cast as the mother of two grown children Liz and Sonny (played by Frances Mercer and Richard Quine). The character was loosely based on the late theatrical agent-turned-producer Elisabeth (Bessie) Marbury, who had given Kern some early showcases for his music in the mid–1910s. Finally, when the show seems to be mired in disaster, May's brother Johnny takes over direction and makes a silk purse of the sow's ear. The happy ending even provides a second chance at love for Winnie, who is reunited after many years with May's father.

Eve was excited about appearing in a Kern and Hammerstein show, and impressed when the latter even encouraged her to suggest any parts of the script where improvement might be needed. Busy on the West Coast with *Abe Lincoln in Illinois,* Max Gordon had produced the show largely in absentia. Not until previews in Wilmington, Delaware, did he see the show, and his response was devastating. Critical response was largely positive, though it was evident that the show needed trimming. Gordon was not swayed: after seeing the show in Washington, he thought he detected a "pattern of impending failure," as he described it in his memoirs, *Max Gordon Presents,* and swung into action. He fired director Vincente Minnelli, brought in a new choreographer, and insisted that Hammerstein provide major script revisions. At Gordon's direction, most of the gangster subplot was removed. As theater historian Gerald Bordman (*Jerome Kern: His Life and Music*) noted, "Whether the new book was tighter is moot, but there is no question that all the color had been drained from Hammerstein's original conception. What survived was a pale, trite backstage story."

The Associated Press's Mark Barron wrote that the return to the Broadway stage of Kern and Hammerstein with a new show was a major event, and audiences were waiting with strong anticipation. "The trouble," Barron noted, "is that such happily-awaited events do not always live up to expectations of audiences who want only one standard out of Kern and Hammerstein, and that is their top one." Barron thought the show had "an excellent cast, headed by Hiram Sherman, Eve Arden, and Donald Brian" (November 26, 1939).

Writing in the *New York Times,* Brooks Atkinson praised the music and the cast, but declared Hammerstein's book a mess. "After a random opening scene," Atkinson said, "it involves the performers in tedious arguments over a fantastic play that is never defined. It strews odds and ends throughout the evening and defeats almost every performer who tries to cope with it" (November 18, 1939). Among those trying, he noted Eve, who "makes an occasional impression on it with her scatter-brained comedy." Critic Burns Mantle, writing in the *Chicago Tribune,* concurred that the show had "a fairly muddled story" (November 26, 1939).

The New Yorker (November 25, 1939) also singled her out among the cast. Noting that the show "manages to achieve a certain maturity in its comedy and, unlike most musicals, actually gets better and funnier as it goes on," the magazine columnist added, "Much of the credit for this must go to Eve Arden, whose looks plus comedy sense plus authority make her an almost incredible mother of two grown children." Others were less certain about the show's prospects, though most critics recognized "All The Things You Are" as a classic Kern song.

With lukewarm reviews, and other popular musicals (like Ethel Merman in Cole Porter's *DuBarry Was a Lady*) doing brisk business, the show struggled. An attempt to drum up business by featuring the cast in a radio broadcast didn't help much, though it was the basis for the "original cast recording" issued on CD in the 1990s. *Very Warm for May,* Kern's last original Broadway show, closed after 59 performances. Stung by the show's failure, Hammerstein refused to authorize revivals of it for many years afterward. (In 2010, however, more than 70 years after its brief Broadway run, *Very Warm for May* was staged in San Francisco by the 42nd Street Moon Theater, as part of an ongoing tribute to Kern's work. It was also cited, more than 50 years after its production, as the introduction to musical theater that would inspire a career choice for the nine-year-old viewer Stephen Sondheim.)

Nearly a decade later, Eve hadn't forgotten the experience of appearing in "probably the worst flop show Oscar Hammerstein ever wrote," and turned it to her advantage, as she told the *Syracuse Herald-Journal*'s Marjorie Turner in a September 1949 interview. Told it would be impossible to get tickets for the red-hot *South Pacific* during her visit to New York, she sent a telegram to Hammerstein with a mock threat. "Get Mary Martin for your hits," she wired him, "but I will not star in your next flop." She had her tickets by return mail.

Only about a month after playing her final performance in *Very Warm for May*, Eve was back in front of Broadway audiences in the musical revue *Two for the Show*. The show, a follow-up to *One for the Money* staged a year earlier, featured sketches by Nancy Hamilton, and was directed by Josh Logan. A strong cast included Betty Hutton, Alfred Drake, Keenan Wynn, Richard Haydn (doing his Edwin Carp characterization), and, of course, Eve. Her talent for mimicry was showcased in the sketches "Destry Has Ridden Again," lampooning Marlene Dietrich, and "To a Skylark," which found her assuming a Gertrude Lawrence pose. The *New York Times*'s Brooks Atkinson termed the results "an intimate revue that retains some of the freshness of amateur skylarking" (February 9, 1940). Atkinson noted Eve, the "rangy blonde who worked so valiantly in *Very Warm for May* last November," as contributing strongly in a dentist's office sketch with Wynn. Walter Winchell, in his February 11, 1940, syndicated column, reported that the show "was voted an enjoyable improvement over its predecessor, which was also good." Finding the show hard on her vocal chords, Eve stayed with *Two for the Show* only until May, when she gave notice and was replaced by actress Grace Coppin.

Eve returned to California in mid–1940, where she spent a busy year acting almost non-stop in films. In quick succession, she played roles at Warner Bros., MGM, and RKO, among others, becoming a familiar and welcome face to moviegoers in a variety of genres.

In the summer of 1941, Eve signed to return to the New York stage with a featured role in *Let's Face It*, which would star Danny Kaye. *Let's Face It* was adapted from the comedy *The Cradle Snatchers*, which had enjoyed a successful Broadway run in the 1920s. By most accounts, the show came together smoothly under the supervision of veteran producer Vinton Freedley. The *New York Times*'s Theodore Strauss reported that the show "has had a charmed life from the very beginning ... there has been no feverish last-minute bedlam, not one of the cast has been changed, no Sheriffs have pursued it, no eternal enmities have

Eve strikes up the band in this sketch from the Broadway revue *Two for the Show*.

come between the writers, directors and composer. If ever a show was born with a golden spoon in its mouth, this is it" (November 16, 1941).

Life magazine raved about the show: "*Let's Face It* is one of those rare shows that has all the ingredients.... Its humor, unabashedly frank and gusty, is given double glitter by Cinema Actress Eve Arden and Broadway's newest funnyman, Danny Kaye. The show's mood is topical and its smoky gags come fast ... the whole performance is fused, with fine theatrical alchemy, into two hours of rough and rowdy fun" (November 10, 1941). *Let's Face It* was a smash hit that ran for well over 500 performances, keeping it open until March 1943. Eve, however, left the show in the fall of 1942 when her one-year contract expired, being replaced by Carol Goodner and, at the very end of the run, Kalita Humphreys in the role of Maggie Watson.

Eve returned to *The Lux Radio Theatre* for its January 11, 1943, segment, which was adapted from her 1941 Columbia film *She Knew All the Answers*. Joan Bennett and Eve recreated their film roles as Gloria and Kitty, while leading man Franchot Tone was supplanted by Preston Foster. A few weeks later, Eve was again heard on *Lux*, although in a slightly different capacity. In "The Show-Off" (February 1, 1943), adapted from George Kelly's comedy, Harold Peary (*The Great Gildersleeve*) and Beulah Bondi headed the cast. Eve was heard during the program's commercial segment, playing the recurring role of fictitious Hollywood columnist Libby Collins, essayed in other segments by Dorothy Lovett, Ynez Seabury, and, most notably, Doris Singleton.

Having previously said no to a long-term movie contact, Eve surprised some observers when she signed a seven-year pact with Warner Bros. in 1944. Her two-picture-a-year deal with one of Hollywood's premier studios gave her a satisfactory number of "outs" for radio work. Though she was tempted into signing on as a contract player by the quirky, distinctive role of Sgt. Natalia Moskoroff in *The Doughgirls* (1944), she was wrong if she assumed that she would be allowed to play a varied lot of characters at the studio. In a 1991 interview with the *Toronto Star,* she described to reporter Jim Bawden the function she played in Jack Warner's eyes, quoting the studio boss as saying of one particular picture, "There's no script, a few fading stars and an indifferent director. So put Eve Arden in it and it may make a few bucks."

The role that would cement her persona in moviegoers' minds came not long after *The Doughgirls.* Late in 1944, she was assigned to play a supporting role as Ida Corwin, wise and witty best friend to Joan Crawford's title character, in *Mildred Pierce*. The phenomenal success of that 1945 release would prove to be something of a mixed blessing. Movie character actors were often valued for their ability to present an identifiable, comfortingly familiar "type" with limited screen time, and this became Eve's fate as well. Her ability to drop a cutting, sardonic line of dialogue with precise timing was unparalleled, but she had not anticipated that she would be locked into this type of characterization for much of her film career.

Eve's Warner Bros. contract allowed her to continue radio work. In 1945, she was cast as a featured player in Danny Kaye's first network series. Having first attained stardom on Broadway, Kaye was offered a lucrative movie contract by producer Samuel Goldwyn. The 1944 release of Kaye's first starring picture, *Up in Arms,* successfully introduced him to national audiences, and was followed a few months later by his radio series. *The Danny Kaye Show* aired its opening installment on January 6, 1945, with guest star Eddie Cantor. Supporting the star were Eve and character actor Lionel Stander, along with Harry James and his orchestra. The show was sponsored by Pabst Beer, and directed by Dick Mack. Among the show's writers was the well-regarded Goodman Ace, of *Easy Aces* fame.

In the series opener, Danny, playing himself, has just signed a contract with Pabst to star in his own radio show. The sponsor (played by Frank Nelson) is a jovial type given to making corny jokes, at which he laughs heartily. When Danny introduces "my manager, Eve Arden," Mr. Pabst urges him to do whatever she says—"After all, we don't want Miss Arden to harden." Hearing that Danny is being given his own show, comedian Eddie Cantor shows up in the hopes of discouraging this new competition, unnerving Danny with dire predictions as to the effect radio work will have on his health. When Danny panics and disappears days before his debut broadcast, it falls to his manager, Eve, to check all his favorite hangouts and track him down. She finally finds him hiding out in the hotel steam room, where the sound of Eddie Cantor happily going on in his place inspires Danny to rush to the studio. The series opener gave listeners the opportunity to hear Kaye sing "Minnie the Moocher" as well as his trademark songs, building to a finale in which he enacts a play providing all the voices-male, female, canine, and otherwise. In the show's closing credits, the announcer notes that Eve "appears through the courtesy of Warner Brothers."

The *New York Times*'s Jack Gould noted, "Neither Miss Arden nor Mr. Stander had much to do on the first broadcast, perhaps due to the exigencies of getting the new series off to a start. In Miss Arden's case in particular it is hoped that this situation will not long prevail, for she is a lady of proved comic abilities on stage and screen, and her smart and acidulous comments should be welcome on the air too" (January 14, 1945). The second broadcast, devoted primarily to a sketch telling Danny's life story ("A Kaye Grows in Brooklyn") did little to improve the situation, again giving Eve only a few meaningful moments. In an unknowing harbinger of things to come, Eve plays Danny's fourth-grade teacher in the sketch, three years before her fame as *Our Miss Brooks*. In addition to the series, Eve and Danny turned up together in *Command Performance,* a project of the U.S. War Department, in which top stars worked for free providing entertainment broadcast, not to civilians at home, but to enlisted men and women overseas.

The Danny Kaye Show was too expensive a proposition for Pabst and CBS to accept anything less than top ratings, which it did not achieve. When *The Danny Kaye Show* returned for a second-and final-season in the fall of 1945, Eve had departed the cast.

In late January 1946, Eve learned that she had been nominated for an Oscar in the Best Supporting Actress category for her role in *Mildred Pierce*. Also nominated was Ann Blyth, for her performance as Veda, along with Angela Lansbury (*The Picture of Dorian Gray*), Joan Lorring (*The Corn Is Green*), and Anne Revere (*National Velvet*). The Associated Press's Rosalind Shaffer predicted Lansbury the likely winner, with Blyth also a strong possibility. Eve was among the more than 2,000 audience members present at the March 7, 1946, ceremony, held at Grauman's Chinese Theatre and emceed by Bob Hope. Revere took home the statuette.

That same year, Eve began her affiliation with another popular radio show, NBC's *The Sealtest Village Store*. This series had evolved from what had originally been Rudy Vallee's popular show of the early 1940s, which featured John Barrymore and comedienne Joan Davis in recurring roles. Barrymore's untimely death in 1942, followed by Vallee's departure for World War II military service, left the comedy in the hands of Davis, who was subsequently joined by co-star Jack Haley. By 1945, Davis was such a hot radio ticket that she jumped ship for her own popular *Joanie's Tea Room* on CBS, and Eve was brought in as the show's new comedienne. Response was sufficiently favorable that *Billboard* reported a movie version of the show in the offing that summer, though nothing came of this.

Syndicated columnist John Crosby, in his December 31, 1946, installment, filed a harsh review of the revamped *Sealtest Village Store*.

Haley and Miss Arden are respectively proprietor and employee of the Village Store in which they spend as little time as possible and apparently do little business. A village store, I guess, just sounded like a good idea to the writers when this series started, which must have been a very long time ago. Neither Mr. Haley nor Miss Arden sound[s] as if they ever saw a village much smaller than Manhattan or would remain in it longer than it takes to buy gasoline. Nevertheless, through some whim of their ice cream making sponsor, they are marooned in this village speaking in their imperturbably metropolitan accents the devious and aged jokes which are cast in their laps.

While thriving professionally, Eve longed for a family. She and husband, Ned, agreed to investigate adoption. At the time, her *Mildred Pierce* co-star Joan Crawford was viewed not as the *Mommie Dearest* that her adopted daughter would later immortalize in a controversial late–1970s bestseller, but as a generous star who had kindly taken in homeless children. Eve knew Crawford slightly, and after working with Joan's then-husband Phillip Terry in RKO's *Pan-Americana* (1945), asked him for advice on adoption. Via Terry, Eve learned about adoption first-hand from none other than Joan Crawford, and the end result was her new daughter Liza, whom she and Ned brought home in 1945.

During the term of her multi-year contract to make films for Warner Bros. (from 1944 to 1951), Eve was unable to take on another long-term Broadway engagement. Still, despite her Hollywood success, she yearned for stage opportunities. Feeling limited in the type of role she was offered in films, Eve found more creative satisfaction in her stage work. She was one of a sizable group of prominent film actors who appeared onstage for minimal pay in the late 1940s at the La Jolla Playhouse. Gregory Peck, one of the Playhouse's guiding lights, later explained to *Time* magazine, "Hollywood is a vacuum in which criticism doesn't exist.... The only way you can get a really honest opinion of your work is to get in front of an audience that pays to see you. Then you know in a minute if you're bad" (August 8, 1949).

Biography, a comedy by S.N. Behrman, was originally produced on Broadway in 1932–33 by the Theatre Guild with Ina Claire in the lead role of Marion Froude. The play concerns a woman painter who agrees to write her autobiography for a magazine, threatening to embarrass the men who've played significant roles in her life. Eve appeared opposite actor Barry Sullivan, and was directed by Harry Ellerbe. The success of the La Jolla Playhouse production led to a booking at the Hollywood Las Palmas Theater. Philip K. Scheuer, reviewing the production for the *Los Angeles Times,* noted, "Miss Arden's role is that of a woman, a painter who, although she has seen much of life, as the saying goes, is able to assurance her acquaintances—and with patent justification—that she is 'casual, not evil.' ... Miss Arden is just fine in the part" (August 29, 1947). *Billboard* liked it also, saying that Eve was "outstanding" in the role. "Her flawless interpretation of the part throws full emphasis on the caustic content of Behrman's lines" (September 6, 1947).

Filling in as star of *The Sealtest Village Store* in the summer of 1947, Eve had four writers turning out her material—Elon Packard, Stanley Davis, Larry Klein, and Jack Elinson. The results didn't much impress *Billboard*'s reviewer, who complained of a July episode with guest star Cesar Romero, "Eve Arden has proved herself in legit, pix, and previous airshows a competent comedienne, a judgment you would never arrive at from hearing her struggle through the material she works with here ... all the bits of business, involving all the players, were consistently unfunny" (August 2, 1947). That fall, she joined the regular cast supporting new leading man Jack Carson. John Crosby, looking in on the show again for his October 28, 1947, column, thought it not much improved by the addition of Carson, whom he accused of modeling his work on that of the more established Jack Benny. As for Eve, Crosby declared, "Miss Eve Arden's function is almost exactly that of Mary Livingstone."

Eve teamed with Jack Carson for the 1947–48 version of radio's *The Sealtest Village Store*.

Eve herself preferred not to listen to her radio work. According to Elizabeth Wilson's profile of her that appeared in *Liberty*, "By accident, she once turned on the radio in her car—she drives a green convertible Studebaker—and heard herself wisecracking with Jack Carson on the Sealtest show. She turned it off so savagely that the radio hasn't worked since" (February 1950).

In July 1947, Eve flew to Reno, where she was granted a divorce from Edward (Ned) Bergen. Her complaint cited mental cruelty as the reason for the separation, but Bergen told reporters outside the judge's chambers that the split was amicable, and Eve was seen leaving with her ex-husband, arm-in-arm. Eve, of course, retained primary custody of daughter Liza, with Bergen granted visitation rights. As a single mother, she further enlarged her small family with the adoption of a second daughter, Connie.

In the spring of 1948, syndicated columnist Sheilah Graham reported that Carson's sponsors had dropped the Sealtest show, leaving Eve free to pursue other radio work. Eve finished her commitment to the show that summer, and only weeks later would begin her starring role in *Our Miss Brooks*. Jack Carson, too, departed for his own show, bringing *The Sealtest Village Store* to a close after a long run.

Meanwhile, she was again onstage at the La Jolla Playhouse, co-starring with Wendell Corey and Beulah Bondi in a production of Robert E. Sherwood's *The Road to Rome*, directed by Norman Lloyd. Eve assumed the role originally played by Jane Cowl in the show's successful 1927–28 run on Broadway. Commented the reviewer for the *Los Angeles Times*, "As Amytis, pleasure-loving wife of Roman Dictator Fabius Maximus, Miss Arden utilizes her generously endowed charms, fortified by a social conscience, to save Rome from Hannibal's Carthaginian army" (July 8, 1948).

Though it's difficult in hindsight to imagine anyone but Eve playing the role of Connie Brooks, *Our Miss Brooks* was not originally intended to be a vehicle for her. The show began as part of CBS's initiative to develop its own shows in-house, decreasing the influence of advertising agencies and/or stars to produce most of radio's entertainment content. *Brooks* was intended to be a vehicle for stage star Shirley Booth (1898–1992), a favorite of radio audiences for her earlier featured role as Miss Duffy on *Duffy's Tavern*. In fact, the show began life with the working title of *Our Miss Booth*. Booth played the role in an audition episode for CBS, aired in April 1948, but the finished product did not quite seem to jell, and didn't attract a sponsor. Some three years later, when Eve's version of *Our Miss Brooks* had become a substantial radio hit, and was being eyed for television, writer Don Ettlinger, who had written the initial script for the Shirley Booth version, sued CBS for damages, claiming he had never been properly compensated for his contribution.

Offered the role of Connie Brooks in the wake of Booth's departure, Eve was initially unenthusiastic, as she told the *New York Times*'s Val Adams in a September 1949 interview: "Before this I'd been in radio shows but all I did was read gag lines. When CBS first approached me about this idea I told them to go away." She finally accepted the lead role in the as-yet-unsponsored summer series provided that CBS would allow her to tape her performances for that first, abbreviated season before her vacation began.

The pilot episode of *Our Miss Brooks,* heard on June 23, 1948, used a heavily rewritten version of the script that Booth had previously essayed. It depicted Connie Brooks's first meeting with new school principal Osgood Conklin, after five years of teaching English at Madison High School. She's excited by the prospect of being promoted to head of the English department, an assignment that would net her an extra $6 per month. Unfortunately (except for the show's comedy), Connie and her new boss are at odds from the get-go. They first meet when Walter Denton, driving Miss Brooks to school, collides with Mr. Conklin's cherished car, a black touring car she terms "a hopped-up hearse." Not knowing this stranger's identity, Connie sasses him when he berates her and Walter, calling him "Barking Boy." Later, at school, she not only makes a nervous mess of her English class while her new supervisor observes, but falls victim to a misunderstanding when Mr. Conklin believes she and Walter are conducting a romantic liaison.

Though he would become an important factor in the success of *Our Miss Brooks,* actor Gale Gordon did not appear in the first broadcasts; Joe Forte originated the role of Osgood Conklin. Gordon later told writer Dina-Marie Kulzer (*Television Series Regulars of the Fifties and Sixties in Interview*) that he was offered the role from the outset, but CBS executives balked at paying what was then his going rate of $150 per show. After he and his wife, Virginia, listened to the first broadcast of the new comedy series, Mrs. Gordon said, "Thank God they didn't pay you the $150 because that's the worst show I've ever heard." Not long afterwards, Joe Forte was out, and CBS met Gordon's salary demands to play Connie Brooks's boss, a role that would last him for the next eight years.

By the time he won the role of Mr. Conklin, Gordon's vocal talents were quite familiar to radio audiences from his supporting role as Mayor LaTrivia on *The Johnson's Wax Show with Fibber McGee and Molly;* his featured role on *The Great Gildersleeve* as Gildersleeve's rival Rumson Bullard; as well as ongoing assignments in popular shows like *The Whistler, Big Town,* and *The George Burns and Gracie Allen Show.* The year 1948 found him taking on not only Osgood Conklin, but roles in *My Favorite Husband* (as boss Rudolph Atterbury) and *The Phil Harris–Alice Faye Show* (portraying the sponsor's representative Mr. Scott). *Our*

Miss Brooks would become perhaps his best-written and most noteworthy version of the actor's prototypical character.

Cast as Eve's love interest, the shy biology teacher Mr. Boynton, was Jeff Chandler, an established radio performer but not yet the movie star he would become by the early 1950s. Chandler, then being heard in the medical serial *The Private Practice of Dr. Dana*, would continue in the radio role opposite Eve for the entirety of his five-year contract, even after Robert Rockwell began playing Boynton on TV. Richard Crenna, who would make a virtual cottage industry of playing nerdy teenagers on radio, earned big laughs as Connie's devoted student Walter Denton. Jane Morgan played Connie's daffy landlady, Margaret Davis, who dishes up a peculiar menu of culinary delicacies (like clam fritters) for her hapless tenant. Not part of the audition show, but added later was Conklin's pretty daughter Harriet, as voiced by Gloria McMillan, who would serve as romantic interest for Walter Denton. McMillan was, in fact, a high school student when she won the role, as was young Leonard Smith, cast as Madison High's addle-brained athlete Stretch Snodgrass.

The series began its regular run on July 19, 1948. The *New York Times*'s Jack Gould, reviewing the initial broadcast of *Brooks* in his July 25, 1948, column, thought the new show had the makings of a hit. Gould, saying that Eve had long deserved her own radio vehicle, added, "As those who saw her in a succession of Broadway musicals will fondly recall, Miss Arden is one of those rare and delightful comediennes who can convey a sense of wonderful worldliness, a lady who with a crackling bon mot can cut a stuffy soul down to size. Her delivery is knowing and sharp, albeit spoken always with a twinkle in the eye." *Billboard* concurred, calling the new show "a winner" and adding, "A hefty portion of the credit belongs to Eve Arden, who seems to have found her niche with this show.... Miss Arden flashed some fancy footwork thru a boff script, making even ordinary lines seem funny" (July 31, 1948).

Variety also gave the show and its star a thumbs-up, saying, "It's certainly a vast improvement over her Sealtest career of the past season on NBC. Cast as a romantic English teacher who's on the make for a biology instructor, she accents all of the script's high points for a maximum laugh payoff" (July 21, 1948).

The job on *Brooks* was a pleasant one for Eve, largely free of tension or strain. "Why, I've seen radio actors in front of a mike whose hands shake like this," she told the *New York Times*'s Val Adams, demonstrating a nervous flutter. "If I found myself that way I'd quit" (September 4, 1949). Within days of the first broadcast, CBS sales executives were entertaining offers to sponsor the show when it began its regular run in the fall. Network president Frank Stanton personally congratulated Eve on the show's high ratings.

The show returned to the airwaves in October 1948, and quickly became a staple of CBS's Sunday night schedule. After that first abbreviated season of transcribed broadcasts, done to accommodate Eve's schedule, it would settle into a regular routine. As radio historian John Dunning (*Tune in Yesterday*) explained, the schedule was an easy one for the cast. "They came to work on Sunday, arriving at the Hollywood studio at mid-morning for an informal reading of the script. Lines and cues were learned, and a more polished rehearsal followed in the early afternoon. At 3:30 Pacific time, the show was broadcast live to the East Coast and taped for later replay in the West." The show's longtime sponsor was Colgate-Palmolive-Peet, Inc., who used it primarily to tout the benefits of Colgate Dental Cream and Luster Crème Shampoo. *Variety* predicted a long, highly rated run for the comedy series. (Still a favorite of Old Time Radio aficionados today, *Our Miss Brooks* provided Eve with her signature character. Eve's accomplishments in the aural medium were recognized in 1995, when she was inducted into the Radio Hall of Fame.)

Eve is pictured with the men in Miss Brooks's radio life: Gale Gordon as Mr. Conklin (left) and Jeff Chandler as Mr. Boynton.

As early as late 1948, there was discussion of a movie adaptation of *Our Miss Brooks*, given the show's quick rise to top radio ratings; however, the movie didn't come about until 1956. In the meantime, the show continued weekly original broadcasts year-round until the summer of 1950, when the cast and crew took their first break after 86 episodes. In the episode first aired March 26, 1950, Connie is looking forward to the start of baseball season, because she has a date with Mr. Boynton to attend Madison High's game against longtime rival Clay City High. As she tells Mrs. Davis, "I figure if he spends enough time looking at curves, and watching other fellows trying to get to first base, it might give him an idea." Unfortunately, thanks to Mr. Conklin's mismanagement of the athletic fund, there's no money to pay for the team's uniforms. He makes an alternate suggestion:

CONKLIN: Do you think our boys could play good ball without uniforms?
CONNIE: I don't know how good they'd play, but they'd certainly draw a nice crowd.

Some of her sharpest wit bounces harmlessly off Philip Boynton, who rarely perceives the point of her most pointed remarks. When Connie tells her erstwhile boyfriend that the baseball game has been canceled, she suggests an after-school movie date instead:

CONNIE: By 4:00, we could be sitting in the balcony at the State Theater.
PHILIP: But the State Theater doesn't open until 6:30.
CONNIE: That's what I say, it might be fun.

When her beau still fails to take the hint, Connie says, "Mr. Boynton, do me a favor. The next time we're sitting in the balcony, borrow the usher's flashlight, and see how your fellow Americans are living."

Her frequent rival for Mr. Boynton's attentions is fellow teacher Daisy Enright (played by Mary Jane Croft), with whom Connie regularly exchanges barbs like, "Miss Enright, if you ever become a mother, I'd love one of the kittens."

In general, life was good for Eve in the late 1940s. Though her marriage hadn't worked out, she was happily raising her two daughters, while enjoying a lucrative screen and radio career that had won her many fans. But, as she confessed to columnist Hedda Hopper, there was still one complaint: if she could "just get out of the hackneyed [movie] roles. I'm getting so I'm allergic to myself on the screen. I terrify me. I'd like to do something that's human and understandable, instead of just having the camera turn on me to give out with a wisecrack, while the boy and girl are tying their shoelaces" (September 19, 1948). While awaiting the release of her most recent films, *One Touch of Venus* and *My Dream Is Yours*, she'd begun to wonder if a return to the stage might be just the cure for her typecasting blues.

During the summer of 1949, while still taping new episodes of *Brooks*, Eve returned to the La Jolla Playhouse to appear in a production of *Here Today*, co-starring Robert Alda. Originally seen on Broadway in 1932 as a vehicle for Ruth Gordon, George Oppenheim's romantic comedy was subtitled "A Comedy of Bad Manners." It told the story of renowned playwright Mary Hilliard, whose ex-husband, novelist Philip Graves, plans to marry Claire, a young woman from a socially prominent family that doesn't approve of him. Mary, with her friend Stanley in tow, takes it upon herself to help Philip's cause, persuading his fiancée's formidable mother that he is a more suitable match than his rival, stodgy Spencer Grant. Instead, as complications build, Mary realizes she is still in love with Philip himself, and has second thoughts just as her campaign to help Philip win Claire's hand is coming to fruition.

Though her work at the La Jolla Playhouse was artistically rewarding, it paid Eve only a minimal salary. In the early 1950s, Eve took the advice of a colleague who suggested that she could more profitably slake her thirst for the stage by taking bookings on the summer stock circuit. Although she couldn't have known it, her decision also had a profound affect on her private life. While auditioning actors to play opposite her in summer stock, she met Brooks West, who would become her second husband.

Eve later described to *Family Circle*'s Harry Evans, in a December 1953 interview, her initial meeting with Brooks. "Our talk lasted for about 20 minutes. After he'd left, I was aware of three reactions. I liked his looks and his voice. The third one will kill you. I liked his sense of efficiency—no wasted words or gestures, no windy personality-kid charm to knock over susceptible Miss Brooks. The next day he read a scene with me, and I knew he was it."

Eve and Brooks first worked together in a production of *Over Twenty-One*, written by Ruth Gordon, who had also starred in its 1944 Broadway run. Harry Ellerbe directed the summer stock production, which also featured Donald Foster and Bert Thorn. Eve's radio popularity as *Our Miss Brooks* made her an easy sell to summer stock audiences, as *Billboard* reported of her engagement in Sea Cliff, New York: "Management reports heaviest advance to date ... nine out of ten pew-buyers referring to [*Brooks*] when they step to the window" (July 29, 1950).

Over Twenty-One takes place over a six-week period in the summer of 1943. Nearly 40 years old, newspaper editor Max Wharton enlists in the armed services, and is dispatched to Miami, where he and other men learn the ins and outs of military life, as they are trained and assessed for future assignments. Eve played Max's wife, Paula, known as Polly, a sophisticated author and screenwriter who accompanies her husband to a shabby little bungalow in Miami, and offers support and encouragement as he tries to make his contribution to the war effort. Though Max has been warned that "over twenty-one, you don't absorb any more," he proves the naysayers wrong, while Paula finds she is needed as well, offering to take over his newspaper job until he's ready to take it up again.

The *Washington Post*'s Richard L. Coe, catching the show at the Olney Country Theatre, noted, in his June 29, 1950, review:

> The part of the wise, witty wife who's pushing her husband through Officer Candidate School ... is right up Eve's particular highway.... For this dry-voiced lady is one of our best comediennes. It is an interesting fact that she has made people like her—the superior, terribly aware female who always, somehow, loses the great Battle of Love.... Eve's admirers will be delighted to have her back in the attractive flesh, with a man all her own.

Eve told United Press's Virginia MacPherson that her in-person appearances around New England sometimes disappointed her fans, who were expecting to see the snappish, wisecracking woman they loved from Warner Bros.' movies. "They'd stand there and look at me expectantly," she explained in the interview published November 4, 1950. "And brother, was I a letdown! I didn't get witchy.... I didn't gossip ... and I couldn't come up with a wisecrack to save my life. I'm afraid they found out the awful truth about Arden. I'm really a horribly innocuous person off the screen." That didn't mean, of course, that she couldn't derive the maximum benefits from Ruth Gordon's best scripted lines, as when a wide-eyed young wife asks Polly if her husband is really nearing 40 years of age. "Yes, he really is," Polly replies. "We've been everywhere about it, but there's nothing they can do."

Back at home after a busy summer, she resumed her weekly performances in *Our Miss Brooks*. A CBS press release announcing the show's third season in 1950 notes, "As gayhearted Connie Brooks, Miss Arden has created for millions of radio fans the model of an ideally popular teacher. Connie is youngish, glamorous, sympathetic, wisecracks with an unusual sense of humor—and has a deep regard for her profession." That same year, Eve was named for the second time Outstanding Comedienne in a poll conducted by *Radio and Television* magazine. She told journalist Alice Pardoe West, who quoted her in an April 1951 interview for West's syndicated "Behind the Scenes" column, "I don't know why people laugh at me. Of course in a show I say the lines and if they laugh—fine. But why, I'll never know."

Now an established radio star, earning a reported $4,000 per week, Eve continued to make occasional guest appearances alongside her role on *Miss Brooks*. She starred in the memorable January 18, 1951, segment of *Suspense,* "The Well-Dressed Corpse," scripted by E. Jack Neumann and John Michael Hayes. The episode cast her as affluent New York advertising executive Ruth Francis, who's found by the police lying half-dressed in an alley in Hell's Kitchen. Questioned by police, she says, "I'm the murderer you're looking for." Flashbacks reveal how the worldly and sophisticated Ruth fell in love with handsome, eligible

Playing prominent members of Madison High's student body were Richard Crenna (center) as Walter Denton, and Gloria McMillan (right) as Harriet Conklin, shown here with Eve.

Roy Moore, and announced her intention of marrying him. When he tells her that he's already engaged to Long Island socialite Elizabeth Granger, Ruth is devastated, and the gossip column reports of her being jilted leave her humiliated and furious. In a heated moment, Ruth shoots Roy and goes on the lam, only to learn from a letter he left behind that there is another surprise in store concerning the elusive Miss Granger. Eve's strong and poignant dramatic performance was directed by Elliott Lewis, who would go on to work with her on TV's *The Mothers-in-Law;* also featured in the broadcast was actor Hy Averback, who would later make several appearances on *Our Miss Brooks.* A few weeks later, Eve appeared opposite William Holden in the *Screen Guild Players'* adaptation of "Miss Grant Takes Richmond," stepping into the role originated by her friend Lucille Ball in the 1949 film.

In December 1950, syndicated columnist Erskine Johnson quoted Eve as admitting that she and Brooks were romantically involved, though denying reports that they had already been secretly married. Johnson provided an update in his April 27, 1951, column: "Eve Arden is no longer denying the possibility of an altar sprint with actor Brooks West, but she vows that it won't be in the immediate future." Meanwhile, she and Brooks toured together for 12 weeks that summer with *Here Today,* the comedy she had previously performed at the La Jolla Playhouse. The *Washington Post* noted of her work, "She snarls, coos, bites and blandishes with hilarious zest. She yawns with inexpressible exhaustion and she stretches like a cat after a midnight prowl. Her long, trim figure and that slick strawberry patch atop her head are the envy of every female in sight, a magnet for every male" (June 28, 1951).

With the tour winding down, Eve and Brooks were married on August 25, 1951, at the Shelton, Connecticut farm home of her friends Stanley and Ann Armster. Brooks accompanied Eve back to California following their wedding, so that the newlywed actress could begin a new season playing one of radio's best-known single women in a new season of *Our Miss Brooks.*

The popularity of *Our Miss Brooks* made it a natural to consider for transfer to the emerging medium of television. The radio series would even outlive the television version, finally breathing its last in 1957. Eve had made appearances on the new medium as early as 1948, when she was a guest star on an early episode of *The Texaco Star Theater.* At least as early as 1949, the idea had been floated of moving *Brooks* to television, but the deal didn't come together quickly. In June 1951, Eve told Erskine Johnson, "They want me to do *Our Miss Brooks* as a live TV show. I want to do it on film. We get into big arguments about it." That fall, *I Love Lucy* made its debut, becoming not only an immediate popular hit but revolutionizing the way television comedy was produced. Only weeks after *Lucy*'s debut, *Billboard* reported that CBS's Harry Ackerman was actively negotiating with Eve for the TV version of *Brooks,* now set to be done on film. The three-camera system of shooting before a live audience that had been developed by the Desilu staff would be put to use when *Our Miss Brooks* came to television the following fall. The rehearsal and shooting schedule for *Brooks* was arranged so that the company could use Desilu cameras and lights on days of the week that they weren't needed for *I Love Lucy.* In April 1952, General Foods signed on to sponsor the TV *Miss Brooks,* providing a budget of $32,000 for each installment.

As with many other early TV sitcoms adapted from radio shows, *Our Miss Brooks* would take advantage of the backlog of scripts accumulated over the four-year radio run. Fond of her radio cast, and knowing how strongly they had contributed to the show's success, Eve wanted as many of them as possible to transfer to the TV version. Gale Gordon (Mr. Conklin) signed to reprise his role on video, as did Jane Morgan (Mrs. Davis) and Gloria McMillan (Harriet Conklin). Leonard Smith, heard as Stretch Snodgrass on radio, would make TV appearances in the same role, as did Mary Jane Croft as Miss Brooks's rival Daisy Enright. Although Richard Crenna had

Eve and Brooks at a party, shortly before their marriage in 1951.

outgrown the teenage role of Walter Denton, and was ready to move on to other projects, Eve persuaded him to help launch the television show, and he ultimately stayed for three years. While most of the radio cast would transfer to the television show, Eve and her producer had to find a new Mr. Boynton. Jeff Chandler's burgeoning career as a movie star made it unlikely that he would accept a part in the TV series, which would occupy his time in a way that a weekly radio broadcast hadn't. Also, all concerned agreed that he was too virile and burly in front of the cameras. Though he would continue to play Boynton on radio until his original five-year contract expired in 1953, Chandler was replaced for the TV ensemble by actor Robert Rockwell. A graduate of the Pasadena Playhouse, Rockwell's career prior to his TV sitcom work included a featured role in the late 1940s Broadway production of *Cyrano de Bergerac*. Following in the footsteps of Jeff Chandler, Rockwell would have no trouble making the role of Philip Boynton his own; in

Featured in both the radio and TV versions of *Our Miss Brooks* was Jane Morgan (right, with Eve) as Connie's daffy landlady Mrs. Davis (courtesy Fredrick Tucker).

fact, he would spend much of the rest of his career struggling to overcome the typecasting he experienced as a result of *Brooks*'s enduring popularity.

The show was scheduled to air Fridays at 9:30 P.M. on CBS. Eve enjoyed the work. "I don't mind TV a bit," she told Associated Press reporter Bob Thomas in August 1952, having completed filming of the first several *Brooks* episodes. "In fact, I like it. It's the nearest thing to summer stock. You get to do a different show every week with competent actors and technicians." Eve and her featured players, many of them veterans of the theater, applied the same discipline to their TV sitcom, rarely missing lines during the live performance and sometimes completing the shoot, costume changes and all, in less than an hour. Each segment was filmed with approximately 300 audience members on hand to provide genuine laughs and applause.

Given the necessity to complete an episode every week, Eve accepted the reality that the TV show would be imperfect. "An actor has to be content in realizing that his show isn't going to be the greatest thing in the world every week," she said in a September 14, 1952, interview with the *New York Times*'s Val Adams. "The audience has to learn this too. If the over-all series is considered good, rather than each individual performance, no one can expect any more. No actor can be great every week on television, particularly if he's a great actor. It's fatal to be a perfectionist in television. It's impossible under the circumstances."

An unnamed crew member told *TV Guide* that Eve was a pleasant colleague. "She doesn't like it when the camera reveals unexpected wrinkles or unflattering lines, but what woman does? Fortunately, Eve isn't hard to photograph, as people who have seen the show can tell you" (May 1, 1953).

Though Gale Gordon's talents as a radio actor had long been recognized, regular TV exposure as Osgood Conklin brought him new appreciation. "It is a delight to hear and see Gale Gordon in action," commented columnist Peg Simpson in December 1952, only a few weeks after the show's video debut. "He is a rare performer with the amazing ability to read lines as if he wrote them. His sense of comedy and the absurd is seldom surpassed and his faultless sense of timing can rarely be imitated." Highly regarded in the industry, Gale would have been busy even if the TV version of *Our Miss Brooks* hadn't succeeded; in fact, Lucille Ball had wanted him to play Fred Mertz on *I Love Lucy*.

Brooks West, too, was busy on TV that season, playing the featured role of Richard Rhinelander III, on CBS's *My Friend Irma*, starring Marie Wilson and Cathy Lewis. Unlike Eve's show, *Irma* was telecast live, airing one hour prior to *Brooks* on Friday nights.

Midway through the first season, John Crosby commented, "*Our Miss Brooks* is still essentially a radio show. That is, the situations are a little too broad, the characters a little too one-dimensional. It wouldn't amount to much without Eve Arden, who is a joy to watch and also to listen to. The television show started out pretty shakily last fall but, I must admit, has steadily improved and in its blither moments it can be awfully funny" (February 26, 1953). Though the show wasn't the ratings powerhouse that Desilu's *I Love Lucy* quickly became, it found favor with viewers, and became a staple of CBS's Friday night schedule.

On February 11, 1954, Eve was named Best Female Star of a continuing series at the annual Emmy Awards, beating out such top-rated names as Lucille Ball, Loretta Young, Imogene Coca, and Dinah Shore. Named top male star was Eve's friend and frequent co-star Donald O'Connor, then appearing on NBC's *Colgate Comedy Hour*. International News Service's Emily Belser, in an article published the day after the ceremony, called the Arden/O'Connor wins "the biggest surprises of the evening," adding that the reading of their names "drew gasps from the audience." Not feeling well, and fairly certain she wouldn't win, anyway, Eve was not in attendance at the awards presentation. A few days later, newspapers all across the country carried photos of Eve, still in bed, clutching her Emmy as Brooks looked on approvingly.

Her personal life was also coming along nicely. Eve and Brooks augmented their family in 1953 with the adoption of an infant son they named Duncan Paris West. Less than a year later, in March 1954, Eve announced that she was pregnant. Though Lucille Ball's real-life pregnancy had been famously written into *I Love Lucy* a year or so earlier, this was not an option for Eve, playing the unwillingly single schoolmarm. Some creative costuming and staging choices helped prevent viewers of *Our Miss Brooks* from sensing anything different in the final episodes of the show's second television season. On September 17, 1954, Douglas Brooks West was born.

The formula of *Our Miss Brooks* called for Connie to wait in vain for a romantic gesture from stodgy Philip Boynton. Many viewers pined to see her win his affections, as acknowledged in *TV Guide*'s April 2, 1954, cover story, "Why Miss Brooks Can't Get Her Man." Writer/director Al Lewis explained, "If we were to allow Boynton to catch on, we'd have to let him react. Then he could do only two things: go for the girl or give her the brush. And the format of a very successful show would have to go out the window. If he went for the girl, they'd get married and we'd be off on the kind of family show of which there are already too many. If he gave her the brush, we'd have to drop him and bring in another man—and no other man could possibly be as naïve as Boynton."

During the show's summer hiatus in 1955, Eve, along with Gale Gordon, Richard Crenna, Robert Rockwell, and Gloria McMillan, reprised their TV roles in the Warner Bros.' feature film version of *Our Miss Brooks*. After spending several years cranking out a weekly TV episode, Eve enjoyed the luxury of a 30-day shooting schedule for the feature film, earmarked for 1956 release. Though rumor had it that the movie would resolve the long-standing standoff between Miss Brooks and matrimony, Eve wasn't telling. "If I gave away too much," she told journalist Bob Thomas in his August 1, 1955, column, "the people wouldn't pay their 65 cents to see the picture."

With ratings on the decline, *Our Miss Brooks* underwent a drastic overhaul at the beginning of its fourth video season. The show's 100th aired episode on television was its last to feature the original cast in the established format. The characters of Walter Denton and Harriet Conklin, as played by Richard Crenna and Gloria McMillan, were dropped completely. The show's time slot shifted slightly, being aired an hour earlier on the Friday night schedule. In that fall's scripts, Connie Brooks and her co-workers lost their jobs at Madison High, which was to be demolished in favor of a new highway. The unemployed schoolteacher found a new assignment, teaching younger children at Mrs. Nestor's Elementary School. After so many years of chafing under the dictatorial rule of Osgood Conklin, Connie was dismayed to learn that he, too, has obtained a job there.

New to the cast in supporting roles were Bob Sweeney as school vice-principal Oliver Munsey, who became Connie's pal, and Nana Bryant as Mrs. Nestor. Child actor-singer Ricky Vera, having already logged a couple of guest appearances on the show, was cast in the recurring role of Connie's adoring student Benny Romero. In perhaps the show's most shocking change, Mr. Boynton was written out of the series, as Robert Rockwell's character was said to have taken a job out of town. In the new format, Connie's love interest was initially the brash new gym instructor Clint Allbright, played by William Ching, but he soon gave way to actor Gene Barry, as the more likable Gene Talbot.

The fourth-season episodes of *Our Miss Brooks* made it all too apparent that the show was having trouble settling into a winning pattern. Another cast change was necessitated by the death on December 24, 1955, of character actress Nana Bryant, who originated the role of Mrs. Nestor in the series. She was replaced by Isabel Randolph as another Mrs. Nestor, this time named Ruth, though the character was indistinguishable from the original. Before the season was out, Gene Barry departed his role, and Robert Rockwell was invited back to reprise the greatly missed Mr. Boynton.

Viewers and critics alike responded negatively to the new format. That spring, an unhappy Eve talked bluntly with columnist Marie Torre about the future of *Our Miss Brooks*.

> The changes in *Brooks* were made pretty much against my will and, even worse, we leaped into the revised format without sufficient preparation. I think the haste affected the show. It just isn't the same to me anymore. Little by little, I've been trying to bring back the old members, but I'm still not satisfied. I honestly have no desire to continue next season under the present setup. Maybe it would do me good to take a year off from TV, anyway [March 12, 1956].

Though *Our Miss Brooks* left the prime time schedule in early fall, viewers could still see Connie Brooks in action. Eve sold the network her interest in the series for a sizable sum. CBS began daytime reruns of the series that fall. The radio series also returned for another season that fall, though it too would be history by the summer of 1957.

With her series canceled, Eve told reporter Aline Mosby (for her July 25, 1956, *Hollywood*

Report column) that she intended to take a hiatus from regular TV work, but meant to return: "Then I'd like to do a fairly different series, but still a comedy. The problem is to pick a character that will last. We did four years of *Brooks* on television, and this will be our eighth year on radio." In the fall of 1956, Eve signed a new multi-year deal to remain a CBS television star.

In short order, *The Eve Arden Show* was added to the network's fall 1957 schedule. The series was based on Emily Kimbrough's 1948 memoir *It Gives Me Great Pleasure,* which detailed the author's experiences on lecture tours. Eve's character, Liza Hammond, was a novelist whose book *Summer's End* brought her to the attention of women's clubs and other organizations looking for a speaker. A widow with two young daughters to support, Liza lives in New York City with her family, including her mother Nora. Given co-star billing in the show's opening titles was character actor Allyn Joslyn, as Liza Hammond's agent, George Howell. Eve had worked with Joslyn in several films prior to his being cast in *The Eve Arden Show.* Frances Bavier, already a veteran of the sitcom *It's a Great Life* (NBC, 1954–1956) but best known for her later work as Aunt Bee on *The Andy Griffith Show* (CBS, 1960–1968), was cast as Liza's mother. Completing the regular cast were child actresses Karen Green and Gail Stone as Liza's twin daughters. Alternate-week sponsors were Lever Brothers and Shulton. The opening installment was penned by comedy writer Sol Saks, and directed by Sheldon Leonard.

Since Lucille Ball and Desi Arnaz had brought their top-rated *I Love Lucy* to an end (as a half-hour sitcom) in 1957, some observers speculated as to which comedienne would take over Lucy's top place. The *Los Angeles Times*'s Cecil Smith, writing on August 18, 1957, just a few weeks before the premiere of *The Eve Arden Show,* noted, "The best bet in my book for Lucy's crown is Eve Arden, who comes back to television this year wearing a brand-new personality and driving a bright and shiny new show. She's combed the chalk dust of *Our Miss Brooks* out of her reddish-blond hair."

Smith heaped more praise upon Eve's shoulders in his September 17, 1957, review of the series premiere. He thought the program showed promise, and found the character of Liza Hammond "somebody I personally like a lot more than Connie [Brooks]." Of the show's premise, he said, "I think it's a funny idea and Lord knows Eve Arden can turn a bright phrase or comic twist with anyone. She's surrounded by some fine comedy actors, including Allyn Joslyn as the lecture circuit manager and Frances Bavier as her mother." *TV Guide* liked it too, noting, "Meeting the harassments which beset a traveling lecturer, Miss Arden is as fast as ever with a quip and Allyn Joslyn makes an excellent foil.... All in all, *The Eve Arden Show* is good clean fun" (December 28, 1957). *Variety* wondered about the show's long-term viability, but praised the pilot, noting, "The Sol Saks-Sherman Marks scripting contrib[ution] was frequently clever without being sophisticated and captured the essence of Miss Kimbrough's style and good-natured kidding-in-earnest, particularly when it comes to clubwomen. And Miss Arden, pro that she is, knows her way with a line or a situation" (September 25, 1957).

Eve told reporters like the *Chicago Tribune*'s Seymour Korman that she had bought some 70 new gowns to wear in her new role. "In *Our Miss Brooks,* I was always chasing one man—Mr. Boynton. As Liza, I have a number of guys chasing me. That's why I got the 70 gowns. Quite pleasant" (December 28, 1957). Though the show allowed for romantic possibilities, however, Eve said there were no immediate plans for Liza Hammond to become half of a couple. "The show's main purpose is comedy—this may be a good season for it, after all—and warm mother-daughters relationships." Like her previous show, *The Eve Arden Show* was filmed three-camera style before a studio audience. Eve liked getting the responses of a live audience but told journalist Cecil Smith it was incumbent upon performers to know when to draw the line. "It's so easy to be seduced by laughter," she explained. "To milk a laugh with a funny face or a fall. You can gain a laugh and lose a scene" (September 17, 1957).

The show faced competition from ABC's popular Western drama *The Life and Legend of Wyatt Earp,* and from the comedy/variety show of George Gobel on NBC. From the beginning, *Earp* emerged victorious, with Eve's show running a distant third in its time slot. In early October, according to *Billboard,* author Emily Kimbrough was being sent to California "to see what could be done about shaking the kinks out of the program." A few weeks later, the same publication reported that "a new production team is currently attempting to overhaul" *The Eve Arden Show,* in the face of "generally weak" ratings.

Profiled in *TV Guide,* Eve admitted that not all her fans embraced her latest role, and her characterization that left Connie Brooks behind. "My hairdresser wouldn't watch the new show. She was mad at me for dropping *Our Miss Brooks.* Finally she told me she did tune in the third show. I asked her how she liked it. She shrugged and said, 'So-so.' But she's coming around. Some *Brooks* fans are like that" (November 30, 1957). The star herself enjoyed playing Liza Hammond, with whom she shared some pertinent characteristics. "Liza is more nearly me than Connie was," Eve said. "After all, I'm a happily married career mother. And most people don't seem to realize I'm an introvert."

Stepping into a role, Eve said in a CBS press release promoting her new show, helped her put her own shyness behind her. "When I'm in character ... all doubts leave me. When I'm being Liza Hammond, novelist and lecturer, on my new show, I completely forget about Eve Arden, the person. This ability to transfer my personality to a non-existent person enables me to perform according to script and to forget what people might think of Eve Arden going through the comedy routines that might be required in any given show."

Though it had been easy enough to sell sponsors on a new sitcom starring Eve Arden, the day-to-day execution of *The Eve Arden Show* proved problematic. Aside from the basic premise of an author on a tour, and the twin daughters, the series drew little on Kimbrough's book. The writer and director who had guided the pilot episode were back to work on their regular shows, and unable to participate in subsequent episodes. Brought in by CBS to help out, screenwriter Edmund L. Hartmann later told his biographer Donald W. McCaffrey (*Bound and Gagged in Hollywood*), "I wrote some of her scripts as I produced the show. She didn't want to do broad comedy."

By January 1958, the *New York Times* was quoting "reliable sources" as saying that the sponsors had pulled the plug on *The Eve Arden Show,* which was posting low ratings. Eve's firm contract for 26 shows, however, meant that it would continue at least through its final first-run broadcast in March. The show brought its first and only season to a close with a segment in which Liza receives a marriage proposal from an old college boyfriend. After airing its last original segment in March, Eve's sitcom gave way to a new quiz show, *Wingo.* Ironically, Eve was nominated for an Emmy just as her show was going down for the third time.

Visited on the set by syndicated columnist Hal Humphrey as the closing episode of *The Eve Arden Show* was filmed, the star said, "We were rushed into this new series ... and that's something which won't happen to me again. When we made the pilot film last summer, we were told that the series would not be offered until January of this year. Then all of a sudden we're told it's sold, and we have to start shooting for September. Because of that, we did not get the same writers, producer, or director who made the pilot film. Naturally, with a different set of people, it is difficult for them to take over and keep the same character and direction of the stories" (February 13, 1958). In hindsight, she also wondered whether the prevalence in reruns of *Our Miss Brooks* had hurt the chances of her new show, either by overexposure or simply confusion for viewers who didn't realize that *The Eve Arden Show* was a separate entity.

Although her television work and her growing family would largely keep her away from the theater in the mid–1950s, Eve made a triumphant stage comeback in 1958, when she assumed the starring role in the West Coast production of *Auntie Mame*. The job offer came at a propitious time, as the recent cancellation of *The Eve Arden Show* left her inclined to steer clear of television for a bit. After considering parts in *The Pink Jungle* and *Marriage-Go-Round*, she decided to accept the role in *Auntie Mame* originated in New York by Rosalind Russell. Eve's husband, Brooks West, assumed the part of Mame's husband, Beauregard Jackson Pickett Burnside; Benay Venuta took the role of Vera Charles; while up-and-coming players like Florence MacMichael and Ray Fulmer, both of whom would make their mark on 1960s television, were to be found in the supporting cast. A number of actors who had previously appeared in the New York production reprised their roles, and Eve enjoyed the guidance of original director Morton da Costa as well.

As Eve explained to columnist Hazel Johnson, she had previously declined an offer to replace Russell in the Broadway production, and likewise said no to a lengthy national tour: "Then they said, how about London, and I was tempted. But I knew that Americans were becoming unpopular there and so I said no again. They also asked me to take a company to Honolulu but then we decided to play in it on the West Coast" (September 23, 1958). Surprised herself that she had taken such a long hiatus from stage work, she told the *Los Angeles Times*'s Cecil Smith, "I consider myself so much a part of theater that I never realize I'm away from it" (August 10, 1958).

Having laid *Our Miss Brooks* to rest only two years earlier, Eve took care to play Mame Dennis as a quite different woman from her famed schoolteacher. "Do you see any of 'Miss Brooks' in my playing of Mame?" she asked the *Oakland Tribune*'s Theresa Loeb Cone during an October 1958 interview. "Please, be frank. I really want to know." Assured that Connie Brooks was nowhere to be seen onstage, Eve explained that she consciously chose to play Mame a bit differently than she came across in Patrick Dennis's bestselling book. "I try to make it apparent that Mame is really interested in the boy and that he

Eve's leading man in the West Coast production of *Auntie Mame* was none other than husband Brooks West.

fills a necessary niche in her hectic life." She told Cecil Smith she had never really known anyone quite like Mame in real life, "although Vera Charles, now ... but I wouldn't want to name any names."

Having opened with a brief run in San Diego, the show played Los Angeles for two months, and then concluded with ten weeks in San Francisco. Eve drew rave notices for her interpretation of Mame Dennis, and the show did strong business in every city it played.

Eve also revived her dormant movie career in the late 1950s, accepting a featured role in Otto Preminger's *Anatomy of a Murder* (1959). Also in the cast was Brooks, making his feature film debut in a solid role as the district attorney prosecuting a controversial murder case. The movie was both well received critically and a big box-office hit. Eve followed it up with another prestigious assignment, playing an unusually unsympathetic and unpleasant character in *The Dark at the Top of the Stairs,* adapted from a play by William Inge.

In 1960, Eve and Brooks were on the summer stock circuit with George Axelrod's *Goodbye Charlie,* with Eve assuming Lauren Bacall's 1959–60 Broadway role as Charlie Sorel, the formerly lecherous playboy who's somehow reincarnated as a woman. Considered risqué in its day, the play was toned down a bit from its Broadway incarnation for the stock audiences. Catching opening night at the Lake Whalom Playhouse in Fitchburg, Massachusetts, the un-bylined critic of the *Fitchburg Sentinel* raved, "Junoesque Eve is quick, she's tart, her lines fit the type of humor that has endeared her to theater, movie, and television audiences.... Mr. West, Miss Arden's real-life husband, is a virile, suave gentleman with talent to burn.... It was refreshing to have Eve Arden out from under the school teacher role and delightful to see a husband-wife combo in action" (July 26, 1960). During the show's engagement at the Ivoryton Playhouse, the *Hartford Courant* reported, "As the swearing, cigar-smoking, scotch-swigging Charlie, Miss Arden is pure delight, and you'll have a wonderful time trying to reconcile her appearance with her attitude" (August 17, 1960). According to an item in Hedda Hopper's syndicated column, Eve grew lonesome for her children during the summer tour, and sent for them to join her (July 21, 1960).

The continuing popularity of *Our Miss Brooks* in reruns had producers interested in doing another series with Eve, but she was hesitant. "We've become a nation of critics," she complained to columnist Vernon Scott. "People seem afraid to laugh and admit they have enjoyed a comedy show. They ask their neighbors how they like a show to check their reaction first. Everyone is afraid of being square. After watching a comedy they feel it should be criticized before expressing any enjoyment of the show" (November 26, 1960).

Though Eve would not return to network television with a weekly series until the debut of *The Mothers-in-Law* in 1967, she did pursue several possible series prospects during the early 1960s. Under the banner of Ardley Productions, she collaborated with producer Stanley Roberts on a pilot called "The Colonel's Lady," an unsuccessful candidate for the 1961–62 schedule. This show was designed to allow Eve an opportunity to co-star with her real-life husband Brooks West, playing a movie star and the soldier who marries her and takes her away from Hollywood. In 1965, she played opposite actor Steve Franken (*The Many Loves of Dobie Gillis*) in another pilot, with the working title of "The Eve Arden Show." Directed by Mitchell Leisen, the sitcom pilot for Universal Television cast Eve as a New York widow who interfered constantly in the lives of her family and friends.

Having conquered virtually every other avenue of show business, Eve surprised some observers when she accepted a Las Vegas nightclub engagement in 1962. Armed with special material written by Sidney Miller, she opened at the Sahara Hotel late that summer. Reported the *Los Angeles Times*'s John L. Scott, "Any skeptics about Miss Arden's versatility soon are set right by the comedienne's combination of humor, hoofing talents and devastating impressions of famous personages" (August 28, 1962). Supporting Eve were four male dancers, as well as vocalist Vic Dana and comic Lennie Weinrib. Scott noted that Eve's show in the Sahara's Congo Room was playing to "capacity audiences."

In the summer of 1963, the *New York Times*'s drama editor Sam Zolotow reported that Eve's agent was in negotiations with the producers of Howard Teichmann's *A Rainy Day in Newark*, which was to feature Eddie Mayehoff in a leading role. "The stint intended for Miss Arden," Zolotow reported, "is a liberal-minded owner of a small New Jersey clock factory." When the play opened that fall, however, the major female roles were being played by Dody Goodman and Mary McCarty, and it closed its doors in less than a week.

Later that year, Eve and her family departed on a year-long trip to Europe. She was mostly inactive professionally while enjoying the opportunity to spend time with her family. However, while in London, she accepted the starring role in a British-made pilot for a new TV sitcom variously known as "The Eve Arden Show" (again) or "He's All Yours." With the network and sponsors hesitant to allow shooting to continue overseas, the pilot didn't sell, though it aired as an episode of *Vacation Playhouse* in the summer of 1964.

Back at home after their year away, Eve went back to work with a revival of *Wonderful Town* at L.A.'s Valley Music Theater. Of her performance as Ruth, the *Los Angeles Times*'s Kevin Thomas remarked, "She creates a character of warmth, vitality, and wry good humor.... She is perfect in a part that suits her so well one might think it had been written with her in mind" (October 29, 1964). The role served not only to win her critical plaudits, but to remind producers that this memorable actress was back on the scene.

In early 1965, Eve filmed a featured role in the youth-oriented AIP comedy *Sergeant Deadhead*, then resumed her theater work. *Beekman Place* had not been a success in its original 1964 Broadway production, closing after only 29 performances, but Eve and Brooks took it to summer stock only a few months later. Samuel Taylor's script outlined a romantic triangle among a professional violinist, his wife, and his old flame. According to an announcement of the show's opening at the Ogunquit Playhouse published in the *Kennebec* (MN) *Journal*, "Urbane epigrams and ticklish embarrassments are traded by a retired concert violinist and a titled widow meeting twenty years after an experience they once shared but don't want to recall, especially within the hearing of the violinist's wife" (July 3, 1965). Eve took the role of Englishwoman Lady Pamela Piper in the comedy, which Arlene Francis had originated on Broadway, while Brooks appeared as Christian Bach-Nielsen, a violinist being pressured by wife Emily (Barbara Berjer) to continue his musical career. Catching the show during its run at the Pocono Playhouse, the *Pocono Record*'s Pat McCain Williams found it "a fast-paced comedy" that was "an excellent vehicle for her comedy talent" (August 11, 1965). In the show's supporting cast as Eve's daughter was actress Alexandra Moltke, soon to become the leading lady of TV's Gothic soap opera *Dark Shadows*. Eve and Brooks were joined on the road that summer by three of their four children. As she explained at a women's club luncheon covered by the *Syracuse Herald-Journal*, "Our boys are swimming in pools coast to coast, and Connie helps me make quick changes back stage" (July 21, 1965).

She accepted the lead role of Dolly Levi in the Chicago company of *Hello, Dolly!* The production was directed and choreographed by Gower Champion, who worked with Eve for a week prior to her debut in the role. When Eve joined the Chicago troupe in the summer of 1966, the New York production, by then starring Ginger Rogers, had recently marked its 1,000th performance and was still going strong. Carol Channing had been playing the role in Chicago for nearly six months to brisk ticket sales. As the *Chicago Tribune*'s William Leonard noted in his June 14, 1966, review of her opening night performance, Eve's interpretation of Dolly was no mimicking of her predecessor's. "Miss Arden," he

Eve returned to weekly television in 1967 as the star of NBC's *The Mothers-in-Law*. At left is TV husband Herbert Rudley.

wrote, "doesn't go in for all that eye rolling and lip smacking and caressing of vowels and scratching of consonants, the alternate roaring and squeaking, the flirting with the galleries, the little girl coyness and the business woman's hard-headedness. She is more of a lady, charming and funny, winning and warm, but never surprising with an explosion or a wild veering in a new direction of personality." In January 1968, after she had left the production and assumed the lead role in TV's *The Mothers-in-Law*, she was presented with the Sarah Siddons Society's award for "Chicago's Actress of the Year." According to the *Chicago Tribune*'s Eleanor Page, Eve accepted the accolades of her peers with grace, saying, "You gave Carol Channing the key to the city. I was afraid I might wind up with her pass key. But when I stepped on stage at the Shubert I knew this Dolly was back where she belongs" (January 14, 1968).

Meanwhile, in Hollywood, her longtime friend and colleague Desi Arnaz was back at work after a lengthy hiatus, and wanted to work with Eve again. Desi returned to active television production in 1966, at the invitation of CBS president William Paley. Having seen what the stress of running Desilu at its peak did to his health, Desi was interested in the creative aspect of working in television, provided he wasn't expected to assume the administrative chores he'd grown to hate. The newly formed Desi Arnaz Productions jumped into the fray with three projects that were pilots for prospective weekly series; the adventure show *Land's End,* and two situation comedies—*The Carol Channing Show* and *The Mothers-in-*

Law. Of the three, it was the latter that quickly emerged as the most promising candidate for a network berth.

From the start, *The Mothers-in-Law* was intended as a starring vehicle for Eve Arden. The concept for the show was developed by Bob Carroll, Jr. and Madelyn Davis, the writers whose work had been integral to the success of *I Love Lucy*. Though the comedic character of the mother-in-law was nothing new in television, Carroll and Davis envisioned a series that told the story from her point of view. It was a role that fit Eve beautifully, though despite being the mother of four children she herself had yet to play mother-in-law in real life.

As their original outline of the format, reproduced in James Elliot Yanizyn's *The Mothers-in-Law: Historical Analysis of a Television Series*, explained, "*The Mothers-in-Law* is the story of two couples, the Hubbards and the Buells—their friendship, and their fights—and the involvement (and let's face it—meddling) in the lives of their married children. It will also be the story of their children, Jim and Suzie, and how it is to go to college when married, and how they react to their meddling in-laws." In characterizing the role that Eve would play, Carroll and Davis wrote, "Eve and Roger [later renamed Herb] Buell are fairly conventional people who do the right things, support worthy causes, and play excellent bridge. Eve's roses are the envy of the neighborhood, and she is an excellent cook, although she sometimes gets over her head with French dishes. She plays golf and is very proud of the fact that she was once an amateur champion and has lots of trophies from club tournaments." At one point, Desi and his colleagues envisioned another favorite 1950s sitcom star, Ann Sothern (*Private Secretary*), playing opposite Eve. They soon came to realize, however, that Sothern was somewhat similar to Eve comedically, and the combination of those two ladies would not generate the sparks that the show needed. Instead, actress-singer Kaye Ballard was chosen to play the mother-in-law who would be both best friend and occasional rival to Eve's character.

Signed to play the role of Eve's TV husband was actor Herbert Rudley, who'd recently been featured in the single-season NBC sitcom *Mona McCluskey* (1965–66). According to notes in Desi's production files, other actors considered for husbandly roles in the series were Morey Amsterdam, who'd recently completed his run in *The Dick Van Dyke Show*, and Eve's husband, Brooks West. Richard Deacon, who would join *The Mothers-in-Law* in its second season, would have been a possibility also, but was committed to an ongoing role in the company's other sitcom project, *The Carol Channing Show*. Once casting for the show was complete, most of the first names originally chosen by Carroll and Davis were dropped, in favor of allowing the actors to use their own given names.

Funding for the pilot episode of *The Mothers-in-Law*, which was filmed in January 1967, was largely provided by Procter and Gamble. The show would be filmed three-camera style in front of a studio audience, the method that had originally been developed for *I Love Lucy*. Davis and Carroll's original outline for the series also called for each family to have a 12-year-old boy, but these characters were dropped before the pilot script was written. In the pilot, Eve's daughter was played by actress-dancer Kay Cole, but Desi replaced her with Deborah Walley before the series launched. Recruited to the show's staff were numerous Desilu veterans, including musical director Wilbur Hatch.

Although Procter and Gamble was enthusiastic about *The Mothers-in-Law*, and willing to provide full weekly sponsorship, CBS executives were dubious. As the outspoken Kaye Ballard later explained in a *New York Times* interview with Rex Reed, "There's this big dum-dum at CBS ... who didn't want this show. I mean they were paying Desi Arnaz something like $50,000 just to *think* and then when he came up with this show *and* both of the original writers of *I Love Lucy* to write it, this dum-dum says, 'Who cares about mothers-in-law?'

Desi said, 'Everybody who has ever had one or is about to have one, which includes most of the human race.'.... There was no loyalty to Desi or to Eve Arden, who had both made so much money for CBS in the past. Even with the sponsor insistent on the show, they still said no" (September 10, 1967).

When the pilot failed to attract a firm offer there, Desi and his compatriots took it to NBC, which agreed to host the series on its Sunday night schedule. Although the sale was cause for celebration, it was apparent that the time slot would be a challenge—that half-hour between Walt Disney and *Bonanza* was a difficult one. Competition from *The Ed Sullivan Show* on CBS and *The FBI* on ABC would be strenuous. As Desi told columnist Vernon Scott, "Every year for six years NBC has slipped a new show in that spot. Five of them were comedies [most recently, *Hey, Landlord!*] and they all died. Sullivan had a half-hour head start on them" (February 4, 1968). Determined to catch viewers' attention before they even considered changing channels, Desi filled the opening titles of *The Mothers-in-Law* with brassy music, sound effects, and a rotating series of action-filled clips from the show.

Having been the sole star of her previous sitcom efforts, Eve now found herself sharing the stage with another actress whose role was of equal importance. Some expected sparks between the two women offstage as well as on. "At first, they eyed each other like a couple of stray dogs," said an anonymous observer in a *TV Guide* profile of Eve. "There might have even been a few hackles up. But they seem to complement each other and are good friends now." In "People Appreciate Comedy," an article that appeared under Eve's byline during the summer of 1968, the star said, "I have loved working with Kaye Ballard. She's sort of a big pixie, always full of fun and always 'up' when it's time to go on. And while we each play a mother-in-law, we are two different people. We complement one another. What she is, she's a very funny girl."

Eve also praised Desi, telling the *Los Angeles Times*'s Walt Dutton, "I feel confident with Desi at the helm. He's a firebrand and sometimes he blows his top, but it's because he fights for something if he believes in it. He's a perfectionist, and that makes it difficult because I am, too" (October 29, 1967). Eve added that she liked Davis and Carroll's scripts, and thought the series' basic setup lent itself to many viable stories.

Madelyn Davis would later tell scholar James Elliot Yanizyn, whose 1974 master's thesis at San Diego State University was a history of *The Mothers-in-Law*, "It was a happy show to work on. There was no temperament.... I believe Eve is the most even-tempered woman. I've never seen her in a bad mood." Another admirer, executive producer Desi Arnaz, told the Associated Press's Cynthia Lowry, "In the past 30 years, how many really attractive women comediennes can you think of? Carole Lombard, Jean Arthur, Roz Russell, Kay Kendall, Lucy, of course—and Eve—that's just about the whole list" (September 3, 1967).

By the late 1960s, some found Desi's style of situation comedy old-fashioned, but he dismissed the criticism. "In comedy, all there is to worry about is the relationships between people," he told Vernon Scott in a February 1968 interview. "You just take the normal things that happen at home and exaggerate them a little bit. If you do it right you won't win the Nobel Prize, but you'll be entertaining people. The toughest thing in the world is to be honest and natural. So if you are going to be funny you can't be bigger than life; you have to make the situations recognizable to all of your audience."

Signed to serve as the show's producer and frequent director was Elliott Lewis, who had previously produced the first two seasons of *The Lucy Show*. In addition to his work behind the camera, Desi made occasional guest appearances in *The Mothers-in-Law*, as a bullfighter named Señor Raphael del Gado, who befriends the Hubbards and the Buells.

Some affiliated with *The Mothers-in-Law* felt that Desi's contribution to the show was marred by his dependence on alcohol. Director Maury Thompson, who had been working with Lucy and Desi since serving as the script clerk on the first season of *I Love Lucy*, told writer Geoffrey Mark Fidelman in *The Lucy Book*, "By this time [1967], I am sorry to say that Desi's disease had gotten out of control. He hardly knew what was going on around him. Eve didn't know how to deal with Desi's condition, but she never raised her voice or made a fuss. When it got to the point where she felt uncomfortable, she said, 'Desi, darling, I'm really tired. I'm going to go home now.'" Editor Dann Cahn concurred: "It was a difficult show because the man in charge had a problem."

Ratings for *The Mothers-in-Law* were decent, and better than some had anticipated in a highly competitive time slot, but not exceptional. Procter and Gamble was willing to sponsor a second season of the show, provided it could be had for the same per-episode price as in season one. This meant that Eve and her co-stars would be expected to forego the customary 5 percent annual pay increase given to actors in an ongoing series. All but actor Roger C. Carmel, cast as Roger Buell, agreed to the plan. Angered, Desi cut Carmel loose, and replaced him with actor Richard Deacon.

From the time Madelyn Davis and Bob Carroll wrote their original proposal for *The Mothers-in-Law*, they had envisioned that the second season would find the young married couple expecting their first child. For the show's second season, Eve and Kaye Ballard were

Eve and Brooks frequently paired for theatrical engagements in the late 1960s and early 1970s.

given billing above the title, though their names still appeared in smaller type than that of "presenter" Desi Arnaz. Ratings did not improve, and the second season was the show's last. The show's 56 segments went into syndication, playing numerous local stations throughout the 1970s.

Freed of her commitment to weekly television, Eve continued to be active onstage. She often teamed with her husband Brooks, who functioned variously as co-star, director, or both. Among the shows that were part of their repertoire were *Cactus Flower*, *Beekman Place*, *Marriage-Go-Round*, and *Critic's Choice*. In *Under Papa's Picture*, a comedy by Joe Connelly and George Tibbles, Eve played a widowed mother who finds herself pregnant after a liaison with an Italian lover (played by Brooks). Catching a 1976 production of the latter at Chicago's Drury Lane North, the *Chicago Herald*'s Genie Campbell called it "relaxed, contemporary, exceedingly delightful theater," adding that Eve was "woven into the play as a star should be, an important asset and not just as a cover-up for stale material" (April 30, 1976).

In 1970, Eve headlined the national touring company of Leonard Gershe's *Butterflies Are Free*. Eve told the *Chicago Tribune*, "It's a very good, interesting, fun play. I think people are put off a little bit that it's a play about a blind boy. It's a comedy, but very touching. I can't remember doing a play so satisfying to an audience." Performing at Los Angeles's Huntington Hartford Theater, Eve played opposite film actor Wendell Burton. Among the well-known guests at a black-tie dance following the opening night performance were Zsa Zsa Gabor, Ann Miller, producer David Merrick and Eve's frequent stand-in Marijane Maricle.

The following year, Eve and Brooks took a new show, Lee Thuna's *Natural Ingredients*, on a tour that was hoped to culminate in a Broadway run. Richard Day's review in the *Bridgeport Post* suggested that the show's future in New York was dubious at best. Calling Thuna's script "trite, feebly cute, and tediously predictable," Day wrote, "Reminiscent of an inflated television play of the sort hopefully denied prime time, Miss Thuna's dreary script boasts Eve Arden's passable, seasoned antics as a comedienne, several mildly odd and obnoxious (if not uncommon) character types, and a vestigial generation gap element, all clustered about an attractive couple in early middle age whose marriage has lost its luster" (July 13, 1971). Indeed, the hoped-for Broadway production never materialized.

Though she was seen frequently as a television guest star in the 1970s, another weekly series never happened. Interviewed by the *Chicago Tribune*'s Pat Colander in 1975, Eve remarked, "I've been considering another series. It's such a difficult time; the business is run by people who don't know much about the business. I've seen two pretty good scripts, but there are always other problems: Will the writers stay with it? Will we have enough autonomy? Will the cast be top notch?" She teamed with Don Knotts for a CBS comedy pilot called "Harry and Maggie," but the series did not sell. Movie-wise, she made her Disney debut with a funny character role in *The Strongest Man in the World*, her first theatrical feature in 10 years.

A disastrous 1976 production of *Applause* in Australia left Eve and her husband stranded a long way from home; the show shut down when producers failed to pay the bills, and their salaries were still owed them. Back home, she replenished the coffers with guest appearances on the some of the most popular shows of the late 1970s and early 1980s, including *Maude*, *The Love Boat*, *Alice*, and *Hart to Hart*.

In early 1978 Eve went into rehearsal for an L.A. production of *Absurd Person Singular*, by Alan Ayckbourn, a trio of one-act plays about a series of Christmas Eve parties attended by three couples. Aside from Eve, the principal players included Stockard Channing, Lawrence Pressman, John McMartin (as Eve's husband), and Roberta Maxwell. Eve told the *Los Angeles Times*'s Wayne Warga, "I saw the play in London at least three years ago and I loved it so I wrote a fan letter to Alan Ayckbourn. I was amazed to find what a young man he was, young enough to be one of my children. The Theatre Guild offered it to Brooks and me but we couldn't do it at the time. This time it all worked and I'm so happy I can do it.... It's a funny play with a lot of symbolism and meaning that isn't hard to take. The last act is ... well, a bit weird. But good!" (February 15, 1978). The *Times*'s theater critic Dan Sullivan wasn't dazzled by the result, but said, "Farce is like champagne, it makes you tolerant, and this is vintage stuff, with no headaches in the morning.... It's three wonderful plays about three terrible parties, period" (February 18, 1978).

Nearly 60 years after making her motion picture debut, Eve had her biggest movie success in years when she played the "guest" role of Miss McGee in the smash hit musical comedy *Grease*. The film's enormous popularity introduced her to a new generation of moviegoers, and amused longtime fans who were pleased to see *Our Miss Brooks* "promoted" from teacher to principal at last.

Eve continued to travel the country for stage appearances into the early 1980s. In the summer of 1980, she was treading the boards in Texas with Donald O'Connor in a production of Patrick Dennis's *Little Me*. The following year, she was seen at San Antonio's Fiesta Dinner Playhouse in the comedy *A Single Indiscretion*.

The year 1982 saw the release of Eve's final two feature films, neither of them a top-flight addition to her résumé. *Pandemonium* made little impact on paying audiences, but *Grease II*, while critically shrugged off, was one of Paramount's major summer releases.

In early 1983, Eve withdrew from a Santa Barbara production of *Barefoot in the Park* when she was offered the starring role in a Broadway show. Eve's final such venture was the disastrous *Moose Murders*. Newcomer Arthur Bicknell's comedy, according to the *New York Times*, was "a mystery farce [that] relates the adventures of Joe Buffalo Dance, Snooks and Howie Keene, Nurse Dagmar, Stinky Holloway, and others pulled together on one stormy night at the Wild Moose Lodge, where several murders take place, Stinky tries to sleep with his mother, and a man in a moose costume is assaulted by a bandage-wrapped quadriplegic."

Eve and a co-star in *Moose Murders*. The moose seems to be winning.

Interviewed by the Associated Press's Jay Sharbutt, Eve said she was happy to be back on Broadway after a 42-year absence, but demurred at discussing the story of *Moose Murders* in detail. "I can tell you it's exhausting because it's kind of a wild farce and there's much running around and falling down in it, and a few people get killed" (February 4, 1983).

Rehearsals for *Moose Murders* soon turned contentious. Eve thought the script needed work but was told she could make no changes. Production personnel complained that the star did not know her lines. Finally reaching an impasse, Eve withdrew from the production prior to opening night. Publicly, the reason given was the customary "artistic differences." She was replaced by actress Holland Taylor (best-known for her later roles in the TV sitcoms *Bosom Buddies* and *Two and a Half Men*).

Filing his opening-night review, the *New York Times*'s Frank Rich still seemed shell-shocked by what he'd witnessed onstage. "From now on, there will always be two groups of theatergoers in this world," Rich wrote, "those who have seen *Moose Murders,* and those who have not.... A visit to *Moose Murders* is what will separate the connoisseurs of Broadway disaster from mere dilettantes for many moons to come." Clive Barnes, in the *New York Post*, wrote, "This murderously uncomic murder comedy was so indescribably bad, that I do not intend to waste anyone's time describing it" (February 23, 1983).

Moose Murders drew ferocious reviews from virtually every corner, and closed after a single disastrous performance. It would go on to achieve a weird sort of cult fame for its sheer awfulness. Actress June Gable, a survivor of the show's one and only performance, later recalled, "After those awful reviews, the box office was flooded with calls. They kept telling them the show had closed and people would say, 'What? We can't buy tickets?' We could have sold out for a month." A quarter-century later, with the benefit of hindsight, the playwright himself told the *New York Times*'s Campbell Robertson, "Was it really that bad? The simple answer is yes" (April 21, 2008).

Though the experience of *Moose Murders* left a bad taste in her mouth, Eve hardly lacked for work. Not long after the disastrous show closed, she was offered a featured role in Woody Allen's next film, ultimately released as *The Purple Rose of Cairo*. Before she could begin work on the film, however, a family crisis intervened. Eve's husband, Brooks, suffered a stroke in December 1983. Unwilling to leave his side during this ordeal, Eve told Woody Allen to recast her role.

Allen later told his biographer Eric Lax (*Conversations with Woody Allen*) of his disappointment that he didn't get the opportunity to work with Eve. "I *hired* her. She came to New York for costume fittings. She was playing the Zoe Caldwell part in *Purple Rose*. At that time I was thinking, My God, I'm working with *Van Johnson* and *Eve Arden!* Whoever thought? I'm playing the outfield with Joe DiMaggio and Babe Ruth! But then her husband died and she pulled out." Eve's beloved husband Brooks died on February 7, 1984, at the age of 67, having never regained consciousness after his debilitating stroke.

As far back as the 1960s, Eve had talked in interviews about wanting to write a book. She had been writing steadily prior to Brooks's illness, but put the book aside during his hospitalization and for several months after his death. In mid–1985, St. Martin's Press published Eve's autobiography, *Three Phases of Eve,* to good reviews.

After losing Brooks, Eve would work only a few more times as an actress. A 1987 appearance on CBS's popular prime time soap opera *Falcon Crest,* working with her old Warners' colleague Jane Wyman, was Eve's last television performance.

Eve died at her home on November 12, 1990, having been in failing health for some time. Heart disease was given as the cause of death, but she had also been diagnosed with cancer. She was buried at the Westwood Village Memorial Park Cemetery in Westwood, where the marker on her grave reads, "Eve Arden West, 1908–1990. Wife-Mother-Actress-Author. The world will remember."

In the days following her death, tributes poured in. On *Entertainment Tonight,* film historian Leonard Maltin said, "Having Eve Arden in a movie was like having comedy insurance. She knew her way around a wisecrack better than anybody in Hollywood." Noted critic Carrie Rickey commented in the *Philadelphia Inquirer,* "Producers came to rely on Arden to move in with a brittle line of dialogue just as their picture threatened to go awash in the soggy flow of the leading lady's tears. In studio parlance, Arden was a 'lifeguard.' She made forgettable pictures memorable and good pictures terrific" (November 13, 1990).

Though she may not have attained the top rung of stardom, she enjoyed nearly 60 years of steady employment and audience affection. Only a few years before her death, Eve told journalist Bob Thomas that she didn't mind being thought of primarily as a comedic actress. "I love making people laugh," she said. "If I'm in a serious play, I often think to myself, 'I could make that line funny.' There has always been such a need for laughter in the world, and never more than today" (May 24, 1985).

II

Filmography

The Song of Love (1929)

Belle Baker (*Anna Gibson*), Ralph Graves (*Tom Gibson*), David Durand (*Buddy Gibson*), Eunice Quedens [Eve Arden] (*Mazie LeRoy*), Arthur Housman (*Joe, the Acrobat*), Charles Wilson (*Traveling Salesman*)
Director: Erle C. Kenton. *Producer:* Edward Small. *Screenplay:* Howard Green, Dorothy Howell, Norman Houston. *Story:* Howard J. Green, Henry McCarthy. *Photography:* Joe Walker. *Songs:* Maurice Abrahams, Mack Gordon, Max Rich, George Weist. *Film Editor:* Gene Havlick. *Assistant Director:* Sam Nelson. *Chief Sound Engineer:* John Livadary. *Sound Engineers:* Edward L. Bernds, Harry Blanchard. Columbia Pictures; released November 13, 1929. B&W; 76 minutes.

Anna and Tom Gibson, along with their young son, Buddy, are successful vaudeville performers in an act called "The Three Musketeers." Anna, however, aspires to better things for Buddy. When he skips a performance one day, and is found playing ball outside the theatre, his mother realizes that work is costing him his childhood. Anna insists that he drop out of the act to complete his schooling, lest he become "just another actor." Needing a new act, Tom takes on a new partner, sexy blonde Mazie, with whom he soon becomes romantically involved, and drowns his sorrows in a bottle or two. Anna supports herself and her son with a job as a café singer at the Paradise Cabaret while Buddy is placed in military school. She later graduates to a high-paying gig at the Palace, while Tom is spiraling downward. The young boy takes it upon himself to see that his parents are reunited, and one day Anna is surprised during her performance to find both her son and her recalcitrant husband in attendance.

Belle Baker (1893–1957) was a singer/actress who played her only leading role in film here. A popular vaudeville star, she was signed by producer Edward Small to make her film debut in the spring of 1929; the film's working title was "Cradle of Jazz." Composer Maurice Abrahams, whose songs are heard in the film, was Baker's real-life husband. According to studio publicity, "Miss Baker has consistently refused to appear on the screen because she felt that the talkies had not reached the point to do justice to the human voice.... Miss Baker feels now that talking films are sufficiently perfected to reproduce the voice so that it is life-like." Filming was completed in September 1929.

The 21-year-old Eve Arden, billed under her real name, Eunice Quedens, makes her film debut playing a *femme fatale*. The *New York Times*'s Mordaunt Hall wrote, "Eunice Quedens makes Mazie quite lifelike" (November 14, 1929). *Variety* thought her role as "the blonde come-between" was "a cinch part" (November 20, 1929).

Sound engineer Edward Bernds, who had recently been hired by Columbia for $85 a week, recalled in his memoir, *Mr. Bernds Goes to Hollywood*, "The first day of production of *Song of Love* went smoothly, and so did the days that followed. The film presented few problems; the members of the cast had good voices, there were no frantic dolly shots or complicated stagings, and each day the rushes were satisfactory." Though he remembered director Erle C. Kenton as "arrogant and condescending," Bernds had a fonder recollection of Eve, writing, "The role of the chorus girl who seduced Ralph Graves was played by a young actress, Eunice Quedens. In her skimpy chorus-girl costume she was truly gorgeous and drew the admiring—and perhaps even the lustful—attention of the crew members. Later, Eunice Quedens became Eve Arden."

Ads proclaimed this "the greatest story of mother love ever," and promised moviegoers "music, drama, love, and heart-throbs skillfully blended." A reviewer for the *Kansas City Star* reported that *The Song of Love* "is unusual and pathetic, so much so that many of the more emotional in the audience frankly wipe tears from their eyes during the scenes of sorrow and sadness. Despite its psychological possibilities and its pathos, the picture is genuinely entertaining and the audiences were so enthusiastic about it when we saw it that applause seemed imminent several times and actually rang out once." Added the reviewer, "Eunice Quedens, who recently went to the movies from Henry Duffy's West Coast stock company ... is capable in her first picture role"(March 9, 1930).

Film historian Richard Barrios, whose *A Song in the Dark: The Birth of the Musical Film* is the definitive account of early musicals, says of Eve's film debut, "Naturally the most interest in seeing her came from it being such a younger and brassier Eve Arden. She's very much in the line of early-talkie tough soubrette types. For a film neophyte, she seems comfortable before the camera and at ease speaking lines and with her musical chores. It's not too difficult, too, to draw a line of progression from this performance to her bit in *Dancing Lady* and then to something like *Ziegfeld Girl*. We can certainly see the Arden personality taking shape with the rough edges slowly smoothed out and that wonderful sardonic/hearty veneer forming."

Long thought to be a lost film, *The Song of Love* received its first public screening in many years when it was featured in the 2001 Cinecon film festival program.

Dancing Lady (1933)

Joan Crawford (*Janie Barlow*), Clark Gable (*Patch Gallagher*), Franchot Tone (*Tod Newton*), May Robson (*Dolly Todhunter*), Winnie Lightner (*Rosette LaRue*), Fred Astaire (*Himself*), Robert Benchley (*Ward King*), Ted Healy (*Steve*), Art Jarrett (*Vocalist*), Grant Mitchell (*Jasper Bradley, Sr.*), Nelson Eddy (*Specialty Singer*), Maynard Holmes (*Jasper Bradley, Jr.*), Sterling Holloway (*Pinky*), Gloria Foy (*Vivian Warner*), Moe Howard (*Moe*), Curly Howard (*Curly*), Larry Fine (*Harry*), Eunice Quedens [Eve Arden] (*Marcia*)
Director: Robert Z. Leonard. *Executive Producer:* David O. Selznick. *Associate Producer:* John W. Considine, Jr. *Screenplay:* Allen Rivkin, P.J. Wolfson, from a book by James Warner Bellah. *Photography:* Oliver T. Marsh. *Special Effects:* Slavko Vorkapich. *Orchestra Conductor:* Lou Silvers. *Rerecording Director:* Douglas Shearer. *Art Director:* Merrill Pye. *Interior Decorations:* Edwin B. Willis. *Gowns:* Adrian. *Film Editor:* Margaret Booth. MGM; released November 24, 1933. B&W; 92 minutes.

Aspiring to a career in the legitimate theater, beautiful dancer Janie Barlow is meanwhile earning her keep in a burlesque show, until it is shut down in a police raid. Bailed out of the pokey by wealthy Tod Newton, who has taken a shine to Janie, the lovely dancer rebuffs his romantic advances but accepts his help getting into the chorus of a Broadway show. Dance director Patch Gallagher, annoyed to have this former burlesque dancer foisted off on him because of her friendship with a wealthy potential investor, tests her to the limit. While Tod conspires behind the scenes to make the show a flop, so that Janie will retire from the theater and marry him, she and Patch are equally determined to build their careers and make *Dancing Lady* into a success.

A dozen years before they so memorably teamed in *Mildred Pierce,* Eve (still known as Eunice Quedens) and Joan Crawford (1905–1977) worked together for the first time in *Dancing Lady.* Her role so brief that she did not receive billing, Eve attracted notice nonetheless for a strong scene in which she plays Marcia, an actress unsuccessfully auditioning for a role in *Dancing Lady.* Janie arrives at the Bradley Theatre just in time to witness Marcia's angry exit, after Patch Gallagher has rejected her for the role of a Southern belle. Stalking through the lobby, she says, "And you all can tell that Mr. Gallagher that cotton will grow black before I come see him again! Where we-all come from, suh, gentlemen know how to speak to ladies." Just as we're thinking the Southern accent sounds a bit overdone, Patch's assistant Steve retorts, "You-all go back to the Mason-Dixon Line, sugar!" Disgusted, Eve's character leaves in the company of her agent, whom she chides bitterly, saying, "Oh, I told you that Southern accent would sound phony!" Joan Crawford, as Janie, looks on wide-eyed as the scene plays out, and notes there is now a sign on the theater door saying, "No more girls wanted." (Being a Joan Crawford heroine, of course, Janie is in no way dissuaded from barging in to request her audition).

Eve, who readily confessed to a longtime crush on Clark Gable, would have a better opportunity to get acquainted with the popular leading man when they were both seen in *Comrade X* (1940).

Fred Astaire (1899–1987), newly arrived in Hollywood after signing with RKO, made his film debut here, loaned to MGM for a brief appearance as one of the performers in Patch Gallagher's show. Ted Healy and His Stooges, newcomers to MGM in 1933, are also seen as members of the company. Clearly unafraid of hyperbole, MGM publicity writers described *Dancing Lady* as "a picture with spectacle and splendor never before attempted and that goes for all film musicals heretofore. *Dancing Lady* is not just another picture. It is the screen's crowning achievement in the production of elaborate musical extravaganzas."

Oh, Doctor (1937)

Edward Everett Horton (*Edward J. "Ned" Billop*), Donrue Leighton (*Helen Frohman*), William Hall (*Rodney Cummings*), Eve Arden (*Shirley Truman*), Thurston Hall ("*Doc*" *Erasmus Thurber*), Catherine Doucet (*Martha Striker*), William Demarest ("*Marty*" *Short*), Edward Brophy ("*Meg*" *Smith*), Minerva Urecal ("*Death Watch*" *Mary Mackleforth*), Wilson Benge (*Butler*), James Donlan (*Mr. Stoddard*), Kitty McHugh (*First Nurse*), Cornelius Keefe (*Ship's Officer*), Ben Taggart (*Policeman*), Edward Le Saint (*Dr. Evans*), Lloyd Ingraham (*Dr. Bower*), Henry Roquemore (*Auto Salesman*), Frank H. Hammond (*First Patient*)

Director: Raymond B. McCarey. *Screenplay:* Harry Clork, Brown Holmes, based on the novel by Harry Leon Wilson. *Associate Producer:* Edmund Grainger. *Director of Photography:* Milton Krasner. *Special Effects:* John P. Fulton. *Art Director:* Jack Otterson. *Associate Art Director:* Loren Patrick. *Film Editor:* Bernard W. Burton. *Musical Director:* Lou Forbes. *Sound:* William R. Fox, Jesse T. Bastian. Universal Pictures; released April 1, 1937. B&W; 72 minutes.

Ned Billop will be a wealthy man in six months, when he is due to inherit $500,000, but the inveterate hypochondriac fears he won't last long enough to collect his reward. Aboard a ship to California, Ned meets four suspicious characters—three con men and their lady friend Shirley Truman. Ned accepts the foursome's offer to sign over his inheritance in exchange for an immediate $50,000, so that he can enjoy what he believes will be his last days. Ned and his new acquaintances take up residence in California, where they hire a pretty nurse, Helen, to attend to his every imagined ache and pain. Attracted to Helen, as is their landlord Rodney, Ned forces himself to overcome his fears so that he can impress her with his derring-do. In turn, Helen learns of the scammers' attempt to defraud Ned, and helps him turn the tables on the felonious foursome.

Eve Arden made her official movie debut under her new name in this Universal comedy. This was the second screen adaptation of Harry Leon Winston's 1920 novel, following in the footsteps of a 1925 silent version with Reginald Denny and Mary Astor.

Universal ads promised Depression Era moviegoers, "What this country needs is a darned good laugh! Here it is!" The *Oakland Tribune*'s Wood Soanes thought the starring role "puts a good deal of strain on Horton who has to spend a good first half of the film relying on his jitters and his facial contortions to make laughs grow where the author didn't plant them" (May 28, 1937). Soanes listed Eve as among the supporting players who "lend a hand" in making the film amusing. *Variety* wasn't too enthusiastic either, but noted, "Smooth dialogue keeps this hokey picture from going completely corkscrew and it's sufficiently swift to please the fans in the multiple trade" (June 23, 1937).

Looking back on the film, Eve didn't rate it highly, but felt amply compensated by the opportunity to work with, and befriend, Edward Everett Horton.

The former Eunice Quedens made her official film debut as Eve Arden in *Oh, Doctor,* starring Edward Everett Horton.

Stage Door (1937)

Katharine Hepburn (*Terry Randall*), Ginger Rogers (*Jean Maitland*), Adolphe Menjou (*Anthony Powell*), Lucille Ball (*Judith Jones*), Eve Arden (*Eve*), Ann Miller (*Annie*), Gail Patrick (*Linda Shaw*), Constance Collier (*Miss Luther*), Andrea Leeds (*Kay Hamilton*), Samuel S. Hinds (*Henry Sims*), Franklin Pangborn (*Harcourt*), Phyllis Kennedy (*Hattie*), Pierre Watkin (*Carmichael*), Jack Carson (*Mr. Milbank*), Margaret Early (*Mary Lou*), Norma Drury (*Olga*), Josephine Whittell (*Miss Arden*), Frank Reicher (*Stage Director*), Jean Rouverol (*Dizzy*), Grady Sutton (*Butch*)

Director: Gregory La Cava. *Producer:* Pandro S. Berman. *Screenplay:* Morrie Ryskind, Anthony Veiller, from the play by Edna Ferber, George S. Kaufman. *Photography:* Robert de Grasse. *Musical Director:* Roy Webb. *Art Directors:* Van Nest Polglase, Carroll Clark. *Set Dressing:* Darrell Silvera. *Gowns:* Muriel King. *Recording:* John L. Cass. *Editor:* William Hamilton. RKO-Radio Pictures; released October 8, 1937. B&W; 92 minutes.

New York City's Footlights Club is a theatrical boardinghouse populated by women aspiring to show business careers. Into this rough-and-tumble world comes Terry Randall, a well-bred newcomer from a socially prominent family who's determined to try her hand as an actress. Terry's high-toned mannerisms fail to impress most of the girls, including her down-to-earth roommate, dancer Jean.

Successful theatrical producer Anthony Powell is casting his newest drama, *Enchanted April,* but most of the women in the Footlights Club can't get their foot in the door with him. Among the hopefuls is vulnerable Kay Hamilton, who achieved fine notices in a show a year or so ago, but is now experiencing a long and discouraging period of unemployment. Powell, who's quite the ladies' man, has been squiring snooty club resident Linda Shaw around town, but now has his eye on Jean Maitland, for reasons less professional than personal. When Terry Randall is offered the star-making role of Jeannette in Powell's new show, she unknowingly provokes a tragedy that leaves her fellow denizens of the boardinghouse embittered toward her, and causes her to consider how badly she wants her chance at stardom.

As Eve, one of the young women at the Footlights Club awaiting her big break, Eve Arden attracted the notice of moviegoers and critics who had mostly overlooked her appearance in *Oh, Doctor*. Even in this unbeatable cast of stars, stars-in-the-making, and lovely newcomers, Eve (playing a character who shares her first name) stands out with her quick wit, sharp delivery, and impeccable timing. As she and her girlfriends endure a long and tiresome wait among a crowd of hopefuls in Mr. Powell's outer office, knowing they will most likely get the brush-off as they usually do, Eve notes, "Imagine opening a great big office like this just *not* to see people." Later, when Jean asks her if she intends to catch Terry's opening night performance in *Enchanted April*, Eve retorts, "No, I'm going tomorrow, and catch the closing." Decorating a number of her scenes is her character's pet cat, a white shorthair she names Henry. Only in the film's closing moments do we learn that Henry has proven to be a misnomer for the feline who's just delivered a litter of kittens, causing Eve to sigh, "I'm so discouraged."

Among the real-life newcomers given bit roles here is Frances Gifford (1920–1994), who would appear some ten years later with Eve in *The Arnelo Affair* (1947). Young Frances Reid (1914–2010), who would find her greatest fame years later as the matriarch of the TV soap opera *Days of our Lives*, appears in the film's closing moments. Also seen briefly is a young Jack Carson

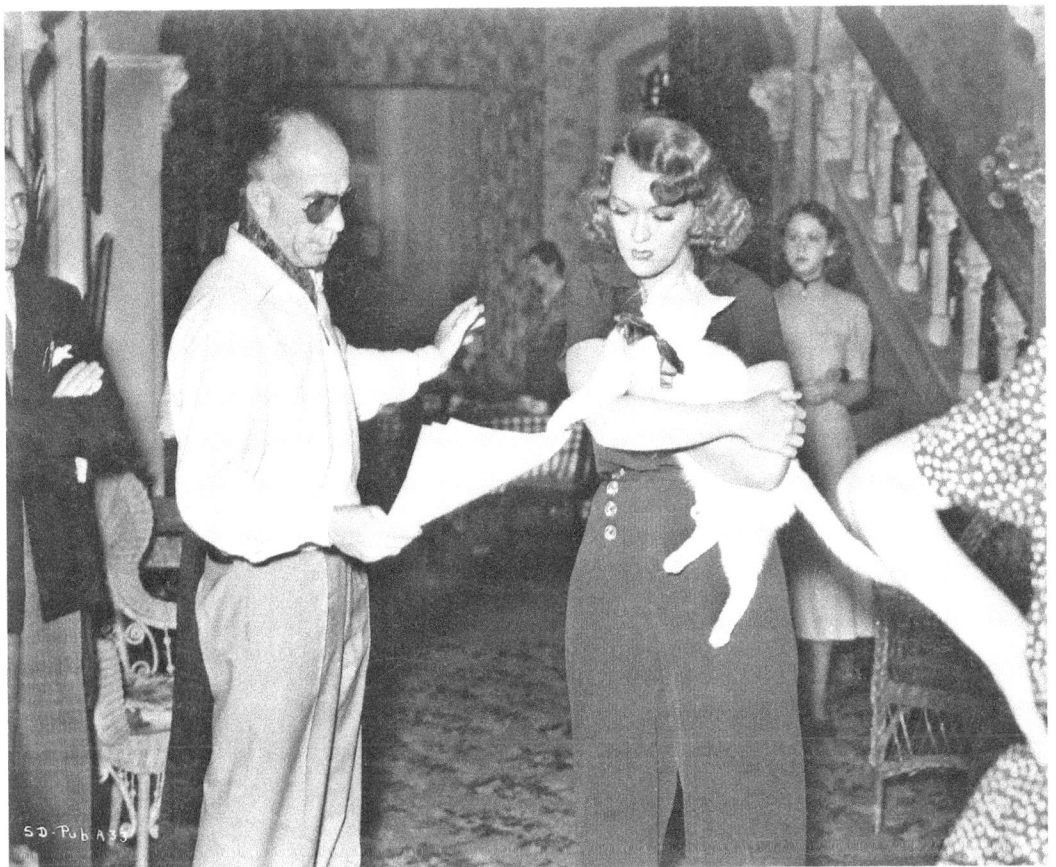

Eve and her feline co-star confer with director Gregory La Cava on the set of *Stage Door*.

(1910–1963), in one of 14 films the screen newcomer would make in 1937. It was only the first of five times that Eve and Jack, both to be Warner Bros. contract players in the 1940s as well as co-stars in a radio show, would share credits in the same film.

It is largely to the credit of director Gregory La Cava that the atmosphere of the boardinghouse, and the attitudes of the women who inhabit it, seem so real and fresh. In a profile of the director that appeared in the *Bright Lights Film Journal,* Eve's co-star Andrea Leeds explained, "Gregory La Cava had all of us girls in the movie come to the studio for two weeks before the shooting started and live as though we were in the lodging house itself. He rewrote scenes from day to day to get the feeling of a bunch of girls together—as spontaneous as possible. He would talk to each of us like a lifelong friend. That gave us a feeling of intimacy." As filming progressed, La Cava was increasingly taken with Eve, and the character that was developing before his eyes. "The cat was a natural ham," Eve later explained of her feline co-star during a *Family Circle* interview, "and the next thing we knew, puss and I were being slipped into extra scenes. I lay awake thinking of cat gags, which *I* would point up with cute lines. Straight man for an alley cat! By the end of the film I found out they were paying the cat $150 a week, which was more than I got. But who's yowling!"

Frank S. Nugent's review in the *New York Times* took the form of rebutting the frequently heard complaints of playwrights George S. Kaufman and Edna Ferber that Hollywood had made a mess of their *Stage Door.* Wrote Nugent, "Script-writers Morrie Ryskind and Anthony Veiller have taken the play's name, its setting and part of its theme and have built a whole new structure which is wittier than the original, more dramatic than the original, more meaningful than the original, more cogent than the original" (October 8, 1937). Opined *Variety,* "It is funny in spots, emotionally effective occasionally, and generally brisk and entertaining. It will do business" (September 15, 1937).

Eve would play in a second version of her *Stage Door,* a radio adaptation heard on *The Lux Radio Theatre* in February 1939.

Cocoanut Grove (1938)

Fred MacMurray (*Johnny Prentice*), Harriet Hilliard (*Linda Rogers*), the Yacht Club Boys (*Themselves*), Ben Blue (*Joe De Lemma*), Eve Arden (*Sophie De Lemma*), Rufe Davis (*Bibb Tucker*), Billy Lee (*Half-Pint*), George Walcott (*Tony Wonder*), Dorothy Howe (*Hazel De Vore*), Red Stanley (*Dixie*), Harry Owens and His Royal Hawaiian Orchestra

Director: Alfred Sentell. *Producer:* George M. Arthur. *Original Story and Screenplay:* Sy Bartlett, Olive Cooper. *Photography:* Leo Tover. *Art Direction:* Hans Dreier, Earl Hedrick. *Editor:* Hugh Bennett. *Sound Recording:* Harry Mills, Don Johnson. *Interior Decorations:* A. E. Freudeman. *Costumes:* Edith Head. *Musical Direction:* Boris Morros. *Songs:* Burton Lane, Frank Loesser, Frederick Hollander, Ralph Freed, Harry Owens, Jock, Bert Kalmar, Harry Ruby, Victor Young, the Yacht Club Boys. *Musical Adviser:* Arthur Franklin. Paramount Pictures; released May 20, 1938. B&W; 85 minutes.

Bandleader Johnny Prentice dreams of success for his little-known troupe, but until now they have had to settle for minor gigs, from which they often get fired because of Johnny's quick temper. When one of his players wins a trailer in a contest, Johnny sets out from Chicago to California with his band, so that they can audition for the annual competition for new bands at the famed Hollywood nightspot, the Cocoanut Grove. Along the way, Johnny's troupe picks up a couple of new members. Pretty Linda Rogers, hired to serve as tutor to Johnny's adopted son Half-Pint, proves to be a singer with a winning voice. When their car breaks down en route, Johnny persuades eccentric tow truck driver Bibb Tucker to drive them the rest of the way to California, promising him a shot at the spotlight for his quirky songs and imitations.

In Hollywood, Johnny's band wins an audition at the Cocoanut Grove alongside their rivals from the Tony Wonder band. Although club owner Mr. Grayson is favorably impressed by the Johnny Prentice outfit, he mistakenly hires the Wonder troupe instead. Johnny's discouraged band members disperse to go their separate ways, until Bibb jumps into action to reunite them.

Eve is teamed here with comedian Ben Blue (1901–1975), playing a husband-and-wife dance

Cast members of *Cocoanut Grove* included (left to right) Harriet Hilliard (later known as Harriet Nelson), Billy Lee, Eve, leading man Fred MacMurray, and Rufe Davis.

team that are among the "novelty" acts Johnny features in his floor show. Their routine features rubber-limbed Blue as the man who tries in vain to impress a hard-edged woman. Sophie, his wife, plays the cigarette-smoking trollop who not only spurns his advances, but strikes a match on his cheek, blows smoke in his face, and tosses knives at him. The apparently indifferent reaction to this number causes Johnny's boss to fire the troupe from an early job playing on an excursion boat touring Lake Michigan.

In terms of dialogue, this is one of Eve's most minor roles. Until Harriet Hilliard's Linda Rogers joins the troupe, she is the only female member of Johnny's company, traveling from gig to gig with the rowdy bunch of musicians. Present throughout the film, her role is disappointingly minor nonetheless, a lackluster follow-up to her appearance in *Stage Door*. She returns in the closing moments to perform a second dance routine with Blue.

This is Eve's only film with popular leading man Fred MacMurray (1908–1991), who acquits himself ably in this early role, though the idea of having him sing to his leading lady Harriet Hilliard wasn't a great one. Hilliard, already the wife of bandleader Ozzie Nelson in real life, wasn't yet using his name professionally, though they had been married since 1935. Later to become enshrined in TV history as the beloved stars of *The Adventures of Ozzie and Harriet* (1952–1966), they were at this time the headliners of a popular dance band. Rufe Davis (1908–1974), known to baby boomers as Floyd Smoot on TV's *Petticoat Junction*, displays his ability to mimic sounds. He had previously been seen alongside Blue and Dorothy Howe in Paramount's *The Big Broadcast of 1938*.

Character actor Charles Lane (1905–2007) is unbilled for his brief role as Mr. Weaver, business associate of the Cocoanut Grove's Mr. Grayson, whose inadvertent flipping of the wrong switch at a critical juncture nearly wrecks the careers of Johnny and his band members. Also uncredited in her minor speaking role as a receptionist is future leading lady Ellen Drew (1915–2003), who would later become the wife of *Grove*'s screenwriter Sy Bartlett.

Director Alfred Sentell, a silent-film veteran whose long list of credits stretched back to 1917, directed Eve in two pictures in a row, also helming *Having Wonderful Time*, released only a few weeks after *Cocoanut Grove*.

The Cocoanut Grove that gives this film its title is not the one in Boston that was the site of a deadly fire in the 1940s, but a Los Angeles nightclub, attached to the ritzy Ambassador Hotel. Popular with motion picture celebrities like Eve's future co-star Joan Crawford, the Grove was also the site of several Academy Award ceremonies in the 1930s and 1940s. (The hotel itself would later go down in history as the location where Senator Robert F. Kennedy was fatally shot by Sirhan Sirhan in 1968. It was demolished in 2005, though the remnants of the Grove itself remain.)

Wood Soanes, reviewing the picture in the *Oakland Tribune*, liked *Cocoanut Grove*, calling it "a gay, light-hearted musical" that offered movie patrons "Cocoanut Grove without that cover charge" (May 27, 1938). Soanes didn't recognize Eve when he screened the film, but thought Blue's "feminine partner ... deserves billing" for her contribution to their "pair of hilarious dance numbers." The *Hartford Courant* deemed this "the smoothest, most plausible and gayest filmusical to emerge from the Paramount studio in some time," crediting Eve and Ben Blue with providing "some rib-tickling comedy and dances" (May 26, 1938).

Having Wonderful Time (1938)

Ginger Rogers (*Thelma "Teddy" Shaw*), Douglas Fairbanks, Jr. (*Chick Kirkland*), Peggy Conklin (*Fay Coleman*), Lucille Ball (*Miriam*), Lee Bowman (*Buzzy Armbruster*), Eve Arden (*Henrietta*), Dorothea Kent (*Maxine*), Richard "Red" Skelton (*Itchy Faulkner*), Donald Meek (*P.U. Rogers*), Jack Carson (*Emil Beatty*), Clarence H. Wilson (*Mr. G*), Allan Lane (*Maxwell "Mac" Pangwell*), Grady Sutton (*Gus*), Shimen Ruskin (*Shrimpo*), Dorothy Tree (*Frances*), Leona Roberts (*Mrs. Shaw*), Harlan Briggs (*Mr. Shaw*), Inez Courtney (*Emma*), Juanita Quigley (*Mabel*), Ann Miller (*Vivian*), Frances Gifford (*Salesgirl*), Dean Jagger (*Charlie*), Russell Gleason (*Waiter*)

Director: Alfred Santell. *Producer:* Pandro S. Berman. *Screenplay:* Arthur Kober, from his play. *Musical Director:* Roy Webb. *Photography:* Robert deGrasse. *Special Effects:* Vernon L. Walker. *Art Director:* Van Nest Polglase. *Associate:* Perry Ferguson. *Set Dressing:* Darrell Silvera. *Gowns:* Edward Stevenson, Renie. *Sound Recorder:* John E. Tribby. *Editor:* William Hamilton. *Assistant Director:* James Anderson. *Songs:* "My First Impression of You," "Nighty Night": Sam Stept, Charles Tobias. RKO-Radio Pictures; released July 1, 1938. B&W; 70 minutes.

Teddy Shaw, employed as a typist in a busy New York City office, is looking forward to her two-week vacation at Camp Kare–Free, described in its brochures as a place "where one can associate with a select number of cultured and sports-loving ladies and gentlemen." Though she has already attracted the attentions of Emil Beatty, a crass but basically decent guy who owns his own business, Teddy wants more from life than she's experienced living in the Bronx with her extended family.

On her arrival at Camp Kare–Free, Teddy is nonplussed to discover a raucous, crowded summer camp unlike the description she read. She is met there by handsome Chick Kirkland, a college graduate who's currently employed as a waiter at the summer camp. Though they initially spar, the two develop a mutual attraction over the days of her visit. Chick quickly falls in love with Teddy, but doesn't feel that his current prospects allow him to propose to her, and she breaks off the relationship after a misunderstanding. When he believes that she has instead taken up with the camp's notorious lothario, Buzzy, Chick comes to her rescue.

According to RKO's publicity, the film offers a "large cast personifying all types of vacationists who hurry to the mountains annually from a short release from their everyday worries ... exhibit[ing] a cross-section of life that has rarely, if ever, been presented on the screen." Location filming took place at Bartlett Lake, in the San Bernardino Mountains, with a mock camp set up for the shoot.

Having Wonderful Time reunites Eve with several of her co-stars from *Stage Door*, notably Ginger Rogers, Lucille Ball, and Jack Carson. Also on hand, making his screen debut, is comedian Red Skelton (1913–1997), cast as the camp's entertainment director. Among the many bit players who make up the camp's guest register are an unbilled Ann Miller, and Lucy's cousin Cleo. Seen as one of Teddy's bunkmates at the summer camp, Eve has regrettably little screen time here, but manages to create a distinctive character nonetheless. Henrietta, as played by Eve, is a wallflower decked out in large glasses and a frizzy hairdo, who affects a ritzy accent and attitude that aren't completely convincing. Though her speech is determinedly high-falutin' ("At what hour are you departing?"), and she daintily cuts her doughnuts with a knife and fork, her nasal Brooklyn tones belie her efforts to project an uppity front. Moments after meeting Teddy, she informs her, "The food here is unbearable. I just had to change my liver!"

Neither Eve (left) nor Peggy Conklin looks to be *Having Wonderful Time.*

Though based on a hit Broadway comedy, and adapted from the screen by the original playwright, this comedy (the *Meatballs* of its day?) sparks relatively few laughs for the contemporary viewer, and drags in spots despite its short running time. The original Broadway production opened in February 1937 and ran for nearly a year. Actress Loise Reichard played Henrietta onstage. The show was almost completely recast for its film adaptation, though comic actor Shimen Ruskin, seen in the film as "Shrimpo," was a veteran of the Broadway cast. The original stage production featured a young John Garfield (then still billed as Jules Garfield) as Chick, whose surname was de-ethnicized from Kessler to Kirkland for the RKO version. Also in the stage cast was future TV producer-director Sheldon Leonard, who noted in his 1995 memoirs that Paramount "goyed it up good." Kober's Broadway script was later used as the basis for *Wish You Were Here*, which enjoyed a very successful run as a musical comedy in 1952–53.

Variety's reviewer, familiar with the Broadway version of *Having Wonderful Time*, wrote, "Much of the charm, romantic tenderness and social problem features of Arthur Kober's stage play ... are missing in the screen version" (June 15, 1938).

Letter of Introduction (1938)

Adolphe Menjou (*John Mannering*), Andrea Leeds (*Katherine "Kay" Martin*), George Murphy (*Barry Paige*), Edgar Bergen & Charlie McCarthy (*Themselves*), Rita Johnson (*Honey*), Ann Sheridan (*Lydia Hoyt*),

Ernest Cossart (*Andrews*), Frank Jenks (*Joe*), Eve Arden (*Cora Phelps*), John Archer, Irving Bacon (*Reporters*), Esther Ralston (*Mrs. Sinclair*), Claire Whitney (*Nurse Ryan*)
Director: John M. Stahl. *Screenplay:* Sheridan Gibney, Leonard Spigelgass, based on an original story by Bernice Boone. *Director of Photography:* Karl Freund. *Art Director:* Jack Otterson. *Associate:* John Ewing. *Film Editors:* Ted Kent, Charles Maynard. *Musical Director:* Charles Previn. *Assistant Director:* Joseph A. McDonough. *Gowns:* Vera West. *Set Decorations:* R.A. Gausman. *Sound Supervisor:* Bernard B. Brown. *Technician:* Joseph Lapis. Universal Pictures; released August 5, 1938. B&W; 100 minutes.

When her apartment catches fire on New Year's Eve, aspiring actress Kay Martin cares about rescuing only one thing—a letter of introduction that she tells her friends will provide her with an entrée to matinee idol John Mannering. Mannering is a 52-year-old leading man from an old show business family whose primary vices are women (he's on the verge of marrying his fourth wife, brassy Lydia), and liquor. What he doesn't know, until he reads the letter of introduction Kay's mother wrote, is that he is also Kay's father.

Kay and her newfound father agree to keep their family relationship a secret for the time being, but her fascination with this well-to-do older man arouses the jealousy of her boyfriend, dancer Barry, who has just asked her to marry him. Believing that Mannering is his romantic rival, Barry proposes to his loyal dance partner Honey on the rebound from Kay, and takes a tour out of town.

To help Kay's career, Mannering signs to co-star with her in a Broadway play called *Return to Paradise*, his first stage role after more than a decade of acting in films. But his drinking and a bad case of nerves cause him to wreck opening night, and Kay's expected triumph is a disaster. Despondent, Mannering steps in front of a taxicab and is badly injured. Though Kay rushes to the hospital on hearing the news, he dies before revealing their family relationship to the press, as he'd intended. Reuniting with Barry, who couldn't go through with his plan to marry Honey, Kay offers him the letter to read, and they are reunited.

Letter of Introduction reunites Eve with two of her co-stars from *Stage Door*, Andrea Leeds and Adolphe Menjou, and has a similar theme about aspiring young performers seeking their career breaks in New York. Though her ninth-place billing (tenth if you count Charlie McCarthy) doesn't suggest it, she has a significant and enjoyable role in this film.

Once again, Eve plays one of the residents of a boardinghouse occupied largely by performers awaiting their big break. The actors, dancers, and other denizens of Mrs. Meggs's boardinghouse call themselves "The Bushel Lighters," since most of their talents are currently hidden under the proverbial bushel. When we meet Cora Phelps, Eve's character, she explains that she is currently employed in a walk-on part in a play: "I appear in the third act and say [melodramatically], 'I'm Jeffrey's wife.... He's killed himself.'" Asked facetiously by another partygoer if she brought the caviar, Cora replies, "No, dear. Woolworth isn't carrying it this year."

When Kay returns from her first evening out with John Mannering, Eve's character asks, "Did he show you his etchings?" Later, when Kay needs the immediate loan of $21 to pay a restaurant check, Cora knocks on the door of fellow boardinghouse resident Edgar Bergen, saying, "Bergen! Open up the penny bank. Snow White's in trouble again!"

Famed ventriloquist Edgar Bergen plays a riff on himself. In real life, Edgar and his dummy Charlie McCarthy were already well known to audiences, thanks to their popular radio show which debuted in 1937. Here, he is presented as a talented but undiscovered newcomer, who gets his first big break on radio thanks to John Mannering. Though it isn't developed to any great extent, there is also a romantic relationship that takes place between Edgar and Eve's character, Cora. (Accompanying Edgar and Charlie to the theater to see Kay's debut, Cora is mistaken by a fan of the ventriloquist as Mrs. Bergen, to which she replies, "Oh, I'm not Mrs. Bergen. I'm Mrs. McCarthy.") Only weeks before this film was released, Edward Bergen and Eve, under her real name, applied for a marriage license in Reno. The similarity in names caused some friends and fans of the well-known ventriloquist to be confused, causing him to explain that it was not he who was marrying Eve.

Andrea Leeds had a short screen career, voluntarily retiring in 1940 after making only a few more films. She and Eve remained longtime friends, as noted in Eve's autobiography. Adolphe Menjou does well with a role that seems to be a lightly disguised John Barrymore.

Given the disparate elements that make up *Letter of Introduction*—the serious father-and-daughter saga of Kay and John Mannering, and a featured role for a ventriloquist and his loquacious dummy—the film works surprisingly well. Modern audiences may wonder why Kay couldn't save everyone a lot of trouble 20 minutes into the film by telling her boyfriend that John Mannering is her father, instead of an old letch.

Eve is nicely photographed here by the great cinematographer Karl Freund, who would later join the staff at Desilu, helping to develop the three-camera system used first to shoot *I Love Lucy* and subsequently for Eve's *Our Miss Brooks*.

While shooting *Letter of Introduction*, Eve told a reporter from the *Los Angeles Times* that she had no interest in becoming a studio contract player. "Why should I sign a contract? I'm making all the money I want. I don't want to tie myself up to a long-term agreement and have other people tell me what pictures I should make. I want to make the choice myself" (July 24, 1938). Not until the mid–1940s would Eve reconsider her stance.

In *Letter of Introduction*, Eve was paired romantically with the popular ventriloquist Edgar Bergen.

According to one Universal ad campaign, *Letter of Introduction* offered "Everything you could ever ask for! Fun! Romance! Story! Even a few tears!" The *Syracuse Herald*'s movie critic Hayden Hickok, in his August 12, 1938, review, thought that Andrea Leeds and Adolphe Menjou did their roles adequately, but raved, "The young lady responsible for the real picture-stealing is Eve Arden, who learned her gag-throwing technique in the 'Follies.'"

Women in the Wind (1939)

Kay Francis (*Janet Steele*), William Gargan (*Ace Boreman*), Victor Jory (*Dr. Tom Wilson*), Maxie Rosenbloom ("*Stuffy*" *McInnes*), Eddie Foy, Jr. (*Denny Corson*), Sheila Bromley (*Frieda Boreman*), Eve Arden (*Kit Campbell*), Charles Anthony Hughes (*Bill Steele*), Frankie Burke (*Johnnie*), Spencer Charters (*Farmer*), Vera Lewis (*Farmer's Wife*), William Gould (*Palmer*), Gordon Hart (*Air Races Official*), Ila Rhodes (*Joan*), Rosella Towne (*Phyllis*), Frank Faylen (*Chuck*)
Director: John Farrow. *Screenplay:* Lee Katz, Albert DeMond, from a novel by Francis Walton. *Dialogue Director:* Jo Graham. *Photography:* Sid Hickox. *Art Director:* Carl Jules Weyl. *Film Editor:* Thomas Pratt. *Sound:* Charles Lang. *Gowns:* Orry-Kelly. *Technical Advisor:* Frank Clark. *Musical Director:* Leo F. Forbstein. Warner Bros.; released April 15, 1939. B&W; 63 minutes.

Ace Boreman is a renowned pilot who's just returned from his latest record-setting 'round-the-world tour. Listening to radio news coverage of Boreman's triumphant flight gives beautiful Janet Steele an idea. Janet and her brother Bill are also accomplished pilots, but he is now paralyzed as the result of a crash. Bill needs treatments from a specialist, but the family can't afford them. Janet asks Ace to let her fly his plane, *Polly,* in a Women's Air Derby competition for which the top prize is $15,000. He refuses initially, despite his attraction to Janet, but finally acquiesces.

Unfortunately for Janet, Ace's estranged wife, Frieda, claims that their Mexican divorce was invalid, and claims *Polly* as community property so that she can enter the derby herself. A guilt-stricken Ace, knowing he has let Janet down, talks his rival, Denny Corson, into letting her pilot his plane instead, which is even faster.

The competition in the cross-country derby, going from Los Angeles to Cleveland, is fierce. Janet's buddy Kit Campbell, piloting an inferior plane, crashes just short of the scheduled stopover in Kansas City. Meanwhile, unscrupulous Frieda, angered that Janet is piloting a faster vehicle than her own, plots with a greedy mechanic to clip her rival's wings as they head toward Cleveland, and snare the $15,000 prize.

Eve's featured role as aviatrix Kit Campbell should have been an interesting one, but there's not much here on which she can chew. Given only a handful of scenes in the film's brief (63-minute) running time, Eve has perhaps her most memorable exchange when she first meets Janet, played by Kay Francis:

> JANET: How's your husband?
> KIT: Eddie?
> JANET: Uhnt-uh.
> KIT: Frank?
> JANET: Uhnt-uh.
> KIT: Oh, you mean Tom. I divorced him three years ago.

Kit also has something of a history with Ace Boreman, whom she says almost made it onto her roll call of husbands. (Janet: "What happened?" Kit: "He said no.") A bit later in the film, we'll meet the woman Ace *did* marry, and realize he'd have been much better off with Kit.

As Eve noted in her autobiography, her big scene in which Kit crashes is rendered unintentionally laughable. The footage of her plane crashing nose-first to the ground in a fiery ball, immediately followed by a shot of her carried out on a stretcher with only minor injuries, resulted in gales of laughter from a preview audience.

Women in the Wind was the swan song of leading lady Kay Francis (1905–1968) under her contract with Warner Bros., filmed in the last few weeks before her contract expired in the fall of 1938. Both the quality of this cheaply made B drama and her under-the-title billing make the studio's disdain for their departing star pretty clear. Still, she's interestingly matched with Eve, and it's a shame the two actresses worked together only this once. The other players are mostly adequate if uninspired, and director John Farrow was clearly wise to limit the "comedy relief" of "Slapsie" Maxie Rosenbloom (1904–1976), cast as Ace's sidekick. This was one of seven films the ex-prize fighter had in release during 1939. Actor John Dilson is billed in the closing credits for playing Sloan, Mrs. Boreman's lawyer, but does not appear in the final cut.

The film was based on the 1935 novel of the same name by Francis Walton, but, as studio publicity acknowledged, "The new Warner picture takes advantage of the popular interest in the most sensational actual happenings in the recent annals of aviation by incorporating somewhat similar incidents in the screen story." The famed real-life female aviator Amelia Earhart was still much in the news during the time that *Women in the Wind* was made and distributed. Missing since she vanished during a 'round-the-world flight in July 1937, Earhart was declared legally dead in January 1939, a few weeks before this film reached theater screens.

Critical response to *Women in the Wind* was not helped by the fact that it followed closely on the heels of a similar women-in-aviation drama from 20th Century–Fox, *Tail Spin.* In that film, which reached theaters in February 1939, the rival pilots were played by Alice Faye and Constance Bennett, and the heroine's best friend (the role often earmarked for Eve) was portrayed by comedienne Joan Davis. *Variety* (April 19, 1939) made particular note of Eve's contribution: "Eve Arden, cast as an aviatrix and about whom the story concerns itself but little, looks like a comer."

Big Town Czar (1939)

Barton MacLane (*Phil Daley*), Tom Brown (*Danny Daley*), Eve Arden (*Susan Warren*), Jack La Rue (*Mike Luger*), Frank Jenks (*Sid Travers*), Walter Woolf King (*Paul Burgess*), Oscar O'Shea (*Paul Daley*), Esther Dale (*Ma Daley*), Horace McMahon (*Punchy Edwards*), Ed Sullivan (*Himself*), Gordon Jones (*Chuck Hardy*), James Flavin (*George Mitchell*), Irving Bacon (*Mr. Frazier*), Buster Phelps (*Boy with Dog*), Frances Robinson (*Flower Shop Clerk*), Oscar Polk (*Arthur*)
Director: Arthur Lubin. *Screenplay:* Edmund Hartmann, from an original story, "Czar of Broadway," by Ed Sullivan. *Associate Producer:* Ken Goldsmith. *Director of Photography:* Elwood Bredell. *Art Director:* Jack Otterson. *Associate:* Richard H. Riedel. *Film Editor:* Philip Cahn. *Musical Director:* Charles Previn. *Sound Supervisor:* Bernard B. Brown. *Technician:* William Fox. *Gowns:* Vera West. *Set Decoration:* R.A. Gausman. Universal Pictures; released May 11, 1939. B&W; 66 minutes.

Gangster Phil Daley, raised in one of New York's toughest neighborhoods, has risen to the top of the shady organization formerly ruled by his mentor, Paul Burgess. Having successfully displaced Burgess, Phil is living high, and is reunited with his kid brother Danny, who's working his way through college as a dishwasher. Phil's ex-girlfriend, Susan Warren, now the proprietor of a successful flower shop, urges him to stay away from Danny, and let him live an honest life, but Phil ignores her advice. Under the influence of his older brother, Danny quits college and joins Phil's gang.

Impressed by his older brother's seemingly glamorous lifestyle, Danny is soon deeply involved with the underworld. Danny pressures boxer Chuck Hardy into throwing a fight, arousing the ire of Phil's chief rival, Mike Luger, who vows revenge. Too late, Phil realizes that he has exposed Danny to danger, and seeks Susan's help in extricating his kid brother from the gang world. Before they can set their plan into place, Danny is shot and killed before their eyes. Ready to leave New York forever, Phil hides out in Connecticut under an assumed name, but is inevitably drawn back toward his former life when he receives what seems to be a summons from Susan.

Big Town Czar is based on an original story by Ed Sullivan (1901–1974), then a columnist for the *New York Daily News* as well as a CBS radio commentator. It was the second of a trio of movie treatments he sold during the late 1930s and early 1940s, in an unsuccessful attempt to establish himself in a film career. Universal purchased the rights to Sullivan's screen story in the summer of 1938, but rejected his title "Czar of Broadway," already used by the studio in an earlier (1930) gangster film. Sullivan also plays himself as a character in the film, sharing several scenes with Barton MacLane and reading from (supposedly) one of his own columns in a framing sequence that opens and closes the film. Like the film's central character, Sullivan himself had a younger brother named Danny, who died at an early age.

Eve is third-billed as Susan, who grew up with the Daley family on Crane Street, living as they do in "the grimiest tenement" New York has to offer. She has a soft spot in her heart for Phil, remembering the days when both were teenagers, and he took her for romantic Sunday walks. She is, however, sufficiently clear-sighted to recognize that Phil is no longer that young man. Having achieved upward mobility as the owner of a flower shop, Susan tries her best to help Danny make his way in the world as well, but concedes defeat when he becomes ensnared with Phil's gang. "I'm a failure," she tells Phil. "I did my best to keep Danny straight, but my best wasn't good enough. So now I turn him over to you, 100 per cent. And I don't want any part of you, or him!"

For those who believe Eve never landed a man in her films, check out the scene in which MacLane's Phil, ready to give up his dangerous life, offers Susan a home in Connecticut that she kindly declines. A studio publicity item claimed that Eve was superstitious about removing her real-life wedding ring, and preferred to have it covered over with adhesive tape and makeup for roles such as this one, in which the character was expected to have a bare ring finger. In general, this is more of a conventional leading lady role for Eve than she typically played. There are virtually no scripted wisecracks for her here, though she pokes gentle fun at Phil's statement that he "ain't been doing so badly," replying, "Ain't you?" She is quite moving in the scene where she, along with Phil, sees Danny shot and killed at close range.

Leading man Barton MacLane (1902–1969), a longtime Warners' contract player, was loaned

Phil Daley (Barton MacLane) is a gangster whose childhood friend Susan (Eve) wants no part of his dangerous lifestyle in *Big Town Czar.*

to Universal for this modest B movie. MacLane enjoyed a long career in film, but may today be most recognizable as General Martin Peterson on TV's *I Dream of Jeannie.* He and Eve would share scenes a second time in *Manpower* (1941). Seen here as a hired killer is Horace McMahon (1906–1971), who would go on to work the virtuous side of Gotham law enforcement as Lt. Mike Parker of television's *Naked City.* This was a relatively early directorial credit for the prolific Arthur Lubin (1898–1995), best-remembered today for directing most of the "Francis the Talking Mule" series as well as producing and directing television's *Mister Ed.*

Frank S. Nugent, reviewing the film in the *New York Times,* called it "a bustling little melodrama, all puffed up with its own unimportance," but did toss a mild compliment Eve's way, saying she "does her best to give some substance to a basically unsubstantial part" (May 4, 1939). In fact, *Big Town Czar* attracted mostly indifferent reviews and didn't sell enough tickets to advance the careers of anyone involved. Some 15 years after its initial run in theaters, *Big Town Czar* was issued by Realart under the title *Fighting the Racketeers,* with Eve, then the star of TV's *Our Miss Brooks,* billed over MacLane in ads.

The Forgotten Woman (1939)

Sigrid Gurie (*Anne Kennedy*), William Lundigan (*Terence Kennedy*), Donald Briggs (*District Attorney Burke*), Eve Arden (*Carrie Ashburn*), Donnie Dunagan (*Terry Kennedy, Jr.*), Elisabeth Risdon (*Margaret Burke*), Paul Harvey (*Charles Courtenay*), Ray Walker (*Marty*), Virginia Brissac (*Mrs. Kimball*), Joseph Downing (*Johnny Bradshaw*), Norman Willis (*Stu Mantle*), George Walcott (*Frank Lockridge*), John Hamilton (*Dr. May*), Grace Hayle (*Woman in Beauty Shop*), Bess Flowers (*Beauty Shop Operator*), Sam McDaniel (*Porter*), Claire Du Brey (*Foxie*)

II. Filmography—The Forgotten Woman (1939)

Sigrid Gurie (center) plays the title character in *The Forgotten Woman*. Featured in the cast are William Lundigan (left) and Eve, who's wondering why her friend keeps a gun around the house.

Director: Harold Young. *Screenplay:* Lionel Houser, Harold Buchman, from a story by John Kobler. *Musical Director:* Charles Previn. *Art Director:* Jack Otterson. *Music:* Frank Skinner. *Sound Supervisor:* Bernard B. Brown. *Gowns:* Vera West. Universal Pictures; released July 7, 1939. B&W; 67 minutes.

Anne Kennedy and her husband, Terry, become unwilling accomplices to a robbery when the escaping criminals commandeer their car for a getaway. Chased by the police, the robbers crash the Kennedys' car, killing Terry. Without her husband to testify to their innocence, Anne is convicted of having been an accessory to the holdup. Prosecuted by up-and-coming young District Attorney Burke, Anne is convicted and sentenced to prison. While serving her sentence, Anne gives birth to a baby boy, whom she names after her late husband. Upon her release from prison three years later, a bitter Anne is forced to give up her son for adoption, as she cannot support him. Eventually the real culprit confesses, absolving Anne of involvement in the robbery. But because District Attorney Burke, who convicted Anne, is now a candidate for governor, he is pressured to suppress the evidence for political reasons. Ads proclaimed, "Framed by men, she fought back with the bitter fury of a love turned to hate!"

The film's title could easily be applied today to leading lady Sigrid Gurie (1911–1969). Discovered by mogul Samuel Goldwyn, she was heavily promoted as an exotic new leading lady, "The Siren of the Fjords," playing her first major role as the leading lady of *The Adventures of Marco Polo* (1938). Though she was indeed of Norwegian stock, she was actually a native of Brooklyn, New York. That fact, which came to light when Gurie sought a divorce from her American husband, caused Goldwyn some embarrassment, and may have contributed to the brevity of her screen career. *The Forgotten Woman* was billed as her first chance to play a contemporary role.

Variety made mention of Eve in a review which, while complimentary, suggested that the critic had missed some of her previous films: "Eve Arden, as the girl's pal and confidante, reveals distinct possibilities in light comedienne roles" (August 9, 1939).

Eternally Yours (1939)

Loretta Young (*Anita Halstead Barnes*), David Niven (*The Great Arturo*), Hugh Herbert (*Benton*), Billie Burke (*Aunt Abbey*), Broderick Crawford (*Don Barnes*), C. Aubrey Smith (*Bishop Hubert Peabody*), Raymond Walburn (*Harley Bingham*), ZaSu Pitts (*Carrie Bingham*), Virginia Field (*Lola de Vere*), Eve Arden (*Gloria*), Ralph Graves (*Mr. Morrisey*), Lionel Pape (*Mr. Howard*), Fred Keating (*Master of Ceremonies*), Dennie Moore (*Waitress*), Walter Sande (*Ralph*), Granville Bates (*Ship's Captain*)

Director: Tay Garnett. *Screenplay:* Gene Towne, Graham Baker. *Art Direction:* Alexander Golitzen. *Associate:* Richard Irvine. *Interior Decorations:* Julia Heron. *Special Photographic Effects:* Ray Binger. *Score and Musical Direction:* Werner Janssen. *Song:* "Eternally Yours," lyrics, L. Wolfe Gilbert; music, Werner Janssen. *Film Editors:* Otho Lovering, Dorothy Spencer. *Miss Young's Gowns:* Irene. *Other Gowns:* Travis Banton. *Sound:* Fred Lau. *Assistant Director:* Charles Kerr. United Artists; released October 7, 1939.

Anita Halstead, granddaughter of a bishop, is engaged to marry dull nice guy Don. On the afternoon of her bridal shower, she attends a performance by stage illusionist The Great Arturo, and falls madly in love with the charismatic performer. After a year and a half on tour with her dashing, mercurial husband, Anita is longing for a home and simpler life, and tired of worrying about the dangerous stunts he performs in his act. By pawning her jewels, Anita has a home built for them in Connecticut—without telling her husband. Unfortunately, Arturo has just signed a lucrative touring contract when he hears of her plans, and quickly dismisses the idea of taking up residence in a country home.

Despondent over their seeming incompatibility, Anita leaves her husband and files for divorce. While on a cruise, she is reunited with her former fiancé, Don, and agrees to marry him. But when Don's employer invites the newlywed couple for a weekend visit, at which the featured entertainment is none other than The Great Arturo, it becomes clear that neither Anita nor her magician ex-husband is ready to put the past behind them.

A dream cast of character actors help stars Loretta Young (1913–2000) and David Niven (1910–1983), who would ultimately make five films together, carry off this charming if insubstantial film. This is the first of three films in which Eve would be featured alongside ZaSu Pitts (1894–1963), though they have no scenes together here. Far down the cast list (tenth-billed), Eve is in and out of *Eternally Yours* in the first 15 minutes. She nonetheless has two sizable scenes as Anita's pal Gloria. As one of the guests at Anita's bridal shower, Eve trades lines with Billie Burke's Aunt Abbey, who finds her behavior a bit brash for the home of a bishop. Drolly comparing the tame shower with the bachelor's party that their husbands will enjoy, Gloria says, "Do *we* clink glasses and howl with glee over Anita's wild oats? If any one of us dropped a wild oat, we'd be darn mum about it."

Eve returns for a later scene in which Gloria meets up with Anita in London, after Anita has married Arturo and taken the place of the pretty assistant in his act. Gloria, who considers her day-to-day suburban life with husband Ben a bit prosaic and predictable, is surprised to learn that her globe-trotting friend Anita is envious of her. Fingering the many expensive dresses and costumes hanging in Anita's dressing room, Gloria says, not unkindly, "Schiaparelli, Worth, Chanel—and the woman complains." Eve plays the scene just right, giving her character warmth and caring alongside her disarming candor.

For the first time here, Eve is directed by Tay Garnett, who will also helm her and Broderick Crawford a year or so later in *Slightly Honorable*.

A *Los Angeles Times* reviewer wrote, "If you can swallow the initial premise of this picture you will do well the rest of the way," predicting that the film "should generate enough laughs in the course of its very madcap and unbelievable proceedings." Noted among its assets by the *Times* was the performance of "the very able Eve Arden" (November 2, 1939).

At the Circus (1939)

Groucho Marx (*J. Cheever Loophole*), Chico Marx (*Antonio*), Harpo Marx (*Punchy*), Kenny Baker (*Jeff Wilson*), Florence Rice (*Julie Randall*), Eve Arden (*Peerless Pauline*), Margaret Dumont (*Suzanna Dukesbury*), Nat Pendleton (*Goliath*), Fritz Feld (*Jardinet*), James Burke (*John Carter*), Jerry Marenghi [Maren] (*Little Professor Atom*), Barnett Parker (*Whitcomb*), Willie Best (*Redcap*), Irving Bacon (*Telegraph Clerk*), Frank Orth (*Chef in Diner*), Emory Parnell (*Ringmaster*)
Director: Edward Buzzell. *Producer:* Mervyn LeRoy. *Screenplay:* Irving Brecher. *Musical Direction:* Franz Waxman. *Lyrics:* E.Y. Harburg. *Music:* Harold Arlen. *Vocal and Orchestral Arrangements:* Murray Cutter, George Bassman, Ken Darby. *Dance Direction:* Bobby Connolly. *Recording Director:* Douglas Shearer. *Art Director:* Cedric Gibbons. *Associate:* Stan Rogers. *Set Decorations:* Edwin B. Willis. *Women's Costumes:* Dolly Tree. *Men's Costumes:* Valles. *Director of Photography:* Leonard M. Smith. *Film Editor:* William H. Terhune. MGM; released October 20, 1939. B&W; 87 minutes.

Jeff Wilson, born to a wealthy and socially prominent Newport family, is making his own way in the world as the owner of the Wilson Wonder Circus. With the circus finally turning a profit, Jeff is ready to pay off his creditors and marry his girlfriend, performer Julie Randall. The plans go awry when Jeff, riding a train along with his entire company of circus cast and crew, is knocked unconscious and robbed of the $10,000 in cash he needs to pay conniving John Carter.

Jeff's pal Antonio summons lawyer J. Cheever Loophole to solve the case. Loophole's suspicions center on Carter, his lady friend Peerless Pauline, and midget Professor Atom. When cozying up to Pauline fails to produce the needed cash, Loophole travels to Newport, in hopes of charming Jeff's rich widowed aunt, Mrs. Dukesbury, into providing the funds. When Mrs. Dukesbury invites all her society friends to a party at which they're expecting a program of highbrow classical music performed by a renowned symphony orchestra, Loophole throws the event into chaos by substituting Jeff's circus as the evening's entertainment.

If not top-flight Marx Brothers, *At the Circus* is nonetheless a delight, with numerous set pieces that gave 1939 movie audiences more than their money's worth in spectacle, laughs, and music. As Peerless Pauline, a circus performer whose act involves walking upside-down while suspended from the ceiling, Eve plays one of her most unusual and memorable roles. Although she is seen briefly in a few other scenes, her major contribution to the film is the hilarious routine in which she's romanced by Groucho Marx's J. Cheever Loophole, trying to recoup the stolen money she's hid-

Ambulance-chasing J. Cheever Loophole (Groucho Marx) meets his match when he encounters the gravity-defying circus star Peerless Pauline (Eve) in *At the Circus*.

ing. From the time Loophole first sets eyes on glamorous Pauline, he's intrigued. "I'll grill her until she's well-done," he says lustily. "She must know something, even if isn't about the case."

Visiting Pauline in her tent later, Loophole finds her practicing her act, hanging from the ceiling. ("Say, you're up early today, aren't you?" he remarks). Suspicious of the fast-talking lawyer, Pauline tries the flirtatious approach:

> PAULINE: Perhaps you'll think I'm forward, but last night, when I first saw you....
> LOOPHOLE: And slammed the door in my face.
> PAULINE: I realized that you're the man I've been dreaming of.
> LOOPHOLE: What do you eat before you go to bed?

As the two play coy with each other, the cagey lawyer finds the wallet full of stolen cash. He's temporarily outfoxed when she retrieves it and tucks it into the bodice of her costume. Looking Pauline over, Loophole then turns and makes an aside to the audience, "There must be some way of getting to that without getting into trouble with the Hays Office." (According to columnist Ed Sullivan, this line resulted in "a three minute yell, wiping out lines of dialog that follow.") The answer, of course, is to persuade Pauline to resume her stroll on the ceiling, in the hopes that gravity will set the hidden wallet loose, but she insists she will do so only if her gentleman friend joins her up high.

Syndicated columnist Harrison Carroll was on the set when the company was filming another key bit. "In the center of the tent," he reported in his July 17, 1939, column, Eve "is about to slide down a rope onto the shoulders of a startled Groucho Marx. Miss Arden has a firm hold on the rope, but if her fingers slip, she won't fall. A piano wire, invisible to the camera, is attached to her middle." Eve slid neatly into place, Groucho delivered his comic line, and it looked like a perfect take—but director Eddie Buzzell called cut and said it would have to be done over. Eve's black tights had acquired a visible shred "from ankle to thigh." Rather than losing time while the tights were repaired or replaced, the resourceful wardrobe mistress smeared lampblack over Eve's leg to cover the hole, and shooting resumed.

After the unforgettable seduction scene, which occurs around the film's halfway point, Eve regrettably vanishes, not to be seen again. Still, despite her limited role, there's plenty to enjoy here, including the wonderful Margaret Dumont (1882–1965), playing her usual role of a stuffy matron outrageously romanced by Groucho; character actor Fritz Feld (1900–1993) as the flummoxed symphony orchestra conductor; and inspired bits like Harpo's chess game in which he's aided and abetted by a trained seal. This is also the film that contains a wonderful production number spotlighting Groucho's song "Lydia the Tattooed Lady."

Writing in the *Washington Post*, Richard L. Coe decreed *At the Circus* "wonderful ... 85 minutes of sheer joy," adding that Eve was "at her best as the human chandelier whom Groucho would like to see lit up" (November 17, 1939).

A Child Is Born (1940)

Geraldine Fitzgerald (*Grace Sutton*), Jeffrey Lynn (*Jed Sutton*), Gladys George (*Florette Laverne*), Gale Page (*Nurse Bowers*), Spring Byington (*Mamie West*), Johnnie Davis (*Ringer Banks*), Henry O'Neill (*Dr. Lee*), John Litel (*Dr. Brett*), Gloria Holden (*Mrs. Kempner*), Johnny Downs (*Johnny Norton*), Eve Arden (*Nurse Pinty*), Fay Helm (*Disturbed Woman*), Louis Jean Heydt (*Steve Kempner*), Nanette Fabares [Fabray] (*Gladys Norton*), Jean Sharon (*Helen Banks*), Hobart Cavanaugh (*Herbie West*), George Irving (*Dr. Cramm*), Edward Gargan (*Sgt. Riley*), Nella Walker (*Mrs. Twitchell*)
Director: Lloyd Bacon. *Executive Producer:* Hal B. Wallis. *Screenplay:* Robert Rossen, based on the play by Mary McDougal Axelson. *Associate Producer:* Samuel Bischoff. *Dialogue Director:* Jo Graham. *Photography:* Charles Rosher. *Film Editor:* Jack Killifer. *Sound:* Charles Lang. *Art Director:* John Hughes. *Makeup Artist:* Perc Westmore. *Gowns:* Milo Anderson. *Technical Advisors:* Dr. Leo Schulman, Evelyn Shepherd, R.N. *Music:* H. Roemhold. *Orchestral Arrangements:* Hugo Friedhofer. *Musical Director:* Leo F. Forbstein. Warner Bros.; released January 6, 1940. B&W; 79 minutes.

The busy seventh-floor maternity ward at an unnamed city hospital plays host to a constant stream of expectant mothers. Middle-aged Mamie West is a veteran of multiple stays in the hospital, having just arrived to give birth for the fifth time. Pretty young Grace Sutton arrives at the hospital handcuffed to a prison matron, as she has just begun serving a 20-year sentence for murder. Florette Laverne is a brassy dancer whose husband says disgustedly of her pregnancy, "This wasn't my idea," and frets that her being out of commission while hospitalized will cost them bookings. Teenaged Gladys Norton is estranged from her family because she married young and had a baby, against their wishes. Also in and out of the ward periodically is a mentally disturbed woman who believes she is pregnant, and helps herself to a momentarily unattended baby belonging to someone else. Keeping watch over them all, and seemingly on 24/7 duty, is calm, efficient Nurse Bowers, who with the help of her assistant, Miss Pinty, keeps the ladies in the ward safe and sound while they await their baby's birth.

Aside from its not inconsiderable entertainment value, *A Child Is Born* is fascinating as social history, showing what was considered a fairly realistic portrait of childbirth and maternity care in 1940. Though Florette is chided for sneaking liquor into the ward, and getting soused as she awaits childbirth, no one seems to have a problem with her puffing away at a cigarette in her hospital bed. Not only are husbands *not* allowed to be involved in the delivery process, brisk Nurse Bowers sends one of them out on a wild goose chase for a nonexistent medicine, just to get him out of the way for an hour or two. Late in the film, when one of the pregnancies results in that standard dilemma of hospital dramas—whether to save the mother or the baby—the staff members talk it over with the parents, and then make up their own minds what to do! We can also tell a little something about movie censorship in the early 1940s by the fact that not one of the actresses playing mothers-to-be has anything like a realistic "baby bump."

Interestingly, by the time she was writing her memoirs, some 45 years after making this film, Eve obviously didn't have the clearest memories of it. She wrote that Gladys George, who's third-billed for her sizable role as Florette, played "little more than a bit" role. George is particularly funny in a scene where her drunken character mocks her fellow patients, mimicking Spring Byington's sprightly and cheerful Mrs. West ("I love babies! I have eight. I'm going to have eight more!"). Byington gives her usual competent and warm performance, though it's a bit of a stretch to accept the 53-year-old actress as a childbearing woman said to be in her mid–30s.

Surrounded by actresses given more colorful characters to play, Gale Page (1913–1983) delivers a subtle and strong performance as the implacable but kindly Nurse Bowers, who takes excellent care of the varied lot of women in her ward. A very young Nanette Fabray (born 1920), who hadn't yet changed the spelling of her last name from the correct-but-usually-mispronounced Fabares, plays a teenaged mother. Lovely Geraldine Fitzgerald, seen by audiences just a few months earlier as best friend to Bette Davis in *Dark Victory* (1939), gets the chance to take the lead here, and is quite touching. Gloria Holden, whose long-term claim to fame proved to be her starring role in *Dracula's Daughter* (1936), plays the patient who desperately wants a baby but cannot have a healthy one. Lloyd Bacon's direction is not showy, but very competent, allowing the drama full play and maintaining a brisk pace. He isn't afraid of the sentiment built into the script, but mostly steers clear of letting the film become maudlin.

As for Eve, her role as Nurse Pinty is distinctly a secondary one in this ensemble, and she receives billing (11th from the top) only in the film's closing credits. She's onscreen fairly often, but rarely the center of attention. To her credit, she plays her rather ordinary role with assurance, giving it just the amount of weight it needs to make Miss Pinty a realistic part of the milieu rather than making unwarranted grabs for attention. Here, she's playing a sensible, capable professional woman, as she would do often on film, but isn't asked to generate laughs.

A Child Is Born was based on the play *Life Begins,* which ran for only eight performances on Broadway in 1932. Mildred Dunnock originated Eve's role of Miss Pinty onstage. That same year, the play was adapted into a film of the same title, with Loretta Young as Grace Sutton, Aline MacMahon as Nurse Bowers, and Mary Philips as Miss Pinty. Only seven years after *Life Begins* played in theaters, Warners recycled it as *A Child Is Born.* A studio publicity release published in the *Panama City News-Herald* claimed, "Never in the history of Hollywood were there as many wedding rings displayed on the beautiful fingers of movie stars as could be seen on the Warner Bros. lot recently. And there was good reason for it, as Sound Stage One was the scene of one of the largest hospital sets ever constructed. But it was more than just a hospital scene that brought out the epidemic of wedding rings—it was the great maternity ward set used in the picture *A Child Is Born*" (January 29, 1940).

Reviewing the film in *Variety,* the obviously male critic (signed "Odec.") seemed squeamishly uncomfortable with what he clearly regarded as a picture for women only. "The film makes childbirth a quite unpleasant affair," he wrote, "but *A Child Is Born* will undoubtedly find a sympathetic reaction in that class of woman who associates the process with martyrdom and self-sacrifice" (January 17, 1940). The *Los Angeles Times*'s Philip K. Scheuer, however, praised the Warner brothers in his January 5, 1940, review: "I thought their film a rather remarkable one, even of its genre— acted with penetration, directed with skill, and playing down the more obvious, sensational aspects with a generally gratifying restraint.... The average maternity ward may not—heaven forbid!— contain so colorful and divergent a group of characters as these, but it is within the license of the playwright to bring them together."

Though the acting opportunities that it offers Eve Arden are limited, *A Child Is Born* stands up well several decades later, still a well-acted, fast-paced and absorbing drama leavened with a touch of comedy.

Slightly Honorable (1940)

Pat O'Brien (*John Webb*), Edward Arnold (*Vincent Cushing*), Broderick Crawford (*Russ Sampson*), Ruth Terry (*Anne Seymour*), Alan Dinehart (*Commissioner Joyce*), Claire Dodd (*Alma Brehmer*), Phyllis Brooks (*Sarilla Cushing*), Eve Arden (*Miss Ater*), Douglass Dumbrille (*George Taylor*), Bernard Nedell (*Pete Godena*), Douglas Fowley (*Madder*), Ernest Truex (*P. Hemingway Collins*), Janet Beecher (*Mrs. Cushing*), Evelyn Keyes (*Miss Vlissingen*), John Sheehan (*Mike Daley*), Addison Richards (*Inspector Fromm*), Cliff Clarke (*Captain Graves*), Howard Hickman (*Senator Scott*), Robert Middlemass (*Senator Berry*), Willie Best (*Art*), Max Rose (*Fingerprint Expert*), Ed Chandler (*Officer Murphy*)

Producer/Director: Tay Garnett. *Screenplay:* Ken Englund, based upon the F.G. Presnell novel *Send Another Coffin. Art Direction:* Alexander Golitzen. *Associate:* Richard Irvine. *Interior Decorations:* Julie Heron. *Director of Photography:* Merritt Gerstad. *Gowns:* Travis Banton. *Film Editors:* Otho Lovering, Dorothy Spencer. *Sound:* Fred Lau. *Assistant Director:* Charles Kerr. United Artists; released January 22, 1940. B&W; 85 minutes.

Young lawyer John Webb and his partner Russ have accepted a $100,000 retainer from clients who are battling for the right to bid on lucrative state highway construction projects. The traffic death of shady Clarence Buckman calls to attention the crony system run by Vincent Cushing, the "head of the state's crooked political machine." Cushing routinely directs highway contracts to his own cronies, a corrupt system that has resulted in roads that are dangerous due to shoddy construction. John is working to pass legislation that will force all highway contracts to be awarded via a sealed bid process.

John uses his friendship with pretty Alma Brehmer, who's involved with Cushing, to infiltrate the powerful man's shady operation. At a party for Cushing and his cronies, John meets ditzy young Anne Seymour, a club dancer who attaches herself to him after he rescues her from an admirer who's pawing her.

When a threatening note is delivered to his office via a tossed knife, John realizes that his enemies will play rough to prevent him shutting down their corrupt business. Shortly afterwards, he's invited to meet Alma at her apartment, only to arrive and find that she's been murdered with the same knife. Considered a prime suspect by the police, he must fight back to prevent himself from being framed for that murder and another one that also cuts close to home.

Slightly Honorable was based on a 1939 mystery novel by author F.G. Presnell. The film switches quickly between comedy and suspense, in a way that seems to intrigue some viewers and unnerve others. Lest we misunderstand, and take the film for a straight crime-drama, it opens with an establishing shot of a lovely tropical island, over which appears the legend: "Eight thousand miles to the southward lies a tiny island paradise—far from the greed, the graft, and the corruption that harass our modern civilization." The visual of the island is pushed away as the remainder of the sentence intrudes: "BUT THAT'S 8,000 MILES AWAY."

II. Filmography—Slightly Honorable (1940)

As secretary to lawyer John Webb (Pat O'Brien, left) in *Slightly Honorable*, Eve is no Della Street. Also pictured is Douglas Fowley.

Eve is featured as Miss Ater, the slightly insolent secretary of "brilliant young attorney" John Webb, played by Pat O'Brien. Webb seems to have something of a romantic past with his office help. She will place phone calls only if he augments his demand with "please," allows him to fetch his own mail because she's busy touching up her makeup, and gives him his messages only when she happens to think of them. Of Miss Ater, Webb says, "One day I'm gonna slip a time bomb in her lunchbox." She is never more than slightly nonplussed at whatever she finds in her bosses' offices, whether it is Russ accompanying himself on the guitar, or a feather-brained showgirl lifting her dress over her head. A genuinely startling and somewhat macabre scene finds John Webb entering his office and being annoyed to find Miss Ater with her ear to his telephone, only to touch her and find a knife protruding from her back.

Other familiar faces in the cast include comic actor Willie Best, unbilled for his featured role as the elevator operator in Webb's building, even though he has several scenes and delivers the film's closing line. Director Tay Garnett appears briefly onscreen as a reporter.

Studio publicity, largely ignoring the film's comedic elements, described *Slightly Honorable* as "not only a fast-moving, suspenseful tale of the upper crust, it is a powerful and articulate indictment of racketeering and political chicanery.... A thrilling climax, packed with punch and surprise, reveals the suave culprit and makes *Slightly Honorable* a 'must' on your picture list."

The *Greeley* (CO) *Daily Tribune*, in its February 9, 1940, "TheaterGuide" column ("Opinions and information guaranteed to be from sources other than the press departments of motion picture producers"), took a different stance. The column quoted a favorable review from the *Motion Picture*

Herald, which called the picture "as funny a comedy as ever made in Hollywood, despite the fact that the underlying plot concerns several murders and an attempt by crooked politicians to frame an innocent person. It is hilarious, and the dialogue improves many of the situations of the popular novel ... which forms the basis."

Variety, however, was less impressed in its January 10, 1940, review. Noting that the film was adapted from a book, the reviewer noted, "Either the writers had little substance to work on from the original, or they muffed the motivation of the book entirely. In any case, story skips along between serious drama and comedy without deftness, and winds up in the aggregate as a whatisit."

Perhaps the harshest review of the film came from director Tay Garnett. In his amusing autobiography, *Light Your Torches and Pull Up Your Tights,* he claims that producer Walter Wanger loused up the film in post-production. Garnett, who made the film under the name of the novel on which it was based, *Send Another Coffin,* was horrified to learn at its San Francisco premiere that it had been retitled. Of the finished product, he wrote, "What we saw was a badly mutilated, un-funny comedy. It had been cut with a jigsaw and reassembled with a Mixmaster. It was AWFUL."

She Couldn't Say No (1940)

Roger Pryor (*Wally Turnbull*), Eve Arden (*Alice Hinsdale*), Cliff Edwards (*Banjo Page*), Clem Bevans (*Eli Potter*), Vera Lewis (*Pansy Hawkins*), Irving Bacon (*Abner Pestler*), Spencer Charters (*Hank Woodcock*), Ferris Taylor (*Judge Jenkins*), Chester Clute (*Ezra Pine*), Zeffie Tilbury (*Ma Hawkins*), George Guhl (*Barber*), Frank Mayo (*Town Marshal*), Creighton Hale (*Jasper*)
Director: William Clemens. *Associate Producer:* William Jacobs. *Screenplay:* Earl Baldwin, Charles Grayson, from the play by Benjamin M. Kaye. *Director of Photography:* Ted McCord. *Dialogue Director:* Hugh MacMullan. *Art Director:* Stanley Fleischer. *Film Editor:* Harold McLernon. *Gowns:* Howard Shoup. *Sound:* Dolph Thomas. *Makeup Artist:* Perc Westmore. *Musical Director:* Leo F. Forbstein. Warner Bros.-First National Pictures; released December 7, 1940. B&W; 62 minutes.

Young lawyer Wally Turnbull's professional practice is seriously in the doldrums, as clients are few and far between. The phone rings mostly with calls from creditors. Wally's fiancée, Alice, also holds a law degree, but is currently working as his secretary, since her husband-to-be "wants to be the only mouthpiece in the family." Therefore, the firm of Turnbull and Johnson (Mr. Johnson being fictitious) exists solely on his efforts, while he tells Alice, "If I ever hear of you even thinking of taking a case...."

Wally gets an unexpected break when he's hired by his former employer to persuade an elderly farmer in the small town of Kerricksville to sell a thousand acres of land to Transatlantic Airways. When he arrives in Kerricksville, however, Wally learns that the farmer, 79-year-old Eli Potter, refuses to see any visitors because of an impending breach-of-promise suit against him by his 65-year-old girlfriend Pansy Hawkins. While Wally is out of town reporting the latest developments in the case, his friend and process server, Banjo Page, coaxes Potter into hiring Turnbull and Johnson to defend him in the lawsuit. If Potter wins his case, he agrees to turn over the deed to the land as payment to his attorney. Rather than lose the opportunity when she's unable to reach Wally, Alice takes Potter's case in her fiancé's absence.

When Wally learns that his lady friend has signed up a client, he's so angry that he offers to defend Pansy Hawkins in the breach-of-promise suit, with the land in question also to be his reward if he wins. Wally and Alice thus find themselves facing off as opposing attorneys in the same case, putting their relationship in jeopardy. The courtroom climax, which turns largely on Eli's response of "mebbe" (maybe) to his lady friend's marriage proposal, ultimately brings together not one but two pairs of lovebirds.

She Couldn't Say No was adapted from a play of the same name by Benjamin M. Kaye, which had only a brief run on Broadway in the fall of 1926. Onstage, the lead role of Alice Hinsdale was played by Florence Moore.

Rarely screened today, this inexpensive B movie, somewhat reminiscent of the far better known *Adam's Rib* (1949), is a delight for fans of Eve, as it represents one of her few leads in motion pictures. Though she's second-billed to leading man Roger Pryor, the film is primarily a

Eve played a rare leading-lady role in *She Couldn't Say No*, co-starring Roger Pryor (center) and Cliff Edwards.

showcase for Eve. Running just over an hour, it moves at a rapid clip and is pleasant, if unexceptional, entertainment. Beautifully dressed and made up, Eve shows herself quite capable of playing the romantic lead, though she retains a touch of her usual persona. The film played the bottom of double bills, often with *Santa Fe Trail* (1940).

Set in the mid–1920s, *She Couldn't Say No* treats the idea of a "lady lawyer" as being slightly less exotic to the people of Kerricksville than a visitor from Mars. Her professional methods are presented as stereotypically female—she dresses to the nines for the courtroom, flirts shamelessly with the small-town judge presiding over the case, makes objections to testimony for no particular reason, and at one point tells a witness, "You're not supposed to think! You're a witness." Her closing argument has her debunking Pansy's claim on Eli by talking about her own experience of being in love with a man who hasn't married her, saying, "I'm a woman. I know."

Eve's leading man Roger Pryor (1901–1974) was an actor and bandleader who, at the time of this role, was the husband of Ann Sothern. Cliff Edwards (1895–1971) has some funny moments as process server "Banjo" Page in a film released only a few months after he was the voice of Jiminy Cricket in *Pinocchio* (1940). Irving Bacon plays Abner, who holds a variety of jobs in the small town of Kerricksville (porter, janitor, bailiff) in a manner reminiscent of his later guest appearance on a 1952 episode of *I Love Lucy*, "The Marriage License," donning a succession of caps to match his ever-changing roles. Future Warners' leading lady Alexis Smith has a bit here as one of several residents of Kerricksville spreading gossip about the Potter-Hawkins affair by telephone.

No fan of watching her own screen work, Eve once told an interviewer that she ran from a movie theater in horror when unexpectedly confronted with a trailer for *She Couldn't Say No*.

Variety noted that the 1940 film version of *She Couldn't Say No* adhered pretty closely to the stage version of almost 15 years previously, but thought the results were adequate: "An entertaining 'B,' full of laughs and hoked-up situations.... Courtroom scene is packed with giggles" (January 22, 1941).

Comrade X (1940)

Clark Gable (*McKinley B. Thompson*), Hedy Lamarr (*Theodore Yahupitz*), Oscar Homolka (*Commissar Vasiliev*), Felix Bressart (*Vanya*), Eve Arden (*Jane Wilson*), Sig Rumann (*Emil Von Hofer*), Natasha Lytess (*Olga Milanava*), Vladimir Sokoloff (*Michael Bastakoff*), Edgar Barrier (*Rubick*), George Renavant (Laszlo), Mikhail Rasumny (*Russian Officer*), Leon Belasco (*Baronoff*)

Director: King Vidor. *Producer:* Gottfried Reinhardt. *Screenplay:* Ben Hecht, Charles Lederer. *Original Story:* Walter Reisch. *Director of Photography:* Joseph Ruttenberg. *Musical Score:* Bronislau Kaper. *Recording Director:* Douglas Shearer. *Art Director:* Cedric Gibbons. *Associate:* Malcolm Brown. *Set Decorations:* Edwin B. Willis. *Special Effects:* Arnold Gillespie. *Gowns:* Adrian. *Men's Costumes:* Gile Steele. *Makeup:* Jack Dawn. *Film Editor:* Harold F. Kress. MGM; released December 1940. B&W; 90 minutes.

American reporter "Mac" Thompson is assigned to cover news in Moscow by a Topeka newspaper. On the surface he seems to be what his ex-girlfriend Jane, a fellow reporter, describes as "a no good, incompetent party boy." In actuality, he's the much sought-after "Comrade X," who enrages Russian officials by spiriting uncensored news and photographs back to the Western

Eve found it no hardship to play the girlfriend of Clark Gable in *Comrade X*.

world. His secret identity puts him at considerable risk, since as Jane says of their contacts at the Kremlin, "Anything to keep the truth out of print is their motto."

Mac's Russian friend Vanya, a valet at his hotel, inveigles him into getting his beautiful daughter Theodore, a streetcar conductor, safely out of the country. Though Theodore is a loyal Russian who holds fiercely to communist views, her father fears that her outspokenness will put her in harm's way unless she escapes to America in Mac's keeping. So as to be granted permission to leave Russia, Mac and Theodore, whom he nicknames Lizzie, are married that night. When the discovery of Mac's spy camera puts Vanya under suspicion of being Comrade X, both men, along with Theodore, are thrown into the Kremlin jail.

Eve plays Mac's lady friend Jane Wilson, who bursts into his room on his wedding night to learn he has married. Though they have been lovers in the past, she now describes herself as "one of the alumni." Jane still has a soft spot for Mac, despite the incident that broke them up, which was "when you waltzed out on me in Tokyo for a bow-legged Geisha girl." Learning that Hedy Lamarr's character Theodore has succeeded in marrying Mac, she shakes her rival's hand and says, "Congratulations, my dear. I didn't think it could be done without a police warrant." After this, her third major scene, Eve unfortunately vanishes from the remainder of the film.

Natasha Lytess (1913–1964), seen as a prim Russian secretary whom Mac gets drunk in order to keep her quiet, has only a handful of film-acting credits to her name. She's better known in her capacity as the trusted acting coach of Marilyn Monroe. Eve would be cast alongside Hedy Lamarr for the second time only a few months later, when both graced the cast of *Ziegfeld Girl* (1941).

As most reviewers and commentators noted, *Comrade X* owed its existence largely to the success of 1939's *Ninotchka*. Bosley Crowther, in the *New York Times*, commented, "Seldom has a film—with the exception of Charlie Chaplin's *The Great Dictator*—satirized a nation and its political system with such grim and malicious delight as does this Yuletide comedy" (December 26, 1940). Going Crowther one better, the *Los Angeles Times*'s Edwin Schallert thought "it out–*Ninotchka*s *Ninotchka* in being a ribald presentation of the funny side of the Communistic regime in the land of the Slavs" (December 4, 1940).

No, No, Nanette (1940)

Anna Neagle (*Nanette Smith*), Richard Carlson (*Tom Gillespie*), Victor Mature (*William Brown*), Roland Young (*'Happy' Jimmy Smith*), Helen Broderick (*Susan Smith*), ZaSu Pitts (*Pauline Hastings*), Eve Arden (*Kitty Revere*), Billy Gilbert (*Styles*), Tamara (*Sonya*), Stuart Robertson (*Stillwater Sr./Jr.*), Dorothea Kent (*Betty*), Aubrey Mather (*Remington*), Mary Gordon (*Gertrude*), Russell Hicks (*Hitch*), Keye Luke (*Sung*), Victor Wong (*John*)
Producer/Director: Herbert Wilcox. *Screenplay:* Ken Englund, based on the musical comedy by Frank Mandel, Otto A. Harbach, Vincent Youmans, Emil Nyitray. *Music:* Vincent Youmans. *Lyrics:* Irving Caesar, Otto A. Harbach. *Director of Photography:* Russell Metty. *Art Director:* L.P. Williams. *Gowns:* Edward Stevenson. *Miss Neagle's Portrait:* McClelland Barclay. *Recording:* Richard van Hessen. *Special Effects:* Vernon L. Walker. *Editor:* Elmo Williams. *Choreography:* Aida Broadbent. *Set Decorations:* Darrell Silvera. *Assistant Directors:* Kenneth Holmes, Lloyd Richards. *Associate Producer:* Merrill G. White. *Musical Director:* Anthony Collins. RKO Radio Pictures; released December 20, 1940. B&W; 97 minutes.

"Happy" Jimmy Smith is a genial older man who lives on the family estate with his wife, Sue, and their pretty young niece, Nanette. Although the family fortune isn't what it used to be, Jimmy has a bad habit of taking on young women as protégées. Unfortunately, when he is unable to completely finance the aspirations of wannabe performer Sonya, painter Kitty, and, finally, the unspecified dreams of "Betty from Bridgeport," the women threaten to expose his relationship with them to his unsuspecting wife.

Nanette does her best to untangle her uncle's affairs, at the expense of her own best interests. She employs her charms to get producer Bill to cast Sonya in his show, *So Long, Sister*. Once that drama is settled, Nanette next has to arrange for Tom Gillespie, a young artist who's infatuated with her, to give art lessons to aspiring painter Kitty. When Tom, whose usual work is commercial art of sexy young women, paints a lovely portrait of Nanette, she is forced to sell it to buy off

Uncle Jimmy's latest blonde. After impulsively accepting Bill's marriage proposal, though it's Tom she really loves, Nanette boards an airline flight that unwittingly will serve as a meeting ground for virtually everyone in Jimmy's complicated life, including his angry wife.

Eve, cast as "Kitty from Kansas," strides into this film at around the half-hour point and picks up its pace considerably. Thanks to Jimmy's generosity, she has transformed herself from a manicurist to a sharply dressed, hoity-toity would-be artist who drags two dogs on a leash everywhere she goes. As she says to Jimmy, in her affected accents:

> KITTY: Remember the old Kitty Revere? Just a simple, naïve girl, clipping your cuticles. Oh, but that's all behind us. To the future, Jimmy! And then, when the Metropolitan Museum is asking for a first from the brush of Katherine Revere, you, Jimmy, will be the happiest man at the hanging!
> JIMMY: Yes, I certainly will.

When Kitty meets handsome Tom, who will be her instructor, she tells him, "Mr. Gillespie, I want to paint—horribly." He's a little unnerved by her, especially when she says dramatically, "When do we begin? I'm ready. Do with me what you will!"

No, No, Nanette originated as a musical comedy on the British stage in the mid–1920s, transferred successfully to Broadway, and was first adapted to film in 1930. A 1971 Broadway revival starring Ruby Keeler, Helen Gallagher, and Patsy Kelly was a hit. In the 1940 film, the music is deemphasized somewhat, though both of the musical's best-known songs, "I Want to be Happy" and "Tea for Two" are present. Leading lady Anna Neagle (1904–1986) was a British subject who first became a star in her native England. Producer-director Herbert Wilcox was a major force in guiding her career, and also became her husband in 1943. Their success in the British Isles convinced executives at RKO to import them to America, where Neagle starred in *Nurse Edith Cavell* (1939) and *Irene* (1940) before taking on the role of Nanette Smith. RKO paid Warners, owners of the film rights to *Nanette*, a reported $200,000 for the property, and also tried (unsuccessfully) to borrow Warners player Dennis Morgan to play the male lead.

It's clear from the opening moments that the film is to be a showcase for Neagle, who even appears live in the opening titles, stepping out onstage to pull a curtain on which the film's credits have been painted. Acclaimed artist McClelland Barclay was commissioned to paint the original picture of Neagle as Nanette that plays a prominent role in the film's plot. Producer-director Wilcox even showcases the star's dancing skills in a rather gratuitous dream sequence. Her performance in *No, No, Nanette,* however, though competent, is almost overshadowed by the skillful comedic support of not only Eve, but ZaSu Pitts, playing the Smiths' maid Pauline. It was a role that should have come naturally to Pitts, who played the same character in the 1930 film version.

Roland Young (1887–1953), best-remembered for playing haunted Cosmo Topper in *Topper* (1937), contributes strongly here. Rather than seeming like a dirty old man, Young makes his character endearing, an innocent who just likes to "spread a little sunshine," especially around attractive younger women. Eve, who towers over him, uses her height to good advantage as her character overwhelms his timid persona. Young, already a film veteran with nearly 200 credits on his filmography, told the United Press's Alexander Kahn (December 18, 1940) that his romantic tussles in *No, No, Nanette* with Eve, Helen Broderick, and others represented his first cinematic love scenes. Broderick reportedly commemorated the occasion by having a newsboy bring a paper to the set prominently headlined, "Pickle-Faced Romeo Runs Rampant."

Eve is also quite good in her scenes with handsome Richard Carlson (Tom), who mostly plays straight man. Torben Meyer appears unbilled as Mr. Furtlemertle, who proves to be a benefactor to Kitty. He and Eve are both seen in *Bedtime Story* (1941). Actor Stuart Robertson, with the help of a good makeup job, plays father-and-son attorneys whose practice seems largely devoted to trying to settle the Smiths' domestic affairs. He was Neagle's real-life brother.

The *New York Times*'s Bosley Crowther didn't much care for this version of *Nanette,* which "uses that airy score for little more than incidental background music, substitutes nothing in its place and meanders tediously through a typical silly musical comedy plot to an exceedingly silly conclusion. Film producers have strange ideas" (December 20, 1940). Crowther did note Eve as one of "a cast of dependable comics" appearing in support, but thought the film made little use of them. The *Washington Post* took a happier view of the film, saying of Eve's performance, "Miss Arden is by far the most provocative of those who are in there for strictly comic purposes" (December 25, 1940).

That Uncertain Feeling (1941)

Merle Oberon (*Jill Baker*), Melvyn Douglas (*Larry Baker*), Burgess Meredith (*Alexander Sebastian*), Alan Mowbray (*Dr. Vengard*), Olive Blakeney (*Margie Stallings*), Harry Davenport (*Mr. Jones*), Sig Rumann (*Mr. Kafka*), Eve Arden (*Sally Aikens*), Richard Carle (*Albert*)

Director/Producer: Ernst Lubitsch. *Screenplay:* Donald Ogden Stewart. *Adaptation:* Walter Reisch, from a play by Victorien Sardou, Emile du Najac. *Music:* Werner R. Heymann. *Director of Photography:* George Barnes. *Art Director:* Alexander Golitzen. *Miss Oberon's Gowns:* Irene. *Assistant Director:* Horace Hough. *Set Interiors:* A.E. Freudeman. *Film Editor:* William Shea. *Sound Technician:* Arthur Johns. Ernst Lubitsch Productions/United Artists; released April 20, 1941. B&W; 83 minutes.

Young corporate wife Jill Baker, married to insurance man Larry for six years, has what would seem to be an ideal life, living in luxurious comfort on Park Avenue. Though their friends see them as an ideal couple (they are known socially as "The Happy Bakers"), Jill and Larry are in a rut that has left her feeling bored and unappreciated. Suffering from a recurring case of hiccups that she cannot shake, Jill agrees to visit a psychoanalyst, but firmly rejects his theory that her condition is somehow related to the state of her marriage.

Legal secretary Miss Aikens (Eve) provides a feminine perspective to her boss Mr. Jones (Harry Davenport, center) and client Larry Baker (Melvyn Douglas) in *That Uncertain Feeling*.

In the analyst's waiting room, Jill meets a fellow patient, classical pianist Alexander Sebastian. The iconoclastic Sebastian, who's completely unlike her nice-guy, run-of-the-mill husband, intrigues Jill by introducing her to a world of music and modern art. Believing that they have grown apart, Jill and Larry agree to a divorce so that she can marry Sebastian. But as they prepare to go their separate ways, and Jill sees more clearly what her future life with her eccentric, impulsive new man will be like, she finds herself wondering if she has made the wrong choice.

Not to be confused with the Bob Hope comedy *That Certain Feeling* (1956), this mild comedy is one of the lesser efforts of the great Ernst Lubitsch (1892–1947), whose classic films include *Trouble in Paradise* (1932), *Ninotchka* (1939), and *Heaven Can Wait* (1943). It is a remake of his 1925 silent film *Kiss Me Again,* which featured Clara Bow in the role played here by Eve. Eve, seen only in the film's second half, has a few scenes as Miss Aikens, secretary to Larry's attorney, Mr. Jones. When Larry confides his marital difficulties to his friend and attorney, Mr. Jones calls in Miss Aikens to give them a woman's point of view. Working for a living herself, Miss Aikens doesn't readily sympathize with the problems of a married woman who's bored with her kind, handsome husband, her mink coat, and her Park Avenue apartment. Later, Miss Aikens is called back into the office to witness a staged quarrel between Jill and Larry, in which he can't quite bring himself to deliver the slap to her face that will provide her needed grounds for divorce.

Screenwriter Donald Ogden Stewart (1894–1980) won an Oscar for his screenplay of *The Philadelphia Story* (1940).

The *Los Angeles Times*'s Philip K. Scheuer found the lead performances of Oberon, Douglas, and Meredith competent, but didn't find anyone else worthy of singling out, "[e]xcept for Eve Arden as a secretary" (May 8, 1941). The *Christian Science Monitor* noted, "Considering that Ernst Lubitsch produced and directed and that Donald Ogden Stewart wrote the screen play, we might have expected something more amusing" (May 16, 1941).

The spring release of *That Uncertain Feeling* launched Eve's busiest year in motion pictures. Regular moviegoers would have had difficulty avoiding her, had anyone wanted to do so; she had ten films released in 1941, encompassing a variety of studios and genres.

Ziegfeld Girl (1941)

James Stewart (*Gilbert Young*), Judy Garland (*Susan Gallagher*), Hedy Lamarr (*Sandra Kolter*), Lana Turner (*Sheila Regan*), Tony Martin (*Frank Merton*), Jackie Cooper (*Jerry Regan*), Ian Hunter (*Geoffrey Collis*), Charles Winninger (*Pop Gallagher*), Edward Everett Horton (*Noble Sage*), Philip Dorn (*Franz Kolter*), Paul Kelly (*John Slayton*), Eve Arden (*Patsy Dixon*), Dan Dailey, Jr. (*Jimmy Walters*), Al Shean (*Al*), Fay Holden (*Mrs. Regan*), Felix Bressart (*Mischa*), Rose Hobart (*Mrs. Merton*), Bernard Nedell (*Nick Capalini*), Ed McNamara (*Mr. Regan*), Mae Busch (*Jenny*), Renie Riano (*Annie*), Josephine Whittell (*Perkins*), Sergio Orta (*Native Dancer*), Joyce Compton (*Miss Sawyer*), Roscoe Ates (*Janitor*), Ray Teal (*Pawnbroker*), Ruth Tobey (*Betty Regan*)

Director: Robert Z. Leonard. *Producer:* Pandro S. Berman. *Screenplay:* Marguerite Roberts, Sonya Levien. *Story:* William Anthony McGuire. *Musical Numbers Director:* Busby Berkeley. *Director of Photography:* Ray June. *Recording Director:* Douglas Shearer. *Art Director:* Cedric Gibbons. *Associate:* Daniel B. Cathcart. *Set Decorations:* Edwin B. Willis. *Musical Presentation:* Merrill Pye. *Gowns and Costumes:* Adrian. *Makeup:* Jack Dawn. *Film Editor:* Blanche Sewell. *Songs:* "You Stepped Out of a Dream" (Nacio Herb Brown, Gus Kahn), "Minnie from Trinidad" (Roger Edens), "I'm Always Chasing Rainbows" (Harry Carroll, Joseph McCarthy), "Mr. Gallagher and Mr. Shean" (Edward Gallagher, Al Shean). *Vocals and Orchestrations:* Leo Arnaud, George Bassman, Conrad Salinger. MGM; released April 25, 1941. B&W; 132 minutes.

As an opening title says, *Ziegfeld Girl* takes us back to the 1920s to depict "that fabulous era—when Florenz Ziegfeld glorified the American girl, and New York wore her over its heart like an orchid—while she lasted." Casting is underway for the latest edition of the *Ziegfeld Follies,* soon to open at the New Amsterdam Theatre. While his office is filled with hopeful young women, Mr. Z (who never actually appears onscreen) has his own methods of discovering new talent. As his beleaguered assistant, Mr. Sage, knows, the boss can find potential Ziegfeld girls almost anywhere—"He found one in a Staten Island ferry, one on the Bronx Express, two in an all-night laundry." Among his latest discoveries are Sheila Regan, elevator operator in a department store

Lana Turner (left), with Eve as "the best horrible example you'll ever see," in *Ziegfeld Girl*.

on Fifth Avenue, minor-league vaudeville performer Susan Gallagher, and Sandra Kolter, gorgeous wife of an impoverished violinist auditioning for a spot in the show's orchestra.

The three young women are hired for the *Follies,* but soon learn that their big break carries some consequences. Sue Gallagher is forced to choose between opportunity with the Ziegfeld organization and her loyalty to her vaudevillian father. Sandra Kolter finds the job straining her relationship with her musician husband. As for Sheila Regan, her future with boyfriend Gil is threatened when she has her head turned by wealth, glamour, and the ready access to alcohol, gambling, and other vices that her success offers.

Patsy Dixon, Eve's character, is a "hardened veteran" in the Follies, who's seemingly heard and seen it all. Early on, boss Mr. Slaton gives the new girls some words of wisdom, saying, "In a few minutes you're going on in your first number. Do you know what that means? It means you're Ziegfeld girls. It means you're going to have all the opportunities of a lifetime crowded into a couple of hours—and all the temptations." Patsy just yawns. As we see from the dazzling array of jewelry Patsy wears, she's been amply rewarded during her time with the Follies. Telling one of the younger girls she should marry for love, Patsy admires her own bejeweled arm and says, "I did!" (Retorts a co-worker: "All five times!")

When Patsy's time in the spotlight comes to an end, she takes it philosophically, saying, "Well, little Patsy's picture is out of the lobby, and little Patsy's out of the show. And this is the first time in five years I haven't been a June bride." Co-worker Jenny suggests that there's nothing wrong with Patsy that another marriage wouldn't fix, to which she replies, "You know, I think I'll settle down and adopt a baby—a boy, about twenty-one." Still, for all her outward cynicism, Patsy does have a decent streak, as when she tries in vain to persuade the inebriated Sheila not to go onstage. When Sheila asks who Patsy is to intercede, the older woman replies, "The best horrible example you'll ever see."

Eve, of course, knew a little about the *Ziegfeld Follies* first-hand, having been a featured player in two editions in the 1930s. She joined the movie cast as a replacement for the originally cast Rita Johnson, who withdrew from the role of Patsy. Incredibly prolific director Robert Z. Leonard had been behind the camera since the 1910s, directing more than 150 films before calling it quits in 1957. MGM advertisements pronounced *Ziegfeld Girl* the "greatest musical extravaganza of all time!" According to contemporary publicity, producer Pandro S. Berman and Leonard auditioned more than 600 young women in order to choose the several dozen used as showgirls in the film.

This star-studded MGM feature attracted mostly positive notices, and did well at the box office. Critic Charles G. Sampas, writing in the *Lowell Sun* took exception to Hollywood's treatment of the Ziegfeld legend, suggesting that the truth was a little harsher than what the film depicted. "It is true," Sampas wrote, "that jewelry was showered upon the Ziegfeld gals—literally tons of it. It is also true that they didn't last long.... The gals were flashes in the pan. And they reached the wastebasket quicker than it took them to reach the spotlight" (May 9, 1941).

Ziegfeld Girl has a huge cast, and Eve's name doesn't even make it into the opening titles. Nonetheless, she plays one of the more memorable characters who passes in front of the viewer's eyes in the course of the film's two-hour-plus running time.

She Knew All the Answers (1941)

Joan Bennett (*Gloria Winters*), Franchot Tone (*Mark Willows*), John Hubbard (*Randy Bradford*), Eve Arden (*Sally Long*), William Tracy (*Benny*), Pierre Watkin (*George Wharton*), Almira Sessions (*Elaine Wingate*), Thurston Hall (*J.D. Sutton*), Grady Sutton (*Ogleby*), Billy Benedict (*Singing Telegram Boy*)
Director: Richard Wallace. *Producer:* Charles R. Rogers. *Screenplay:* Harry Segall, Kenneth Earl, Curtis Kenyon, based upon the *Cosmopolitan* story by Jane Allen. *Director of Photography:* Henry Freulich. *Film Editor:* Gene Howlick. *Art Direction:* Lionel Banks. *Montage Effects:* Donald Starling. *Musical Director:* M.W. Stoloff. *Assistant to Producer:* William A. Pierce. Columbia Pictures, released May 14, 1941. B&W; 85 minutes.

Young millionaire playboy Randy Bradford is on the verge of eloping with chorus girl Gloria Winters when he is threatened with the loss of his inheritance by his guardian, stuffy Wall Street banker Mark Willows. Gloria persuades Randy to postpone the wedding so as not to forfeit his millions. Using her roommate's name, she bluffs her way into a temporary job as receptionist and switchboard operator at the firm of Bradford, Willows and Wharton. She intends to hold the job only long enough to impress Mark into writing her a letter of recommendation that they hope will force him to release Randy's inheritance. Instead, Gloria unexpectedly becomes enmeshed in the company's stock market fortunes. Nearly fired for her ineptitude, Gloria instead becomes the heroine of the company's directors when an error on her part causes them to turn a tidy profit in the market.

Working closely alongside Mark Willows, Gloria finds a likable man underneath his stern and proper demeanor. He likewise finds himself attracted to this endearing young woman, unaware she is the same one he assumed was a gold-digger. After an evening out, in which they pay a visit to Coney Island, Mark and Gloria both realize they are attracted to each other. Sensing that he may be in danger of losing his girl to Willows, Randy decides to take a job at his late father's company, and soon reveals his true relationship to Gloria. Though Mark acquiesces to letting Gloria and Randy go forward with their wedding plans, almost all concerned are secretly hoping that something gives before she exchanges vows with the wrong man.

Fourth-billed Eve has a decent-sized (though unspectacular) role as Gloria's best friend and roommate in this agreeable comedy, which Columbia Pictures promoted as "one of the gayest, giddiest, and grandest love-and-laugh comedies of the year." The film had its origin in a magazine story called "A Girl's Best Friend Is Wall Street," which according to the *Los Angeles Times*'s Edwin Schallert had been "the subject of spirited bidding" by studios (November 4, 1940). Leads

Joan Bennett and Franchot Tone were set by the fall of 1940. At the time Eve's casting was announced in February 1941, the film's intended title was *A Girl's Best Friend Is Broadway*. According to the closing credits, Eve plays Sally Long, but her character is referred to in the film only as Katherine (or Kitty) Long. Among her few scenes is a lengthy one in which she is forced to pose as Gloria's invalid sister, giving scant respect to Mark Willows's impassioned speech about overcoming her illness through willpower.

A number of recognizable character faces turn up in smallish or even bit roles in the film. Grady Sutton plays vague Ogleby, a staff member at Bradford, Willows and Wharton, who knows he recognizes Gloria but can't quite figure out why. Frequent Bowery Boys co-star Billy Benedict croons an insulting singing telegram that Randy sends to his rival Mark, while Thurston Hall is seen briefly as a competing stockbroker. Perennial movie drunk Jack Norton has an unbilled bit, as do Dick Elliott and Roscoe Ates, among others.

Joan Bennett (1910–1990) is a lovely and charming heroine, though her patrician speech patterns ("fast" comes out as "fahst") don't quite suggest a veteran of rough-and-tumble New York City nightclubs. Franchot Tone (1905–1968), already divorced from Joan Crawford, nicely conveys Mark's transformation from stuffy to a more personable and engaging character. He's yet another Crawford spouse to share the screen with Eve, who later appeared opposite Phillip Terry in *Pan-Americana*. Director Richard Wallace would work with Eve again a year or so later in *Obliging Young Lady*.

The *Oakland Tribune*'s Wood Soanes, in his July 10, 1941, review, didn't award *She Knew All the Answers* a prize for originality, saying the screenwriters "have been going to the movies in earnest and borrowing freely from hither and yon," but admitted that the movie was nonetheless "a lot of fun." A bit less enthusiastic, the *New York Times*'s Bosley Crowther called it "a proper and inconsequential little comedy which one may take or leave and no harm done either way" (June 20, 1941).

Writing in the *Chicago Tribune*, reviewer "Mae Tinée" opined, "Here's a comedy that has an edge on a lot more pretentious and widely heralded films that I could name. It's fast. It's droll. It's unexpected.... Eve Arden plays Gloria's roommate. THERE'S an actress! And SO easy to look at!" (July 15, 1941). *Variety* concurred that "Eve Arden catches attention as the showgirl blonde" (May 21, 1941).

Eve reprised her film role as Kitty when *She Knew All the Answers* was adapted for an episode of *The Lux Radio Theatre*.

San Antonio Rose (1941)

Jane Frazee (*Hope Holloway*), Robert Paige (*Con Conway*), Eve Arden (*Gabby Trent*), Lon Chaney, Jr. (*Jigsaw Kennedy*), Shemp Howard (*Benny the Bounce*), The Merry Macs (*Mary Lou Cook, Joe McMichael, Ted McMichael, Judd McMichael*), Richard Lane (*Charles Willoughby*), Elaine Condos (*Elaine*), Louis Da Pron (*Alex*), Charles Lang (*Ralph*), Peter Sullivan (*Don*), Richard Davies (*Eddie*), Luis Alberni (*Nickolas "Nick" Ferris*)

Director: Charles Lamont. *Associate Producer:* Ken Goldsmith. *Screenplay:* Hugh Wedlock, Jr., Howard Snyder, Paul Gerard Smith. *Original Story,* Jack Lait, Jr. *Director of Photography:* Stanley Cortez. *Art Director:* Jack Otterson. *Associate Art Director:* Ralph M. DeLacy. *Film Editor:* Milton Carruth. *Set Decoration:* R.A. Gausman. *Musical Director:* Charles Previn. *Orchestration:* Frank Skinner. *Sound Supervisor:* Bernard B. Brown. *Technician:* Charles Carroll. *Gowns:* Vera West. *Musical Numbers Staged by* Nick Castle. Universal Pictures; released June 20, 1941. B&W; 63 minutes.

Showgirls Hope Holloway and Gabby Trent, who have a sister act, are stranded outside the town of Bentridge after their show closes unexpectedly. Acting on a tip from a truck driver who gives them a lift, Hope and Gabby try to get jobs at a roadhouse called the Plantation. The joint's owner, Nick Ferris, is intimidated by a couple of thugs hired by the competition, the Harmony House, and abandons his business outright, leaving the two showgirls stranded. Hope and Gabby team up with a quartet called Con Conway and His Texans, the next scheduled act at the Plantation, and agree to try running the place themselves.

Hope, Gabby, and their friends manage to convince a local radio station to broadcast their live musical performances at the Plantation, augmented by sound effects records to make it appear that the place is bustling with appreciative, applauding customers. After the initial radio broadcast, the Plantation is besieged with customers once it truly opens its doors the following night.

Low-rent bad guy Jigsaw Kennedy and not-too-intimidating sidekick Benny the Bounce, who have promised the owner of the Harmony House that they can shut down the Plantation, get themselves hired on as waiters on opening night and do their best to make a shambles of the evening. Luckily for Gabby and her friends, Jigsaw and Benny's efforts to insult the customers, who assume that all of this is part of the zany club's floor show, only help make the Plantation a success. Hope has a happy ending in her love life as well, having won the heart of Con.

Seven musical numbers fill much of the running time in this amiable, low-budget second feature, which tells its familiar but enjoyable story in just over an hour. Universal's trailer promised moviegoers, "You'll sing out and swing out as youth gets gay!" (which, of course, meant something rather different in 1941).

With five principal players, plenty of music, and only an hour or so of film, none of the characters is more than lightly sketched, including Eve's. Third-billed, she has a very typical best-friend-of-the-heroine role as Gabby Trent, playing most of her scenes with Jane Frazee's Hope, and knocks off a few good cracks. Of her pal Hope's romantic rival, singer Mona, she remarks, "She's two-faced, and I don't like either one of them."

Gabby is hardly intimidated by the likes of Jigsaw and Benny (Lon Chaney and Shemp Howard), knocking the gun out of Jigsaw's hand and tossing the bullets out the window. As Howard's Benny crawls through the window to make his exit, she gives him a swift kick in the hindparts, saying "Need some help?" Later, when they promise they've gone straight, she allows them to take temporary jobs as waiters at the Plantation, promising, "I'll pay you union scale. I'll give you a check tonight. And if business is good next week, I'll sign it." (A few years later, of course, Eve will have a much more famous job in the hospitality industry when she plays best pal to Joan Crawford in *Mildred Pierce* [1945].)

Though she's prominent onscreen throughout the majority of the film's brief running time, Eve is mostly on the sidelines for the slapstick climax of the film, in which waiters Jigsaw and Benny make a shambles of opening night at the Plantation. She probably didn't mind, as she's one of the few players in this scene who doesn't end up on the receiving end of a seltzer bottle.

This was the first of several on-screen teamings for Universal contract players Robert Paige (1911–1987) and Lon Chaney, Jr. (1906–1973). Two years later, they would have their most famous collaboration on *Son of Dracula*. Only a few months after the release of *San Antonio Rose*, the release of Universal's *The Wolf Man* would give Chaney a major boost toward his 1940s career as a horror star.

Also prominently seen are the Merry Macs, a musical quartet recently signed by Universal who were already a popular attraction on radio. Brothers Judd, Joe, and Ted McMichael are the nucleus of the group, joined by Mary Lou Cook. Cook, as Mona, capably plays a bad-girl role in addition to performing musically. The film's musical director, Charles Previn, then head of Universal's music department, was a second cousin to composer-conductor André Previn.

Not widely reviewed, *San Antonio Rose* was generally received as the pleasant, enjoyable B picture it was. The *Salt Lake Tribune* called it "a tune-filled mélange of fast and wacky entertainment" (August 27, 1941).

Whistling in the Dark (1941)

Red Skelton (*Wally Benton*), Conrad Veidt (*Joseph Jones*), Ann Rutherford (*Carol Lambert*), Virginia Grey (*Fran Post*), "Rags" Ragland (*Sylvester*), Henry O'Neill (*Phillip Post*), Eve Arden (*"Buzz" Baker*), Paul Stanton (*Jennings*), Don Douglas (*Gordon Thomas*), Don Costello (*"Noose" Green*), William Tannen (*Robert Graves*), Reed Hadley (*Beau Smith*), Mariska Aldrich (*Hilda*), Lloyd Corrigan (*Harvey Upshaw*), George Carleton (*Deputy Commissioner O'Neill*), Will Lee (*Herman*), Ruth Robinson (*Mrs. Robinson*)

Director: S. Sylvan Simon. *Producer:* George Haight. *Screen Play:* Robert MacGunigle, Harry Clork, Albert Mannheimer. *Based Upon the Play by* Laurence Gross, Edward Childs Carpenter, presented on the stage by Alexander McKaig. *Director of Photography:* Sidney Wagner. *Musical Score:* Bronislau Kaper. *Recording*

II. Filmography—Whistling in the Dark (1941)

Director: Douglas Shearer. *Art Director:* Cedric Gibbons. *Associate:* Gabriel Scognamillo. *Set Decorations:* Edwin B. Willis. *Gowns:* Kalloch. *Film Editor:* Frank E. Hull. MGM; released August 8, 1941. B&W; 78 minutes.

Radio star Wally Benton, known to his listeners as "The Fox," has a popular nightly show in which he dramatizes the solutions to fictitious crimes. Joseph Jones, the leader of a religious cult bilking lonely women, stands to receive a million-dollar inheritance from one of his late followers if he can eliminate the only other heir, her nephew Harvey Upshaw. Jones and his cronies kidnap Wally so that they can force him to dream up a foolproof way to eliminate Upshaw. Along with Wally, the crooks kidnap the two women in his life—his radio leading lady, Carol Lambert, whom he planned to marry, and the sponsor's daughter, Fran Post, whom his agent Buzz wants Wally to romance so as to keep his contract.

Held captive at the cult's headquarters, a gloomy mansion called the Silver Haven, Wally devises a viable murder plot to get himself and the women released. Instead, Jones and his henchmen refuse to let them go even after the work is done. Managing somehow to rewire a portable radio at the mansion, Wally broadcasts a remote that alerts authorities as to their whereabouts, and prevents Mr. Upshaw from ingesting the poison that was intended to kill him.

Eve has a relatively minor role as Wally's businesslike manager Buzz. After a couple of good early scenes, Eve disappears from the midsection of the film, but resurfaces near the end, as Wally and his lady friends are rescued. Buzz is not a sufficiently important character for the screenwriters to provide any background on her; she functions merely as the impetus to keep Wally involved with Fran Post. Reminding Wally that his radio contract is up for renewal, she advises him to show some interest in Miss Post, so that her father will keep him employed. Ignoring his protests that he intends to marry Carol that evening, Buzz dissuades him from doing so, informing him that practically every viable sponsor has a daughter, most of them not nearly as presentable as Fran.

Having delivered that news, Eve will soon recede into the background. Her best moment in the film comes a few minutes later, when she accompanies Fran to a nightclub at which they expect Wally to join them shortly. As they're being seated, Buzz addresses the maître d':

BUZZ: If a gentleman arrives asking for Miss Post, show him over here, will you?
MAÎTRE D': One gentleman for two ladies?
BUZZ: Oh, it's all right. I'm just going to watch.

It's a prophetic line, as indeed her character will be sidelined for much of the film's running time. Midway through the film, Eve pops up long enough to have a brief argument with Fran's father, once the disappearance of Wally and his lady friends has attracted attention. Virginia Grey and Ann Rutherford, playing the two romantic interests in Wally's life, get substantially more screen time than Eve does. Conrad Veidt, an émigré to Hollywood from Germany, spent most of his time playing menacing characters in films like *A Woman's Face* (1941) and *Casablanca* (1942). This rare appearance in a comedy allows him to bring genuine menace in the midst of a silly script.

Whistling in the Dark was loosely based on a Broadway comedy that ran for just over a year in the early 1930s. MGM released a film adaptation of the stage show in 1933, with Ernest Truex recreating the lead role he'd played on Broadway. It was recycled less than a decade later as a vehicle for Skelton. Made after he'd been an MGM contract player for only a year, *Whistling in the Dark* was Skelton's first leading role, and performed well enough at the box office to merit two sequels: *Whistling in Dixie* (1942) and *Whistling in Brooklyn* (1943). Ann Rutherford reprised her role as Wally's fiancée in both, but Eve's character did not recur in the second and third film. She did, however, make guest appearances on Red Skelton's popular TV show in later years, usually cast as the nagging, domineering wife to Red's George Appleby character.

The *Washington Post*'s Nelson B. Bell raved about *Whistling in the Dark* and its star, saying, "His previous film assignments have given rich promise of a spectacular Skelton future on the screen. *Whistling in the Dark* clinches it.... There will be no stopping the fellow now." Eve was among the supporting players Bell credited with "keep[ing] the thing popping like a bunch of firecrackers," delivering "high-speed performances" (August 8, 1941).

Manpower (1941)

Edward G. Robinson (*Hank McHenry*), Marlene Dietrich (*Fay Duval*), George Raft (*Johnny Marshall*), Alan Hale (*Jumbo Wells*), Frank McHugh (*Omaha*), Eve Arden (*Dolly*), Barton MacLane (*Smiley Quinn*), Ward Bond (*Eddie Adams*), Walter Catlett (*Sidney Whipple*), Joyce Compton (*Scarlett*), Lucia Carroll (*Flo*), Egon Brecher (*Pop Duval*), Cliff Clark (*Cully*), Joseph Crehan (*Sweeney*), Ben Welden (*Al Hurst*), Barbara Pepper (*Polly*), Dorothy Appleby (*Wilma*)

Director: Raoul Walsh. *Executive Producer:* Hal B. Wallis. *Associate Producer:* Mark Hellinger. *Screenplay:* Richard Macaulay, Jerry Wald. *Director of Photography:* Ernie Haller. *Dialogue Director:* Hugh Cummings. *Film Editor:* Ralph Dawson. *Art Director:* Max Parker. *Sound:* Dolph Thomas. *Gowns:* Milo Anderson. *Special Effects:* Byron Haskin, H.F. Koenekamp. *Makeup Artist:* Perc Westmore. *Technical Advisor:* Verne Elliott. *Music:* Adolph Deutsch. *Musical Director:* Leo F. Forbstein. *Song:* "He Lied and I Listened," lyrics, Frank Loesser, music, Frederick Hollander. Warner Bros.; released August 9, 1941. B&W; 103 minutes.

Crew members employed by the Bureau of Power and Light are charged with the demanding and often dangerous job of repairing downed power lines. Foreman Hank McHenry is a good guy who doesn't have much success with women. When Hank meets his co-worker Pop Duval's beautiful daughter Fay, recently released from a brief stretch in prison, he is immediately attracted. When Pop is killed on the job, Hank and his buddy Johnny try to look after Fay, who sloughs off their help and takes a job in a sleazy clip joint called the Midnight Club.

When Johnny warns Fay against taking advantage of Hank's infatuation with her, she rebels by accepting her would-be lover's marriage proposal. As she gets to know both Johnny and her new husband better, Fay realizes that she is falling in love with Johnny, and decides to give up her loveless marriage and leave town. While visiting the club where she used to work, Fay is caught up in a raid, while Hank is injured on the job.

Eve has a small featured role here as Dolly, one of Fay's two pals and co-workers at the Midnight Club. (Dumb-blonde specialist Joyce Compton plays the other, Southern-accented Scarlett). We first meet Dolly when she sticks up for Marlene Dietrich's Fay, saying to their boss, "Leave the kid alone. She buried her old man this afternoon." The line is skillfully delivered, but sounds a little odd, as the 40-year-old leading lady doesn't really qualify as any kind of "kid," and in any event is barely registering enough emotion on her face to justify Eve's dialogue.

A hard-boiled, world-weary veteran of the nightclub, Dolly says, "I'm 25, look 35, and feel 50." (Eve was 33 at the time.) Dolly urges her friend Fay to accept Hank's marriage proposal even though she doesn't love him, claiming she herself would happily accept an offer from anyone who wore pants and held a job.

In her few scenes, Eve plays well not only with Compton and Marlene Dietrich, but also with Barton MacLane (previously her co-star in *Big Town Czar*), cast as her rough-hewn boss Smiley. Smiley is a pretty tough customer, but that cuts no ice with Dolly. Unimpressed with him and his establishment, Dolly tells her boss, "You know, Smiley, there's one grand consolation about working in this dump. You can't get any lower." Later, when Fay wants a referral to seek work in Chicago, Smiley tips her off about a club run by a friend of his, calling it "a sophisticated joint, just like this one." Dolly responds, "I suppose that means they serve their Mickeys in champagne glasses."

The *Los Angeles Times*'s Edwin Schallert thought *Manpower* rather similar to several other Warner Bros.' pictures he'd already seen, but concluded that it "holds up well enough to entertain and satisfy" (July 4, 1941). Eve, along with Walter Catlett, Ward Bond, and Joyce Compton, among others, was mentioned as one of the supporting players worthy of note.

Last of the Duanes (1941)

George Montgomery (*Buck Duane*), Lynne Roberts (*Nancy Bowdrey*), Eve Arden (*Kate*), Francis Ford (*Luke Stevens*), George E. Stone (*Euchre*), William Farnum (*Maj. McNeil*), Joseph Sawyer (*Bull Lossomer*), Truman Bradley (*Capt. Laramie*), Russell Simpson (*Tom Duane*), Don Costello (*Jim Bland*), Harry Woods (*Sheriff Red Morgan*), Andrew Tombes (*Sheriff Frank Taylor*), Tim Ryan (*Bartender*), Ann Carter (*Lucy Cannon*), J. Anthony Hughes (*Cannon*), Harry Hayden (*Banker*), Arthur Aylesworth, Lew Kelly (*Old Timers*)

Director: James Tinling. *Executive Producer:* Sol M. Wurtzel. *Screenplay:* Irving Cummings, Jr., William

Kate, played by Eve, is proprietor and star performer of the Last Chance Saloon in *Last of the Duanes*.

Conselman, Jr., from the story by Zane Grey. *Director of Photography:* Charles Clarke. *Art Directors:* Richard Day, Chester Gore. Set Decorator: Thomas Little. *Film Editor:* Rich DeMaggio. *Costumes:* Herschel. *Sound:* W.D. Flick, Harry M. Leonard. 20th Century–Fox; released September 26, 1941. B&W; 57 minutes.

    Jim Duane, candidate for sheriff in the town of Welleston, Texas, in 1870, is shot and killed just prior to the election. His son Buck shows up to avenge his father's death. Buck kills the man responsible for his father's murder, but must go on the lam from the town's corrupt lawmen. Befriended by a grizzled old outlaw, Luke Stevens, Buck learns some tricks of the trade just before his new friend is killed.
    In the rowdy "outlaw town" of Rimrock, Buck meets Kate, proprietress of the Last Chance Saloon, and learns that outlaws there have taken captive pretty young Nancy Bowdrey, whose family was friendly with the Duanes. With some help and advice from Kate, Buck frees Nancy, but learns that there is now a substantial price on his head. Falsely accused of a murder in the town of Huntsville, Buck clears himself of that charge, but the Texas Rangers aren't through with him yet. Major McNeil of the Rangers offers Buck a "conditional pardon" from the governor if he can successfully infiltrate the Cheseldine gang.
    Unbeknownst to Buck, the real brains behind the Cheseldine gang is none other than Kate herself. After participating in one holdup with the gang so as to prove his worth, Buck is next instructed to take part in a bank robbery in Huntsville. Knowing he is being set up for an ambush, Kate makes him a surreptitious proposition to run away together to Mexico. Kate explains, "We're the same kind of people, Buck. We've both been kicked around a lot, and I guess folks think we're

pretty bad, but we know that maybe they got the wrong idea." When he declines, she sees him off with tears in her eyes, saying, "All right, then, go on out and stop a few bullets. Maybe they can dent that thick hide of yours."

This was no less than the fourth film adaptation of famed Western author Zane Grey's 1913 story, originally published as *The Lone Star Ranger*. Fox trumpeted this as "a new Western star in the most exciting of all Zane Grey's action-packed stories!" The star in question was George Montgomery (1916–2000), signed to a Fox contract just a year earlier, and being actively promoted as a leading man. (Two years after this film was released, he became the husband of singer Dinah Shore.) Fox apparently liked this story so much that they released yet another version in 1942, this time called *Lone Star Ranger*.

Despite her prominent billing, ingénue Lynne Roberts has only two scenes of any consequence, giving Eve little competition for the feminine acting laurels. William Farnum, seen here as Major McNeil of the Texas Rangers, played the lead role of Buck Duane in the 1919 version of *The Last of the Duanes*, making it a bit of an in-joke when his character here meets the leading man and remarks, "I know quite a bit about you, Duane." Child actress Ann Carter, a few years before she played a leading role in *The Curse of the Cat People* (1944), has an unbilled bit here as the witness who clears Buck Duane of wrongdoing in the death of her mother. Francis Ford, seen as the outlaw, expires after delivering one of the chattiest deathbed speeches in motion picture history.

Variety rated this a decent if unexceptional Western, but did note, "Eve Arden is convincing as the lone dance hall entertainer" (September 10, 1941).

Sing for Your Supper (1941)

Jinx Falkenburg (*Evelyn Palmer*), Charles "Buddy" Rogers (*Larry Hays*), Bert Gordon ("*The Mad Russian*"), Eve Arden (*Barbara Stevens*), Don Beddoe (*Wing Boley*), Bernadene Hayes (*Kay Martin*), Henry Kolker (*Myron T. Hayworth*), Benny Baker (*William*), Dewey Robinson (*Bonzo*), Sig Arno (*Raskalnikoff*), Lloyd Bridges (*Doc*)
Director: Charles Barton. Producer: Leon Barsha. Screenplay: Harry Rebuas. Director of Photography: Franz F. Planer. Film Editor: Arthur Seid. Art Director: Lionel Banks. Columbia Pictures; released December 4, 1941. B&W; 66 minutes.

Bandleader Larry Hays is about to be evicted from the dance hall where he and his orchestra play. Wealthy Evelyn Palmer, owner of the building, overhears Larry's conversation with her property manager, Myron Hayworth, and decides to pay the club a visit. On arrival there, she hides her true identity and persuades Larry to hire her as a hostess. With help from fellow hostess Barbara, who befriends the newcomer, Evelyn makes a success of the job and arranges for the impending eviction to be halted. Discovering that Evelyn is a talented singer, Larry makes her part of his act. Wanting to give Larry's career a boost, Evelyn arranges for the band to perform at an upscale club. Opening night is a success, and Evelyn's singing talent is recognized, but so is she. The resulting headlines, exposing Evelyn as a slumming heiress, cause a major falling-out between Evelyn and Larry. Two of Larry's friends, his manager Wing Boley and band member The Mad Russian, scheme to reunite the lovers with an elaborate plot that involves slipping the hapless bandleader a Mickey.

Eve is featured as dance hall hostess Barbara Stevens in this obscure, rarely seen Columbia B picture. Studio publicists described her role as "a sharp-tongued dime-a-dancer who teaches the Park Avenue debutante the tricks of taxi-dancing." Romantically, she is paired with comedian Benny Baker (1907–1994), playing Evelyn's chauffeur William. The plot, and Eve's function in it, are reminiscent of her later film *Earl Carroll Vanities* (1945). *Sing for Your Supper* was originally announced under the title *Ten Cents a Dance*, and according to the *Hollywood Reporter* was intended to be a vehicle for Harriet Hilliard.

Leading lady Jinx Falkenburg (1919–2003) was a former fashion and pin-up model who would become a popular talk show host, teaming with husband Tex McCrary in a show called *Hi Jinx*. Her co-star Buddy Rogers (1904–1999), perhaps best-remembered for his early hit *Wings*

(1927), led a jazz band in real life as well as acting in films, and was the longtime husband of actress Mary Pickford.

Variety blasted this little movie with both barrels, noting, "This is 66 minutes of humdrum romantic comedy carrying two song numbers, neither of which means anything. Faces a struggle as a business-getter, and doubtlessly will be hard to move." Added the reviewer, "Minor cast members include Eve Arden, who gets no chance at all as a dancery hostess" (December 10, 1941). Of the cast, the *New York Times* reviewer commented, "We wish them well. In fact, we wish that Columbia could put them to better use" (December 1, 1941).

Bedtime Story (1941)

Fredric March (*Lucius "Luke" Drake*), Loretta Young (*Jane Drake*), Robert Benchley (*Eddie Turner*), Allyn Joslyn (*William Dudley, Jr.*), Eve Arden (*Virginia Cole*), Helen Westley (*Emma Harper*), Joyce Compton (*Beulah*), Tim Ryan (*Mac*), Olaf Hytten (*Alfred*), Dorothy Adams (*Betsy*), Clarence Kolb (*Collins*), Andrew Tombes (*Billy Wheeler/Pierce*), Pierre Watkin (*Eccles*), Torben Meyer (*Dinglehoff*)

Director: Alexander Hall. *Producer:* B.P. Schulberg. *Screenplay:* Richard Flournoy. *Story:* Horace Jackson, Grant Garrett. *Film Editor:* Viola Lawrence. *Art Direction:* Lionel Banks. Columbia Pictures; released December 25, 1941. B&W; 86 minutes.

On closing night of her latest hit play, leading lady Jane Drake announces to the audience that this is not only her last performance in this show, but in any show. After seven years of

Eve puddles up in *Bedtime Story*, to the consternation of Fredric March and Loretta Young.

working toward their professional goals, Jane and her playwright husband Luke have agreed to retire. They have purchased a farm in Connecticut and intend to enjoy a more relaxing existence.

Before their new life can even begin, however, Jane realizes that Luke does not intend to give up his career—or hers. He is putting the finishing touches on what he believes is his best play yet, *Bedtime Story*, which has a lead role earmarked for Jane. When she discovers that Luke is continuing to make plans for the new production, intending to give her only a few days' rest before beginning rehearsals, Jane decamps for Reno and files for divorce.

Their marriage now dissolved, Luke goes forward with plans for *Bedtime Story*, believing that he can eventually persuade Jane to return. Meanwhile, Jane accepts the attentions of a nice, dull banker who seems willing to give her the quieter life she craves. When Luke tries to undermine Jane's relationship with her new beau, William Dudley, an infuriated Jane responds by impulsively marrying Mr. Dudley.

Although Luke isn't able to prevent his ex-wife's remarriage, he does manipulate her into temporarily assuming the star role in his new production. Meanwhile, Jane, having rued her hasty second marriage, has a secret weapon at her disposal—a credit card receipt that shows her residency in Reno, which made that marriage possible, was actually invalidated by an overnight trip she took with Luke. While Jane connives to get the receipt into Luke's hands, he takes steps to assure that her wedding night with Dudley isn't conducive to consummating their marriage.

Supporting Loretta Young for the second time, Eve's presence in both films makes the resemblance in plot structure between this and *Eternally Yours* (1939) that much more noticeable. Both cast Young as a loving wife who divorces her too-busy-for-her husband, and then marries a dull nice guy in haste. Here, though, Eve isn't playing the usual friend of the heroine. Instead, she has an enjoyable role as comedienne Virginia Cole, who's cast by Luke as the leading lady of *Bedtime Story* after Jane refuses the part. "Virgie," making her dramatic debut in the play, isn't up to the demands of the role, which Luke fully anticipates. With her willing (though somewhat implausible) assistance, miscast Virgie stays with the production only long enough for Jane to step in at a critical juncture and take her place.

Another character actress given a good showcase here is Helen Westley, who's quite funny as the impecunious older actress who has a featured part in Luke Drake's play. Westley shares a funny drunk scene with Fredric March and Robert Benchley. Dumb-blonde specialist Joyce Compton earns some laughs as yet another of Luke's cast members, Beulah, whose trumped-up credentials as a pianist are exposed when she struggles through an awkward rendition of "Chopsticks." Clarence Kolb, probably best-remembered as grouchy Mr. Honeywell from TV's *My Little Margie* (1952–1955), appears briefly as an actor hired by Luke to make Jane believe her second marriage is invalid.

Though they have little interaction onscreen, this is Eve's first film with veteran character actor Allyn Joslyn (1901–1981), who will be her leading man in TV's *The Eve Arden Show* (1957–58). His performance as the bland banker (disdainfully referred to by Luke as "Six Percent Dudley") is quite good. Eve and Joslyn worked together again in *The Lady Takes a Sailor* (1949).

Studio publicity promised audiences "one of the gayest, giddiest love-and-laugh hits ever filmed, "featuring a "superb comedy cast." Well-received critically, *Bedtime Story* attracted positive reviews from multiple sources, among them *Variety*, which termed it "a wide-awake, racy, and spontaneous farce that will get plenty of audience attention and ... strong box-office returns." Eve, Allyn Joslyn, and others were credited with "good support" (December 10, 1941).

Obliging Young Lady (1942)

Joan Carroll (*Bridget Potter*), Edmond O'Brien ("*Red" Reddy*), Ruth Warrick (*Linda Norton*), Eve Arden ("*Space" O'Shea*), Robert Smith (*Charles Baker*), Franklin Pangborn (*Professor Gibney*), Marjorie Gateson (*Mira Potter*), John Miljan (*George Potter*), George Cleveland (*Clarence, Hotel Manager*), Luis Alberni (*Riccardi*), Charles Lane (*Smith*), Fortunio Bonanova (*Chef*), Andrew Tombes (*Train Conductor*), Almira Sessions (*Maid*), Pierre Watkin (*Markham*), Florence Gill (*Miss Hollybud*), Sidney Blackmer (*Attorney*), Virginia Engels (*Bonnie*), George Watts (*Judge Hilburn Knox*), Jed Prouty (*Judge Rufus*), George Chandler (*Skip*)

II. Filmography—Obliging Young Lady (1942)

Director: Richard Wallace. *Producer:* Howard Benedict. *Screenplay:* Frank Ryan, Bert Granet. *Story:* Arthur T. Horman. *Music:* Roy Webb. *Musical Director:* C. Bakaleinikoff. *Director of Photography:* Nicholas Musuraca. *Special Effects:* Vernon L. Walker. *Art Directors:* Albert D'Agostino, Carroll Clark. *Gowns:* Renie. *Recording:* Hugh McDowell, Jr. *Editor:* Henry Berman. *Assistant Director:* Sam Ruman. RKO Radio Pictures; released January 30, 1942. B&W; 80 minutes.

Young Bridget Potter is caught in the crossfire of her parents' acrimonious divorce and has become the object of a bitter custody battle. Fed up with the Potters's bickering, the judge awards temporary custody of Bridget to her mother's attorney, Mr. Markham. Hoping to avoid newspaper publicity, Markham tells his pretty young secretary Linda Norton to hide out with Bridget at a mountain lodge.

Ex-newspaper reporter "Red" Reddy, now an aspiring novelist, takes a shine to Linda and follows her to the lodge, concealing his true identity. Though Linda, who already has a boyfriend, Charles, shows no interest in Red, he befriends young Bridget. To throw off a detective hired by Bridget's mother, Red claims to be noted sportsman and game hunter Professor Stanley, while Linda and Bridget are forced to pose as his wife and daughter.

Red's cover as Professor Stanley is put to the test when a party of bird watchers checks into the lodge, pestering him to share stories of his adventures in Africa. Even worse, Red's friendly rival "Space" O'Shea, reporter for the *Tribune*, turns up, having deduced that Bridget is in hiding with Linda there. When Space informs Linda that her friend Red is a journalist, Linda wrongly concludes he's there to betray her secret. Linda, Bridget, and Charles make a speedy exit from the lodge, launching a wild chase that culminates in the offices of small-town Judge Knox, who does his best to untangle the confusion.

"Space" O'Shea, Eve's character, has a longstanding professional rivalry with Red Reddy, though he swears he's through with the newspaper business. There's also a hint that she has more than a professional appreciation for Red, as when he says disparagingly to her, "Look, why don't you give up trying to be the world's worst reporter, and marry some substantial dope?" He turns away and doesn't hear her quiet reply, "Why don't you get substantial, dope?"

Eve's screen time is unfortunately limited, but she does score a couple of good scenes. In the first, she bluffs her way into the office of attorney Markham by posing as Linda's honey-dripping cousin Suwannee Rivers (!) from Memphis, badgering the attorney into disclosing Linda's whereabouts. (On her way out the door, she drops the act just in time to shock the receptionist with her distinctly un–Southern exit line, "So long, Toots!")

Later, at the Lake Mohawk Lodge, the determined reporter lets nothing stand in the way of phoning in her exclusive story about Bridget Potter's hideaway. Red, trying to protect the woman with whom he's fallen in love, drags Space forcibly from the phone booth, landing both of them in an inelegant heap on the floor. Still hot on the trail of the story when it lands in Judge Knox's office, Space finally gets at the truth, and may be just the woman to console a rejected—and "substantial"—Charles as well.

A minor bit of fluff, *Obliging Young Lady* mostly played the bottom half of double bills. It was the first starring role for young Joan Carroll, signed by RKO with visions of a Shirley Temple-type setup. RKO publicists modestly described it as "a fast moving romantic comedy, crammed with laugh-provoking situations, each designed to top the one before and all building to a side-splitting climax. It is the kind of comedy that causes a refreshing relaxation because each gentle tug of the heart is made richer by the humorous situations developed when a child of nine connives to play Cupid." Filming took place in the summer of 1941.

Eve works here for the first time with RKO contract player Ruth Warrick, who had made her film debut a year or so earlier with the controversial *Citizen Kane*. The two ladies would be reunited onscreen almost a decade later, in *Three Husbands* (1951). Child actress Joan Carroll was already a veteran of the Broadway hit *Panama Hattie*, starring Ethel Merman, with whom she sang a memorable duet of "Let's Be Buddies."

Variety didn't think much of *Obliging Young Lady*, calling it "a strikeout ... very little boxoffice value," but did take note of Eve, saying, "The bit Eve Arden does when posing as a Memphis belle is well done by this clever comedienne" (November 5, 1941).

After filming *Obliging Young Lady,* Eve relocated to New York to take up a featured role in the Broadway comedy *Let's Face It,* resulting in her absence from movie screens until early 1943.

Hit Parade of 1943 (1943)

John Carroll (*Rick Farrell*), Susan Hayward (*Jill Wright*), Gail Patrick (*Toni Jarrett*), Eve Arden (*Belinda "Lindy" Wright*), Melville Cooper (*Bradley Cole*), Walter Catlett (*J. MacClellan Davis*), Mary Treen (*Janie*), Tom Kennedy (*Westinghouse*), Astrid Allwyn (*Joyce Germaine*), Tim Ryan (*Brownie May*), Dorothy Dandridge, the Golden Gate Quartette, Count Basie and His Orchestra, Ray McKinley and His Orchestra, Freddy Martin and His Orchestra, Nick Stewart (*Willie*)

Director: Albert S. Rogell. *Associate Producer:* Albert J. Cohen. *Screenplay:* Frank Gill, Jr. *Additional Dialogue:* Frances Hyland. *Director of Photography:* Jack Marta. *Musical Director:* Walter Scharf. *Music & Lyrics:* Jule Styne, Harold Adamson. *Orchestrations:* Marlin Skiles. *Dance Director:* Nick Castle. *Film Editor:* Thomas Richards. *Art Director:* Russell Kimball. *Set Decorations:* Otto Siegel. *Wardrobe:* Adele Palmer. *Miss Patrick's Gowns:* Adrian. *Song:* "Yankee Doodle Tan," music, J.C. Johnson; lyrics, Andy Razaf. *Optical Effects:* Consolidated Film Industries. Republic Pictures; released March 26, 1943. B&W; 82 minutes.

Aspiring songwriter Jill Wright comes to New York after interesting a music publisher in her work. On her first night in town, Jill visits a swanky nightclub with her cousin Lindy and sees the co-owner of the Miracle Publishing Company, Rick Farrell, performing her song and taking the credit for it. When she confronts Rick, he offers Jill a job, saying that they should collaborate and use his contacts to further her career. His idea of collaboration, however, proves to be signing his name to songs that Jill creates, a better alternative to his previous practice, which was to create clichéd songs with the aid of a wheel he calls "the Lyric Master."

Jill accepts Rick's offer just to give him enough rope to hang himself, intending to hold him responsible for stealing her copyrighted work. Rick, meanwhile, equally sure he is successfully stringing Jill along, does his best to romance her while continuing to keep company with his girlfriend, nightclub singer Toni. Toni, in turn, has an advantageous relationship with wealthy, older Bradley Cole, who gives Rick's work exposure in his nightclubs and keeps her employed as a singer.

The professional collaboration of Jill and Rick is quite successful, due mostly to her abilities. Despite their best intentions, both Rick and Jill fall in love for real. When he senses that her newest song, "A Change of Heart," has the potential to make the Hit Parade, he decides to do right by his lady friend—once the song has caught on, he will publicly give her attribution for all the successful songs she has written, on the occasion of their wedding. Though Lindy is skeptical that Rick has really reformed, Jill gives her heart to him, and is devastated when a jealous Toni sabotages their relationship. Desperate to set things right with his beloved, Rick ponies up a $10,000 war bond to have "A Change of Heart" played on a national radio show, where he will set the record straight once and for all.

Hit Parade of 1943 followed in the footsteps of previous *Hit Parade* films released in 1937 and 1941, and a popular radio show dating back to 1935. The film's primary selling points to contemporary audiences are probably the opportunity to see early performances by Susan Hayward and Dorothy Dandridge (the latter playing a band singer), as well as to see the real-life musical stars (Count Basie, dance bandleader Freddy Martin) who appear onscreen during the fairly lavish (for Republic) production numbers. Dandridge and Basie are spotlighted in a lengthy production number near the film's halfway point that revolves around a song called "Harlem Sandman" that Jill and Rick purportedly create. Rick and Jill have one of the odder "meet cute" scenes you're likely to see, as their first encounter comes when he accidentally lights her coat on fire in a busy lobby.

Eve plays the leading lady's cousin and roommate, providing a needed dose of wit and common sense from time to time. Her persona meshes nicely with that of Susan Hayward's Jill, who also has sass and spirit but is also a little more romantically inclined than her seen-it-all cousin. Lindy is dismayed when her starry-eyed cousin comes home late from an evening out with Rick and confesses that she now wants to be with him. Pointing out that Rick is not only dishonest, but a wolf, Lindy reminds a besotted Jill, "And you were going to fatten him up, skin him, and then hang his pelt out to dry, remember?" Finally giving up on persuading her cousin, Lindy says with disgust, "I'm going to bed and have a nightmare with my own cast of characters." Later, she earns another laugh when she sits down with a thump on the keyboard of a piano, listens to the resulting clamor, and says ruefully, "Two octaves. I'd better reduce."

Eve is reunited here with her *Stage Door* co-star Gail Patrick (playing the nasty Toni), though they don't have a scene together. Nick Stewart, probably best known for playing Lightnin' on the TV version of *The Amos 'n' Andy Show* (1951–1953), appears unbilled in a small role as "Weary Willie," the janitor who gives Jill and Rick some late-night inspiration for their "Harlem Sandman" number. Character actress Mary Treen is amusing in a brief appearance as Rick's no-nonsense secretary.

On its re-release in 1949, *Hit Parade of 1943* was known as *Change of Heart,* after the Jule Styne-Harold Adamson number that becomes a plot point in the film, and was cut by some 15 minutes. During the interim since its initial release, leading lady Susan Hayward had become a top star, and an Oscar winner. Audiences watching the reissue in 1949 undoubtedly knew they were being served leftovers, what with the script's by-then dated references to war bonds, food rationing, and air raids.

Cecil Smith, writing in the *Chicago Tribune,* found the film "hamstrung by an inane, improbable story and by a group of peculiarly unlovable principal characters.... Poor Eve Arden, who knows how to make dry comedy register well when she has some good lines, is deserted by the script" (July 7, 1943). Sounding as if he'd seen a completely different film, the *Washington Post*'s Nelson B. Bell raved about *Hit Parade of 1943,* saying it "embodies everything that a Grade-A musical should have—a richly diversified score, a well-balanced and engaging cast, humor, romance, three 'name' bands, a half-dozen or so top-flight specialty artists and, most amazing of all, a coherent, logical and thoroughly interesting story." He noted that "the comedy score is run up by Eve Arden, as Jill's cynical pal" (July 10, 1943).

Let's Face It (1943)

Bob Hope (*Jerry Walker*), Betty Hutton (*Winnie Porter*), Dona Drake (*Muriel*), Cully Richards (*Frankie Burns*), Eve Arden (*Maggie Watson*), ZaSu Pitts (*Cornelia Figeson Pigeon*), Marjorie Weaver (*Jean Blanchard*), Raymond Walburn (*Julian Watson*), Phyllis Povah (*Nancy Collister*), Joe Sawyer (*Sgt. Wiggins*), Dave Willock (*Barney Hilliard*), Nicco & Tanya (*Dancers*), Andrew Tombes (*Judge Henry Pigeon*), Arthur Loft (*George Collister*), Grace Hayle (*Mrs. Wigglesworth*), Evelyn Dockson (*Mrs. Taylor*), Barbara Pepper (*Daisy*), George Meader (*Justice of the Peace*), Phyllis Ruth (*Lulu*)
Director: Sidney Lanfield. *Associate Producer:* Fred Kohlmar. *Screenplay:* Harry Tugend, based on the musical play by Dorothy Fields, Herbert Fields, Cole Porter, suggested by a play by Norma Mitchell, Russell G. Medcraft. *Songs:* Cole Porter. *Musical Direction:* Robert Emmett Dolan. *Vocal Arrangements:* Joseph J. Lilley. *Musical Assistant:* Arthur Franklin. *Song,* "Who Did It? I Did! Yes I Did!": Jule Styne, Sammy Cahn. *Dance Staging:* Seymour Felix. *Director of Photography:* Lionel Lindon. *Art Direction:* Hans Dreier, Earl Hedrick. *Special Photographic Effects:* Gordon Jennings. *Process Photography:* Farciot Edouart. *Editor:* Paul Weatherwax. *Costumes:* Edith Head. *Makeup Artist:* Wally Westmore. *Sound Recording:* Hugo Grenzbach, Don Johnson. *Set Decoration:* Ray Moyer. Paramount Pictures; released August 5, 1943. B&W; 79 minutes.

Soldier Jerry Walker, perennially short on money, is forced to postpone his wedding to girlfriend Winnie for the umpteenth time when he is confined to quarters for damaging an Army Jeep. Winnie works as an instructor at the Alicia Allen Milk Farm, a health retreat whose latest arrivals are three middle-aged married women who suspect their husbands dropped them off there so that they could indulge in some unhindered philandering.

Maggie Watson, the unofficial leader of the trio, concocts the idea of making their husbands jealous with the help of three young soldiers from nearby Camp Arthur. Swayed by the $300 Maggie offers him, Jerry agrees to furnish himself and two buddies as paid companions for the weekend. Jerry's buddies Frankie and Barney, who help sneak him out of the Army base, aren't too enthusiastic once they get a look at their dates, but go along with the routine to help their friend. Maggie and her friends deduce that their husbands will show up with lady friends at the summer place in Southampton that belongs to Cornelia's family. Within a few hours, the summer house contains not only Maggie, her friends, and their doughboy dates, but the ladies' husbands, the bimbos they invited over, and the soldiers' jealous girlfriends. The party moves to a nightclub, where Maggie and her friends live it up with Jerry, Frankie, and Barney, while Winnie and her companions decide to teach their boyfriends a lesson with the help of the older women's husbands. With the party getting out of hand once his commanding officer arrives on the scene, Jerry and his AWOL buddies make a strategic retreat by boat that proves to have a surprisingly beneficial outcome to their fledgling military careers.

Let's Face It was loosely adapted from the hit Broadway show in which Eve appeared opposite Danny Kaye, which in turn was adapted from a 1925 comedy called *The Cradle Snatchers*. With Kaye signed to a movie contract by Sam Goldwyn by the time the film went into production, *Let's Face It* was revamped to make a vehicle for funnyman Bob Hope (1903–2003). High-energy Hope is well-matched here with the bouncy Betty Hutton (1921–2007), whose movie career would really take off a year or so later with *The Miracle of Morgan's Creek* (1944). In her third film with ZaSu Pitts, Eve works more closely with the veteran character actress than she did in their two previous ventures. Pitts assumes the role played by Edith Meiser onstage, while Phyllis Povah, best-remembered for her supporting role in *The Women* (1939), takes the place of Vivian Vance as Nancy.

There's a regrettably harsh tone to much of the comedy here, to the film's detriment. Screenwriter Harry Tugend and director Sidney Lanfield don't convey a great deal of respect for the fairer sex, their treatment of ZaSu Pitts's character Cornelia being particularly unkind. Jerry's buddies, no matinee idols themselves, yelp in horror at their first sign of Cornelia, making a crack about her resemblance to Boris Karloff. When Lanfield first shows us the health retreat where Winnie works, we see a shot of the cows who supply guests with milk, cutting directly from a view of the cows' hindparts to an unflattering rear view of the chubby women Winnie is training. Even the sympathetic character of Winnie refers to her clientele as "those blimps."

Though Eve doesn't have too many choice lines here, she gives sass and bite to the ones she does get, as when she decides with relish to beat her husband at his own game: "I'll show that middle-aged Henry Aldrich of mine that I can buy my way into kindergarten, too!" She delivers her usual assured performance, but is a bit oddly cast as an older woman casting a lecherous eye at Bob Hope, who was 40 to her 35 when the film was made. Seen as Eve's onscreen husband is the veteran character actor Raymond Walburn (1887–1969), 21 years her senior.

Unbilled for a bit part as a chorus girl here is up-and-coming Yvonne De Carlo (1922–2007). Only a few years later, Eve would be playing a supporting role in *Song of Scheherazade* (1947), by which time De Carlo was an established leading lady and the film's top-billed star. Another pretty face passing quickly by the camera in *Let's Face It* was a young Noel Neill, later to establish herself as Lois Lane on TV's *The Adventures of Superman*.

Hardly afraid of superlatives, Paramount publicity men advertised *Let's Face It* as "the funniest thing since they invented laughing gas! The rowdiest, the rollickingest, the raciest riot of comedy you'll ever see!" *Variety* largely concurred, saying, "The laughs ... come so often and so fast as to be stepping on one another, with the audience estimated at missing 25 percent of the gags" (August 11, 1943).

Cover Girl (1944)

Rita Hayworth (*Rusty Parker/Maribelle Hicks*), Gene Kelly (*Danny McGuire*), Lee Bowman (*Noel Wheaton*), Phil Silvers (*Genius*), Leslie Brooks (*Maurine*), Eve Arden (*Cornelia "Stonewall" Jackson*), Otto Kruger (*John Coudair*), Jinx Falkenburg (*Herself*), Jess Barker (*Young Coudair*), Anita Colby (*Miss Colby*), Curt Bois (*Chef*), Edward Brophy (*Joe*), Thurston Hall (*Tony Pastor*), Jean Colleran, Francine Counihan, Helen Mueller, Cecilia Meagher, Betty Jane Hess, Dusty Anderson, Eileen McClory, Cornelia B. Von Hessert, Karen X. Gaylord, Cheryl Archibald, Peggy Lloyd, Betty Jane Graham, Martha Outlaw, Susann Shaw, Rose May Robson (*Cover Girls*)

Director: Charles Vidor. *Producer:* Arthur Schwartz. *Screenplay:* Virginia Van Upp. *Adaptation:* Marion Parsonnet, Paul Gangelin. *Story:* Erwin Gelsey. *Directors of Photography:* Rudolph Maté, Allen M. Davey. *Music:* Jerome Kern. *Lyrics:* Ira Gershwin. *Musical Director:* M.W. Stoloff. *Dance Numbers Staged by* Val

Raset, Seymour Felix. *Assistant to Producer:* Norman Deming. *Art Direction:* Lionel Banks, Cary Odell. *Set Decorations:* Fay Babcock. *Gowns:* Travis Banton, Gwen Wakeling, Muriel King. *Hats:* Keneth [sic] Hopkins. *Makeup:* Clay Campbell. *Hair Styles:* Helen Hunt. *Montages and "Cover Girl" Presentation:* John Hoffman. *Magazine Covers Created by* Hoffman & Coburn. *Magazine Covers Photographed by* Robert Coburn. *Orchestrations:* Carmen Dragon. *Music Recording:* P.J. Faulkner. *Song:* "Poor John," Fred W. Leigh, Henry E. Pether. *Film Editor:* Viola Lawrence. *Technical Color Director:* Natalie Kalmus. *Associate:* Morgan Padelford. *Technical Advisors:* Harry Conover, Anita Colby. *Assistant Director:* Oscar Boetticher, Jr. Columbia Pictures; released March 30, 1944. Color; 107 minutes.

Beautiful redhead Rusty Parker is one of the featured dancers at her boyfriend Danny McGuire's Brooklyn nightclub. While working at the nightclub provides legitimate, entry-level employment in show business, Rusty and her fellow dancers aspire to bigger things, despite his warnings that real success is not gained quickly. Another dancer, Maurine, tells Rusty about a contest to select *Vanity* magazine's "Golden Wedding Girl," whose face will grace the cover of its 50th anniversary issue. Miss Cornelia Jackson, assistant to the magazine's suave publisher, John Coudair, has auditioned countless young women for the prestigious cover assignment, but hasn't been able to find one that suits her employer.

Though Miss Jackson notices Rusty's beauty when she arrives for the audition, she is less impressed by the young dancer's brash, chatty persona, which she has assumed thanks to some malicious advice from jealous Maurine. As Maurine seems to be the leading candidate for the magazine cover, John accompanies Miss Jackson to see her perform at Danny's slightly seedy club. But instead of being taken with Maurine's charms, John Coudair instead is immediately intrigued by Rusty's talent and beauty.

It seems that Rusty's lookalike grandmother, Maribelle Hicks, was also a performer, and won the heart of John Coudair during his youth, 40 years earlier. But when his upper-crust family snubbed her, she refused his hand in marriage, and instead enjoyed a happy, simpler life with a man who wasn't wealthy or famous. Not knowing why Mr. Coudair is so taken with her, Rusty accepts the modeling assignment he offers, and her *Vanity* magazine cover opens new doors for her. Soon it appears that her career is on the upswing, and that she may be ready to move beyond her job at Danny's nightclub.

Mr. Coudair's friend, Broadway producer Noel Wheaton, offers her a starring role in his next show. Coudair and Wheaton persuade Danny that it would be wrong to stand in his girlfriend's way, and that she deserves a better life than he can give her. When Danny and Rusty quarrel over her career aspirations, she impulsively accepts the Broadway role, while he and his roommate, comedian Genius, take off for an Army tour. While on the road, Danny learns that Rusty has accepted a marriage proposal from Noel Wheaton, and rushes back to New York to see if there is still hope for the two of them.

Once again, Eve is playing the sharp-tongued, well-dressed woman who works behind the scenes in show business. This was moviegoers' first chance to see her in a color feature, and the film's splashy Technicolor visuals nicely highlight the eye-catching outfits she wears as Miss Jackson. She shares most of her scenes with actor Otto Kruger, cast as her magazine publisher boss. She shows up at her office just as he is explaining his idea for a new cover girl—"I want a new face," he says. In walks Stonewall, who responds, "I don't blame you. So do I." Though loyal to her boss, even hard-boiled Miss Jackson is disturbed by the efforts of Coudair and Wheaton to lure Rusty away from her boyfriend. "You're trying to do something you'll never do—lure a girl away from a guy she loves with *things*," she says, adding that she's "just dame enough to be glad" that such a plan is doomed to failure. However, 45 more minutes of film will unspool before Miss Jackson is proven correct.

According to Eve's autobiography, she suggested the gag in which Miss Jackson, playing billiards with Coudair and Wheaton, accidentally tears a gaping hole in the pool table cover.

Screenwriter Virginia Van Upp, in a May 1944 interview with journalist Robbin Coons, admitted that the story of *Cover Girl* was not designed to keep an audience in suspense. "What we have," Van Upp said, "is a simple fairy tale, laid in Brooklyn. You know how it's going to turn out; you can relax on that score and just enjoy what's happening while it turns out that way."

Other Cover Girls seen in the film include 15 young models representing popular magazines of the 1940s—*Cosmopolitan, Liberty, Collier's,* and even *Farm Journal.* Actress-model Jinx Falkenburg, who would be a ubiquitous presence on early TV as a talk show hostess (alongside her husband, Tex McCrary) has a small role as herself. Character actor Edward Brophy is, surprisingly, unbilled for his featured role as proprietor of a Brooklyn joint where Danny, Genius, and Rusty like to hang out after the show. Also unbilled is Jack Norton in yet another bit as a drunk.

Credited as technical advisors on the film are Harry Conover, real-life owner of the very successful modeling agency that bore his name, and actress-model Anita Colby, who appears briefly onscreen as another Coudair employee. Colby, once a much sought-after cover girl herself (having been discovered by Conover), served as chaperone to the 15 models featured in the picture, and was also press agent for the film. Oscar-nominated for its music, art direction, color cinematography, and sound, *Cover Girl* took home only one statuette, for the musical direction and orchestrations of Morris Stoloff and Carmen Dragon.

The Doughgirls (1944)

Ann Sheridan (*Edna Stokes Cadman*), Alexis Smith (*Nan Curtiss Dillon*), Jack Carson (*Arthur Halstead*), Jane Wyman (*Vivian Marsden Halstead*), Irene Manning (*Sylvia Cadman*), Charlie Ruggles (*Stanley Slade*), Eve Arden (*Sgt. Natalia Moskoroff*), John Ridgely (*Julian Cadman*), Alan Mowbray (*Breckenridge Drake*), John Alexander (*Warren Buckley*), Craig Stevens (*Lt. Tom Dillon*), Barbara Brown (*Elizabeth Brush Cartwright*), Francis Pierlot (*Mr. Jordan*), Donald MacBride (*Judge Franklin*), Regis Toomey (*Agent Walsh*)
Director: James V. Kern. *Executive Producer:* Jack L. Warner. *Producer:* Mark Hellinger. *Screenplay:* James V. Kern, Sam Hellman. *Additional Dialogue:* Wilkie Mahoney. *From the Stage Play by* Joseph Fields. *Director of Photography:* Ernest Haller. *Film Editor:* Folmer Blangsted. *Dialogue Director:* Jack Gage. *Sound:* Stanley Jones. *Art Director:* Hugh Reticker. *Technical Advisor:* Nicholas Kobliansky. *Set Decorations:* Clarence Steensen. *Special Effects:* William McGann. *Montages:* James Leicester. *Gowns:* Milo Anderson. *Makeup Artist:* Perc Westmore. *Musical Director:* Leo F. Forbstein. Warner Bros.-First National Pictures; released November 25, 1944. B&W; 102 minutes.

Newlyweds Vivian and Arthur Halstead arrive in wartime Washington, D.C., to take up residence in the honeymoon suite of the Hotel Grayson. Although Arthur has assured Vivian that news reports of a housing shortage in the nation's capital have doubtless been exaggerated, they learn that another couple, the Cadmans, are being evicted from the honeymoon suite in order to make room for the new arrivals. At first Vivian is offended when Mrs. Cadman, who's in the middle of taking a bath, refuses to vacate the honeymoon suite, until she catches a glimpse of her. It seems that Edna and Vivian are old friends who used to perform together in a chorus line. Although Vivian just wants to be alone with her new husband, she finds herself sharing the bridal suite with not only Mr. and Mrs. Cadman, but also another old friend, Nan, who turns up in the hotel lobby seeking accommodations.

Shortly after the Halsteads' arrival, brassy Edna is angered to learn that her new husband, Julian, married her before his interlocutory decree legally ended his first marriage. The first Mrs. Cadman turns up to triumphantly tell her successor that her marriage is invalid. In short order, it turns out that none of the three friends is legally married—not only did Nan's fiancé, Tom, go into quarantine with measles before the ceremony could be performed, but the justice of the peace who married Vivian and Arthur turns out to be an impostor.

Peeved, Arthur refuses to remarry Vivian until she clears their honeymoon suite of the parade of friends and hangers-on now occupying it, who have grown to include Natalia, "the great guerrilla fighter," a hard-boiled sergeant in the Russian army. In short order, the ladies have run up several hundred dollars' worth of hotel bills for room service, beauty salon treatments, and assorted other luxuries, which Arthur refuses to pay. Meanwhile, their suite continues to be only slightly less populated than Union Station, with regular interruptions from Arthur's lecherous boss, a pompous radio war correspondent, several babies from a war nursery, an FBI man, and a hapless stranger seeking in vain a place to sleep.

Eve's screen test for the role of Natalia, the Russian soldier, won her not only that role but a seven-year contract with Warner Bros. that would elevate her to the top ranks of Hollywood character actors. She receives a relatively rare billing above the title here, and plays easily the

The ladies known as *The Doughgirls* are (left to right) Ann Sheridan, Alexis Smith, Jane Wyman, Irene Manning, and Eve.

most distinctive character, though she doesn't make her initial entrance until more than a half-hour into the film.

Natalia, who totes a gun everywhere she goes, and shoots pigeons from the terrace of the bridal suite, proves to be unexpectedly helpful to her new friends. Though her gunplay nearly gets them evicted from the hotel, she proves to have a particular talent for dealing forcefully with the neighborhood pawnbroker, which comes in handy when the ladies find themselves unable to pay their hotel bill.

The Doughgirls was adapted from the highly successful Broadway comedy that opened in late 1942 and ran for more than 600 performances. Arlene Francis, best-remembered today for her long panel show stint on *What's My Line?*, was considered by Broadway producers to have a knack for accents, and originated the role of Natalia onstage. The play was directed by George S. Kaufman, and represented another success for Joseph Fields, who had already racked up impressive runs for *My Sister Eileen* and *Junior Miss*. Warners paid $250,000 for the film rights to the hit play. Among the tasks facing adapters Kern and Hellman were to insert situations that would make the three leads believe they are married, when in fact they are not, a change from the original production.

Leading ladies Ann Sheridan (1915–1967) and Jane Wyman (1917–2007) get their share of laughs, with Wyman cast as the type of likable-but-featherbrained nincompoop that was her early stock in trade at Warners. Third lead Alexis Smith (1921–1993) gets a less memorable role, though she does play opposite her real-life love, Craig Stevens, whom she married in the summer of 1944. Eve's frequent costar Jack Carson plays the frustrated husband of Wyman, while actor John Ridgely, who's wed to Eve in *My Reputation* (1946), appears as Sheridan's spouse-to-be. Charlie Ruggles (1886–1970) plays Arthur's smarmy boss with a twinkle in his eye that helps make the potentially offensive character more endearing.

Director James V. Kern, who also co–authored the film script, helmed only a handful of films, but enjoyed a long career in television comedy, notably directing multiple episodes of *I Love Lucy* and *My Three Sons*.

Time, found the screen version of *The Doughgirls* "even louder than the stage original, but not so fast and not so funny" (October 16, 1944). Coming on the heels of films like *The More the Merrier* (1943), many reviewers felt that comedy arising from the wartime housing shortage was no longer fresh by the time *The Doughgirls* landed in theaters. It's likely that some of its humor worked better on stage than it does on film. The scene in the film's opening minutes when the mention of a vacancy at the hotel's registration desk causes an immediate stampede is amusing here, but probably played funnier in a theater. The reviewer for the *New York Times* enjoyed it purely as a "mad farce," noting, "The picture as a whole sets out to make no sense, and it accomplishes that negative aim beautifully and delightfully" (August 31, 1944).

Pan-Americana (1945)

Phillip Terry (*Dan Jordan*), Audrey Long (*Jo Anne Benson*), Robert Benchley (*Charlie Corker*), Eve Arden (*Helen "Hoppy" Hopkins*), Ernest Truex (*Uncle Rudy*), Marc Cramer (*Jerry Bruce*), Isabelita [Lita Baron] (*Lupita*), Rosario & Antonio, Miguelito Valdes, Harold & Lola, Louise Burnett, Chinita Marin, Chuy Castillon, Padilla Sisters, Chuy Reyes & His Orchestra, Nester Amaral & His Samba Band (*Specialty Acts*)

Director/Producer: John H. Auer. *Executive Producer:* Sid Rogell. *Screenplay:* Lawrence Kimble. *Original Story:* Frederick Kohner, John H. Auer. *Musical Director:* C. Bakaleinikoff. *Songs:* Ary Barroso, Margarita Lecuona, Gabriel Ruiz, Pepe Guizar, Carlos Castellanos, Antonio Fernandez, Bobby Collazo. *Orchestral Arrangements:* Gene Rose. *Musical Numbers Staging:* Charles O'Curran. *English Lyrics:* Mort Greene. *Director of Photography:* Frank Redman. *Special Effects:* Vernon L. Walker. *Art Directors:* Albert D'Agostino, Al Herman. *Set Decorations:* Darrell Silvera, Michael Ohrenbach. *Recording:* Richard Van Hessen. *Editor:* Harry Marker. *Gowns:* Renié. *Rerecording:* Terry Kellum. *Assistant Director:* Ruby Rosenberg. RKO-Radio Pictures; released March 22, 1945. B&W; 84 minutes.

The editorial staff of *Western World* magazine takes a trip through Central and South America, preparing a special issue to be called "Pan-Americana," which will showcase the people and sights of the region. Along for the ride with foreign editor Charlie Corker and managing editor Helen Hopkins (known to all as Hoppy) is ace photographer Dan Jordan, a slick charmer whose favorite professional activity is shooting glamour photos of beautiful women. For reasons not completely professional, Dan chooses pretty staff writer Jo Anne as his collaborator on the project. Although Dan and Jo Anne flirt with each other from the get-go, both are playing a cat-and-mouse game. Playboy Dan resists commitment, having broken off three previous engagements, while she is stringing him along only to get a free ride to South America, where her fiancé, Jerry, awaits her.

Jo Anne tells her friend and boss, Hoppy, that she and Dan are "sort-of engaged," not foreseeing the complications that will arise. As the trip through various Latin American capitals progresses, Jo and Dan grow closer, until he learns from an unexpected telephone call that her fiancé is awaiting her in Rio de Janeiro. Upon arrival in Rio, the two men compete for Jo's attentions, and Hoppy, knowing Dan's playboy nature, takes it upon herself to look after her young friend's interests.

With much of its 84 minutes devoted to musical and dance numbers, there's not much time for the actors here to shine. They spend a fair amount of time seated around various white-clothed nightclub tables, applauding enthusiastically whatever specialty act is performing. The action cuts back and forth between the live stage show sponsored by the magazine in New York, and emceed by Charlie, and flashbacks to the trip where the acts were located.

Eve's character, Hoppy, is another of the dry-witted, intelligent working women she so often

Eve casts a knowing eye on leading lady Audrey Long in *Pan-Americana*.

portrayed. Hoppy has no romantic interest in the film, though she has a friendly relationship with Robert Benchley's character Charlie, her co-worker on *Western World* magazine. She also, of course, serves as the slightly older and wiser friend of the heroine, and dishes out some good advice. (When Hoppy and Jo are the midst of a tête-à-tête while watching yet another nightclub act, Charlie starts listening, and asking questions, just long enough for Hoppy to pat him on the wrist, point him back in the direction of the stage, and say, "Drink your rum, Charlie, and look at the pretty girls.")

Personable Phillip Terry (1909–1993) was then the husband of Joan Crawford, whom he'd married in 1942, though they would announce their impending divorce by the end of the year. Eve, who has some nice scenes with Terry here, has now worked with all three of Crawford's actor husbands. Eve and Joan would, of course, team for *Mildred Pierce* only a few months after *Pan-Americana* was completed. Humorist Robert Benchley (1889–1945), in real life a dear friend of Eve's, introduces the musical revue that frames the film, in his typically confused and uncertain style. He died of a cerebral hemorrhage only a few months after *Pan-Americana* was released. Eve says in her autobiography that Benchley, who'd written admiringly of her stage performances while reviewing for the *New Yorker*, once made a light-hearted proposal of marriage to her.

The fine character actor Ernest Truex (1889–1973), who previously worked with Eve in *Slightly Honorable*, has a small role here as Jerry's uncle, who plays host to the group in Rio. Jane Greer (1924–2001), then still known as Bettejane, appears unbilled in an early scene as Eve's assistant, Miss Downing, a nervous type who catches herself calling the boss "sir" instead of "ma'am." In Cuba, the star attraction is a handsome, dark-haired singer who comes onstage to the beat of drums and launches energetically into a number called "Babalu." No, it's not Desi Arnaz—it's bandleader Miguelito Valdes, who popularized the song with audiences South of the border long before Arnaz took it up.

This modest programmer attracted OK reviews. *Variety* called it "routine ... as inoffensive as it is unimportant." Wrote the reviewer, Eve and co-star Robert Benchley "struggle with some feeble lines and situations for comedy relief" (February 21, 1945).

Earl Carroll Vanities (1945)

Dennis O'Keefe (*Danny Baldwin*), Constance Moore (*Drina*), Eve Arden (*Tex Donnelly*), Otto Kruger (*Earl Carroll*), Alan Mowbray (*Grand Duke Paul*), Stephanie Bachelor (*Claire Elliott*), Pinky Lee (*Pinky Price*), Mary Forbes (*Queen Mother Elena*), Parkyakarkus (*Parky*), Leon Belasco (*Baron Dashek*), Tom Dugan (*Waiter*), Chester Clute (*Mr. Weems*), Jimmy Alexander (*Singer*), Tom London (*Tom*), Beverly Loyd (*Cigarette Girl*), Edward Gargan (*Policeman*), Robert Greig (*Vonce*), Wilton Graff (*Mr. Thayer*), Tommy Ivo (*Tommy*), Liliane & Mario (*Specialty Dancers*), Woody Herman and His Orchestra
Director: Joseph Santley. *Associate Producer:* Albert J. Cohen. *Screenplay:* Frank Gill, Jr. *Original Story:* Cortland Fitzsimmons. *Photography:* Jack Marta. *Musical Director:* Walter Scharf. *Musical Supervisor:* Albert Newman. *Music and Lyrics:* Walter Kent, Kim Gannon. *Film Editor:* Richard L. Van Engel. *Dances Staged by* Sammy Lee. *Sound:* Dick Tyler, Howard Wilson. *Art Directors:* Russell Kimball, Frank Hotaling. *Set Decorations:* Earl Wooden. *Costume Supervisor:* Adele Palmer. *Special Effects:* Howard Lydecker. *Makeup:* Bob Mark. Republic Pictures; released April 5, 1945. B&W; 91 minutes.

Young princess Drina and her mother, royals from the small European state of Turania, are in New York City trying to arrange a loan for their impoverished country. Though expected to live a sheltered life among a select class of people, Drina is allowed to take music lessons from nightclub owner Tex Donnelly. While the royal mother assumes her daughter is studying classical music, Drina actually enjoys learning boogie-woogie, and sneaking out to visit Tex's Wolf Club.

At the club one night, all is abuzz because legendary producer Earl Carroll is visiting to see the latest floor show written by Danny Baldwin and featuring singer Claire Elliott. When Danny and Claire are late arriving due to a traffic accident, Drina agrees to sing the lead number as a lark. Danny arrives at the club just in time to hear Mr. Carroll say he wants to produce the show, and especially likes Drina's singing. Rather than lose the deal, Danny tries in vain to hire the incognito princess, who takes a dislike to his brash, no-nonsense manner. Tired of being held captive in her "glamorous straitjacket" as a royal, Drina decides to accept the gig until Claire is able to resume work, intending to teach Danny a lesson. Instead, Danny and Drina fall in love.

When a jealous Claire reveals Drina's hidden life to her horrified mother, the queen insists that her daughter sever all ties with the show, without revealing her true identity. Danny and Drina are both miserable until their friends concoct a plan to set matters right once again.

Two years after *Hit Parade of 1943*, Eve returned to Republic for this derivative musical comedy featuring many of the same behind-the-scenes players. Here, the balance between music and story is weighted a bit more in the favor of story, and overall the film works better. Eve is featured as Drina's pal Tex, shrewd nightclub owner who provides an entrée to New York City nightlife that proves very appealing to the princess.

For the purposes of this film, Carroll's shows are presented as if they are fairly standard musical revues. The real Earl Carroll died in a plane crash three years after this film's release. According to contemporary studio publicity, the girls seen in the film were primarily from Carroll's current shows, though some of them were young Republic contract players.

As a nightclub owner, Tex is quick with a quip as usual. Of one waiter, Eve remarks in passing, "I must remember to fire that man." The presence of a cigarette girl, with no cigarettes to peddle, is explained by Tex: "She's putting her grandmother through welding school." Smart as always, Eve's character quite sensibly refuses to believe there is such a place as Turania, until she's shown it on a map.

Pinky Lee (left) and Eve (right) provided most of the comedy in *Earl Carroll Vanities*. Also pictured is leading man Dennis O'Keefe.

Leading lady Constance Moore (1920–2005), a Republic stalwart during the war years, would return for a followup, *Earl Carroll Sketchbook* (1946), also written by Gill, before retiring from films in 1947. *Vanities* received an Oscar nomination for the song "Endlessly" that Moore sings in the film's finale. Male lead Dennis O'Keefe would work with Eve again in *The Lady Wants Mink* (1953). Director Joseph Santley, whose credits stretched back to the late-silent era, directed a number of musicals and comedies.

Aside from Eve, the film's main comedic presence is Pinky Lee (1907–1993), who would become a mainstay of early television with his comedy show. Eve teams up with the diminutive Lee for a song-and-dance routine in which he's cast as "The Last Man in Town." More than one reviewer noted this number as one of the film's highlights. The film also provides a role for comic Harry Parke (1904–1958), billed as Parkyakarkus, who appears as the argumentative owner of a cheap diner to which Danny takes Drina on a date. Parke, the father of actor-director Albert Brooks, was playing a similar character on his popular radio comedy in the mid–40s, *Meet Me at Parky's*.

The movie editor of the *Hutchinson* (KS) *News-Herald* dismissed it as "one of those standard assembly jobs in which lavish sets and two-story headdresses make up for lack of inventiveness" (July 15, 1945). The *New York Times* thought the plot ludicrous, but said, "Discounting the strain on credulity, this royal lark is merely an innocuous, unimportant entertainment in which no one gets hurt—or even excited" (April 2, 1945).

Patrick the Great (1945)

Donald O'Connor (*Patrick Donahue, Jr.*), Peggy Ryan (*Judy Watkins*), Frances Dee (*Lynn Andrews*), Donald Cook (*Patrick Donahue, Sr.*), Eve Arden (*Jean Mathews*), Thomas Gomez (*Max Wilson*), Gavin Muir (*Prentis Johns*), Andrew Tombes (*Sam Bassett*), Irving Bacon (*Mr. Merney*), Emmett Vogan (*Alsop*), the Jivin' Jacks and Jills (*Themselves*)
Director: Frank Ryan. *Producer:* Howard Benedict. *Screenplay:* Bertram Millhauser, Dorothy Bennett. *Original Story:* Jane Hall, Frederick Kohner, Ralph Block. *Director of Photography:* Frank Redman. *Songs Directed by* Edward Ward. *Dance Director:* Louis da Pron. *Music Score:* H.J. [Hans] Salter. *Art Direction:* John B. Goodman, Abraham Grossman. *Director of Sound:* Bernard B. Brown. *Technician*: Jess Moulin. *Set Decorations:* Russell A. Gausman, E.R. Robinson. *Film Editor:* Ted Kent. *Gowns:* Vera West. *Assistant Director:* William Holland. *Songs:* Inez James, Sidney Miller. *Song:* "For the First Time," by Charles Tobias, David Kapp. Universal Pictures; released May 4, 1945. B&W, 84 minutes.

Young Pat Donahue and his girlfriend, Judy, are in the audience on the closing night of *Gypsy Love,* the hit Broadway musical that stars his father—Pat, Senior. Pat persuades his father's producer, Max Wilson, to lend scenery and costumes from the closing show to his amateur group in the Berkshires, the Red Barn Theatre Workshop Players. In exchange, Pat and his friends agree to try out scenes from *Everything Goes,* Wilson's next production. When Wilson and playwright Prentis Johns see young Pat play the lead role, they decide to cast him in his Broadway debut, not telling him that they'd already promised the job to his father.

Wanting to concentrate on nothing but his big break, Pat breaks things off with Judy, returning her sorority pin, and follows his father on his vacation to Pine Valley Lodge. In order to put over his big love song, "For the First Time," in the new show, Pat's been told that he needs more experience with women, so that he can portray "a grown-up romance, from an adult point of view." Conveniently enough, among the other vacationers at the lodge, with her secretary Jean in tow, is pretty Lynn Andrews, a slightly older woman who works as a food writer. Father and son are both taken with Lynn, who befriends Pat *fils* on a lark, but doesn't take him seriously as a lover. Because father and son are so close, neither wants to hurt the other, but all works out for the best in the end as Pat, Senior, decides to marry Lynn and take a few months off, while Pat, Junior, lands the prize role in *Everything Goes* and reunites with loyal Judy.

When a movie heroine tells her assistant, "You're the sassiest secretary I ever had," it's a pretty safe bet she's addressing Eve Arden, who plays a typical mid-40s role as sardonic Jean. Her heart of gold is a little tougher to see under her brassy exterior this time, as when she listens to young Pat sing and remarks, "He's a tenor. He deserves to be hit." Her best moments come midway through the film, when she feigns illness in order to save Lynn from her dinner date with Pat, Senior, only to learn that her boss is having a fine time and no longer wants her to intercede.

Not making her first entrance until almost half an hour into the film, Eve is also missing in the finale. She has little interaction with top-billed O'Connor, aside from a running gag in which they bump into each other on the stairs of the lodge, finding themselves doing an impromptu dance to avoid colliding. Although two marquees seen in the film spell father and son's last name as Donohue, it is spelled in the closing credits as Donahue.

The singing and dancing team of Donald O'Connor (1925–2003) and Peggy Ryan (1924–2004) teamed for the last time here, after making multiple joint appearances for Universal as an ersatz Mickey Rooney and Judy Garland. Hyperkinetic Ryan is something of an acquired taste, making it easy to understand why Pat is so taken with Frances Dee's Lynn. O'Connor was actually serving in the U.S. Army at the time of the film's release. Universal held it back for more than a year after filming was completed in the spring of 1944, so as to keep him on movie screens and in fans' thoughts during his absence from the studio.

The paths of Eve Arden and Donald O'Connor would continue to cross with some regularity over the next several decades. They were reunited onscreen five years later, when both were seen in *Curtain Call at Cactus Creek* (1950). By 1954, both were working steadily in television, and won Emmys. In the early 1980s, they appeared together onstage in *Little Me,* and in 1982, both were guest stars in *Pandemonium.*

Lovely Frances Dee (1909–2004), cast as Lynn, was the wife of actor Joel McCrea, and is probably best remembered for her role in *I Walked with a Zombie* (1943). Co-scenarist Frederick Kohner is better known for creating the character of Gidget in the 1950s, based on the exploits of his own teenaged daughter.

Shortly after this film was released, syndicated columnist Erskine Johnson noted that he had seen Eve featured in glamorous layouts in five different magazines of late, and commented, "It's about time. Eve can hold her own with the best of the siren trust" (June 1, 1945).

Universal's copywriters promised moviegoers attending *Patrick the Great* "hilarious fun ... with music ... gals ... entertainment galore!" Writing in the *Los Angeles Times*, reviewer John L. Scott called *Patrick the Great* "a pleasant piece of cinema entertainment ... lighthearted, musical, and amusing" (January 14, 1945).

The playwright, Prentis, has the most apropos line concerning *Patrick the Great* when he remarks, "I used this plot in a play once, and no one would believe it."

Mildred Pierce (1945)

Joan Crawford (*Mildred Pierce Beragon*), Jack Carson (*Wally Fay*), Zachary Scott (*Monte Beragon*), Eve Arden (*Ida Corwin*), Ann Blyth (*Vera Pierce Forrester*), Bruce Bennett (*Albert Pierce*), Lee Patrick (*Maggie Biederhof*), Moroni Olsen (*Inspector Peterson*), Veda Ann Borg (*Miriam Ellis*), Jo Ann Marlowe (*Kay Pierce*), Butterfly McQueen (*Lottie*), Chester Clute (*Mr. Jones*), George Tobias (*Mr. Chris*), John Compton (*Ted Forrester*), Charles Trowbridge (*Mr. Williams*), Garry Owen (*Policeman on Pier*), Barbara Brown (*Mrs. Forrester*), James Flavin (*Detective*)

Director: Michael Curtiz. *Executive Producer:* Jack L. Warner. *Producer:* Jerry Wald. *Screenplay:* Ranald MacDougall, based on the novel by James M. Cain. *Music:* Max Steiner. *Director of Photography:* Ernest Haller. *Film Editor:* David Weisbart. *Art Director:* Anton Grot. *Montages:* James Leicester. *Sound:* Oliver S. Garretson. *Set Decorations:* George James Hopkins. *Dialogue Director:* Herschel Daugherty. *Special Effects:* Willard Van Enger. *Wardrobe:* Milo Anderson. *Makeup Artist:* Perc Westmore. *Orchestral Arrangements:* Hugo Friedhofer. *Musical Director:* Leo F. Forbstein. Warner Bros.-First National Pictures; released October 20, 1945. B&W; 111 minutes.

Summoned to the police station in the middle of the night, well-heeled Mildred Pierce Beragon is informed that her husband, Monte, has been murdered. Learning that the detective in charge of the case suspects her ex-husband, Bert, Mildred insists that he cannot have committed the crime, and recounts (via flashbacks) the events leading up to the murder.

Four years earlier, Mildred was a middle-class housewife whose husband, Bert, had just lost his job in real estate. While Mildred's own needs are simple enough, she devotes herself solely to her two daughters, especially older daughter Veda, who craves only the best things in life. After Mildred and Bert quarrel over the children, and the attention he pays to neighbor Maggie Biederhof, Bert moves out, leaving Mildred to go it alone. Faced with a stack of bills, Mildred takes a waitress job and, over the next several months learns the restaurant business from the ground up. Mildred's hard work finances singing lessons, new clothes, and other luxuries for Veda, but the pretty teenager still keeps her mother at arm's length, and is embarrassed by her mother's job. When Mildred's younger daughter Kay dies of pneumonia, the grief-stricken mother becomes even more determined to win the love of her surviving daughter.

With the help of Bert's former real estate partner, Wally, who has always had his eye on Mildred, she purchases a run-down house to convert into her own restaurant. The owner of the property, Monte Beragon, is the scion of a wealthy family fallen on hard times. The restaurant, Mildred's, is a roaring success, with the help of business manager Ida Corwin, a friend who gave Mildred her first job as a waitress. In order to protect Mildred's investment from the bill collectors still chasing Bert, Wally insists that she end her marriage. Having reluctantly done so, Mildred falls in love with charming Monte, a self-proclaimed loafer who's only too happy to live off a woman's hard work. Fascinated when Monte introduces her to the high-society world he inhabits, Veda craves acceptance there, and becomes his steady companion until Mildred tells him to stop seeing her.

Cut off from her chance at wealth, Veda maliciously marries a boy from a wealthy family,

Eve (left) takes a telephone call from *Mildred Pierce*, as Zachary Scott gives Ann Blyth a look-see.

and lies that she is pregnant so that his snobbish mother will buy her off. When Mildred foils that scheme, an angry Veda leaves home, later turning up as a singer in a tacky roadhouse. Knowing that only wealth and social position can win Veda's heart, Mildred buys a luxurious home and asks Monte to marry her, so as to give her greedy daughter the lifestyle she wants. On the fateful night in question, Mildred not only learns that her extravagant spending to support Monte and Veda has cost her the restaurant business she built up, but realizes that her husband and her daughter are romantically involved.

A marvelous picture that rewards multiple viewings, *Mildred Pierce* is bolstered by a top-notch supporting cast headed by Eve as Ida Corwin, and featuring such heavy hitters as Butterfly McQueen, Lee Patrick, Moroni Olsen, and young Ann Blyth as the dreadful Veda. It was adapted from author James M. Cain's 1941 novel of the same name, and found its way to movie screens on the heels of *Double Indemnity* (1944), which proved to be an enormous popular and critical success for Paramount.

Eve's character, like most of the others, originated in the novel, but has been revised somewhat for the screen. In Cain's novel, Mildred initially resents Ida, who rides herd on her as she learns to be a waitress, and Mildred's "dislike of Ida was intense." Cain's Ida is married, to an unemployed plasterer, and when the chips are down will not prove to be as loyal a friend to Mildred as she is in the screenplay. Though only one screenwriter is credited, several worked on this project at various stages, among them Catherine Turney, who knew Eve from their work together in the early 1930s with the Bandbox Repertory Theatre. According to scholar Albert J. LaValley, in his introduction to the published screenplay of *Mildred Pierce* (University of Wisconsin Press, 1980), "Turney's [draft] scripts follow the book closely, particularly in its clearer early parts, but it is she who determines which scenes are dramatized and which omitted, where the emphasis will fall, how the scenes should be dramatically linked, and what the overall structure should be. Most of her choices are followed in all the other scripts, even to reworking her original scenes."

Mildred Pierce contains not only one of Eve's best-known performances, but also one that solidified her typecasting in the eyes of viewers and studio executives alike. She was nominated for an Academy Award as Best Supporting Actress, but lost to Anne Revere for her role in *National Velvet*. Ranald MacDougall's script endows her richly with sharp, sassy lines, some of them still remembered and quoted today ("Personally, Veda's convinced me that alligators have the right idea. They eat their young.") A shrewd businesswoman and a good friend to Mildred, Eve's Ida is often the only one who can tell her the truth—and the one with whom she commiserates, as when they share a drink accompanied by Ida's rueful toast, "To the men we've loved—the stinkers!"

A large step up in quality from the pictures she'd done recently as a freelance artist (*Pan-Americana, Patrick the Great*), *Mildred Pierce* also served to fix in the minds of Warners' executives what they thought Eve did best. Over the next several years, Joan Crawford's best pal would be seen by moviegoers as the supportive friend or colleague to Barbara Stanwyck, Doris Day, Jane Wyman, Lizabeth Scott, and even (in a change of pace) Dane Clark. Eve and Joan would also be teamed again, in *Goodbye, My Fancy* (1951), reportedly at Crawford's request.

Although critical response to *Mildred Pierce* was mixed upon its initial release, Alton Cook of the *New York World-Telegram* wrote, "There is never a slackening of the exciting pace and rush of episode. Two hours seldom have slipped by faster or more eventfully in a movie theater" (September 28, 1945). Added the *New York Sun*'s Eileen Creelman, "There is plenty of comedy, rich real comedy, with Eve Arden ... and Butterfly McQueen supplying much of the fun." The reviewer for the *New York Times* had his doubts about the picture overall, finding Mildred's unwavering support for Veda unconvincing, but noted, "Eve Arden is her customary hardboiled self, and that's all right with us" (September 29, 1945).

In a 1985 interview with the Associated Press's Bob Thomas, Eve confessed that she had yet to see her own performance in *Mildred Pierce*: "I never went to see the picture. I couldn't stand seeing myself on the screen. In the theater I could envision myself as wonderful because of the audience response to my lines. But I was always disappointed with myself on the screen."

My Reputation (1946)

Barbara Stanwyck (*Jessica Drummond*), George Brent (*Maj. Scott Landis*), Warner Anderson (*Frank Everett*), Lucile Watson (*Mary Kimball*), Eve Arden (*Virginia "Ginna" Abbott*), John Ridgely (*Cary Abbott*), Jerome Cowan (*George Van Orman*), Esther Dale (*Anna*), Bobby Cooper (*Keith Drummond*), Scotty Beckett (*Kim Drummond*), Leona Maricle (*Riette Van Orman*), Janis Wilson (*Penny Boardman*), Ann Todd (*Gretchen Van Orman*), Cecil Cunningham (*Stella Thompson*), Durwood Kaye ("*Droopy*" *Hawks*), Marjorie Hoshelle (*Phyllis*), Sam McDaniel (*Johnson*), Robert Shayne (*Hank Hawks*)
Director: Curtis Bernhardt. *Executive Producer:* Jack L. Warner. *Producer:* Henry Blanke. *Screen Play:* Catherine Turney, from the novel *Instruct My Sorrows* by Clare Jaynes. *Director of Photography:* James Wong Howe. *Music:* Max Steiner. *Dialogue Director:* Jack Gage. *Film Editor:* David Weisbart. *Art Director:* Anton Grot. *Sound:* Everett A. Brown. *Barbara Stanwyck's Gowns:* Edith Head. *Gowns:* Leah Rhodes. *Special Effects:* Roy Davidson. *Makeup Artist:* Perc Westmore. *Set Decorations:* George James Hopkins. *Musical Director:* Leo F. Forbstein. Warner Bros.-First National Pictures. Released January 26, 1946. B&W; 94 minutes.

Well-to-do Jessica Drummond is widowed at the age of 33, leaving her with two young sons. In the rarefied social world Jessica and her family have occupied in Lake Forest (near Chicago), there are strict expectations of how a widow should behave. To the disapproval of her stern mother, Mrs. Kimball, Jessica refuses to wear mourning (as her mother has done for the past 25 years). Desperately lonely without the companionship of her husband, Jessica nonetheless resists the urgings of her mother and friends to accept the romantic attentions of longtime family friend Frank Everett, a good and kind man who would provide security, but whom she does not love.

Her down-to-earth friend Ginna invites her to a vacation at Lake Tahoe, where Jessica meets Major Scott Landis on the ski slopes. Once back in Chicago, Jessica learns that Major Landis is now stationed nearby, and renews her acquaintance with the handsome soldier. Jessica decides to continue seeing Scott, though she knows her friends will disapprove, and despite his warning that he is not the marrying type. When one of her mother's gossip-loving friends sees her meeting Scott at his apartment, Jessica soon finds her friends turning against her, and spreading rumors behind her back that hurt her relationship with her sons. When Scott receives his orders to ship out from New York, Jessica pledges to go with him, but can't go through with it after she sees that her sons need her.

Though this is in some ways a typical Eve Arden role of the period, as her character Ginna is the heroine's supportive best friend, in other ways it stands apart. Unlike most Arden characters, Ginna is happily married to a good man (Cary, played by John Ridgely), with whom she enjoys an easy, comfortable relationship that stands in contrast to Jessica's loneliness. Mr. and Mrs. Abbott are even seen in bed together, unusual for 1946, where they banter lightly after Cary realizes that his wife has been interfering in her friend's love life. "You're a hardboiled mug," Ginna tells her husband fondly in response to his criticism; he answers, "And you are a matchmaking nuisance." Neither is offended, as is clear when he follows his comment with "Good night, my pet."

While Ginna is not particularly a wisecracker to the degree that some of Eve's characters are, she's plainspoken just the same. At one point, she chides her good friend Jessica, saying, "It just makes me sick the way you've let everyone manage you all your life. You've got to start being yourself for a change." Eve makes her first entrance more than 20 minutes into the film, and is present mostly in its midsection.

Set in 1942, the film had multiple references to wartime activities such as Victory Gardens and gasoline rationing. Though this film fits neatly into the type of roles for which Warners placed Eve under contract, it was actually shot in 1944, prior to her signing on as a salaried

Jessica (Barbara Stanwyck) gets some good advice from pal Ginna (Eve) in *My Reputation.*

employee. In later years, Barbara Stanwyck would name this film among her favorite roles. Once the film was released, Warners' publicity department tried to make Jessica's story sound sexier and more outrageous than it really was, with lines in the trailer such as, "Why can't a woman love more than once?" and "Happiness means more to me than my reputation."

Variety's mixed review thought "femme moviegoers" would enjoy themselves with *My Reputation*, saying the picture began slowly but built to "a well-architected buildup to a dramatic blow off that's certain to have a lot of handkerchiefs moist when the lights go up." Eve, along with Warner Anderson, was credited as one of the supporting players who "turn in neat jobs" (January 9, 1946).

Less impressed was the *New York Times*'s Bosley Crowther, who thought the film's premise of societal disapproval "much ado about nothing—or practically nothing ... the mere demonstration of behavior and social conventions herein is so thoroughly stilted and stuffy that the whole thing lacks common sense" (January 26, 1946). A friendlier reaction came from the *New York Sun*'s Eileen Creelman, who praised *My Reputation* as "a consistently interesting picture. It tells of likable people, real people, in terms that are neither melodramatic nor caricaturing" (January 26, 1946).

The Kid from Brooklyn (1946)

Danny Kaye (*Burleigh Sullivan*), Virginia Mayo (*Polly Pringle*), Vera-Ellen (*Susie Sullivan*), Steve Cochran (*Speed McFarlane*), Eve Arden (*Ann Westley*), Walter Abel (*Gabby Sloan*), Lionel Stander (*Spider Schultz*), Fay Bainter (*Mrs. E. Winthrop LeMoyne*), Clarence Kolb (*Wilbur Austin*), Victor Cutler (*Photographer*), Charles Cane (*Willard*), Jerome Cowan (*Fight Announcer*), Don Wilson, Knox Manning (*Radio Announcers*),

Eve comes between Danny Kaye and Walter Abel in *The Kid from Brooklyn*.

Kay Thompson (*Matron*), Johnny Downs (*Master of Ceremonies*), George Chandler, Billy Wayne (*Reporters*), Pierre Watkin (*E. Winthrop LeMoyne*)

Director: Norman Z. McLeod. *Producer:* Samuel Goldwyn. *Adaptation:* Don Hartman, Melville Shavelson, *from a screenplay by* Grover Jones, Frank Butler, Richard Connell, *based on a play by* Lynn Root, Harry Clork. *Director of Photography:* Gregg Toland. *Art Direction:* Perry Ferguson, Stewart Chaney. *Associate:* McClure Capps. *Film Editor:* Daniel Mandell. *Musical Director:* Carmen Dragon. *Musical Supervisor:* Louis Forbes. *Dances:* Bernard Pearce. *Vocal Arrangements:* Kay Thompson. *Costume Designer:* Miles White. *Clothes Designer:* Jean Louis. *Set Decorations:* Howard Bristol, Clifford Porter. *Makeup:* Robert Stephanoff. *Hair Stylist:* Marie Clark. *Technicolor Color Director:* Natalie Kalmus. *Associate:* Mitchell Kovaleski. *Sound Recorder:* Fred Lau. *Technical Adviser:* John Indrisano. Samuel Goldwyn, Inc.; released March 21, 1946. Color; 113 minutes.

Nebbishy milkman Burleigh Sullivan, doing his best to defend his sister's honor, gets into a melee on the street with two drunks following her home from her nightclub job. When the smoke clears, middleweight boxing champion Speed McFarlane, one of the guys harassing Susie Sullivan, is knocked out cold, and to all appearances it was puny Burleigh who clocked him. The next morning, newspaper headlines proclaim, "Milkman Curdles Champ."

With his prizefighter made a laughingstock overnight, fast-talking promoter Gabby Sloan concocts a scheme to launch Burleigh's ring career as "The Fighting Milkman." As Burleigh himself readily admits, he's no fighter—his best talent is for ducking when he sees a punch coming. But having been fired from the Sunflower Dairies, he agrees to take on a fight career in hopes of landing lovely singer Polly Pringle. Thanks to a few carefully fixed fights, Burleigh actually rises in the middleweight rankings, leading up to a bout with Speed himself. Gabby, who's bet heavily against odds-on favorite Burleigh in the match, plans to clean up big when Speed wins the bout. But various complications, including Polly's disapproval of the changes that fame brings to her unassuming boyfriend, and an inadvertent dose of sleeping pills fed to Speed minutes before the match, conspire to leave the outcome of the fight unexpectedly in question.

Cast as Gabby Sloan's dry-witted girlfriend, Ann, Eve looks terrific in some colorful Jean Louis outfits that seem to have been given more thought and effort than her dialogue in *The Kid from Brooklyn*. Her impeccable timing nails down the laughs whenever there's one to be had. Part of an entourage being given the bum's rush out of Burleigh Sullivan's apartment by his angry sister, Ann strolls coolly by the camera and observes, "Brooklyn hospitality!" Later, after gruff coach Spider is having a tough time turning the shy milkman into "Tiger" Sullivan at training camp, Ann employs a less orthodox method. Having kissed the boo-boos he sustained at Spider's hands, Ann asks Burleigh if he knows how to dance. Told yes, she shows him how to adapt his dance floor moves to prizefighting, to the accompaniment of the Blue Danube Waltz: "Tra la la la la, boom boom, boom boom! Tra la la la la, boom boom, boom boom!"

Eve and Danny Kaye worked together for the first time in the Broadway hit *Let's Face It*. The success of that show resulted in a lucrative motion picture contract with Samuel Goldwyn for Kaye. Over the next few years, Danny and Eve would team frequently, on Kaye's CBS radio show, and here.

The Kid from Brooklyn was a remake of the 1936 Harold Lloyd comedy *The Milky Way*, which in turn was adapted from a Broadway comedy that ran only a few weeks in the late spring and early summer of 1934. (Gladys George played Eve's role of Ann onstage; Verree Teasdale in the Lloyd film version.) Kaye's version was an expensive film, and looked it. The shooting of the climactic prize fight reportedly took two weeks and employed some two thousand atmosphere players. Musical numbers featured the beauteous Goldwyn Girls, and songs furnished by Jule Styne and Sammy Cahn.

Aside from Kaye, the film gives a few moments in the spotlight to lovely leading lady Virginia Mayo (1920–2005), who would ultimately appear opposite the comedian in five films in the mid- to late 1940s. In her second film, dancer Vera-Ellen (1921–1981), as Kaye's sister, does a couple of strenuous routines that will make you tired just watching her.

Steve Cochran (1917–1965), in this early role, shows an unexpected flair for comedy that wouldn't often be seen in his later tough-guy parts. Clarence Kolb (1874–1964), who'd previously shared a screen credit with Eve in *Bedtime Story* (1941), is strongly featured here as irascible dairy owner Mr. Austin, presenting the same blustery persona he would bring to playing Charles Farrell's boss on TV's *My Little Margie*. Seen briefly as one of the announcers at ringside is Don Wilson, famed for his longtime stint on Jack Benny's radio and television shows. Lionel Stander (1908–1994), best known to modern audiences as Max in TV's *Hart to Hart*, played Spider Schultz in both film versions.

The *Washington Post*'s Nelson B. Bell called *The Kid from Brooklyn* Danny Kaye's "best picture to date." Crediting the performances of Walter Abel, Lionel Stander, and Steve Cochran as "top-drawer," Bell added that they were "easily matched by Eve Arden's as their acidly stimulating feminine accomplice" (September 3, 1946).

Night and Day (1946)

Cary Grant (*Cole Porter*), Alexis Smith (*Linda Lee Porter*), Monty Woolley (*Himself*), Ginny Simms (*Carole Hill*), Jane Wyman (*Gracie Harris*), Eve Arden (*Gabrielle*), Victor Francen (*Anatole Giron*), Alan Hale (*Leon Dowling*), Dorothy Malone (*Nancy*), Tom D'Andrea (*Bernie*), Selena Royle (*Kate Porter*), Donald Woods (*Ward Blackburn*), Henry Stephenson (*Omar Cole*), Paul Cavanagh (*Bart McClelland*), Sig Ruman (*Wilowski*), Jimmie Dodd (*Red*), Carlos Ramirez (*Specialty Singer*), Milada Mladova (*Specialty Dancer*), George Zoritch (*Specialty Dancer*), Adam & Jane Di Gitano (*Specialty Dancers*), Estelle Sloan (*Specialty Dancer*), Mary Martin (*Herself*)

Director: Michael Curtiz. Executive Producer: Jack L. Warner. Producer: Arthur Schwartz. Screenplay: Charles Hoffman, Leo Townsend, William Bowers. Adaptation: Jack Moffitt. Based on the Career of Cole Porter.

Eve attending the premiere of *Night and Day* with then-husband Ned Bergen.

Production Numbers Orchestrated and Conducted by Ray Heindorf. *Dance Numbers Created and Directed by* LeRoy Prinz. *Directors of Photography:* Peverell Marley, William V. Skall. *Technical Color Director:* Natalie Kalmus. *Associate:* Leonard Doss. *Musical Director:* Leo F. Forbstein. *Film Editor:* David Weisbart. *Sound:* Everett A. Brown, David Forrest. *Art Director:* John Hughes. *Dialogue Director:* Herschel Daugherty. *Montages:* James Leicester. *Additional Music:* Max Steiner. *Set Decorations:* Armor Marlowe. *Makeup Artist:* Perc Westmore. *Wardrobe:* Milo Anderson. *Dance Costumes:* Travilla. *Special Effects:* Robert Burks. *Vocal Arrangements:* Dudley Chambers. Warner Bros.-First National Pictures; released August 3, 1946. Color; 127 minutes.

Young Cole Porter, scion of a well-to-do family, drops out of Yale Law School to pursue his interest in music. With the help of his former professor, Monty Woolley, Cole stages his first musical production, *See America First,* only to have its opening night ruined by the news that the *Lusitania* has been sunk. As he hits the pinnacle of success, Cole begins to be a neglectful husband to Linda, throwing all his attention to his work, until they separate. When Cole is critically injured in a riding accident, however, Linda rushes to his side, and they are reunited.

Made while Porter was at the height of his fame and popularity, *Night and Day* presents a highly selective view of the famed composer's life, notably avoiding the topic of his bisexuality. Though not released until 1946, it had been in the works for more than two years, delayed by script revisions as well as Cary Grant's hesitation to take on the lead role. Eve's role in *Night and Day* was what would today be termed a cameo role. In a film that runs a little more than two hours, she is onscreen for approximately three minutes, and has only two scenes. Nonetheless, it is an interesting performance in which she plays a role quite unlike her usual screen type, and does so quite memorably. As Gabrielle, a French revue star, she is approached by Linda to sing the still-unknown Cole's song "I'm Unlucky at Gambling" in her next show. Gorgeously gowned and coiffed, sporting a charming French accent, Gabrielle reluctantly agrees to do her friend the favor, saying, "But let me warn you, darling. If there ees a man involved, he weel fall in love with me. I don't know how eet happens, but eet happens!" Realizing that Linda is working on behalf of the man she loves, Gabrielle agrees to speak to her producer about using the song, saying perplexedly, "I, Gabrielle, take such a chance on a young man, and somebody else's young man! I think I am losing my mind, *non?* However, anything for *l'amour,* I understand.... I was in love myself once—many times!"

As it turns out, Gabrielle's producer, M. Giron, likes the song, but after Gabrielle tries it to lukewarm reaction in front of an audience, cuts it from the show, telling Cole, "Your lyrics are too smart, too sophisticated." Cole is also embarrassed to learn that his wife invested money in the show in the hopes of placing his music.

Eve reportedly told a journalist, "This is honestly the hottest number I have ever done." This was, in fact, quite true, as she performed the song on a sweltering soundstage wrapped in a heavy costume under blazing lights. Shooting was delayed by some disagreements between her and director Michael Curtiz over the accent she was using.

Warner Bros. promoted *Night and Day* as a celebration of its 20th anniversary making sound films, saying in newspaper advertisements, "It's the last word in pictures since pictures spoke their first word!" The film was Oscar-nominated for its musical score. *Time* thought the film was OK, but wondered why it couldn't have delved a bit more truthfully into Porter's real life, instead of "steamrolling the man himself with the same deadpan, posthumous reverence that the movies used on Zola, Pasteur, Woodrow Wilson, and Mme. Curie" (July 8, 1946). The *Oakland Tribune*'s Wood Soanes, in his August 5, 1946 review, thought the opulent, lavishly produced extravaganza "far too long," but mostly successful, and predicted great box-office success. Eve was among the featured players he mentioned as "actors of great skill who make important contributions to the general success of the piece." Likewise, the *New York Times* found Eve, who "plays a French songstress in broad burlesque ... very amusing" (July 26, 1946).

The Arnelo Affair (1947)

John Hodiak (*Tony Arnelo*), George Murphy (*Ted Parkson*), Frances Gifford (*Anne Parkson*), Dean Stockwell (*Ricky Parkson*), Eve Arden (*Vivian Delwyn*), Warner Anderson (*Detective Sam Leonard*), Lowell Gilmore (*Dr. Avery Border*), Ruth Brady (*Dorothy Alison*), Ruby Dandridge (*Maybelle*), Joan Woodbury (*Claire Lorrison*)

Director/Screenplay: Arch Oboler. *Producer:* Jerry Bressler. *Story:* Jane Burr. *Director of Photography:* Charles Salerno. *Film Editor:* Harry Komer. *Musical Score:* George Bassman. *Recording Director:* Douglas Shearer. *Art Direction:* Cedric Gibbons, Wade Rubottom. *Set Decorations:* Edwin B. Willis. *Associate:* Thomas Theuerkauf. *Costume Supervision:* Irene. *Makeup:* Jack Dawn. MGM; released February 13, 1947. B&W; 86 minutes.

Pretty Anne Parkson is the neglected wife of rising attorney Ted Parkson, who seems more concerned with his career than his family. Though she has a lovely home, a nine-year-old son she adores, and financial security, Anne is restless. When Ted brings home his newest client, suave nightclub owner Tony Arnelo, he instantly takes an interest in her. Hiring Anne to redecorate his apartment, the sleazy Tony plays on her loneliness to draw her into a relationship. She visits him in the afternoons at his apartment, and accepts a key to his place, but cuts off the relationship when she has an unpleasant encounter with another of Tony's lady friends, actress Claire Lorrison.

The next day, Anne learns from the morning newspaper that Claire has

In *The Arnelo Affair*, leading lady Frances Gifford (left) takes some fashion tips from her pal, "the eminent dress shop industrialist," played by Eve.

been murdered, and knows Tony is responsible. Because she dropped a compact given to her by Ted at the crime scene, Anne may also be implicated, especially after Tony threatens her with an incriminating letter she wrote him after their breakup. The detective doggedly pursuing the case soon learns of the Parksons' connection to Tony Arnelo, and questions them both in an effort to solve the murder.

Writer-director Arch Oboler (1909–1987) was primarily known for his radio work, notably his enduring suspense series *Lights Out*. His radio success led him to attempt a motion picture career, with spotty results. This was his third venture behind the motion picture camera since starting with *Bewitched* (1945); perhaps his most effective film was the nuclear holocaust drama *Five* (1951). Most viewers of this film won't be surprised to learn, if they didn't already know it, that Arch Oboler was a radio man. It's the only possible explanation for the breathy, intrusive, and unnecessary voiceover narration by Anne that plays through the first half of the film.

Eve is featured as the Parksons' upstairs neighbor Vivian, who is also Anne's closest friend. A dress designer who owns her own shop (Ted calls her "the eminent dress shop industrialist"), Vivian is chic, impeccably dressed, slightly caustic, but a good friend to Anne. Far more sure of herself than her friend, Vivian explains over a breakfast, "You know, Anne, just give me a plate of bacon and eggs, a full pocketbook, a chinchilla coat, and a man, and I'm happy. I'm such a simple girl." Sensing that Anne is getting in over her head with sleazy Tony Arnelo, Vivian gives her friend a warning ("canaries and hawks don't make good playmates") that she fails to heed. Late in the film, she not only helps the stolid Ted understand what has gone wrong in his relationship with Anne, telling him a little about how marriage can look from the woman's vantage point, but also provides a vital clue that sets him on the track toward clearing his wife's name.

Having both directed and co-authored *The Arnelo Affair,* Arch Oboler can be safely blamed to a large extent for the film's shortcomings. Sad to say, though, he received a considerable assist in lousing it up from leading lady Frances Gifford, whose performance largely involves a number of vacant stares into space. Her face is lovingly bathed in light as she emotes to distressingly little effect.

One of the picture's better reviews came from *Variety,* which thought it "may become one of this season's sleepers" (February 12, 1947). The *Chicago Tribune*'s "Mae Tinee" complained that "this murder story consists of little except talk, most of it affected and repetitious" (March 1, 1948). Bosley Crowther, writing in the *New York Times,* called the film "unmercifully slow and somber and utterly devoid of surprise" (September 13, 1947).

Oddly enough, this is only the first of Eve's 1947 releases that is basically a rehash of *The Letter* (1940). About three months after this hit theaters, *The Unfaithful* came along to plow largely the same ground.

Song of Scheherazade (1947)

Yvonne De Carlo (*Cara de Talavera*), Brian Donlevy (*Captain Vladimir Gregorovitch*), Jean-Pierre Aumont (*Nikolai Rimsky-Korsakov*), Eve Arden (*Madame Conchita Manuela de Talavera*), Philip Reed (*Prince Mischetsky*), John Qualen (*Lorenzo*), Richard Lane (*Lieutenant*), George Dolenz (*Pierre*), Elena Verdugo (*Fioretta*), Terry Kilburn (*Midshipman Lorin*), Charles Kullmann (*Dr. Klin*), Robert Kendall (*Hassan*)

Writer/Director: Walter Reisch. *Producer:* Edward Kaufman. *Associate Producer:* Edward Dodds. *Musical Adaptation and Direction:* Miklos Kozsa. *Directors of Photography:* Hal Mohr, William V. Skall. *Technical Color Director:* Natalie Kalmus. *Associate:* William Fritzche. *Film Editor:* Frank Gross. *Art Direction:* Jack Otterson, Eugene Lourie. *Director of Sound:* Bernard B. Brown. *Technician:* Joe Lapis. *Set Decorations:* Russell A. Gausman, E.R. Robinson. *Costumes:* Yvonne Wood. *Dialogue Director:* Joan Hathaway. *Choreographer:* Tillie Losch. *Hair Stylist:* Carmen Dirigo. *Director of Makeup:* Jack P. Pierce. *Lyrics:* Jack Brooks. *Assistant Director:* William Holland. Universal-International Pictures; released February 26, 1947. Color; 106 minutes.

In 1865, a Russian naval ship docks at Morocco and its crew is given shore leave. Among the crew members is young Nikolai Rimsky-Korsakov, who's already begun composing the music that will eventually make him world famous. Looking for a piano on which to play his latest composition, Nikolai makes the acquaintance of flighty socialite Madame de Talavera, and her beautiful daughter Cara. To all appearances enjoying a lavish lifestyle, Cara and her mother are actually deeply in debt, and making ends meet only because Cara spends her evenings dancing at a local café.

Though he has always preferred working on his music to female companionship, Nikolai falls in love with Cara, and she with him. When the sailors' shore leave is nearing an end, they concoct a plan to hide Cara aboard the ship, and take her back to Russia where she can study ballet. The plan fails, and the young lovers are separated—until the night Rimsky-Korsakov's *Scheherazade* makes its triumphant public debut.

By the end of her seven-year contract with Warners, Eve would be unhappy with the lack of variety she found in her movie roles. *Song of Scheherazade,* however, which she filmed on loan-out to Universal-International, gives her the chance to play quite a different character from her usual best-friend-of-the-heroine type. Madame de Talavera is a vague, silly, fanciful creature who spends her days flouncing about her palatial home in lavish outfits that would embarrass a drag queen, fluttering a mantilla as she flirts with every man in sight, and blithely ignoring the realities of her existence. Delighted to make the acquaintance of an aspiring musician, she proceeds to unfurl a series of highly suspect stories about the musical greats she has known: "Mendelssohn! I met him in London. He was a very dear friend of my husband's. Confidentially, he composed the Wedding March for me." When Paganini is mentioned, she says, "Oh, that wicked Paganini! At one time he and I ... [laughs merrily] ... well, it's quite a story."

Interviewed at Universal in the spring of 1946, Eve told the *Los Angeles Times*'s Philip K. Scheuer she was pleased with the opportunity to take a break from her usual type of movie role:

"It's quite a departure for me. She's a divine nutsy character, more like the kind I've played on the stage, who doesn't make much sense but is a lot of fun. Her hacienda, or whatever they call it in Morocco, is run down and she has lost all her money—but she acts as if she still has it."

Needless to say, verisimilitude takes quite a beating in *Song of Scheherazade*. Though it's true that Rimsky-Korsakov served in the Russian navy, and was composing music while on a lengthy voyage in the early to mid-1860s, the accuracy of this film biography pretty much ends there. Apparently executives at Universal-International saw no good reason why the Russian composer couldn't be played by an actor with a strong French accent. The script is full of ripe dialogue, as when Nikolai tells his lady love, "You *are* music! How was I able to write before I met you?" If we are to believe this film, the great composer wrote several of the major works of his career in the course of a single week. Still, there are occasional signs that we're not meant to take any of this too seriously—Madame de Talavera has a brightly colored parrot who, when's she been blathering on too long, chirps, "Yak, yak, yak, yak!"

Eve, all dolled up as Madame de Talavera, in *Song of Scheherazade.*

Perhaps the best approach to enjoying this colorful film is to heed the advice Eve's character offers her daughter—"Oh, that's one thing I never do, darling—*think.*"

Serving as both director and screenwriter of this cheesy epic was Walter Reisch (1903–1983), who earned writing credits on two of Eve's previous films, *Comrade X* (1940) and *That Uncertain Feeling* (1941). He would subsequently win an Oscar for his screenplay of *Titanic* (1953). *Song of Scheherazade* represents one of his few stints in the director's chair, those assignments far outnumbered by his screenwriting credits.

Gorgeous Yvonne De Carlo, a bit player in Eve's film *Let's Face It,* rose quickly through the ranks at Universal after the success of her film *Salome, Where She Danced* (1945), and an attendant publicity campaign that labeled her "The Most Beautiful Girl in the World." In reality, Eve would have been an awfully young mother to have given birth to De Carlo, her junior by only 14 years. Yvonne's leading man, actor Jean-Pierre Aumont, was at the time married to another exotic U-I leading lady, Maria Montez. Among the young actors playing bit parts as midshipmen here is William Ching, who later appeared as lecherous athletic director Clint Albright on *Our Miss Brooks.*

Writing in the *Winnipeg Free Press,* Frank Morriss noted, "That gentleman revolving around and around in his grave these spring days would be Nikolas Rimsky-Korsakoff, who lived and died a rather austere gentleman in Russia. What has set him rotating is the fact that Universal-International has concocted a musical movie about him which has him writing practically the whole output of a lifetime during a few days stopover at a Moroccan port ... the movie's scenarists have turned dizzy and jumped into space" (April 5, 1947). The critic did acknowledge, however, that Metropolitan Opera tenor Charles Kullmann sang beautifully in the film, and that Eve was "shrewdly funny" in her role.

The Unfaithful (1947)

Ann Sheridan (*Christina Hunter*), Lew Ayres (*Larry Hannaford*), Zachary Scott (*Robert Hunter*), Eve Arden (*Paula*), John Hoyt (*Detective Lieutenant Reynolds*), Jerome Cowan (*Prosecuting Attorney*), Steven Geray (*Martin Barrow*), Peggy Knudsen (*Claire*), Marta Mitrovich (*Mrs. Tanner*), Douglas Kennedy (*Roger*), Claire Meade (*Martha*), Frances Morris (*Agnes*), Jane Harker (*Joan*)
Director: Vincent Sherman. *Executive Producer:* Jack L. Warner. *Producer:* Jerry Wald. *Screenplay:* David Goodis, James Gunn. *Director of Photography:* Ernest Haller. *Film Editor:* Alan Crosland, Jr. *Art Director:* Leo K. Kuter. *Sound:* Francis J. Scheid. *Dialogue Director:* Felix Jacoves. *Wardrobe:* Travilla. *Special Effects:* William McCann, Robert Burks. *Set Decorations:* William Wallace. *Makeup Artist:* Perc Westmore. *Music:* Max Steiner. *Orchestral Arrangements:* Murray Cutter. *Musical Director:* Leo F. Forbstein. Warner Bros./First National Pictures; released June 5, 1947. B&W; 109 minutes.

Real estate man Bob Hunter arrives home early from a business trip to learn that his wife, Chris, has stabbed and killed an intruder at their home. Chris tells the police that the man, Michael Tanner, was unknown to her, and that he tried to steal her jewelry. Tanner's bitter widow believes that Chris's act was a murder, not a case of self-defense. Chris's friend and attorney, Larry Hannaford, takes on the challenge of proving her innocence.

Sleazy art dealer Martin Barrow provides the first crack in Chris's case when he offers to sell Larry a bust of Chris sculpted by Michael Tanner. Faced with this evidence of their prior acquaintance, Chris eventually confesses to Larry that Michael Tanner was her lover while Bob was away at war. Although Chris hopes to buy the incriminating statue and prevent Bob from learning of her unfaithfulness, a bitter Mrs. Tanner tells Bob the truth.

Eve plays Bob's cousin Paula, who moves in a sophisticated social circle. When we first meet her, she's throwing an elegant party to celebrate the fact that, with Larry's help, Paula has just won a divorce from her husband of six years and was "pardoned, or was it paroled?" she asks. Possessed of a quick wit and a sharp tongue, Paula employs both freely, saying at one point of a friend, "Isn't that Joan stupid? Poor dear, she's just not smart enough to be an idiot." The shocking facts of Bob's wife having killed a burglar makes for some tantalizing gossip among Paula and her friends, much to the displeasure of Bob and Larry. "Those witches—they ought to be measured for broomsticks," Larry says of Paula and her friends after they confront a harried Chris at a restaurant. But when the chips are down, Paula plays a surprising role in helping Bob look at his marriage in a new light.

Eve is directed here for the first time by Vincent Sherman, who would go on to guide her performance in *Goodbye, My Fancy* (1951). She and Sherman worked together again many years later when he directed her in the 1980 television miniseries *The Dream Merchants*. Ironically, Eve was on theater screens as the newly divorced Paula just as her own first marriage, to literary agent Ned Bergen, came to an end via a Reno divorce.

The *New York Times* thought *The Unfaithful* was "a better than average murder mystery," benefiting from "some uncommonly persuasive acting and skillful direction" (June 28, 1947). *Variety* named Eve "among others in cast who register strongly" (May 28, 1947). Taking especial note of Eve's contribution to the film was the *Los Angeles Times*'s Edwin Schallert, who not only praised the film overall but wrote, "Eve Arden is splendid and sparkling. There is not her equal for the type of part she enacts—brittle yet human at the right moments" (June 26, 1947).

The Voice of the Turtle (1947)

Ronald Reagan (*Sgt. Bill Page*), Eleanor Parker (*Sally Middleton*), Eve Arden (*Olive Lashbrooke*), Wayne Morris (*Cmdr. Ned Burling*), Kent Smith (*Kenneth Bartlett*), John Emery (*George Harrington*), Erskine Sanford (*Storekeeper*), John Holland (*Henry Atherton*)
Director: Irving Rapper. *Producer:* Charles Hoffman. *Screenplay:* John Van Druten, based on his play. *Additional Dialogue:* Charles Hoffman. *Director of Photography:* Sol Polito. *Film Editor:* Rudi Fehr. *Art Director:* Robert Haas. *Sound:* Stanley Jones. *Dialogue Director:* Richard Barr. *Montages:* James Leicester. *Special Effects:* Harry Barndollar, Edwin DuPar. *Set Decorations:* William Kuehl. *Wardrobe:* Leah Rhodes. *Makeup Artist:* Perc Westmore. *Music:* Max Steiner. *Orchestral Arrangements:* Murray Cutter. *Musical Director:* Leo F. Forbstein. Warner Bros.-First National Pictures; released December 25, 1947. B&W; 103 minutes.

II. Filmography—The Voice of the Turtle (1947)

Glamorous actress Olive Lashbrooke (Eve, right) offers a few words of wisdom to her less worldly friend Sally (Eleanor Parker) in *The Voice of the Turtle*.

Sally Middleton is a young, beautiful, but rather naïve actress living in wartime New York. Her relationship with producer Kenneth Bartlett comes to an abrupt and painful end when she realizes that, for him, it was just intended to be a fling, not "a great romance." Heartbroken Sally, left alone at Christmastime by a man with whom she believes she was in love, resolves to close off her emotions and stop making herself vulnerable to men.

The polar opposite of Sally, especially in her attitudes toward men, is Sally's friend Olive Lashbrooke. Also an actress, glamorous Olive neatly juggles a variety of men, most of whom she takes not at all seriously. One of them, Sergeant Bill Page, is in town while on a weekend furlough, and has plans with Olive that she throws over at the last minute in favor of someone she likes better. Embarrassed by her friend's machinations, Sally agrees to accompany Bill to dinner after Olive sloughs him off. Later, reluctant to send nice-guy Bill out into a raging snowstorm to look for a hotel room late at night, Sally offers him the use of the daybed in her living room on his first night in New York.

Though Bill, who was once jilted by the girl he loved, seems to be just the ticket for the slightly pixilated Sally, she has a difficult time opening her heart once again. But after a happy weekend spent in his company, she finds the strength to stand up to her friend Olive when it appears that she's not yet done toying with Bill's affections.

One of Eve's best supporting performances, her role in *The Voice of the Turtle* has been somewhat overlooked, largely because of the film's relative unavailability. Though she was often stuck in a rut of playing the heroine's unglamorous, usually man-less best friend, here she shows clearly that she has the beauty and the talent to play a glamorous type, one who deftly keeps men on her string. She shares billing above the title with Ronald Reagan, Eleanor Parker, and Wayne Morris.

Strongly present in the film's first half hour, Eve's character becomes secondary as the romance between Eleanor Parker's Sally and Ronald Reagan's Bill escalates. But she charges full force into a third-act climax that finds her squaring off against her girlfriend, and the man she thought was hers whenever she wanted him.

Eve recognized this as one of the stronger roles she'd been given under her Warners' contract, and she plays the juicy role of Olive with fervor. It's to her credit that the character, selfish and cynical as she is, is also surprisingly endearing. She's quite funny as the competitive actress who doesn't trouble to hold back a malevolent chuckle when reading a scathing newspaper review of a rival's performance. "Oh, how awful," Olive says happily. "Oh, poor Virginia ... she couldn't have been *that* bad!" Later, when she finds herself gently but firmly told off by her erstwhile beau Bill, Olive delivers one last stinger on her way out the door: "Now if a woman said that, you know what they'd call her, don't you?" (Onstage, the line was a more direct, "I never knew men could be such bitches!")

The role of Olive Lashbrooke in *The Voice of the Turtle* is also noteworthy for helping Vivian Vance land her iconic role of Ethel Mertz in TV's *I Love Lucy*. Recommended to Lucy and Desi for the role of Ethel by her friend, original *Lucy* director Marc Daniels, Vivian was hired after Desi saw her onstage in a California production of *Turtle*. Though the roles of Olive and Ethel could hardly be less alike, Desi admired Vivian's performance, and felt sure she could play the role.

Eleanor Parker (born 1922) brings a lovely vulnerable quality to the role of Sally, contrasted sharply with Eve's delineation of Olive. Ronald Reagan's natural geniality makes him well suited to the role of Bill, though at 36 he was arguably a bit too old for the part. The release of *Voice of the Turtle* followed close on the heels of his embarrassing co-starring turn opposite Shirley Temple in *That Hagen Girl*. Offscreen, his romantic life was complicated, as well, as he was in the final stages of his troubled marriage with another Arden co-star, Jane Wyman, who would sue him for divorce in 1948.

Nick Stewart, previously seen in a small role in Eve's *Hit Parade of 1943*, appears unbilled here as Sam, the elevator operator in Sally's apartment building. Frank Wilcox, who had a recurring role as an oilman in the 1960s TV hit *The Beverly Hillbillies*, is seen briefly as another of Olive's men, a fellow actor who means little to her, but who came in handy carrying her bags during a road company tour.

John Van Druten's play *The Voice of the Turtle* was a smash hit on Broadway, running more than 1,500 performances. The three-character play, which took place entirely in Sally's apartment, opened in December 1943, with Margaret Sullavan playing Sally and Audrey Christie cast as Olive, closing finally in early 1948, just as the film version was going into general release. Christie was later replaced by film actress Betty Field in the role of Olive. The show also represented an early career break for the great Eileen Heckart, who served as Assistant Stage Manager and understudied both female roles. It also toured successfully, despite some mild controversy over the story point of a young woman allowing a man she'd just met to share her apartment overnight.

Warner Bros. bought picture rights to the hit play in 1944, though production wouldn't get underway until early 1947. Producer Charles Hoffman was charged with the task of "opening up" the play, working with Van Druten to add scenes taking place in a French restaurant, a diner, and the Broadway theater where Sally is being considered for a job. Veteran Broadway producer Alfred de Liagre, Jr., who went to Hollywood to assist in adapting his stage hit to film, was dismayed by Jack Warner's insistence on casting Parker and Reagan, both of whom he considered miscast. As he told syndicated columnist Norman Nadel in a 1980 interview, "So we fought about it for two months, daily, and finally Jack said, 'I paid you half a million dollars to do this, and it's my privilege to louse it up if I want to.'" Unhappy with how Hollywood treated what he considered "the most enchanting romantic comedy of all time ... a great piece of play craftsmanship," de Liagre would largely steer clear of filmmaking until he agreed to work with Sidney Lumet on *Deathtrap* more than 30 years later.

By the time of the film's release in late 1947, the wartime setting was no longer current, necessitating an opening title that explains, "It was December 1944 in New York, and it seemed that the war and the winter were never going to end...." When released to television, the film was retitled with the meaningless monicker *One for the Book.* The original title is a Biblical quote taken from the Song of Solomon.

Already nominated once as Best Supporting Actress for *Mildred Pierce*, it's surprising that Eve didn't earn another nod for this standout role. It was, however, a year marked by some strong female performances, among them Marjorie Main's debut as Ma Kettle in *The Egg and I*, and the featured roles of Anne Revere and the ultimately victorious Celeste Holm in *Gentlemen's Agreement.*

The Voice of the Turtle received a rave review from the *Los Angeles Times*'s Edwin Schallert, who "enthusiastically recommended [it] as one of the brightest comedies of the season" (February 21, 1948). *Variety* called it "an infectious, fluffy mirth-maker with sturdy boxoffice prospects," and also noted Eve's contribution: "Miss Arden registers importantly" as Olive (December 31, 1947).

In 1951, Eve reprised the role of Olive Lashbrooke in a stage production of *Turtle* that toured ten military bases on the West Coast. She appeared opposite Diana Lynn (with whom she made *Paid in Full*) and Mel Ferrer.

Among the many moviegoers who would find the film memorable was a young Woody Allen. Allen, who cast Eve nearly 40 years later in one of his own films (from which she subsequently had to withdraw), told author Eric Lax (*Conversations with Woody Allen*) that *The Voice of the Turtle* "just played right into my fantasy of what life in New York would be. I was impressed with it because Eve Arden was in it and I always loved Eve Arden."

One Touch of Venus (1948)

Robert Walker (*Eddie Hatch*), Ava Gardner (*Venus*), Dick Haymes (*Joe Grant*), Tom Conway (*Whitfield Savory II*), Eve Arden (*Molly Stewart*), Olga San Juan (*Gloria*), James Flavin (*Det. Kerrigan*), Sara Allgood (*Mrs. Fogarty*), George Meeker (*Mr. Crust*), Gino Corrado (*Headwaiter*)

Director: William A. Seiter. *Producer:* Lester Cowan. *Associate Producer:* John Beck. *Based on the musical play produced by* Crawford & Wildberg, *staged by* Elia Kazan. *Music:* Kurt Weill. *Book:* S.J. Perelman, Ogden Nash. *Lyrics:* Ogden Nash. *Musical Score & New Lyrics:* Ann Ronell. *Suggested by* "The Tinted Venus" by F. Anstey. *Screenplay:* Harry Kurnitz, Frank Tashlin. *Director of Photography:* Frank Planer. *Art Direction:* Bernard Herzbrun, Emrich Nicholson. *Dance Director:* Billy Daniels. *Songs Arranged and Conducted by* Leon Arnaud. *Film Editor:* Otto Ludwig. *Sound:* Leslie J. Carey, Joe Lapis. *Set Decorations:* Russell A. Gausman, Al Fields. *Gowns:* Orry Kelly. *Hair Stylist:* Carmen Dirigo. *Make-Up:* Bud Westmore. *Assistant Director:* William Holland. *Special Photography:* David S. Horsley. Universal-International, released August 1948. B&W; 82 minutes.

The owner of Savory's Department Store has just spent $200,000 to have a statue constructed of Venus, the Goddess of Love. The statue, intended to be the centerpiece of the in-store art gallery, is being tended by lowly window dresser Eddie Hatch. When Eddie kisses the statue, it comes to life as the beautiful, voluptuous goddess herself. Venus follows Eddie home to the apartment he shares with his best friend, Joe. Eddie is blamed for the disappearance of the statue, and Savory sics a detective on him to track it down, over the objections of his sensible secretary of ten years, Molly Stewart, who addresses him variously as "Lord and Master," "Sire," and the like.

Eddie's girlfriend, Gloria, is so marriage-minded that he says when he takes her out to dinner that "the only thing she ever eats is rice." To keep himself out of trouble with Gloria, Eddie takes Venus back to the department store, and leaves her overnight in the store's model home. Told in the morning by Molly that an unknown young woman was found sleeping in the store, owner Whitfield Savory intends to throw her out, but instead is smitten with the beautiful stranger. At his urging, Molly has Venus outfitted with the store's best clothes, makeup, and hair styling. However, she resists Savory's blandishments, being interested only in Eddie. Thanks to Venus's influence, Savory agrees to drop the charges against Eddie. She also proceeds to successfully rearrange the love lives of all the denizens of Savory's Department Store—causing Gloria to realize that it is Joe, not Eddie, whom she loves, and helping Savory see that he is actually in love with his devoted aide Molly.

Molly Stewart (Eve) loves her boss Mr. Savory (Tom Conway), but he's infatuated with a drowsy Ava Gardner in *One Touch of Venus*.

Set to turn back into a statue at midnight, Venus pleads with the gods for a few extra moments, but Eddie finds his way back to her only to discover she has resumed her former form. Soon afterwards, however, he meets a lovely new store employee named Venus Jones, who looks remarkably familiar to him.

Molly's feelings for her boss are suggested in the film's first few minutes, when he is re-introduced to a pretty young lady he has not seen since she was a little girl. Told by the young woman's mother that Whitfield Savory used to bounce her daughter Brenda on his knee, Molly retorts, "Well, bully for Brenda. I've been his secretary for ten years, and I haven't made it yet."

Eve's character has a running set-to with James Flavin's officious Detective Kerrigan, to whom she says at one point, "Hi, Gumshoe. Your handcuffs are showing." Veteran character actress Sara Allgood (1879–1950) has one scene as Mrs. Fogarty, Eddie Hatch's nosy landlady from whom he has to hide Venus when she barges into his apartment.

One Touch of Venus was adapted from the Broadway hit musical comedy starring Mary Martin (1913–1990), which ran for more than 500 performances between October 1943 and February 1945. Paula Laurence played the role of Molly, whose last name was Grant, in the stage version. For the film, producer Lester Cowan commissioned sculptor Joseph Nicolosi to make a life-sized statue of Ava Gardner costumed as Venus. According to publicity at the time, Gardner's Venusian robes, which she wore for the majority of her time onscreen, weighed a mere 13 ounces.

Eve's casting as Molly Stewart was announced in January 1948, and the film was in production by February. In March, columnist Erskine Johnson reported that Eve would get "full co-star billing for the first time" in *Venus*, "her reward for stealing most of the scenes." In the finished film, however, she is billed at the top of the supporting cast, sharing a "with" card with James Flavin and others.

Commented Theresa Loeb of the *Oakland Tribune*, "The contributor of the best acting in the comedy and the gal who rates the most laughs for expert delivery of lines plus appropriate gestures is Eve Arden as a highly efficient secretary to Tom Conway, owner of the store" (November 15, 1948). *Time* added, "Director William Seiter extracts some dry comedy from the Milquetoastian terror of the little clerk and from Venus' languid, Olympian indifference to the uproar she creates.... Eve Arden is good as a secretary who understands her wolf of a boss all too well" (September 27, 1948).

The acclaim she received for her performance, along with some publicity from her agent, evidently rubbed screenwriter Harry Kurnitz the wrong way, as reported in Edith Gwynn's syndicated column. Kurnitz had apparently gotten wind of the fact that Eve's sharp line delivery led some to believe that she had augmented her role with clever ad-libs. "You will be delighted to know," Kurnitz wrote in an open letter to Eve, "that your part in the new Warner picture, which I am also writing, is being left blank. I am enclosing a new pen, The Ego Special, which writes under press-agents" (March 31, 1948).

In the summer of 1948, with *One Touch of Venus* in the can awaiting release, Eve began her starring role in radio's *Our Miss Brooks*.

Whiplash (1948)

Dane Clark (*Michael Gordon*), Alexis Smith (*Laurie Durant*), Zachary Scott (*Rex Durant*), Eve Arden (*Chris Sherwood*), Jeffrey Lynn (*Dr. Arnold Vincent*), S.Z. Sakall (*Sam*), Alan Hale (*Terrance O'Leary*), Douglas Kennedy (*Costello*), Ransom Sherman (*Tex Sanders*), Fred Steele (*Duke Carney*), Robert Lowell (*Trask*), Don McGuire (*Markus*), Tommy Garland (*Rocky*), Maudie Prickett (*Mrs. Gruman*), John Harmon (*Kid McGee*), I. Stanford Jolley (*Artist*), Jimmie Dodd (*Bill*)

Director: Lewis Seiler. *Producer:* William Jacobs. *Screenplay:* Maurice Geraghty, Harriet Frank, Jr. *Adaptation:* Gordon Kahn. *Story:* Kenneth Earl. *Director of Photography:* Peverell Marley. *Film Editor:* Frank Magee. *Art Director:* Charles H. Clarke. *Sound:* Dolph Thomas. *Montages:* James Leicester. *Dialogue Director:* Felix Jacoves. *Special Effects:* William McGann, Edwin DuPar. *Technical Adviser:* Mushy Callahan. *Set Decorations:* Jack McConaghy. *Wardrobe:* Milo Anderson. *Makeup Artist:* Perc Westmore. *Music:* Franz Waxman. *Orchestral Arrangements:* Leonid Raab. *Musical Director:* Leo F. Forbstein. Warner Bros.-First National Pictures; released December 24, 1948. B&W; 91 minutes.

Prizefighter Mike Angelo, in the middle of a bout at Madison Square Garden, seems to be on the verge of losing. Seemingly going down for the count, he finds himself thinking back to how his unlikely athletic career began.

Aspiring painter Mike Gordon is surprised when his friend, bar owner Sam, sells one of Mike's paintings for $75. Meeting the beautiful stranger who bought his painting, Mike tells her she overpaid for it, and tries to buy it back. The woman insists on keeping it, but tries to stay aloof from Mike, who is instantly attracted to her. Despite her hesitation, Mike insists on taking her out to dinner. By the end of their first evening together, he is already in love with the beautiful, enigmatic stranger, whose name he discovers to be Laurie.

When Laurie abruptly checks out of her hotel and vanishes, Mike uses his only clue—a package she forwarded—to trace her to New York City. Taking up temporary residence there, he paints a portrait of Laurie that he considers his best work yet, but is thwarted in his efforts to locate the woman herself. One night, Mike accompanies his friend Chris to a nightclub where Laurie is the featured singer. When he goes backstage, Laurie rebuffs him, telling him she doesn't want to see him hurt. Mike persists in knocking on her dressing room door until he is knocked out cold by one of the club's bouncers. Waking in the private office of club owner Rex Durant, Mike soon learns that the woman he has been pursuing is Mrs. Durant.

Rex Durant is a former prize fighter who is now disabled. Impressed by the way Mike used his fists to defend himself, he offers to sponsor him as a boxer. Not willing to let go of Laurie yet, Mike accepts the offer, adopting the professional name "Mike Angelo" to emphasize his gimmick as a painter/fighter. Though Laurie clearly doesn't love her husband, she stays with him for

Just for a change of pace, Eve plays best pal to a man (Dane Clark) in *Whiplash*.

reasons that have to do with her brother, a doctor who has a serious drinking problem. Badly concussed after his fight with Rex's stooge, Mike nonetheless agrees to go forward with his championship match when Laurie's sadistic husband promises to release his hold on her if Mike wins.

Though Eve is most often remembered for playing the best friend of leading ladies in movies, here she performs a similar function for the leading man. She is featured as Chris Sherwood, Mike's neighbor who becomes his first friend in New York. Sympathetic to his unrequited love for another woman, she offers him an alternative he probably would have been wise to take: "Mike, look, I'm not exactly beautiful, but I am available. I'm kind to my mother, and I make very good spaghetti." (Ironically, she happens to look quite lovely as she's saying these self-deprecating lines.) Though the character of Chris is regrettably not central to the film, Eve continues to pop up periodically until the closing moments, and draws an occasional good line. When she encounters a battered Mike after one of his set-tos with Rex's henchmen, Chris looks him up and down and remarks, "Golly Moses, where do you want the remains sent?"

Brooklyn-born Dane Clark (1912–1998), a Warner Bros.' contract player since 1943, makes his only film with Eve here. Clark, born Bernie Zanville, was reportedly given his screen name by Humphrey Bogart, with whom he appeared in *Action in the North Atlantic* (1943). Clark aside, many of the remaining players were familiar faces to Eve. She's making her third film with Zachary Scott, and also with Alexis Smith, who co-starred with Eve in *The Doughgirls* (1944). Jeffrey Lynn, with whom Eve appeared in *A Child Is Born* almost a decade earlier, gets a meatier-than-usual role here as Laurie's alcoholic brother.

Maudie Prickett, the fine character actress seen often in TV sitcoms like *The Andy Griffith*

Show (1960–1968) and *Bewitched* (1964–1972), is unbilled for her brief appearance as Mrs. Gruman, the stern landlady who threatens to rent Mike's apartment out from under him when he is late with the rent. Eve's character handily disposes of the threat with her offhand remarks about the various rodents inhabiting the building. Ransom Sherman plays the uncouth Texas oil millionaire who is avidly courting Chris, who'd rather be with Mike. Coaching Dane Clark in his boxing moves was retired prizefighter Mushy Callahan, a champion fighter of the 1920s.

The *Los Angeles Times*'s Philip K. Scheuer thought *Whiplash* a bit dated, but admitted it wasn't dull, saying, "It is loaded with plot — so much so that toward the end one has the impression he is simultaneously viewing two or three movies of the past at once — and is performed with an enthusiasm that would have done justice collectively to all of them." Noting the many familiar members of the Warners' stock company playing "roles they could probably tear through without ever [having] consulted a script," Scheuer noted among them "Eve Arden as Eve Arden" (January 8, 1949).

My Dream Is Yours (1949)

Jack Carson (*Doug Blake*), Doris Day (*Martha Gibson*), Lee Bowman (*Gary Mitchell*), Adolphe Menjou (*Thomas Hutchins*), Eve Arden (*Vivian Martin*), S.Z. Sakall (*Felix Hofer*), Selena Royle (*Freda Hofer*), Edgar Kennedy (*Uncle Charlie*), Duncan Richardson (*Freddie Gibson*), Sheldon Leonard (*Grimes*), Franklin Pangborn (*Manager*), Paul Maxey (*Man at Club*), Sandra Gould (*Mildred*), Iris Adrian (*Peggy*), John Berkes (*Character Actor*), Ada Leonard (*Herself*), Frankie Carle (*Himself*)

Producer/Director: Michael Curtiz. *Screen Play:* Harry Kurnitz, Dane Lussier. *Adaptation:* Allen Rivkin, Laura Kerr. *Associate Producer:* George Amy. *Music:* Harry Warren. *Lyrics:* Ralph Blane. *Musical Director:* Ray Heindorf. *Directors of Photography:* Ernest Haller, Wilfred M. Cline. *Art Director:* Robert Haas. *Film Editor:* Folmar Blangsted. *Sound:* C.A. Riggs, David Forrest. *Dialogue Director:* W. Zolley Lerner. *Set Decorations:* Howard Winterbottom. *Second Unit & Montage Director:* David Curtiz. *Special Effects:* Edwin DuPar. *Wardrobe:* Milo Anderson. *Cartoon Sequence Director:* I. Freleng. *Technicolor Color Director:* Natalie Kalmus. *Associate:* Richard Mueller. *Musical Numbers Staging:* LeRoy Prinz. Warner Bros.; released April 16, 1949. Color; 101 minutes.

Singer Gary Mitchell, the popular star of radio's *Hour of Enchantment*, refuses to sign a new contract with his sponsor Mr. Hofer, leaving both the show and his longtime manager Doug Blake high and dry. In search of a new star, Doug goes to New York and discovers young Martha Gibson, a beautiful war widow with a young son. Bringing Martha to Hollywood, Doug does everything he can to win her a break in show business, but with no luck. Just as a discouraged Martha is ready to give up and return to New York, Doug realizes that he has been promoting her the wrong way, giving her novelty songs to perform when her real strength lies with romantic ballads.

On one of his last performances for Mr. Hofer's show, Gary turns up drunk, and Doug persuades the boss to let Martha perform in his place. Soon her talent has been recognized, and she is well on her way to stardom. Though Doug hopes to win Martha's love, and become stepfather to her son, she is entangled in a hopeless relationship with the unreliable and egotistical Gary instead.

My Dream Is Yours is a remake of the 1934 hit *Twenty Million Sweethearts*, in which the aspiring radio singer was a man, played by Dick Powell.

Eve has a sizable supporting role here as Vivian Martin, Doug's co-worker on *The Hour of Enchantment*. Once again, she's playing the highly competent professional woman, Technicolor photography accentuating her sharp wardrobe, with lots of green. (So as not to compete with star Doris Day, Eve's blonde hair was dyed red).

Financially more stable than Doug, Vi allows herself to be talked into investing in his plan to make Martha Gibson a star. Promised half of his business in exchange for her support, Vi agrees, saying to herself with a sigh, "Somehow I always knew he'd be giving me the business." She allows Martha and her little boy to move into her apartment. Later, when still more money is required to keep Martha's career afloat, Vi sees Doug hungrily eying her mink coat, on which she just made the last payment. Against her better judgment, Vi grudgingly comes through once

Doug Blake (Jack Carson) tries to sell another bill of goods to his friend Vivian Martin (Eve) in *My Dream Is Yours.*

more, saying, "If there's $50 left over from this deal, I'd like to have my head examined." Eve's scenes with Jack Carson have an energy that help keep this longish film entertaining.

Coming out of left field about an hour into the film is an Easter-themed dream sequence, in which Martha's little boy conjures up images of his mom and Doug cavorting with Bugs Bunny. The entire sequence, directed by the great Friz Freleng, is an odd intrusion into the musical comedy, though you haven't lived until you've seen Jack Carson in a bunny suit with giant floppy ears.

With both Jack Carson and Lee Bowman intrigued with the beautiful Doris Day (still in her mid-twenties), Eve has to settle for a few glances that come her way courtesy of 59-year-old Adolphe Menjou's character, Hutch. Menjou and Eve are making their third and last film together, more than ten years after *Letter of Introduction*.

My Dream Is Yours marked Eve's third collaboration with Michael Curtiz, who directed her Oscar-nominated performance in *Mildred Pierce*. She would work again with rising Warners star Doris Day in *Tea for Two* (1950), as she came into the home stretch of her Warners' contract. According to Sheilah Graham's syndicated column, Eve called in sick for one day of shooting on *My Dream Is Yours*, with a temperature of 103. Returning the next day, she still wasn't feeling well, and "had to stagger home again for two more days. 'I spent the time pricing quilted coffins,' cracks Eve, who is still feeling low but is back at work" (May 27, 1948).

Time wasn't overly impressed with the picture—"It has all been done before—frequently much better," but did enjoy Day's singing, and "some mildly astringent lines about radio advertising, mostly delivered by Eve Arden" (May 9, 1949). In a similar vein, John L. Scott, writing in the *Los Angeles Times*, thought the film's basic story trite and a bit shopworn, but found Doris Day a charmer who "really knows how to sell a tune," and added, "Eve Arden delights in her brittle comedy characterization" (April 16, 1949). Tom Santopietro, in his career study, *Considering Doris Day*, credits Eve with delivering the film's best performance: "Arden cuts through the idiocy of the screenplay with each well-timed bon mot and in the process delivers a master class in comic timing."

Also among those singing Eve's praises was the *Washington Post*'s Richard L. Coe, who considered the picture "a supremely dull achievement," but praised Eve's performance, adding: "And speaking of Eve, why is it that she, strikingly attractive, wittier and more human than other females in her pictures, is always pictured as lonely, unwanted, unsung? In real life, I'm sure, Eve is the belle of the ball" (April 18, 1949).

The Lady Takes a Sailor (1949)

Jane Wyman (*Jennifer Smith*), Dennis Morgan (*Bill Craig*), Eve Arden (*Susan Wayne*), Robert Douglas (*John Tyson*), Allyn Joslyn (*Ralph Whitcomb*), Tom Tully (*Henry Duckworth*), Lina Romay (*Raquel Riviera*), William Frawley (*Oliver Harker*), Frank Cady (*Mr. Wentworth*), Harry Cheshire (*Judge Varden*), Fred Clark (*Victor Santell*), Bob Jellison (*Mr. Crane*), Grandon Rhodes (*Dr. Newman*), Olan Soule (*Tyson's Assistant*), Ruth Lewis (*Miss Clark*), Dick Ryan (*Apartment House Clerk*)
Director: Michael Curtiz. *Producer:* Harry Kurnitz. *Screenplay:* Everett Freeman. *Story:* Jerry Gruskin. *Director of Photography:* Ted McCord. *Art Director:* Edward Carrere. *Film Editor:* David Weisbart. *Music:* Max

The Lady Takes a Sailor found Eve playing best friend to leading lady Jane Wyman (right), with Dennis Morgan the sailor in question.

Steiner. *Orchestrations:* Murray Cutter. *Sound:* Everett A. Brown. *Dialogue Director:* Norman Stuart. *Set Decorator:* George James Hopkins. *Special Effects:* Roy Davidson, H.F. Koenekamp. *Wardrobe:* Milo Anderson. *Makeup Artist:* Perc Westmore. Warner Bros.; released December 16, 1949. B&W; 99 minutes.

Jennifer Smith heads a nonprofit organization called the Buyers' Research Institute, which, as a tour guide tells visitors to the Institute, stands "as a bulwark between the consumer and inferior merchandise." Jennifer's public reputation has made the phrase "endorsed by Jennifer Smith" roughly equivalent to the Good Housekeeping Seal of Approval. With the help of her lawyer—and fiancé—Ralph Whitcomb, Jennifer is about to secure the future of her institute with major funding from the Tyson Foundation, whose board members have been impressed by her unstinting record for truth and integrity.

After receiving the happy news that she has been fully funded by the Tyson Foundation, Jennifer sets out for a beachside vacation on Long Island with her best friend, Susan Wayne. While relaxing on the ocean, Jennifer and her small craft are capsized by a strange man operating an experimental submarine. The man, who identifies himself only as "Davey Jones," takes Jennifer aboard to protect her from a brewing storm, keeping her below water in the submarine for several hours and doping her with sleeping pills to keep her calm. A worried Susan, afraid Jennifer has been lost at sea, reports her missing, launching a major search by the police and Coast Guard.

When a groggy Jennifer is found on the beach the next day, the story she tells of the night she spent occupying an experimental submarine in the Long Island Sound with Davey Jones, not to mention the giant octopus they spotted, sounds ludicrous, and newspaper reports play it to the hilt. Because her professional reputation is so centered on absolute truth, headlines like "Truth Girl Tells Big Fish Story" cause the Tyson Foundation to sever its relationship with Jennifer's institute.

Determined to prove the veracity of her story, Jennifer resolves to find the mysterious stranger, and the roll of film she shot during the overnight adventure. In reality, "Davey Jones" is actually Bill Craig, a submarine engineer working on a secret government project. While realizing he has inadvertently damaged Jennifer's reputation, he cannot compromise the security of his project by corroborating her wild story. A series of slapstick misadventures follows after Jennifer hires a detective to track down "Mr. Jones," and the two fight tooth and nail over possession of the incriminating film.

Eve is first-billed among the supporting cast of this amiable, slap-happy romantic comedy, originally announced under the working title of *The Octopus and Miss Smith*. Cast as Jane Wyman's best friend, Susan, she is once again the sensible, dry-witted career woman. Late in the film, when Jennifer has endured a series of wild escapades with Bill, leading everyone around her to question her sanity, the sound of an approaching ambulance siren causes Susan to advise her friend, "If a man gets out with a big net, don't struggle, just give yourself up quietly." Playing a businesswoman who heads a cosmetics company, Eve is impeccably coiffed and clothed, though her dialogue here isn't as sharp and witty as it has been in other recent films.

Also on hand is Eve's frequent co-star Allyn Joslyn, cast yet again as the slightly stuffy fiancé of the leading lady. Anyone who has seen his previous films won't rate highly his chances of making it to the altar with Wyman. Robert Douglas bears the brunt of the film's slapstick as John Tyson, dignified head of the foundation who finds himself caught in the middle of the war between Jennifer and Bill. Various scenes find him doused with water, served a pancake breakfast in his lap, and stripped to his underwear by Bill, who wrongly thinks he has the film canister. Tom Tully has a few funny moments as the incompetent detective Jennifer hires to find Bill. Though the gumshoe brags incessantly about his safecracking and lock-picking skills, he can't seem to get anything open. William Frawley of *I Love Lucy* fame has a funny bit as the president of the New York Liars' Club, who presents an insulting plaque to Jennifer Smith after her story hits the newspapers. A young and unknown Jack Lemmon plays a bit as a plasterer, while Warners' contract player Craig Stevens has an unbilled cameo as a newspaper reporter. Some recognizable character faces (Fred Clark, Frank Cady) turn up in unbilled small roles as well.

The reviewer for the *New York Times* welcomed the picture's broad physical comedy, and while noting that its strength did not lie primarily in dialogue, the "wonderfully caustic Eve Arden never falters when running with a quip" (December 17, 1949).

Paid in Full (1950)

Robert Cummings (*Bill Prentice*), Lizabeth Scott (*Jane Langley*), Diana Lynn (*Nancy Langley Prentice*), Eve Arden (*Tommy Thompson*), Ray Collins (*Dr. Fredericks*), Frank McHugh (*Ben*), Stanley Ridges (*Dr. P.J. Winston*), Louis Jean Heydt (*Dr. Carter*), John Bromfield (*Dr. Clark*), Kristine Miller (*Miss Williams*), Laura Elliot (*Tina*), Laura Lee Michel (*Betsy*), Ida Moore (*Dorothy*), James Nolan (*Charlie Malloy*), Rolland Morris (*Bunny Howard*), Geraldine Wall (*Miss Ames*), Margaret Field (*Joanne's Mother*), Jane Novak (*Mrs. Fredericks*)
Director: William Dieterle. *Producer:* Hal B. Wallis. *Screenplay:* Robert Blees, Charles Schnee, suggested by a *Reader's Digest* story by Frederick M. Loomis, M.D. *Director of Photography:* Leo Tover. *Art Direction:* Hans Dreier, Earl Hedrick. *Special Photographic Effects:* Gordon Jennings. *Process Photography:* Farciot Edouart. *Set Decoration:* Sam Comer, Bertram Granger. *Editor:* Warren Low. *Costumes:* Edith Head. *Makeup Supervisor:* Wally Westmore. *Assistant Director:* Richard McWhorter. *Sound Recording:* Gene Merritt, Walter Oberst. *Music Score:* Victor Young. *Song:* "You're Wonderful"; music, Victor Young, lyrics, Jay Livingston, Ray Evans, sung by Dean Martin. Paramount Pictures; released February 15, 1950. B&W; 98 minutes.

A pregnant woman using an assumed name collapses outside a hospital. The doctor summoned to treat her tells her that he can likely save either her or her baby, but not both. Unhesitatingly, she tells him, "My baby comes first.... Any future I have, my baby will live it for me."

Flashbacks reveal that the woman is Jane Langley, employed at Dorton's Department Store. Jane is in love with her co-worker, Bill, but he has fallen for her younger sister, Nancy, employed as a model at the store. Nancy, raised from childhood by her older sister, is a selfish young woman who doesn't really love Bill. Having made inquiries into his earning power, however, she decides he will make an adequate husband, and accepts his proposal. Believing that her sister is really in love with Bill, Jane hides her own feelings for him, and endeavors to be supportive of the marriage. Once they are married, however, Nancy finds married life disappointingly dull, as Bill spends many hours trying to further his career. At Jane's urging, Nancy gives Bill a daughter, Deborah, but the marriage is still shaky.

Too late, Bill, who's been asked for a divorce by Nancy, realizes that he actually loves Jane. However, Jane urges him to save his marriage for the sake of their daughter. A family tragedy leaves Jane feeling that she must make amends in the only way she can, leading to the final scenes in which she is reunited with the man she loves and her newly matured sister.

Originally announced under the title *Bitter Victory,* the film was ultimately released as *Paid in Full.* It is in some ways reminiscent of *Mildred Pierce,* not only for Eve's presence but because the relationship between Jane and her spoiled younger sister is not unlike that between Mildred and her ungrateful daughter Veda. Steeped in melodrama, the script and direction are effective in the early scenes, but careen dangerously close to parody in the later reels, as the story grows increasingly absurd and campy. Lizabeth Scott does her best with the role of heroic Jane, to which she's not particularly well suited. Diana Lynn's head-snapping performance as a mental patient who can no longer bear to have her sister's name spoken in her presence is likely to elicit snickers from all but the most forgiving viewers. Other scenes evoke laughs that they wouldn't have in 1950. Jane's repeated addressing of her family physician as "Dr. Phil" is good for a few giggles, as is the innocently intended but slightly icky scene in which camera bug Bill, on his honeymoon, shows his desire for a family by enthusiastically focusing his lens on a passing little girl at the hotel pool. By about the halfway point, *Paid in Full* is beginning to seem like a ripe target for one of those *Carol Burnett Show* skits in which Carol herself would have played unfortunate Jane, with Vicki Lawrence as nasty Nancy and Harvey Korman the clueless Bill.

Providing most of the intentional laughs in the film is, of course, Eve. Winning first billing among the supporting cast, her name in larger type than those of Ray Collins and others, Eve once again plays the supportive best friend and co-worker of the heroine. Not for the first time, she is given a mannish nickname ("Tommy"). Tommy, who's depicted as working hard to obtain her M.R.S., is involved with a commitment-shy man she refers to as "Perky," who doesn't appear onscreen. Though the role is one she could have done in her sleep by this point, she does get some good lines. Most prominent in the first half-hour of the film, Eve's role dwindles as the film progresses.

By the time *Paid in Full* hit theaters, Eve was beginning to acknowledge openly that she was tiring of the monotonous roles in which Warners' cast her. Interviewed by syndicated columnist Erskine Johnson, Eve claimed she had stopped counting how many leading ladies she had supported as the cheerful best friend. "When they throw Shirley Temple at me," she said, "I'm going to quit" (April 15, 1950).

Ray Collins, seen as the kindly doctor in the opening and closing sequences, is better known as Lt. Arthur Tragg on TV's *Perry Mason*. Young Paramount contract player Laura Elliot, who has little more than a bit here, would have her best film role in *Strangers on a Train* (1951) before changing her professional name to Kasey Rogers and winning featured TV roles in *Peyton Place* and *Bewitched*. Producer Hal B. Wallis, at this time grooming Dean Martin and Jerry Lewis for movie stardom, makes a romantic song sung by Martin (via a bar's jukebox) a key element in romantic scenes between Bill and Jane.

Time called *Paid in Full* "competently played" but "the kind of story that can be heard on the radio any afternoon" (March 6, 1950).

Curtain Call at Cactus Creek (1950)

Donald O'Connor (*Edward Timmons*), Gale Storm (*Julie Martin*), Walter Brennan (*Rimrock Thomas*), Vincent Price (*Tracy Holland*), Eve Arden (*Lily Martin*), Chick Chandler (*Ralph*), Joe Sawyer (*Jake*), Harry Shannon (*U.S. Marshal Clay*), Rex Lease (*Yellowstone*), I. Stanford Jolley (*Pecos*), Ferris Taylor (*Maxwell*)
Director: Charles Lamont. *Producer:* Robert Arthur. *Screenplay:* Howard Dimsdale. *Story:* Stanley Roberts, Howard Dimsdale. *Director of Photography:* Russell Metty. *Technicolor Color Consultant:* Robert Brower. *Art Direction:* Bernard Herzbrun, John F. DeCuir. *Set Decorations:* Russell A. Gausman, Ruby A. Levitt. *Sound:* Leslie I. Carey, Richard DeWeese. *Film Editor:* Frank Gross. *Dance Director:* Louis Da Pron. Universal-International Pictures; released May 25, 1950. Color; 86 minutes.

Old West bank robber Rimrock Thomas and his gang arrive in the town of Cactus Creek just as the citizens are looking forward excitedly to the upcoming performance by members of a traveling theater troupe, the Tracy Holland Repertory Company. Longtime leading man Tracy Holland is an egotistical, self-centered aging ham. Leading lady Lily Martin, that "great star of the New York stage," was a great beauty in her youth, and is now a cynical veteran who is the aunt to pretty ingénue Julie. Julie is in love with the company's lone stagehand, naïve, goodhearted young Edward Timmons, who does all the work behind the scenes while selfish Tracy refuses to give him the performing break he craves.

Bank robber Thomas figures that the Holland company's performance of "The Curse of Drink" provides the perfect distraction to keep everyone occupied while he knocks over the town bank. Unfortunately, when the two events coincide, the theatrical performance is thrown askew by the robbery, and both actors and bank robbers are run out of town on a rail. On the lam after the Cactus Creek robbery, Rimrock takes a job with the Holland company under an assumed name, hiding out with them while they travel to their next scheduled stop in Powder River. He soon learns that a federal marshal is on the trail of the Holland company, sure that another robbery will take place while they are in Powder River. Having successfully evaded Marshal Clay for the past several years, Rimrock defiantly takes the challenge of carrying off another robbery under the lawman's nose. Meanwhile, in his capacity as Edward's assistant, he gazes adoringly at Lily Martin, whom he has loved since seeing her picture in the *Police Gazette* some 15 years earlier, and helps Edward get his big break onstage. When the Powder River bank is successfully robbed, Edward is held accountable, and sentenced to hang, unless his new pal Rimrock Thomas intercedes.

As glamorous Lily Martin, Eve has the opportunity to perform a Cockney-accented novelty song and play a leading role in a *Drunkard*-type melodrama. She resurrects her *Doughgirls* Russian accent to play Catherine the Great in a funny seduction scene opposite Donald O'Connor's Eddie. In her first scene, she carries on a spirited exchange with Vincent Price's vain Tracy Holland:

> LILY: Tracy, you're a very romantic man. You're conducting one of the great love affairs of all time — with yourself.

Co-stars in *Curtain Call at Cactus Creek*, Eve (left) and Gale Storm went on to become two popular sitcom leading ladies in the early 1950s.

>   TRACY: That, coming from you—a second-rate music hall performer who never had any talent.
>   LILY: With what I had a few years ago, I didn't *need* any talent.

Curtain Call at Cactus Creek reunites Eve with her co-star from *Patrick the Great* (1945), who's top-billed here as the hapless but likable Edward. O'Connor's tireless energy is given a good workout in the amusing scenes showing Edward rushing around during the troupe's performance, as he is solely responsible for providing the show's sound effects, music, props, special effects, and the star's costume changes. It's interesting to see Eve here alongside B-movie queen Gale Storm (1922–2009), only two years before both would achieve TV sitcom stardom (with *Our Miss Brooks* and *My Little Margie*, respectively). Not far behind in the switch to television would be Walter Brennan, whose situation comedy *The Real McCoys* (1957–1963) would enjoy a long and profitable run. Speaking of TV players, character actor Paul Maxey, later a featured player on *The People's Choice* (1955–1958), is unbilled for his small role as the banker of Powder River.

All and sundry are directed here by the workhorse Charles Lamont (1895–1993), who would spend much of the next decade helming entries in Universal's bread-and-butter items like Ma and Pa Kettle, Francis the Talking Mule, and the later, lesser films of Abbott and Costello. Lamont had previously directed Eve in *San Antonio Rose* (1941). Principal photography on the film was completed in early 1949, though the film wouldn't go into general release until the following year.

"All's Riot on the Western Front!" promised Universal's ads for this amiable comedy, which produced mostly mild reviews. *Variety* gave Eve a slightly backhanded compliment for her work in the film, saying she "is well cast as the passé thesper [and] capably warbles 'Waiting at the Church.'" The trade paper found *Cactus Creek* overall "slick entertainment ... tailored to the family trade" (May 24, 1950). Less impressed was the *New York Times*'s Bosley Crowther, who recommended the film primarily to fans of Donald O'Connor, and wrote, "The best to be said for this picture is that it has a few bright burlesque spots, is in color, and comes to a finish in a reasonable length of time" (September 22, 1950).

Tea for Two (1950)

Doris Day (*Nanette Carter*), Gordon MacRae (*Jimmy Smith*), Gene Nelson (*Tommy Trainor*), Eve Arden (*Pauline Hastings*), Billy De Wolfe (*Larry Blair*), S.Z. Sakall (*J. Maxwell Bloomhaus*), Bill Goodwin (*William Early*), Patrice Wymore (*Beatrice Darcy*), Virginia Gibson (*Mabel Wiley*), Elinor Donahue (*Lynne Smith*), Crauford Kent (*Stevens*), Johnny McGovern (*Richard Smith*)
Director: David Butler. *Producer:* William Jacobs. *Screenplay:* Harry Clork. *Musical Direction:* Ray Heindorf. *Musical Numbers Director:* LeRoy Prinz. *Dances Staged by* Eddie Prinz, Al White. *Director of Photography:* Wilfrid M. Cline. *Art Director:* Douglas Bacon. *Film Editor:* Irene Morra. *Sound:* Dolph Thomas, David Forrest. *Set Decorator:* Lyle B. Reifsnider. *Wardrobe:* Leah Rhodes. *Technical Color Consultant:* Mitchell Kovaleski. Warner Bros.-First National Pictures; released September 2, 1950. Color; 98 minutes.

Aspiring singer-actress Nanette Carter, a wealthy heiress, is persuaded to invest $25,000 in a Broadway-bound musical in which she will play the lead. Although it's 1929, and the stock market has just crashed, Nanette believes her uncle has safely invested her fortune in government bonds. Unable to tell her that her financial situation is too precarious to allow the investment,

Eve (at right) looks on dubiously as Billy De Wolfe sweet-talks Doris Day in *Tea for Two*.

Nanette's Uncle Max instead tries to dissuade her by making a bet. In order for him to approve the expenditure, she must say "no" to everything she is asked for a 48-hour period. Assigned to keep her company everywhere she goes, and see whether she keeps the bargain, is Nanette's friend and secretary, Pauline.

Sure that she can win the bet, Nanette hosts the cast and crew of the Broadway musical at her estate over the weekend while the bet plays out. Unfortunately, the requirement of saying "no" regardless of the question causes problems for Nanette's burgeoning romance with the show's songwriter, Jimmy. When Nan ultimately emerges victorious despite the havoc it creates, Uncle Max's stuffy attorney, Mr. Early, is forced to break the news of her financial insolvency. Realizing that Mr. Early is far too conservative to have overextended himself in the stock market, Pauline plots to charm him into financing the show that is finally called *No, No, Nanette*.

Tea for Two is a *very* loose remake of *No, No, Nanette*, previously filmed in 1930 and 1940. Though the plot of *Tea for Two* bears almost no resemblance to the original, Eve does play a character with the same name as ZaSu Pitts's comic maid in the 1940 version of *Nanette*.

Coming into the home stretch of her seven-year contract with Warners, Eve supports young leading lady Doris Day for the second time. Eve's astringent wit nicely balances Day's youthful charm and innocence, making them a winning team. Fond of sweet, slightly naïve Nan, Eve's character, Pauline, nonetheless says, "You don't need a secretary, you need a keeper." Of Nan's seemingly silly bet with her uncle, Pauline cracks, "If I'd said yes and no in the right places, I'd be wearing mink."

Eve also plays effectively opposite Day's frequent co-star Billy De Wolfe, cast here as Larry Blair, the smarmy, dishonest producer of the musical show. "What this character won't do for a dime!" she says disgustedly of De Wolfe's character. Her first entrance in the film finds her displeased to find the sleazy producer on her boss's doorstep:

> PAULINE (opening the door to Blair): Well, as I live and try not to breathe, Larry Blair.
> BLAIR: Still don't like me, eh?
> PAULINE: That wins you the honeymoon to Burma and the home in fashionable Hell's Kitchen.
> BLAIR: Never mind the *bon mots*. I want to see Nanette.
> PAULINE: I believe she was vaccinated against you. I'll see if it took.

For most of the film's running time, this seems to be yet another role casting Eve as the sexless secretary of the heroine. (When Nan, sharing a room with Pauline for the night, says, "Put out the light," her secretary says, "Why does a *girl* always say that to me?") But in the closing reel, it is Pauline whose charm comes to the rescue, not only saving the day but winning her a well-heeled husband.

Elinor Donahue, who would spend much of the 1950s playing Betty "Princess" Anderson on *Father Knows Best*, appears unbilled as the teenage daughter of Nan and Jimmy, seen in the flash-forward sequences that bookend the film's main story. "Cuddles" Sakall is almost unbearably cutesy as Day's uncle. Bill Goodwin, cast as the lawyer who takes a shine to Eve's character, was the longtime announcer of Burns and Allen's shows on radio and in the early television years. He later played another romantic interest for Eve in two guest appearances on her 1957–58 TV sitcom, *The Eve Arden Show*.

John L. Scott, in the *Los Angeles Times* called *Tea for Two* "a charming piece of musical froth," noting that both Eve and Billy de Wolfe did well in roles tailored to their familiar screen personas (September 2, 1950).

Three Husbands (1951)

Emlyn Williams (*Maxwell Bard*), Eve Arden (*Lucille McCabe*), Howard da Silva (*Dan McCabe*), Shepperd Strudwick (*Arthur Evans*), Ruth Warrick (*Jane Evans*), Vanessa Brown (*Mary Whittaker*), Robert Karnes (*Kenneth Whittaker*), Billie Burke (*Jenny Bard Whittaker*), Louise Erickson (*Matilda Clegg*), Jonathan Hale (*Edward Wurdeman*), Jane Darwell (*Mrs. Wurdeman*)

A trio of married couples—and one interloper—makes up the primary cast of *Three Husbands* (left to right): Robert Karnes, Vanessa Brown, Shepperd Strudwick, Ruth Warrick, Emlyn Williams, Howard da Silva, and Eve.

Director: Irving Reis. *Producer:* I.G. Goldsmith. *Screenplay:* Vera Caspary, Edward Eliscu. *Story:* Vera Caspary. *Director of Photography:* Frank Planer. *Production Designer:* Rudolph Sternad. *Music:* Herschel Burke Gilbert. *Song:* "Poor Chap," music, Herschel Burke Gilbert; lyric, Edward Eliscu. *Orchestrations:* Joseph Mullendore. *Production Supervisor:* Ben Hersh. *Film Editor:* Louis H. Sackin. *Set Decorations:* Edward G. Boyle. *Sound Recording:* Leon Becker, Mac Dalgleish. *Assistant Director:* Emmett Emerson. Gloria Film Productions; a United Artists release. B&W; 78 minutes.

Newly arrived in Heaven, suave and sophisticated Maxwell Bard asks permission to look down on Earth and follow the lives of his closest friends for the next 24 hours. Bard has directed his attorney, Mr. Wurdeman, to deliver a confidential letter to each of his three closest male friends. Arthur Evans, the first of three to receive the missive, is shocked to read the letter, which begins: "Conscience impels me to write this. After years of friendship, I feel it my duty to make a confession. Your wife and I...." (The remainder of the text is never read or shown in the film, leaving the exact wording of Bard's confession unspecified.) Evans rushes home to confront his wife, while young Kenneth Whittaker becomes the second husband to receive such a note. After delivering the shocking news to the first two men, Mr. Wurdeman hands a similar letter to middle-aged, rough-hewn Dan McCabe. Unlike the other men, McCabe refuses to take the "confession" seriously, saying, "I can smell a gag ten miles away, and that's what this is."

Flashbacks, however, reveal that each of three wives in question enjoyed a warm friendship with the late Mr. Bard. A well-to-do Britisher, he lived a luxurious life in which he frequently enjoyed feminine companionship, though within certain guidelines: "I love women far too much to make wives of them," he said. To sophisticated Jane Evans, he was her favorite companion for an evening at the theater or the symphony, one who tries to prevent her from learning that her husband has a girlfriend on the side. For young wife Mary Whittaker, married only two years,

Max Bard was the patient she nursed through four heart attacks, and a good friend to her when she tires of the way her weak-willed husband lets his mother dominate their lives.

Lucille McCabe (Eve's character) is a plain-spoken, down-to-earth woman from humble stock who has changed little despite the financial successes that her husband's business has brought them. Dan would like his wife, who enjoys drinking beer, betting on horses, and snacking on all her favorite foods, to develop a tonier demeanor in keeping with their new circumstances. He suggests that she do as other well-placed wives do, and join committees, but she demurs: "Not me. My mother was scared by a committee."

Lucille turns to Max, who readily helps her select a fancier wardrobe, and teaches her French, but enjoys her uncomplicated nature in a way that her husband can't seem to do. Her pride is hurt when her husband considers Max's "confession" nothing more than a big joke, and she refuses to confirm that she and Max were just friends.

Called to the lawyer's office the following day for the reading of the will, the three wives are thrilled to learn that the bulk of Max's sizable estate has been divided among the three of them. Rendered financially independent by this revelation, the three friends now realize they can choose to reconcile with her husbands—or not. A final coda to Max's will reassures their husbands that the story of having an affair was not true, that he simply wanted them to better appreciate their wives.

The only one of the lead actresses to be billed above the title, Eve gives the most interesting performance of the three. Ruth Warrick, still playing the kind of flawless-but-rather brittle wife she first essayed in *Citizen Kane* (RKO, 1941), shows little sign of the more interesting persona she will develop in later years as one of the founding stars of the daytime soap opera *All My Children*. Vanessa Brown's performance as young wife Mary is competent but unremarkable. Howard da Silva, cast as Eve's husband, is making one of his last film appearances before his listing in *Red Channels* would have him blacklisted from the motion picture industry for more than ten years.

Two familiar sitcom faces appear in brief, uncredited roles. Character actor Jerry Hausner, seen in a recurring role as Ricky Ricardo's agent Jerry in the early years of *I Love Lucy*, plays a bartender who advises Ken Whittaker to solve the dispute with his fist, while Frank Cady (*Green Acres*'s Sam Drucker) is the elevator operator in the office building where the lawyers work.

The basic structure and setup of *Three Husbands* clearly derive from the 1949 film *A Letter to Three Wives*, whose scenarist, Vera Caspary (married to producer I.G. Goldsmith), also wrote this independent film. The obvious connection irked executives at 20th Century–Fox, whose protests forced producer Goldsmith to enter into arbitration to resolve his right to proceed with *Three Husbands*. Caspary told the *New York Times*'s Thomas F. Brady that she conceived the film to balance out "the terrible overemphasis on male infidelity in the women's magazines" (March 26, 1950). *Three Husbands* takes a more humorous stance on the scenario, though the out-and-out laughs are few. The flashbacks take up the bulk of the running time, roughly dividing the film into thirds. Eve's second-billed role as Lucille McCabe comes into focus in the film's last half-hour. As recorded in her autobiography, she enjoyed the opportunity to play this uncharacteristic role.

The *New York Times* thought the film seriously outclassed by its predecessor, *A Letter to Three Wives*, and "chucklesome only in spots," but did think Eve's segment with Howard da Silva the best of the lot (March 9, 1951).

Goodbye, My Fancy (1951)

Joan Crawford (*Agatha Reed*), Robert Young (*Dr. James Merrill*), Frank Lovejoy (*Matt Cole*), Eve Arden (*Woody*), Janice Rule (*Virginia Merrill*), Lurene Tuttle (*Ellen Griswold*), Howard St. John (*Claude Griswold*), Viola Roache (*Miss Shackelford*), Ellen Corby (*Miss Birdshaw*), Morgan Farley (*Dr. Pitt*), Virginia Gibson (*Mary Nell Dodge*), John Qualen (*Prof. Dingley*), Ann Robinson (*Clarice Carter*), John Alvin (*Jack White*), Bill McLean (*Russ Hughes*)

Director: Vincent Sherman. *Producer:* Henry Blanke. *Screenplay:* Ivan Goff, Ben Roberts, based on the play by Fay Kanin. *Director of Photography:* Ted McCord. *Musical Direction:* Ray Heindorf. *Art Director:* Stanley

Six years after *Mildred Pierce*, Eve (right) supported Joan Crawford again in *Goodbye, My Fancy*.

Fleischer. *Film Editor:* Rudi Fehr. *Sound:* Charles Lang. *Set Decorator:* G.W. Berntsen. *Wardrobe:* Sheila O'Brien. *Makeup Artist:* Gordon Bau. Warner Bros.-First National Pictures; released May 19, 1951. B&W; 107 minutes.

    Congresswoman Agatha Reed is pleased to be offered an honorary degree by Good Hope College, a school she once attended. The event reunites her with two men who were very important to her in the past — college president, Dr. James Merrill, who taught history when Agatha was a student 20 years earlier, and *Life* magazine photographer, Matt Cole, with whom Agatha was romantically involved several years earlier. Only after the invitation to accept the honorary degree is extended, and accepted, does the chair of the school's board of trustees, Claude Griswold, learn that Agatha was actually expelled from the school for being out all night with a man. Dr. Merrill tells the angry Griswold that the special commencement ceremony is Good Hope's opportunity to make amends to Miss Reed for an old wrong.

    With her pragmatic secretary, Woody, in tow, Agatha arrives at Good Hope, and is overcome with nostalgia as she is housed in the same dormitory she used years earlier. No one now at Good Hope knows that the man with whom Agatha was involved 20 years earlier was Dr. Merrill himself, whom she protected so as to save his academic career. Dr. Merrill, now a widower, proposes to Agatha all over again, and she happily accepts. But both Woody and Agatha's ex-boyfriend, Matt, believe that the marriage would be a mistake, and that Agatha is in love with a memory, not the man himself. Over the course of the weekend, Agatha realizes that Good Hope is in the midst of a battle for academic freedom. Many believe Dr. Merrill too weak to stand up to the conservative Claude Griswold, having "long ago given up battles in exchange for buildings." Matters come to a head when Griswold refuses to permit the scheduled showing of *Command to the Future,* a documentary made by Agatha that details the dangers of curtailing access to information and open debate.

Goodbye, My Fancy was based on the play of the same name that had a successful Broadway run of more than a year, beginning in the fall of 1948. The stage production originally starred Madeleine Carroll (later replaced by Ruth Hussey) as Agatha Reed, Conrad Nagel and Sam Wanamaker in the male leads, and Shirley Booth (1898–1992) as Woody. This was, of course, not the first time that the careers of Eve and Shirley Booth had intersected, as Miss Booth had been originally been cast as Connie Brooks in the audition show for radio's *Our Miss Brooks*. Booth won a Best Supporting Actress Tony for the role of Woody. According to the play, Woody's full name is Grace Woods, but the first name is never heard in the film.

When Warners purchased the film rights to Fay Kanin's hit play, it must have seemed a no-brainer to cast contract player Eve as the sardonic but caring secretary to Joan Crawford's congresswoman character. As Agatha Reed says of her valued but outspoken assistant, "You mustn't mind Woody. Her mind's always on the tip of her tongue." Endlessly patient, Woody does whatever task is needed of her, including calling *Life* magazine founder Henry Luce to demand that Matt Cole not cover the commencement ceremony. (Reaching the media giant by phone after tracking him halfway across the country, only to realize that it's too late to prevent Cole's arrival, Woody says coolly, "Mr. Luce? You'll be delighted to know we're renewing our subscription," hanging up the receiver with a clatter.) In one of the best bits of dialogue transferred from play to screenplay, cynical Woody can't quite figure out why her boss is so taken with the idea of revisiting her youth, saying, "I don't believe in looking at the past. I was born in Newark, New Jersey. Every time I go through on a train, I pull down the shade."

The *Los Angeles Times*'s Edwin Schallert found *Goodbye, My Fancy* "mixes rather good romantic and dramatic values, and is on the upper level as a starring vehicle for Joan Crawford." Of Eve, he noted, "Miss Arden is sharply amusing" (May 12, 1951). Less impressed was the *New York Times*'s Bosley Crowther, who found the film's supporting characters "nimble and limpid creations that might easily be taken for caricatures.... The lady's secretary, whom Eve Arden angularly performs, is a perfectly packaged wisecracker right out of the glittering Broadway bin" (May 30, 1951).

Like some of Eve's previous films, *Goodbye, My Fancy* was adapted for the popular radio show *The Lux Radio Theatre*, but she did not reprise her role of Woody, though the show was done in 1952 and again in 1954. Both times, radio actress Joan Banks played Woody, supporting first Barbara Stanwyck and later Rosalind Russell in Crawford's role of Agatha Reed.

This was Eve's final role under the terms of her seven-year contract with Warners. From this point forward, her film work would become more sporadic, as she began to concentrate her attentions on her burgeoning television career, as well as her stage work.

We're Not Married! (1952)

Ginger Rogers (*Ramona Gladwyn*), Fred Allen (*Steve Gladwyn*), Victor Moore (*Justice of the Peace Melvin Bush*), Marilyn Monroe (*Annabel Jones Norris*), David Wayne (*Jeff Norris*), Eve Arden (*Katie Woodruff*), Paul Douglas (*Hector Woodruff*), Eddie Bracken (*Willie Reynolds*), Mitzi Gaynor (*Patsy Reynolds*), Louis Calhern (*Frederic Melrose*), Zsa Zsa Gabor (*Eve Melrose*), James Gleason (*Duffy*), Paul Stewart (*Mr. Stone*), Jane Darwell (*Mrs. Bush*)
Director: Edmund Goulding. *Producer/Screenplay:* Nunnally Johnson. *Adaptation:* Dwight Taylor. *Story:* Gina Kaus, Jay Dratler. *Music:* Cyril Mockridge. *Director of Photography:* Leo Tover. *Art Direction:* Lyle Wheeler, Leland Fuller. *Set Decorations:* Thomas Little, Claude Carpenter. *Film Editor:* Louis Loeffler. *Wardrobe Direction:* Charles LeMaire. *Costume Design:* Elois Jenssen. *Musical Direction:* Lionel Newman. *Orchestration:* Bernard Mayers. *Makeup Artist:* Ben Nye. *Special Photographic Effects:* Ray Kellogg. *Sound:* W.D. Flick, Roger Heman. 20th Century–Fox; released July 11, 1952. B&W; 86 minutes.

Newly appointed small-town justice of the peace Melvin Bush performs his first marriage ceremony on Christmas Eve, tying the knot for two radio performers whose union will help them win a lucrative contract for a "Mr. and Mrs." breakfast show. Over the next week, Bush performs a total of six ceremonies. Not until two-and-a-half years later does he discover that he jumped the gun, that his appointment didn't take effect until the first day of the new year. Consequently, the governor's office is obliged to send a letter to the couples involved, telling them that their marriages are invalid. As Bush and his wife think back on the couples he married between December 24 and December 31, he says, "When these people get that letter from the governor, they'll have a choice that other people never get. Now if they like each other, all they got to do is say yes again. If they don't, well, it's all over and that's the end of it."

Steve and Ramona Gladwyn are earning $5,000 a week as the lovey-dovey co-hosts of radio's *Breakfast with the Glad Gladwyns*. Off mike, Steve and Ramona are married in name only, barely able to tolerate each other when they aren't reading from a script. Acerbic Steve is delighted to receive the letter telling him his marriage to Ramona is invalid, until his producer warns him that their radio career hinges on their legally being man and wife.

The governor's letter arrives at a critical turning point in the lives of several other couples as well. Among them are the Norrises, whose marriage is imperiled by Annabel's burgeoning career as a beauty pageant winner, which is currently taking precedent over her home life, husband, and young son. For young soldier Willie Reynolds, declaring his marriage to Patsy null and void threatens to leave her an illegitimate mother if they can't find the chance to repeat their vows before he's shipped out. And for wealthy socialite Eve Melrose, the news comes just as she is putting into place a lucrative plan to divorce her nice-guy husband and take him for everything he's got.

Eve Arden plays middle-aged wife Katie Woodruff. Although JP Bush remembers the Woodruffs as "that gabby couple that came down from New York. Talk, talk, talk all the time, nothing but talk," they have now settled into a comfortable, rather dull married life. Sitting around home on a quiet evening, they have little to say, other than to make noncommittal remarks about the weather, or this month's selection from the Book-of-the-Month Club. Hector, who thoroughly enjoyed his time as a swinging bachelor before settling down with Katie, opens the letter from the governor. Immediately, the idea of having his marriage eradicated causes him to think back on the happy days when he was out with a different girl every night. But after a few moments of fantasizing, he destroys the letter and decides to maintain his steady life with Katie.

What's the proper response when a middle-aged married couple, Eve and Paul Douglas, finds out *We're Not Married!*

Though *We're Not Married!* is pleasant, enjoyable entertainment, it's a bit of a letdown for an Eve Arden fan. Eve's segment with Paul Douglas runs for less than ten minutes; her best lines come when she brings him down to earth from his happy reverie with some less-than-flattering descriptions of his old girlfriends—Barbara ("that girl with those wonderful big gums") and Francesca ("that fat one you picked up at a bus stop ... looked like a bag full of watermelons"). After that, she's seen only in a brief, wordless closing segment that shows them, along with several other couples, having a second wedding ceremony. Her brief time onscreen limits her ability to develop a fleshed-out character, and little of her dialogue is memorable.

Better-served by Nunnally Johnson's hit-and-miss screenplay are Ginger Rogers and Fred Allen as the bickering radio stars, the Gladwyns. In the studio just before airtime, the acrimony between the Gladwyns is so intense that their producer asks if they can't fight at home instead, but Steve explains, "We can't fight at home. We don't speak there." Their syrupy program is sponsored by an array of dubious products, of which Steve says, "With all this muck we're peddling, Mrs. Gruesome and I are going to end up in electric loveseats yet." Aside from a breakfast food of questionable virtue ("Is his widow still kicking up a fuss?" Steve asks about one hapless user), their other sponsors include a daily newspaper, the *Morning Record,* which proudly boasts "32 columnists, 28 pages of comics, and no news." While Ginger Rogers is effective as the cynical Mrs. Gladwyn, it's also a role that would have been right up Eve's alley. Also effective is the sequence in which golddigging Zsa Zsa Gabor gets a well-deserved comeuppance from her seemingly meek husband.

During production of *We're Not Married!* Fred Allen told syndicated columnist Bob Thomas that it would be his last film appearance: "I was never any good in pictures, and I never really had pictures written for me" (January 6, 1952). However, he did play a role in another Fox ensemble piece, *O. Henry's Full House* (1952), before his untimely death of a heart attack in 1956.

A few more recognizable faces turn up in unbilled bit parts. Jester Hairston *(Amos 'n' Andy, Amen)* is seen as the leader of a group of carolers singing "Silent Night," Byron Foulger appears as the clerk who issues a marriage license to Willie and Patsy Reynolds, and Gloria Talbott *(I Married a Monster from Outer Space)* is one of the pretty girls in Hector Woodruff's fantasy sequence.

We're Not Married! filmed in late 1951 and early 1952, was in wide release across the country during the summer of 1952, just before Eve made her debut in the television version of *Our Miss Brooks.* Fox publicity termed the picture "The Merriest Marital Mix-Up of All Time!" Reviews were generally favorable, with the *New York Times*'s Bosley Crowther terming *We're Not Married* "a tailored entertainment that is one of the snappiest of the year" (July 12, 1952). *Life* called it "the brightest spot in a sad cinematic summer" (July 28, 1952).

The Lady Wants Mink (1953)

Dennis O'Keefe *(Jim Connors),* Ruth Hussey *(Nora Connors),* Eve Arden *(Gladys Jones),* William Demarest *(Harvey Jones),* Gene Lockhart *(Mr. Heggie),* Hope Emerson *(Mrs. Hoxie),* Hillary Brooke *(Evelyn Cantrell),* Tommy Rettig *(Richie Connors),* Earl Robie *(Sandy Connors),* Mary Field *(Janie),* Isabel Randolph *(Mrs. Frazier),* Thomas Browne Henry *(Mr. Swiss),* Brad Johnson *(Bud Dunn),* Mara Corday *(Model),* Robert Shayne *(Cecil),* Jean Fenwick *(Faye),* Jean Vachon *(Doris),* Vicki Raaf *(Daisy),* Mary Alan Hokanson *(Marian),* Barbara Billingsley *(Peggy),* Frank Gerstle *(Jim's Co-Worker),* Bobby Diamond *(Melvin Potts),* Angela Greene *(Marge),* Rodney Bell *(Dave)*
Director/Associate Producer: William A. Seiter. *Screenplay:* Dane Lussier, Richard Alan Simmons. *Story:* Leonard Neubauer, Lou Schor. *Director of Photography:* Reggie Lanning. *Art Director:* Martin Obzina. *Music:* Stanley Wilson. *Assistant Director:* Lee William Lukather. *Sound:* Earl Crain, Sr., Howard Wilson. *Costume Supervisor:* Adele Palmer. *Set Decorations:* John McCarthy, Jr., Otto Siegel. *Film Editor:* Fred Allen. *Special Effects:* Howard & Theodore Lydecker. *Makeup Supervisor:* Bob Mark. *Hair Stylist:* Peggy Gray. *Technical Advisor:* Elizabeth K. Parsons. Republic Pictures; released March 30, 1953. Color, 92 minutes.

Young husband Jim Connors, employed in the credit department at Danfield's Department Store, gives his wife Nora a $79.50 camel's hair coat for her birthday. Though Nora tells her husband she loves the coat, Jim can't help feeling upstaged when he sees the $7,000 mink coat their friend and neighbor Gladys Jones is sporting. Gladys's husband, Harvey, is far more successful in business than Jim, being the well-to-do proprietor of Crazy Harvey's used car lot.

Jim wants to provide a more lavish lifestyle for Nora and their two sons, but he lacks the killer instinct to advance in the corporate world. Having difficulty displaying the "calculated aggression" his boss, Mr. Heggie, wants, Jim either fails to collect overdue bills from customers, or inadvertently insults important ones. When Gladys makes a joke about Nora raising mink so that she can have a fur coat of her own, the younger woman calls her bluff. Visiting mink rancher Mrs. Hoxie, Nora purchases a starter set of one male mink (for $150) and three females (for $75 each). She's told that, within three years, she can breed enough mink to have her own coat. Despite Jim's skepticism, Nora begins her breeding operation in their suburban backyard, resulting in visits from the Zoning Commission, the annoyance of neighbors, and, finally, their eviction

It's obvious that *The Lady Wants Mink*—but this one is only borrowed. Pictured (left to right) are Ruth Hussey, Eve, and Dennis O'Keefe.

from the house. Wrongly believing that Gladys reported her zoning infraction after they'd had a quarrel, Nora moves away with their friendship in tatters.

Since Jim has just been fired from his department store job, and doesn't make a successful used-car salesman, Nora decides they should relocate to the country and become full-time mink breeders. Though Jim initially rebels at the broken-down farmhouse she purchases on an impulse, they eventually settle in and realize they are quite happy raising their family out of the suburban scene. A birthday visit to the farmhouse from Harvey and Gladys Jones leads to a happy fadeout for all concerned.

Though this is a very pleasant, enjoyable comedy, it is really only secondarily about a woman's desire for a fur coat. Nora makes it plain from the first time the subject is raised that her happy home life and her family are more important to her than a mink coat, though she'd enjoy having one. Eve's character, Gladys, is infatuated with her new coat, but is also a childless woman who envies Nora's family. While there are a few brief scenes depicting incidents in which Jim is bitten by one of the minks, there is little effort to mine the kind of broad comedy Lucy Ricardo might have made of mink ranching. Not surprisingly, given the era in which the film was made, the idea of killing animals for fur coats is treated matter-of-factly here, though the scriptwriters don't dwell on the inevitable outcome of raising livestock for their skins.

The underlying theme is really the conformity and competition of life in the suburbs. There's a reference made to "keeping up with the Joneses," and in this film it's quite literal. Eve and William Demarest (1892–1983) play the Connors' next-door neighbors and best friends Harvey and Gladys Jones, a well-to-do middle-aged couple. His business venture has left them very well-fixed financially, and able to enjoy the finer things in life, though it's implied that he has profited from people's financial naïveté and greed.

Though Eve is almost exactly the same age as leading man Dennis O'Keefe (both were in their mid–40s at the time of the film's release), she is paired here not with him but with character actor William Demarest, 16 years her senior. She's very funny as the plain-spoken, somewhat domineering wife whose easygoing husband usually defers to her. When Harvey tactlessly brings up the expensive fur coat in front of Jim, Gladys lets him have it with both barrels, deriding "that large mouth of yours. Not that I mind your opening it, it's all those stupid words that come out of it when you do." Annoyed by his *faux pas,* Gladys says, "Just for that, I *will* cook dinner for you. Come on in and help with the can opener." In Eve's capable hands, the potentially harsh character is still quite endearing, and William Demarest's Harvey occasionally gets off a mild reply, as when she complains that he never listens to her. "I heard you when you said 'mink,' didn't I?" he dryly responds.

Interestingly, Eve misremembered the time period when she made this film when it came time to pen her autobiography, her chronology suggesting that she made it in the early 1960s. Actually, this is very easily identified as an artifact of its era (1953), as the script is replete with references to such matters as the encroachment of television on family life (Jim complains that he never has a conversation with his children anymore, because they are too absorbed in "Kukla, Fran, and Uncle Miltie."). Lots of early TV faces are along for the ride as well, not only Eve but also Hillary Brooke (*My Little Margie*), Tommy Rettig (a year or so before he became the juvenile star of *Lassie*), and Isabel Randolph, who would turn up a few years later in a recurring role on *Our Miss Brooks*. Given the film's emphasis on 1950s suburbia, it's particularly appropriate that we catch a glimpse of Barbara Billingsley (TV's June Cleaver), who has an unbilled bit as one of the birthday party guests oohing and aahing over Gladys's mink. Mary Field, seen occasionally on *Topper,* is good in a small role as one of Jim's co-workers, though director Seiter clearly wasn't watching her when she did a very unconvincing "startled" reaction in a scene where Jim pulls the chair out from under his boss and makes him fall.

Beautiful actress/model Mara Corday (born 1930), soon to become a starlet at Universal-International and the scream queen of monster movies like *Tarantula* (1955) and *The Deadly Claw* (1957), has a bit as a store model who shows off the coat Jim buys for his wife. She also shows off the bathing suit she's wearing underneath, providing a fairly gratuitous bit of cheesecake that the screenwriters do their best to justify ("I was modeling swimsuits when they sent me up here," she explains).

The *New York Times* termed it "a harmless but slapdash family comedy," adding that it was "bolstered by the surefire histrionics of four of the best supporting players in Hollywood"—in addition to Eve, William Demarest, Hope Emerson, and Gene Lockhart (April 6, 1953). *Variety* reacted similarly, terming it "a passable little domestic comedy," but noting that the actors "have to depend on frantic antics to get what laughs there are to be found in the screenplay" (March 25, 1953).

Our Miss Brooks (1956)

Eve Arden (*Constance Brooks*), Gale Gordon (*Osgood Conklin*), Don Porter (*Lawrence Nolan*), Robert Rockwell (*Philip Boynton*), Jane Morgan (*Margaret Davis*), Richard Crenna (*Walter Denton*), Nick Adams (*Gary Nolan*), Leonard Smith (*Fabian "Stretch" Snodgrass*), Gloria McMillan (*Harriet Conklin*), Joe Kearns (*Mr. Stone*), William Newell (*Dr. Henley*), Philip Van Zandt (*Mr. Webster*), Marjorie Bennett (*Mrs. Boynton*) Director: Al Lewis. Producer: David Weisbart. Screenplay: Al Lewis, Joseph Quillan, from an idea by Robert Mann. Director of Photography: Joe LaShelle. Art Director: Leo K. Kuter. Film Editor: Frederick Y. Smith. Sound: Francis Stahl. Set Decorator: William Wallace. Makeup Supervisor: Gordon Bau. Music: Roy Webb. Orchestrations: Gus Levene. Assistant Director: Ralph Slosser. Warner Bros.; released April 24, 1956. B&W; 85 minutes.

Connie Brooks arrives to take up her job as English teacher at Madison High School and immediately falls for shy biology teacher Philip Boynton. As a teacher, Connie's biggest challenge is Gary Nolan, a bright student who isn't applying himself in her classroom. Summoned for a conference by Gary's wealthy father, newspaper publisher Lawrence Nolan, Connie agrees to tutor the boy after school.

Along with her extracurricular tutoring, Connie is also tapped to serve as campaign manager for her blustery principal, Mr. Conklin, who's running against his boss, Mr. Stone, for the newly created office of Coordinator of Education. Though "Old Marblehead" is none too popular with either Connie or the student body, his campaign picks up steam when she devises the tantalizing slogan, "Get Mr. Conklin into Public Office—and Out of Madison."

Although Connie and Lawrence Nolan spar with each other initially, she finds herself attracted to the handsome widower, especially when it appears that her relationship with Mr. Boynton is permanently stalled in second gear. Mr. Nolan, a workaholic who's been neglecting his son, reforms his ways and gives Mr. Boynton some competition for Connie's affections. Meanwhile, Connie's lovable landlady, elderly Mrs. Davis, does her best to bring the two lovebirds together. But Connie's joy at learning that Mr. Boynton is buying a house in the neighborhood, which she believes will be her honeymoon cottage, is shattered when she realizes her bashful beau intends to share the abode with his widowed mother.

Just as the television version of *Our Miss Brooks* was in its final months of original broadcasts on CBS-TV, this Warner Bros. film version unspooled in theaters across the country. In less than 90 minutes, the film not only encapsulates Miss Brooks's life at Madison High from day one, but also provides a resolution never achieved in eight years on radio and television.

Studio publicity quoted Eve as saying, "This is my first picture in three years, and it's the first time in ages I haven't been playing the wise-cracking friend of the heroine. I'd usually wind up with the comic relief while my friend went off into the sunset with the handsome hero."

Included among the film's cast are several Madison High stalwarts who had already been phased out of the TV show. Richard Crenna, on the verge of turning 30, reprises the role of Walter Denton here, though his part is fairly minor. Gloria McMillan's role as Harriet Conklin is even smaller, rendering her little better than a bit player. Adding insult to injury, McMillan, making her big-screen debut, has her name misspelled (as "MacMillan") in the film's opening titles. Leonard Smith and Joseph Kearns also appear, as dopey Stretch Snodgrass, and Board of Education chair Mr. Stone, respectively.

Actor Don Porter (1912–1997), seen as Connie's romantic interest, Larry Nolan, was a veteran of the popular TV sitcom *Private Secretary* (a.k.a. *Susie*), in which he played leading man to actress Ann Sothern. Lovely June Blair, who would go on to become a *Playboy* Playmate as well as the wife of *Ozzie and Harriet*'s David Nelson, is seen briefly as the gorgeous new Miss Lonely-hearts columnist of the *Madison Express*.

The *Christian Science Monitor*'s Rod Nordell wasn't too impressed by the theatrical version of *Our Miss Brooks*: "The improbable characters serve the purposes of a half-hour farce, but they become rather wearing during the course of 85 minutes." Of Eve's performance, Nordell wrote, "Perhaps Eve Arden's long experience in the role has led to her mechanical presentation of it. Each look and gesture appears calculated. She delivers the quips, such as they are, with knife-edge accuracy, but they share the lack of spontaneity of the rest of the film" (March 16, 1956). Richard L. Coe, writing in the *Washington Post*, wasn't enthralled by the movie either, but as a fan of the TV show found a silver lining. Unhappy, as many other viewers were, with the fourth-season revamp of *Brooks* that was then unfolding weekly on CBS-TV, Coe noted, "While her movie isn't very good, it's so much better than this year's TV version you almost feel it's the Good Old Days" (March 9, 1956).

Anatomy of a Murder (1959)

James Stewart (*Paul Biegler*), Lee Remick (*Laura Manion*), Ben Gazzara (*Lt. Frederick Manion*), Arthur O'Connell (*Parnell McCarthy*), Eve Arden (*Maida Rutledge*), Kathryn Grant (*Mary Pilant*), Joseph N. Welch (*Judge Weaver*), George C. Scott (*Asst. State Attorney Gen. Claude Dancer*), Orson Bean (*Dr. Matthew Smith*), Russ Brown (*George Lemon*), Murray Hamilton (*Alphonse Paquette*), Brooks West (*District Attorney Mitch Lodwick*), Ken Lynch (*Det. Sgt. James Durgo*), John Qualen (*Deputy Sheriff Sulo*), Howard McNear (*Dr. Dompierre*), Alexander Campbell (*Dr. W. Gregory Harcourt*), Ned Wever (*Dr. Raschid*), Jimmy Conlin (*Clarence Madigan*), Royal Beal (*Sheriff Battisfore*), Joseph Kearns (*Lloyd Burke*), Don Ross (*Duane "Duke" Miller*), Lloyd Le Vasseur (*Court Clerk*), James Waters (*Army Sergeant*), Duke Ellington

Director/Producer: Otto Preminger. *Screenplay:* Wendell Mayes, based on the novel by Robert Traver. *Music:* Duke Ellington. *Production Design:* Boris Leven. *Director of Photography:* Sam Leavitt. *Camera Operator:* Irving Rosenberg. *Production Manager:* Henry Weinberger. *Lighting Technician:* James Almond. *Key Grip:* Leo McCreary. *Makeup:* Del Armstrong, Harry Ray. *Hairdressing:* Myrl Stoltz. *Wardrobe:* Michael Harte, Vou Lee Giokaris. *Editor:* Louis R. Loeffler. *Sound:* Jack Solomon. *Script Supervisor:* Kathleen Fagan. *Music Editor:* Richard Carruth. *Set Dressing:* Howard Bristol. *Assistant to the Producer:* Max Slater. *Costume Coordinator:* Hope Bryce. *Assistant Director:* David Silver. *Title Design:* Saul Bass. Carlyle Productions/Columbia Pictures; released July 1, 1959. B&W; 160 minutes.

Small-town lawyer Paul Biegler, whose practice is in the doldrums, agrees to defend Army lieutenant Fred Manion, who killed local bar owner Barney Quill in what he claims was a case of temporary insanity. Although Lt. Manion says his beautiful wife, Laura, was raped by the victim, there is no evidence to support this claim. Many of the locals consider Manion a hothead, and Laura a promiscuous woman who was most likely having an affair with Quill. With the help of his trusted aides, secretary Maida Rutledge and heavy-drinking older lawyer Parnell McCarthy, Biegler sets out to defend a man who has all the odds stacked against him.

Eve, making a return to the type of film character roles she played in the years before *Our Miss Brooks,* is cast as Maida Rutledge, Biegler's loyal if slightly cynical secretary. Biegler's practice isn't on the firmest ground financially, as the former district attorney, now back in private practice, spends most of his time fishing. In her first major scene, Maida tells her boss, "I was going over your checkbook yesterday. I can't afford to pay me my salary." This is her second film with the legendary James Stewart (1908–1997), some 18 years after they worked together in *Ziegfeld Girl* (1941).

In some ways, *Anatomy of a Murder* is not unlike a jumbo-sized episode of *Perry Mason,* with Eve playing Della Street to Stewart's version of Mason, the brilliant, cagey defense attorney. That is to say, she's playing Della as she might have been 15 or 20 years later, a little more world-weary and down-to-earth. Upon learning that Paul may defend Fred Manion in what's considered an open-and-shut case, Maida can't help warning her boss about getting his pay up front, commenting, "Those professional soldiers never have a dime. I ought to know. I was married to one." (Only later will Stewart's character fully appreciate the wisdom of this advice.)

Eve's character keeps her ears open at the beauty parlor while getting a manicure, picking up some local gossip that her boss finds helpful. After a handful of good scenes early on, Eve's role largely calls on her to sit in the courtroom behind the defense table and react to the lengthy trial. She is sympathetic to McCarthy's problems with the bottle, even when it makes him unreliable, and doesn't back down even when an exasperated Biegler tells her she's fired, retorting, "You can't fire me till you pay me."

Aside from reviving her career as a character actress in films, *Anatomy of a Murder* was particularly meaningful to Eve for the chance to work with her actor-husband Brooks West (1916–1984), in his only feature film appearance. Though his billing reflects his status as a newcomer to films, placing him deep in the supporting cast, he actually has more to do onscreen than his fifth-billed wife. This was Eve's only film with the noted director Otto Preminger.

The film also finds Eve acting opposite the up-and-coming generation of actors who would come to prominence in the 1960s, among them Lee Remick (1935–1991) and Ben Gazzara (born 1930), both playing one of their first major film roles. George C. Scott (1927–1999), in his second film, makes a strong impression as well. Both Scott and Arthur O'Connell, cast as Parnell McCarthy, were Oscar-nominated for their supporting turns, as was Stewart for Best Actor in a Leading Role.

This somber courtroom drama might not be the film in which you'd expect to see Eve reunited with a cast member from *Our Miss Brooks,* but, in fact, actor Joseph Kearns (1907–1962), seen in a recurring role on that series as Board of Education chairman Mr. Stone, appears briefly here as a witness. Sitting in the judge's chair is, interestingly, real-life attorney Joseph N. Welch (1890–1960), famed for his role in bringing down Senator Joseph McCarthy during the Army-McCarthy hearings of 1954. Duke Ellington provides the film's jazzy score and appears briefly onscreen.

Anatomy of a Murder was based on a 1958 novel attributed to Robert Traver, which was a national bestseller. Traver was the pen name of real-life judge and attorney John D. Voelker (1903–1991), who based the novel on his own experiences defending a similar case in the early 1950s. To give his film verisimilitude, Preminger obtained permission to shoot in and around Marquette County, Michigan, site of Voelker's real-life case, and even in the courtroom where the trial had taken place.

In the fall of 1959, the *Los Angeles Times* reported that Eve would follow this picture with a role as Mario Lanza's manager in *That's My Man*, with filming to take place in Italy and West Berlin, but no such film eventuated.

Anatomy of a Murder drew a rave review from the *Los Angeles Times*'s Philip K. Scheuer, who called it "one of the most extraordinary films ever made for general exhibition ... it grips the imagination for nearly its entire two hours and 40 minutes of play ... it is acted out with such complete believability that you feel you are actually there in that Michigan courtroom where the case (based on fact) was tried."

The Dark at the Top of the Stairs (1960)

Robert Preston (*Rubin Flood*), Dorothy McGuire (*Cora Flood*), Eve Arden (*Lottie Lacey*), Angela Lansbury (*Mavis Pruitt*), Shirley Knight (*Irene "Reenie" Flood*), Lee Kinsolving (*Sammy Golden*), Frank Overton (*Morris Lacey*), Robert Eyer (*Sonny Flood*), Penney Parker (*Flirt Conroy*), Ken Lynch (*Harry Ralston*), Dennis Whitcomb (*Punky Givens*), Peg La Centra (*Edna Harper*), Helen Wallace (*Lydia Harper*), Mary Patton (*Mrs. Ralston*)
Director: Delbert Mann. *Producer:* Michael Garrison. *Screenplay:* Harriet Frank, Jr., Irving Ravetch, based on the play by William Inge. *Director of Photography:* Harry Stradling, Sr. *Art Director:* Leo K. Kuter. *Film Editor:* Folmar Blangsted. *Sound:* Stanley Jones. *Costume Designer:* Marjorie Best. *Set Decorator:* George James Hopkins. *Dialogue Supervisor:* Norman Stuart. *Makeup Supervisor:* Gordon Bau. *Music:* Max Steiner. *Orchestrations:* Murray Cutter. *Assistant Director:* Russell Llewellyn. Warner Bros.; released September 22, 1960. Color; 123 minutes.

In 1920s Oklahoma, salesman Rubin Flood is too proud to tell his wife Cora he's been let go from his job. In middle age, he begins to feel that life is passing him by—he doesn't have enough education to get a better job, while his relationship with his wife has been strained by disagreements about money, sex, and his frequent absences for sales trips. Unhappy at home, Rubin stirs up gossip because of his friendship with local beauty parlor proprietor Mavis Pruitt, a widow whom he has known since they were both young. When Rubin refuses to pay for an expensive party dress that Cora bought their shy teenaged daughter Reenie, the resulting fight causes him to move out temporarily.

Vowing to take their children and leave Rubin, Cora reaches out to her well-to-do sister Lottie, wife of a successful dentist. Lottie is fond of her younger sister, but balks at allowing Cora and her kids to move in with her and husband Morris. Meanwhile, distressed at the quarreling of her parents, Reenie rushes out of the house, and meets a military cadet who's the first young man to ever take an interest in her. Though there is a mutual attraction between Rubin and Mavis, he kisses her but goes no further. Returning home to find Lottie in residence, Rubin nonetheless tries to set things right with his wife.

Given co-star billing after Robert Preston and Dorothy McGuire, Eve shines playing one of the most complex film roles she's ever been handed. As with most of the characters in this excellent William Inge drama, Lottie is multi-layered. Initially, we see her as merely hateful. She's a domineering wife who shows her husband little respect, as well as a chatterbox who never stops talking, and displays an appalling array of prejudices and superstitions. Lottie is displeased by her nephew Sonny's collection of movie star photos ("I hear they're just a bunch of trollops"), believes Catholics are malevolently plotting takeover of the world, and bluntly asks Reenie's party date, "Are you of the Jewish faith?"

Her anti–Catholic diatribe finally causes her brother-in-law Rubin to look her in the eye and declare, "Woman, you oughta get yourself a broom and ride over the housetops! You oughta buy yourself a sheet and poke two holes in it, and go around setting fires. Or better still, get yourself a big piece of tape and put it over your mouth, 'cause you're too ignorant to live!" Even

Lottie's own husband, who admits he's too much of a coward to stand up to her, says (when she's out of the room), "I am pretty sick and tired of the sound of her voice."

Just when we've dismissed Lottie as thoroughly unlikable and with no redeeming qualities, however, Eve plays a lovely scene with Dorothy McGuire's Cora that takes us aback. Lottie quietly confesses to her younger sister that she's always envied her for being able to have children, and tells Cora that she and Morris have not had a sex life in years. While she's not unsympathetic to Cora's situation, and to the fact that Rubin slapped his wife's face in a heated moment, Lottie says, "I wish someone loved me enough to hit me. You and Rubin fight. God, I'd love a good fight. Anything would be better than this— nothing." Acknowledging her own tendency to ramble on, Lottie says, "I talk just to remind myself I'm alive."

Uniformly fine performances, under the guidance of Oscar winner Delbert Mann (*Marty*), help make *The Dark at the Top of the Stairs* a film not easily forgotten. Robert Preston (1918–1987), who took a leave of absence from his stage hit *The Music Man* to play this role, is excellent as the prototypical Inge man who's restless in middle age, fundamentally decent but longing for a change. Dorothy McGuire skillfully plays not only the vulnerable side of Cora that wins her our sympathy, but also the weak, overprotective, and slightly self-pitying woman who's dissatisfied with her life, smothers her young son with excessive attention, and tries too hard to live vicariously through her daughter. Talented Shirley Knight (born 1936) was Oscar-nominated in the Best Supporting Actress category for this early performance. Angela Lansbury (born 1925), given only a few minutes onscreen to sketch the character of Rubin's lady friend Mavis (who never appeared onstage in the play), takes a woman we are prepared to dislike (thinking that she may be his backstreet mistress), and gives her warmth and solidity. Penney Parker (born 1941), as shy Reenie's worldlier best friend, plays a character not unlike the one she would assume in the 1961–62 television sitcom *Margie,* also set in the 1920s.

William Inge's play *The Dark at the Top of the Stairs* opened in December 1957 and played for 468 performances. Inge won a Tony Award for Best Play. Onstage, Eve's role of Lottie Lacey was played by the veteran actress Eileen Heckart (1919–2001), who won her first Tony for the featured role. This wasn't the first time Arden and Heckart had played the same role; during the original Broadway run of *Voice of the Turtle,* Eileen understudied both key female roles, including the character of Olive Lashbrooke that Eve would portray in the 1947 film adaptation.

Back at Warner Bros.' studio for her first assignment in several years, former contract player Eve asked if she could inhabit her old dressing room, but was reportedly told that it was now the lair of the studio's TV leading man, Efrem Zimbalist, Jr. (*77 Sunset Strip*). She commuted daily from her family's farm to the studio for shooting.

The role in *The Dark at the Top of the Stairs* was anything but a typical Eve Arden character. Quoted in studio publicity for the film, Eve commented, "Roles are not being written for a particular actor or actress these days. I don't believe there are any more Joan Crawford roles, Clark

Portrait of a troubled marriage: Eve and Frank Overton as Mr. and Mrs. Lacey in *The Dark at the Top of the Stairs.*

Gable roles, or any other specific type to suit a particular player. Those days are over and I think it is a step forward. Parts are no longer one-dimensional. Audiences expect full characterizations of real people."

In making the film version of Inge's play, director Delbert Mann employed an unusual technique he first adopted when shooting *Marty* (1955). According to an Associated Press story appearing in the *Cumberland* (MD) *Times*, "The cast first ran through the entire script, and then turned to rehearsing on stage before the actual filming" (July 10, 1960). Reported syndicated columnist Hedda Hopper, once Eve had completed filming *The Dark at the Top of the Stairs*, she "couldn't resist a fabulous offer" to appear in a summer stock production of the play, opposite husband Brooks West (March 23, 1960).

The *New York Times*'s Bosley Crowther rated this a flawed adaptation of the original stage play, calling Eve "showy and shallow" in the role of Lottie (September 23, 1960). However, in *Film Daily*'s annual poll of some 1,850 critics, Eve's performance was rated among the year's top five for supporting actresses.

Sergeant Deadhead (1965)

Frankie Avalon (*Sergeant O.K. Deadhead/Sergeant Donovan*), Deborah Walley (*Airman Lucy Turner*), Cesar Romero (*Admiral Stoneham*), Fred Clark (*General Rufus Fogg*), Gale Gordon (*Captain Weiskopf*), Harvey Lembeck (*Airman McEvoy*), John Ashley (*Airman Filroy*), Buster Keaton (*Airman Blinken*), Reginald Gardiner (*Lt. Commander Talbott*), Pat Buttram (*The President*), Eve Arden (*Lt. Charlotte Kinsey*), Romo Vincent (*Tuba Player*), Donna Loren (*Susan*), Ed Faulkner (*Lt. Dixon*), Ed Reimers, John Hiestand (*Newsmen*), Mike Nader, Norman Grabowski, Tod Windsor, Patti Chandler, Luree Holmes, Mary Hughes, Salli Sachse, Bobbi Shaw, Sue Hamilton, Ray Atkinson, Bob Harvey, Jerry Brutsche, Andy Romano, Don Edwards, Bruce Baker, Ray Sittin, Taggart Casey, Jo Collins, Astrid de Brea, Jean Ingram, Peggy Ward, Stephanie Nader, Lyzanne Ladue, Janice Levinson, Alberta Nelson, Sallie Dornan
Director: Norman Taurog. *Writer:* Louis M. Heyward. *Producers:* James H. Nicholson, Samuel Z. Arkoff. *Co-Producer:* Anthony Carras. *Production Supervisor:* Jack Bohrer. *Director of Photography:* Floyd Crosby. *Musical Supervision:* Al Simms. *Musical Score:* Les Baxter. *Songs:* Guy Hemric, Jerry Styner. *Choreography:* Jack Baker. *Art Direction:* Howard Campbell. *Film Editors:* Ronald Sinclair, Eve Newman, Fred Feitshans. *Music Editor:* Milton Lustig. *Sound Editors:* James Nelson, Gene Corso. *Costume Supervisor:* Richard Bruno. *Special Effects:* Roger George. *Assistant Director:* Claude Binyon, Jr. *Dialogue Director:* Michael Hoey. *Properties:* Karl R. Brainard, Richard M. Rubin. *Sound:* Don Rush. *Makeup:* Ted Coodley. *Hair Stylist:* Ray Foreman. *Set Decorator:* Robert G. Nelson. *Construction Coordinator:* Ross Hahn. *Production Assistant:* Jack Cash. American International Pictures; released August 18, 1965. Color; 89 minutes.

Well-intended fumbler O.K. Deadhead of the U.S. Air Force is accidentally launched into orbit with "Project Moon Monkey," which finds him sharing a space capsule with a chimpanzee. Rather than admit they fouled up, General Fogg and his colleagues agree to pretend that this was planned all along, and treat Sergeant Deadhead as a military hero. They also make plans to give him his much-delayed wedding to pretty girlfriend Lucy.

Upon his landing, nice-guy Deadhead has somehow assumed the arrogant, playful, incorrigible personality of the chimp, and refuses to cooperate with the cover-up plans. When General Fogg locates another enlisted man who's a dead ringer for Deadhead, they convince Sergeant Donovan to assume the identity of the man who's now well on his way to becoming famous. The ruse works until Deadhead breaks out of the guardhouse where he's been kept captive, and a nervous Sergeant Donovan balks at taking his new "bride" Lucy on her honeymoon.

Sergeant Deadhead is a harmless comedy (with a few musical numbers) from the youth-oriented American International Pictures, which cleaned up at box offices of the 1950s and 1960s with low-budget films aimed squarely at the teenage market. Leading man Frankie Avalon, already popular with moviegoers as the leading man of AIP's *Beach Party* (1963) and multiple follow-ups (opposite Annette Funicello), is surrounded here by numerous other familiar players from the beach movies. As with many of their 1960s movies, AIP stocks this comedy with familiar older players.

Eve has a sizable role as General Fogg's assistant, Lieutenant Kinsey. She is also the general's clandestine lady friend, who sometimes forgets and calls him Rufus (or "Rufie") during business

Eve is about to cause a big explosion in *Sergeant Deadhead*, as Buster Keaton (center) and Fred Clark look on.

hours. Eager to hook the general as her husband, Charlotte Kinsey sympathizes with Lucy's desire to get Deadhead to the altar, and conspires to help her young charge.

Eve is reunited here with her longtime co-star from *Our Miss Brooks*, Gale Gordon, who plays a psychiatrist. She also teams with young AIP stalwart Deborah Walley, two years before they were cast as mother and daughter in their TV sitcom *The Mothers-in-Law*. But Eve works most closely with her romantic interest, actor Fred Clark (*The George Burns and Gracie Allen Show*). Eve's song, "You Should've Seen the One That Got Away," choreographed by Jack Baker, finds her sharing her own romantic woes with Lucy as the younger woman tries on her wedding dress.

Billed as "Special Cameo Star," actor Pat Buttram, his face mostly obscured, plays the president of the United States, who sounds a bit like Lyndon Johnson. Buttram filmed this role not long before beginning his run as duplicitous Mr. Haney on the long-running CBS sitcom *Green Acres* (1965–1971). The great Buster Keaton appears briefly as a rather superannuated airman, looking weary as he does a couple of slapstick routines for which he hopefully received a nice paycheck.

Variety liked *Sergeant Deadhead* pretty well, deeming it "above-average formula fare for youth situations." Calling Eve and Fred Clark "the comedy keystones" of the production, the reviewer added, "It's good to see her back on the theatre screen" (August 11, 1965). Likewise, *Film Daily* noted, "Eve Arden contributes a pleasant characterization as a lieutenant with a penchant for singing" (August 19, 1965).

The Strongest Man in the World (1975)

Kurt Russell (*Dexter Riley*), Joe Flynn (*Dean Eugene Higgins*), Eve Arden (*Harriet Crumpley*), Cesar Romero (*A.J. Arno*), Phil Silvers (*Kerwood Krinkle*), Dick Van Patten (*Harry Crumpley*), Michael McGreevey (*Richard Schuyler*), William Schallert (*Professor Quigley*), Harold Gould (*Dietz*), Benson Fong (*Ah Fong*), Dick Bakalyan (*Cookie*), James Gregory (*Police Chief Blair*), Kathleen Freeman (*Officer Hurley*), Ann Marshall (*Debbie*), Don Carter (*Gilbert*), Christina Anderson (*Cris*), Paul Linke (*Peter "Porky" Peterson*), Jack David Walker (*Slither Roth*), Melissa Caffey (*Melissa*), John Debney (*John*), Derrel Maury (*Hector*), Matthew Conway Dunn (*Matthew*), Pat Fitzpatrick (*Pat*), David Richard Ellis (*David*), Larry Franco (*Larry*), Roy Roberts (*Mr. Roberts*), Fritz Feld (*Mr. Frederick*), Ronnie Schell (*Referee*), Raymond Bailey (*Regent Burns*), John Myhers (*Mr. Roscoe*), James E. Brodhead (*Edward*), Dick Patterson (*Mr. Secretary*), Irwin Charone (*Irwin*), Roger Price (*Roger*), Jack Bailey (*Jack*), Larry Gelman (*Larry*), Eric Brotherson (*Eric*), Jonathan Daly (*TV Announcer*), Iggie Wolfington (*Mr. Becker*), Ned Wertimer (*Mr. Parsons*), Milton Frome (*Mr. Lutkin*), Laurie Main (*Mr. Reedy*), Mary Treen (*Mercedes*), Eddie Quillan (*Mr. Willoughby*), Jeff DeBenning (*Mr. Rogers*), Henry Slate (*Mr. Slate*), Byron Webster (*Mr. Webster*), Burt Mustin (*Regent Appleby*), Arthur Space (*Regent Shaw*), Bill Zuckert (*Policeman*), Larry J. Blake (*Pete*), William Bakewell (*Professor*), Art Metrano (*TV Color Man*), Pete Renoudet (*Reporter*), Lennie Weinrib (*State Coach*), Danny Wells (*Drummer*), James Beach (*TV Man*)
Director: Vincent McEveety. *Producer:* Bill Anderson. *Writers:* Joseph L. McEveety, Herman Groves. *Director of Photography:* Andrew Jackson. *Art Directors:* John B. Mansbridge, Jack Senter. *Set Decorator:* Bill Calvert. *Second Unit Director:* Arthur J. Vitarelli. *Film Editor:* Cotton Warburton. *Music:* Robert F. Brunner. *Orchestration:* Walter Sheets. *Special Effects:* Art Cruickshank, Danny Lee. *Titles:* Art Stevens, Guy Deel. *Sound Supervisor:* Herb Taylor. *Sound Mixer:* George Ronconi. *Unit Manager/Assistant Director:* Dick Caffey. *Second Assistant Director:* Pat Kehoe. *Costumes:* Chuck Keehne, Emily Sundby. *Makeup:* Robert L. Schiffer. *Hair Stylist:* LaRue Matherson. *Music Editor:* Evelyn Kennedy. Walt Disney Productions; released February 6, 1975. Color; 92 minutes.

Dean Higgins of Medfield College has been given 30 days by the board of regents to shape up the school's finances or be forced out. Deciding that waste is particularly problematic in the Science department, Higgins fires Professor Quigley, who has been coaching his students, including ringleaders Dexter Riley and Richard Schuyler, in an expensive research project involving nutrition for cows. Storming out of the science lab after giving Quigley his walking papers, the dean causes a massive spill that inadvertently creates a formula found to give any human or animal super-strength.

Seeing a huge profit potential, Dean Higgins takes the formula to the Crumpley Crunch Cereal Company. Owner Harriet Crumpley is intrigued by his presentation, during which he demonstrates the temporary super-strength he gets from downing some Crumpley Crunch cereal laced with the secret formula. Harriet challenges her chief business rival, the bombastic president of the Krinkle Krunch Cereal Company, to co-sponsor a televised weightlifting competition between his alma mater, State University, and Medfield. The athletes from Medfield will have their performance augmented by the secret formula, which Harriet expects will boost sales of her company's cereal. Harriet's double-crossing nephew enlists two bungling ex-cons to steal the formula for Krinkle, but they're unsuccessful.

At the competition, Dexter Riley and his classmates who make up the school's weightlifting team, are horrified to discover that the secret formula no longer seems to work. But when Dexter realizes there is one missing ingredient, he races against time (and the town police) to locate the ingredient. He manages to fortify himself just in time to lift barbells weighing more than 1,000 pounds and win the competition for Medfield.

Billed behind Kurt Russell, as Dexter, and Joe Flynn, as the hapless dean, Eve delivers her usual professional performance in a rather sketchily written role that gives her little opportunity to shine. She makes her first entrance about 30 minutes into the film, with a lengthy scene showing Dean Higgins demonstrating the super-strength formula to the Crumpley Crunch board of directors. She's the only woman present in the giant board room, presiding confidently over a passel of gray-suited underlings who are mostly family members and sycophants. When Dick Van Patten's Harry has the temerity to call the meeting to order before she's arrived, she soon walks in and puts him firmly in his place, saying with a smile, "But remember, just because you're a relative doesn't mean I can't fire you." With that scene behind us, her presence in the film is

Harriet Crumpley (Eve) cheers on the weightlifters of Medfield College in *The Strongest Man in the World.*

relatively minor until the closing segment, when she is a highly visible onlooker at the weightlifting competition (smashing a sign over the head of Flynn's Dean Higgins when things go wrong).

The third and last in Disney's series of special-effects comedies featuring college student Dexter Riley (following *The Computer Wore Tennis Shoes* and *Now You See Him, Now You Don't*) delivers decent entertainment to its intended audience. Anyone who doesn't enjoy Joe Flynn's typical neurotic fussbudget performance (à la Captain Binghamton in *McHale's Navy*) should avoid this film like the plague, as he is onscreen virtually nonstop, even more than Kurt Russell. James Gregory, playing the chief of police not long before he joined the cast of *Barney Miller*, strains for laughs in a poorly written and rather offensive sequence involving the cop's ham-handed speech in Chinatown. An almost inexhaustible supply of recognizable character actors drop in for minor roles, but most of them are not given enough screen time to noticeably aid the comedy. This is Eve's only appearance in the series, though Russell, Flynn, Cesar Romero, and others are reprising roles they played in previous entries.

Interviewed by syndicated columnist Vernon Scott during the summer 1974 shooting of *The Strongest Man in the World,* Eve said, "It's the first time I've ever worked at Disney, and I love every minute of it."

Reviewing the film in the *Chicago Tribune,* Gene Siskel remarked of Eve, "It sure is good to see her again" (February 14, 1975). Vincent Canby, in the *New York Times,* found it "reassuring" to see Eve and Phil Silvers in their featured roles as business rivals "whose industrial spy networks recall the worst bungling of the Watergate burglars" (July 10, 1975).

Grease (1978)

John Travolta (*Danny Zuko*), Olivia Newton-John (*Sandy Olsson*), Stockard Channing (*Betty Rizzo*), Jeff Conaway (*Kenickie*), Barry Pearl (*Doody*), Michael Tucci (*Sonny*), Kelly Ward (*Putzie*), Didi Conn (*Frenchy*), Jamie Donnelly (*Jan*), Dinah Manoff (*Marty Maraschino*), Eve Arden (*Principal McGee*), Frankie Avalon (*Teen Angel*), Joan Blondell (*Vi*), Edd Byrnes (*Vince Fontaine*), Sid Caesar (*Coach Calhoun*), Alice Ghostley (*Mrs. Murdock*), Dody Goodman (*Blanche*), Sha-Na-Na (*Johnny Casino and the Gamblers*), Susan Buckner (*Patty Simcox*), Lorenzo Lamas (*Tom Chisum*), Fannie Flagg (*Nurse Wilkins*), Dick Patterson (*Mr. Rudie*), Eddie Deezen (*Eugene Felnic*), Darrell Zwerling (*Mr. Lynch*), Ellen Travolta (*Waitress*), Annette Charles (*Cha Cha DiGregorio*), Dennis C. Stewart (*Leo*), Michael Biehn (*Mike*)

Director: Randall Kleiser. *Producers:* Allan Carr, Robert Stigwood. *Screenplay:* Bronté Woodard, based on the original musical by Jim Jacobs, Warren Casey. *Adaptation:* Allan Carr. *Dance and Musical Sequence Staging and Choreography:* Patricia Birch. *Associate Producer/Unit Production Manager:* Neil A. Machlis. *Music Supervision:* Bill Oakes. *Editor:* John F. Burnett. *Production Designer:* Phil Jefferies. *Director of Photography:* Bill Butler. *Music Post-Scoring:* Michael Gibson. *Costume Designer:* Albert Wolsky. *Set Decorator:* James Berkey. *Makeup Artists:* Dan Striepeke, Eddie Allen. *Hair Stylist:* Christine George. *Music Editor:* June Edgerton. *Assistant Director:* Jerry Grandey. *Second Assistant Directors:* Lynn Morgan, Paula Marcus. *Script Supervisor:* Joyce King. *Sound Effects Editor:* Charles Moran. *Sound Mixer:* Jerry Jost. *Re-Recording Mixer:* Bill Varney. *Assistant Film Editor:* Robert Pergament. *Property Master:* Richard Valesko. *Key Grip:* George Hill. *Gaffer:* Colin Campbell. *Stunt Coordinator:* Wallace Dwight Crowder. *Construction Coordinator:* Gene Kelly. *Women's Wardrobe:* Betsy Cox. *Men's Wardrobe:* Bruce Walkup. *Unit Publicist:* Gary Kalkin. *Assistant Choreographer:* Carol Culver. *Dance Consultant:* Tommy Smith. *Casting:* Joel Thurm. *Electronic Visual Effects:* Ron Hays. *Musical Engineering Consultant:* David J. Holman. *Main Titles Animation:* John Wilson. *Location Manager:* Alan B. Curtiss. *Looping Editor:* Sean Hanley. *Opticals:* Modern Film Effects. *End Title Design:* Wayne Fitzgerald. Paramount Pictures; released June 16, 1978. Color; 110 minutes.

Miss McGee (Eve) dances up a storm with Coach Calhoun (Sid Caesar) in *Grease*.

It is 1959, and teenagers Danny and Sandy have a romantic interlude on the beach during summer vacation. When pretty, innocent Sandy, who's Australian, arrives for her first day as a transfer student to rambunctious Rydell High, she's surprised to learn that Danny is also enrolled there. Interested in rekindling the romance, she's hurt when leather-jacketed Danny, who's the epitome of cool to his friends, is reluctant to have his friends see him getting seriously involved with a nice girl.

While Danny spends his time with a group of buddies known as the T-Birds, Sandy is befriended by the Pink Ladies, led by tough-talking Rizzo. The biggest event of the school year is a dance competition that will be televised live on the *National Bandstand* TV show. Sandy is intensely jealous when Danny and another girl are crowned the best dancers. With the help of her pal Frenchy, Sandy reinvents her look, introducing a sexy new persona that Danny can't resist.

One of the box office hits of the summer of 1978, *Grease* was adapted from the long-running stage musical that opened in early 1972 and ran for more than 3,000 performances. Producers Allan Carr and Robert Stigwood changed the stage show considerably for the film adaptation, including altering the character of Sandy so that Australian singer-actress Olivia Newton-John could be cast in the role.

Eve is one of several veteran performers cast in "Special Guest Appearances" to boost the film's nostalgic flavor. Other 1950s TV favorites on hand include Sid Caesar (*Your Show of Shows*) as Rydell's athletic coach, Edd Byrnes (*77 Sunset Strip*) as the smarmy host of the TV dance show, and Dody Goodman as Miss McGee's hapless assistant, while longtime Warners' contract player Joan Blondell, in one of her last film roles, appears briefly as a waitress. Eve's role was created for the film, and did not exist in the stage version.

Exactly 30 years after she entered the field of education as Miss Brooks, she's promoted here from teacher to principal. Eve's role, little more than a cameo, mostly calls for her to issue silly announcements over the school intercom, and ride herd on her incompetent helper Blanche. Later, Miss McGee tackles a problem Osgood Conklin never could have imagined at Madison High when the live broadcast of *National Bandstand* unexpectedly features three of the T-Birds mooning the camera. In high dudgeon, Miss McGee takes to her PA system to issue a stern warning to the unknown miscreants who bared their rears on TV: "We have pictures of you so-called 'mooners,' and just because the pictures aren't of your faces doesn't mean we can't identify you! At this very moment, those pictures are on the way to Washington, where the FBI has experts in this type of identification. If you turn yourselves in now, you may escape a federal charge." In another of her well-remembered lines from the film, she urges the student body to lend their support to Rydell's sports program, saying, "If you can't be an athlete, be an athletic supporter!"

Billboard correctly predicted box-office success for *Grease,* saying the picture "lives up to its pre-release hype." The review noted that Eve and the other guest players "come across with a sense of humor and warmth" (July 1, 1978). *Grease* surprised even some of its participants, Eve among them, with its box-office clout, which eventually found it ranked as the most successful movie musical ever.

Four years later, Eve would be one of the few cast members from *Grease* to reprise her role in the ill-fated sequel, which would be her final theatrical release.

Under the Rainbow (1981)

Chevy Chase (*Bruce Thorpe*), Carrie Fisher (*Annie Clark*), Eve Arden (*The Duchess of Luchow*), Adam Arkin (*Henry Hudson*), Billy Barty (*Otto Kriegling*), Robert Donner (*The Assassin*), Cork Hubbert (*Rollo Sweet*), Joseph Maher (*Leopold, the Duke of Luchow*), Mako (*Nakomuri*), Pat McCormick (*Tiny*), Peter Isacksen (*Homer*), Jack Kruschen (*Louie*), Freeman King (*Otis*), Richard Stahl (*Lester Hudson*), Louisa Moritz (*Hotel Telephone Operator*), Bennett Ohta (*Akido*), Gary Friedkin (*Wedgie*), Michael Lee Gogin (*Fitzgerald*), Pam Vance (*Lana*), Anthony Gordon (*Inspector Collins*), Leonard Barr (*Pops*), John Pyle (*Steward*), Bill Lytle (*Mail Clerk*), Theodore Lehmann (*Adolf Hitler*), Patty Maloney (*Rosie*), Zelda Rubinstein (*Iris*), Bobby Porter (*Ventriloquist*), Charles Messenger (*Hitler's Aide*), Robert Murvin (*Lefty*), David Haney (*Dispatcher*), Gordon Zimmerman (*Man at Radio*), Jim Boeke (*Whittler*), Tony Ballen (*Truck Driver*), Geraldine Papel

The Duchess of Luchow (Eve) thinks nothing's too good for her beloved Streudel in *Under the Rainbow*.

(*Waitress*), Ruth Brown (*Cleaning Lady*), Art Hern (*Studio Guard*), Bobby Porter (*Ventriloquist*), Charlie Messenger (*Hitler's Aide*), Peter W. Wooley (*Studio Lot Director*), Gary Wayne (*Studio Lot Actor*), Suzanne Leonard (*Studio Lot Actress*), Deloris Crenshaw (*Studio Lot Servant*), Twink Caplan (*Cigarette Girl*), John F. Goff (*Bartender*), Beth Nufer (*Prostitute*), Denise Cheshire, Victor Hunsberger, Jr. (*Flying Monkeys*) *Director:* Steve Rash. *Executive Producer:* Edward H. Cohen. *Producer:* Fred Bauer. *Screenplay:* Pat McCormick, Harry Hurwitz, Martin Smith, Pat Bradley, Fred Bauer. *Story:* Fred Bauer, Pat Bradley. *Associate Producer:* Frances Avrut-Bauer. *Background Production:* Maggie Rash. *Director of Photography:* Frank Stanley. *Production Designer:* Peter Wooley. *Music:* Joe Renzetti. *Costume Designer:* Mike Butler. *Film Editor:* David Blewitt. *Production Manager:* Don Goldman. *Unit Production Manager:* John Lytle. *First Assistant Director:* Robert J. Smawley. *Second Assistant Directors:* Maggie Rash, James S. Simons. *Production Coordinators:* Kelly Marshall, Karen Altman. Orion Pictures; released July 31, 1981. Color; 97 minutes.

It's 1938, and Secret Service agent Bruce Thorpe has been assigned to guard visiting royalty, the Duke and Duchess of Luchow, during their trip to California. The duke lives in fear of assassination attempts, and frequently adopts ludicrous disguises intended as camouflage. His wife, the duchess, is devoted to her dog Streudel. Because the duchess is quite nearsighted, she doesn't realize that the original Streudel died quite awhile ago, and has been replaced more than once since with lookalikes. In Hollywood, Thorpe and the royal couple take up residence at the Culver Hotel, which is also serving as the temporary home of several dozen midgets—the supporting cast of a new movie to be called *The Wizard of Oz*. While remaining constantly vigilant in his bodyguard duties, Bruce takes a liking to pretty Annie Clark, the hapless young lady whose job as special talent coordinator for *The Wizard of Oz* entails keeping the midget actors under control. The presence of a would-be assassin, as well as a diminutive Nazi agent sent to retrieve a valuable map showing American war defenses, adds to the chaos that erupts over a long weekend.

The premise of *Under the Rainbow*, in which the midget actors hired to play the Munchkins in *The Wizard of Oz* prove to be a wild, undisciplined bunch of rabble-rousers, apparently originated with a television interview *Oz* star Judy Garland did in the 1960s. There seem to be two schools of thought where *Under the Rainbow* is concerned. Not to be counted among its fans is Leonard Maltin, whose annual movie guide terms it "astoundingly unfunny and tasteless." Some viewers find it an outrageous comedy that mocks stereotypes, rather than purveying them. Freeman King, as bellboy Otis, is playing the type of character Willie Best might have essayed in an actual 1938 film. The busload of camera-snapping Japanese tourists are said to be members of the Japanese Amateur Photographers Society, aka JAPS.

To its credit, it offers Eve one of the most sizable featured roles of her latter-day film career, as well as another opportunity to demonstrate her facility for accents. She heads an alphabetical list of co-stars. Her pairing with stage actor Joseph Maher (1933–1988), as her duke, works beautifully, and she garnered some of the few critical plaudits the film earned on its initial release.

The *New York Times*'s Janet Maslin thought Eve "played [the Duchess] very amusingly," but was lukewarm about the picture overall: "For a while ... the film seems to have ingenuity and momentum, or at least enough of the bizarre to hold an audience's attention. Later on, the energy runs out, but the gags keep cranking along anyhow" (July 31, 1981).

Peter Isacksen (born 1954), seen as Carrie Fisher's bumbling assistant, was previously a regular on TV's *CPO Sharkey* (1976–1978), where, as here, his above-average height was used for comic contrast. Adam Arkin (born 1956) gives a skillful performance as the hotel's frenetic temporary manager, who comes unglued trying to keep peace as the midgets run amok. Aside from Billy Barty (1924–2000), who has a strong featured role, the other little people in the cast include Zelda Rubinstein (1933–2010), a year before her breakout role in *Poltergeist* (1982), and Felix Silla (born 1937), remembered for his role as Cousin Itt on TV's *The Addams Family*.

This was the feature film debut of director Steve Rash, who would go on to direct Pauly Shore's *Son-in-Law* (1993), *Eddie* (1996), starring Whoopi Goldberg, and several direct-to-video features.

Pandemonium (1982)

Tom Smothers (*Cooper*), Carol Kane (*Candy*), Miles Chapin (*Andy*), Debralee Scott (*Sandy*), Marc McClure (*Randy*), Judge Reinhold (*Glenn*), Teri Landrum (*Mandy*), Candy Azzara (*Bambi*), David L. Lander (*Pepe*), Paul Reubens (*Johnson*), Gary Allen (*Dr. Fuller*), Eve Arden (*Warden June*), Kaye Ballard (*Glenn's Mom*), Eileen Brennan (*Sandy's Mom*), Tab Hunter (*Blue Grange*), Sydney Lassick (*Man in Bus Station*), Edie McClurg (*Blue's Mom*), Jim McKrell (*Mandy's Dad*), Lenny Montana (*Coach*), Donald O'Connor (*Glenn's Dad*), Richard Romanus (*Jarrett*), Izabella Telezynska (*Salt*), Tammy Alverson, Pamela Harlow, Lynn Herring, Jan Speck, Sallee Sunshine Young (*60s Cheerleaders*), Suzanne Kent (*Crying Woman*), Phil Hartmann (*Reporter*), Michael Kless (*Photographer*), Bradley Lieberman (*Chip, Jr.*), Victoria Carroll (*Mandy's Mom*), Alix Elias (*Joe, the Fry Cook*), Ebbe Roe Smith (*Pete*), Randy Bennett (*Male Driver*), Pat Ast (*Bus Driver*), David Becker (*President*), Don McLeod (*Male Nurse*), David McCharen (*Chicken Patient*), Richard C. Adams (*Shock Treatment Patient*), Nancy Ryan (*Fig Leaf Woman*), Jim Boeke (*Fletcher*), Shirley Prestia (*Morgue Attendant*), Michael Tucci (*Man Leaving Restaurant*), Candi Brough (*Crystal*), Randi Brough (*China*), Lynne Marie Stewart (*Stewardess*), Mae Hi (*Passenger on Plane*), Mildred T. Ogata (*Passenger on Plane*), John Paragon, Vern Rowe, Rob Sullivan (*Prisoners*), Joe Shea (*Man in Gas Chamber*), Daniel Davies, Jaime Klein, Richard Whitley (*Men in Restaurant*)
Director: Alfred Sole. *Executive Producer:* Barry Krost. *Producer:* Doug Chapin. *Writers/Associate Producers:* Richard Whitley, Jaime Klein. *Director of Photography:* Michel Hugo. *Music:* Dana Kaproff. *Costume Design:* Roberta Weiner. *Editor:* Eric Jenkins. *Production Design:* Jack de Shields. *Art Director:* James Clayton. *Unit Production Manager:* Bill Watkins. *First Assistant Director:* Ed Milkovich. *Second Assistant Director:* Jack Clements. *Script Supervisor:* Marjorie Mullen. *Assistant to the Producer:* Nancy Walker. *Stunt Coordinator:* Jim Halty. *Set Decorator:* Chuck Graffeo. *Production Coordinator:* Roz Catania. *Location Manager:* Tony Amatullo. *Camera Operator:* Bill Asman. *First Assistant Cameraman:* Glenn Shimada. *Second Assistant Cameraman:* Mako Koiwai. *Production Sound Mixer:* Keith A. Wester. *Supervisory Sound Editor:* Keith Stafford *Sound Editors:* Carl Mahakian, William Manger. *Assistant Sound Editor:* Jeffrey Wilhoit. *Music Editor:* John Mick. *Boom Operator:* Jock Putnam. *Cable Man:* George Tyson. *Assistant Film Editor:* Arthur W. Forney. *Apprentice Editor:* Cari Coughlin. *Property Master:* Ace Holmes. *Makeup:* Bob Mills, Dorinda Carey. *Unit Publicist:* Kimberley Coy. United Artists; released April 1982. Color; 77 minutes.

The opening of Bambi's Summer Cheerleading Camp, on the campus of It Had to Be U, makes locals nervous. Since 1963, the school has suffered periodic outbursts of violent murder whenever cheerleading takes place (a newspaper headline reads, "Exploding Pompons Claim More Cheerleaders: Search Continues for Missing Feet.") Undeterred, Bambi assembles a co-ed group of cheerleading trainees that include snooty Sandy, dopey potheads Andy and Randy, squeaky-clean Glenn and Mandy, and Candy, who possesses telekinetic powers. When escapees from the local prison and mental institution threaten to put the members of Bambi's camp at risk, policeman Cooper (a Mountie) springs into action to save the day.

Given the surprise box office success of *Airplane!* (1980), other filmmakers concluded there was an audience for outrageous, spoofy parodies of movie clichés, peppered with goofy cameo appearances by name actors. *Pandemonium,* somewhat in the vein of later efforts like *Scary Movie,* parodies one of the hottest movie genres of the early 1980s: the "Dead Teenager" slasher movie first popularized by *Friday the 13th* (1980). Known in pre-production as *Saturday the 12th, Pandemonium* draws not only on conventions of that genre, but horror films in general, with gags based on *Carrie,* Maria Ouspenskaya's character in *The Wolf Man* (1941), and a variety of others.

Like some other films of this type, *Pandemonium* is a grab bag of clever in-jokes, silly puns, sophomoric bathroom humor, over-the-top ethnic stereotypes, and pretty much anything else that could be crowded into an unsubtle comedy. Less raunchy than others that would follow in its wake, the film has some clever touches—and some real groaners. The (allegedly) teenaged members of Bambi's camp are introduced onscreen with labels, starting with Sandy as "Victim #1." When Candy Azzara, as Bambi, delivers a lengthy speech explaining her status as a former student at the university who was never permitted to be a cheerleader, the screen flashes, "EXPOSITION ... STILL MORE EXPOSITION." The screenwriters aren't afraid to throw in obvious gags, as when a character who's just been described as "the black sheep of the family" turns out to be—a black sheep.

Eve is one of several name actors signed for cameo appearances; among the others are her frequent co-star Donald O'Connor, and her *Mothers-in-Law* cohort Kaye Ballard. Eve's two scenes were most likely shot in one day, as were most of the other cameo roles, and she does not interact with the other guest players. Eileen Brennan, who appears briefly in a send-up of Piper Laurie's role in *Carrie,* chose to be billed as "A Friend." Like Eve, Tab Hunter played cameo roles in this as well as *Grease 2,* which followed not far behind.

Eve plays "Warden June," ineffectual leader of the state prison who's been taken hostage during a takeover by the inmates. When we first see her, 20-some minutes into the film, she's talking on the phone with Tom Smothers's Mountie character, alerting him that a dangerous inmate has escaped from the institution:

> JUNE: Jarrett killed Gilbert, one of our guards, and made his escape with some power tools.
> COOPER: Jarrett! Is Jarrett the one who murdered his entire family with a hand drill?
> JUNE: That's right, then varnished them and made a lovely set of bookshelves.
> COOPER: Despicable!
> JUNE: Yes, but very talented.

As for Eve's second and final scene, which involves Warden June being sentenced to the "Gas Chamber," with flatulence helpfully provided by a fat, swarthy prisoner, the less said, the better.

Aside from Eve, the film offers an opportunity to see some up-and-coming young performers (Judge Reinhold, Paul "Pee-Wee Herman" Reubens) in early appearances, as well as others familiar to audiences through their 1970s TV roles (*Laverne & Shirley*'s David L. Lander and *Mary Hartman, Mary Hartman*'s Debralee Scott). The former star of the *Smothers Brothers Comedy Hour* and Carol Kane, veteran of the slasher film *When a Stranger Calls,* are billed above the title.

Grease 2 (1982)

Maxwell Caulfield (*Michael Carrington*), Michelle Pfeiffer (*Stephanie Zinone*), Adrian Zmed (*Johnny Nogerelli*), Peter Frechette (*Louis DiMucci*), Christopher McDonald (*Goose McKenzie*), Leif Green (*Davey Jaworski*), Lorna Luft (*Paulette Rebchuck*), Maureen Teefy (*Sharon Cooper*), Alison Price (*Rhonda Ritter*), Pamela

Segall (*Dolores Rebchuck*), Didi Conn (*Frenchy*), Eve Arden (*Miss McGee*), Sid Caesar (*Coach Calhoun*), Dody Goodman (*Blanche Hodel*), Tab Hunter (*Mr. Stuart*), Connie Stevens (*Miss Mason*), Eddie Deezen (*Eugene Felnic*), Matt Lattanzi (*Brad*), Jean & Liz Sagal (*Sorority Girls*), Dennis C. Stewart (*Balmudo*), Brad Jeffries (*Preptone*), Vernon Scott (*Henry Dickey*)
Director/Choreographer: Patricia Birch. *Executive Producer:* Bill Oakes. *Producers:* Robert Stigwood, Allan Carr. *Writer:* Ken Finkleman. *Associate Producer:* Neil A. Machlis. *Music Producer/Arranger:* Louis St. Louis. *Costume Designer:* Robert DeMora. *Editor:* John F. Burnett. *Production Designer:* Gene Callahan. *Director of Photography:* Frank Stanley. Paramount Pictures; released June 11, 1982. Color; 115 minutes.

It's now 1961 at Rydell High School, and a new school year begins with the arrival of transfer student Michael Carrington. Michael, a cousin of alumna Sandy Olsson, is a genteel young Britisher not quite accustomed to the rowdy ways of American high schools. Another alumna, Frenchy, who's dropped back in long enough to take a chemistry course, serves as Michael's tour guide.

Michael is instantly attracted to blonde, beautiful Stephanie, leader of the current group of Pink Ladies. Though he's informed that Pink Ladies only date motorcycle-riding members of the T-Birds, Michael pursues her nonetheless, but gets the brush-off. Resolving to transform himself into the kind of man Stephanie wants, Michael launches a thriving business writing term papers for other students so that he can afford his own motorcycle. On his cycle, with his face obscured behind a helmet and goggles, Michael can project a cool persona that catches Stephanie's attention, and turns the tables on the T-Birds' rivals, the Cycle Lords. But when he butts heads with the T-Birds, who guard their territory, and their women, jealously, the stage is set for a confrontation.

Given the unprecedented popularity of *Grease*, a sequel was probably inevitable. *Grease 2* treads much the same territory as its predecessor, though with lesser-known players, inferior music, and an overall sense of déjà-vu. Many of the scenes, jokes, and songs seem calculated to remind viewers of the first film. Instead of a blonde nice girl falling in love with a leather-jacketed greaser boy, here it's a blonde nice guy paired with a greaser girl (Michelle Pfeiffer, in one of her first important film roles). Substituting for the *National Bandstand* competition is a school talent show, while the diner in the first film gives way to a bowling alley here. Eve's character is still making loopy announcements over the school intercom, this time drawing snickers with an unintended reference to masturbation in place of the "athletic supporter" line from the original film. Patricia Birch, whose choreography was important to the success of the first film, steps into the director's chair here. As in the first film, her choreography is masterful, though here it sometimes takes center stage in a way that detracts from the overall film.

Without John Travolta, Olivia Newton-John, or most of the other young performers who helped make the first film a hit, Eve's return engagement as hapless principal Miss McGee becomes one of the key elements tying the two films together. She and Dody Goodman are given the film's opening lines as they raise the school flag on the first day of a new year. Though she's credited once again with a "Special Guest Appearance," Eve is allotted more screen time here, and billed in the opening titles.

New in this go-round are two more nostalgic faces playing faculty members—Connie Stevens (TV's *Hawaiian Eye*) as the sexy teacher who catches all the boys' eyes, and Tab Hunter as nerdy science teacher Mr. Stuart (not unlike an updated version of Mr. Boynton from *Our Miss Brooks*). Sid Caesar is back as Coach Calhoun, though his footage in the finished film is so minimal that, as the saying goes, he could have phoned it in. Didi Conn is awkwardly jammed into a few scenes as Frenchy, to little effect. Cast as the male lead is actor Maxwell Caulfield (later a cast member of TV's *Dynasty II: The Colbys*), making his film debut. Screenwriter Ken Finkleman was responsible for not one but two disappointing movie sequels in 1982, serving as writer/director of *Airplane II*.

Once again, Eve does what she can—which is quite a bit—with a sketchily written character who pops in and out intermittently. Much of her role calls for her to exhibit shocked reactions to the wild goings-on at Rydell High. Startled to see that Mr. Stuart is offering sex education to his students, she warns him, "They have *drives*, Mr. Stuart, *lustful* drives!" Perhaps her best line comes after that same class, when a worried co-ed takes Miss McGee aside to confide, "I'm a little worried. I missed my last two periods." Miss McGee pats her on the shoulder and says,

"That's all right, dear. You can make them up after school," then does a double-take as the true meaning of the girl's statement registers.

This was Eve's final theatrical release, bringing her motion picture career to a close 45 years after her official debut in *Oh, Doctor.*

In addition to the feature films listed above, Eve also appeared in several short subjects, including *Broadway Highlights* (Paramount, 1936). Columbia's long-running "Screen Snapshots" series featured her in two installments — *Off the Air* (1947) and *Hollywood Life* (1954).

III

Television Performances

Our Miss Brooks

Eve Arden (*Connie Brooks*), Gale Gordon (*Osgood Conklin*), Robert Rockwell (*Philip Boynton*), Richard Crenna (*Walter Denton*), Jane Morgan (*Mrs. Margaret Davis*), Gloria McMillan (*Harriet Conklin*), Leonard Smith (*Stretch Snodgrass*), Jesslyn Fax (*Angela Devon*), Isabel Randolph (*Ruth Nestor*, season 4), Bob Sweeney (*Oliver Munsey*, season 4), Ricky Vera (*Benny Romero*, season 4), Gene Barry (*Gene Talbot*, season 4)
Directors: Al Lewis, John Rich. *Producer/Production Executive:* Larry Berns. *Writers:* Arthur Alsberg, Al Lewis, Joe Quillan. *Directors of Photography:* Robert deGrasse, Karl Freund. *Camera Directors:* John Claar, Sheldon Leonard. *Production Manager:* Argyle Nelson. *Film Editors:* Douglas Hines, John Woodcock. *Art Directors:* Claudio Guzman, Theobold Holsopple. *Set Decorator:* Theo. Offenbecker. *Camera Coordinator:* Maury Thompson. *Assistant Director:* Bert Spurlin. *Property Master:* Reggie Smith. *Makeup Artist:* Robert Cowan. *Music:* Wilbur Hatch. *Editors:* Dann Cahn, Bud Molin.

Aired Fridays at 9:30 P.M. on CBS-TV (through June 1955), then Fridays at 8:30 P.M. on CBS-TV. First aired October 3, 1952; last aired September 21, 1956.

First Season (1952–53)

1. *Trying to Pick a Fight* (October 3, 1952). In the series pilot, Connie is frustrated that her relationship with Mr. Boynton seems stalled after four years of dating, and takes Walter's advice to liven it up with a passionate quarrel. The advice backfires for Miss Brooks, and for Mr. Conklin, who fears that his wife has gone home to Mother after they argue.

2. *The Loaded Custodian* (October 10, 1952). Trying to impress the school board with his parsimony, Mr. Conklin turns down all the faculty's requests for new equipment, and refuses to pay for the broken window in the custodian's office. But when a rumor spreads that the previous janitor hoarded a stash of cash in that office, Connie and her co-workers decide there may be a better way to finance their needs.

3. *The Embezzled Dress* (October 17, 1952). Miss Brooks has been entrusted with $25 earmarked for students' savings accounts, which Mrs. Davis unwittingly spends on a new dress for her tenant. Now all Connie has to do is find someone at Madison High who wants a dress in her size, before the cash is missed.

Character actress Kathleen Freeman (1919–2001), perhaps most recognizable for her featured roles in several Jerry Lewis comedies, makes an early television appearance here as Madison High's home economics teacher, Miss Atterbury.

4. *The Birthday Bag* (October 24, 1952). Connie's birthday is approaching, and her friends want to buy her the green alligator bag she admired at Sherry's Department Store. But when she tells Mrs. Davis she plans to buy it for herself, everyone agrees to prevent this by convincing Connie to lend them her money instead.

Mr. Conklin notes the irony of his agreeing to host a surprise birthday party for Miss Brooks, describing her as "the main obstacle to my peace of mind." Conversely, in the next episode, he will spring into action when he believes Connie might marry and leave her job, saying she would be difficult to replace. Remake of a 1948 radio episode.

5. *Boynton Playacts* (October 31, 1952). Mr. Boynton is being considered for a professorship at State University, but the dean prefers to hire family men. Connie offers to help by impersonating Mrs. Boynton, not realizing she's been cast as Philip's mother, not his wife. Meanwhile, Mr. Conklin, hearing some unreliable gossip from Harriet, jumps to the conclusion that Connie and Philip are getting married for real.

This episode features an unusually straightforward explanation of Mr. Boynton's reluctance to commit. Asked by Dean Faraday whether he ever intends to get married, Philip replies that he hopes to do so when his financial situation allows it, and even implies that Connie is the woman he would choose. Remake of a 1950 radio episode.

6. *Living Statues* (November 7, 1952). *Cast:* Paul Harvey (*Mr. Stone*). In the doghouse for breaking Mr. Conklin's eyeglasses—twice—Connie is assigned to spruce up his office. When she decides to use the new paint that Walter Denton just invented, not knowing one of the active ingredients is liquid cement, the result is a sticky situation for all involved.

Conklin's supervisor, Superintendent Stone, makes his first appearance in the TV series, though he's not yet played by Joseph Kearns, who will ultimately assume the role.

7. *Madison Country Club* (November 14, 1952). *Cast:* Isabel Randolph (*Mrs. Grabar*). Jealous that his rival at Clay City High School was given a sizable charitable contribution by a local philanthropist, Mr. Conklin invites the wealthy donor to visit Madison High. But his plan to convince the woman that the school is in dire financial straits goes awry when a misunderstanding finds Connie, Philip, and Walter dressed to the nines in costumes from the school play.

Isabel Randolph will later return to the series in the recurring role of Mrs. Nestor.

8. *Mr. Whipple* (November 21, 1952). *Cast:* Thurston Hall (*Mr. Whipple*), Parley Baer (*Mr. Bennett*). Retired nurse Mrs. Davis is asked by her former employer to assist him in treating eccentric Mr. Whipple, who has eaten nothing for the past ten days. Wrongly believing that the patient is destitute, Mrs. Davis has all the denizens of Madison High sacrificing their own needs to attend to a man who's actually known to Wall Street as "The Wizard of Finance."

9. *The Big Game* (November 28, 1952). "Snakehips" Geary, a football hero at Madison High some 40 years earlier, is now working as an assistant coach at the school. But when his lack of a high school diploma puts his job in jeopardy, Connie is assigned the task of giving him a crash course in English before the team's next game.

Character actor Burt Mustin (1884–1977), cast as Geary, would continue to play older men for another quarter-century, wrapping up his career with a featured role in *Phyllis* (CBS, 1975–1977).

10. *Blue Goldfish* (December 5, 1952). Walter, Harriet, and Mr. Boynton enlist Connie to persuade Mr. Conklin to purchase some needed equipment for the school, and to provide more heat in the chilly facility. Unfortunately for Miss Brooks, her boss is on the verge of instituting "an economy wave the likes of which this school has never seen," and refuses his staff and students' requests. Connie concocts a plan to persuade Mr. Conklin that the frigid conditions in the school have rendered her and her friends sick with colds.

Remake of a 1949 radio episode.

11. *The Stolen Aerial* (December 12, 1952). *Cast:* Hy Averback (*Felix Seymour*). Mrs. Davis asks Connie to take her TV aerial to Mr. Seymour's shop for repair. Connie does so reluctantly, because Mr. Seymour is "a wolf," but Mrs. Davis knows the shop owner will do the work for free because he likes Connie. When others at school hear that Miss Brooks can get them good prices at Seymour's, she finds herself loaded down with aerials and TV sets needing repair—the morning after Mr. Conklin's aerial has been stolen from his roof. Seeing the stash of TV equipment she has collected with Walter and Mr. Boynton's help, Conklin concludes that the hapless English teacher is a "female Fagin" on a crime wave.

The writers manage to work in a Desilu plug when Mrs. Davis tells a story about their next-door neighbor, who became tangled in "crossed wires" attempting to take down his own aerial. Hearing that, on his way to the hospital last Monday night at nine, Mr. Zimmerman was projecting a clear image of Channel 2, Connie cracks, "Oh, I'm sorry I didn't see him. I wanted to catch *I Love Lucy* that night."

12. *The Hobby Show* (December 19, 1952). Connie's friends feel she is stressed from overwork and should find a relaxing hobby. Mr. Conklin organizes a hobby afternoon at Mrs. Davis's house, where she is introduced to several possible choices—model trains (Walter), knitting (Mrs. Davis), chess (Mr. Boynton), finger painting (Harriet), and repairing toys for needy children (the Conklins). Her efforts to participate in multiple activities simultaneously prove not to be the stress reliever Connie's friends had hoped to give her.

13. *Christmas Show* (December 26, 1952). *Cast:* Virginia Gordon (*Mrs. Conklin*), Florence Bates (*Mrs. Carney*). Broke during the holiday season, Connie plans to finance her friends' gifts by opening her own early and exchanging them at Sherry's Department Store. Crotchety Mrs. Carney, employed in the store's Gift Exchange department, soon wearies of Connie and her friends as they spend the day exchanging one another's gifts. That evening, Christmas Eve dinner at Mrs. Davis's house comes a cropper when Mrs. Conklin invites a guest, who turns out to be her good friend Mrs. Carney.

The great movie character actress Florence Bates (1888–1954), seen as Mrs. Carney, had previously made a guest appearance on Desilu's *I Love Lucy*.

14. *The Pet Shop* (January 9, 1953). Connie is hurt when she thinks Mr. Boynton stood her up for their after-school date to meet in front of the pet shop. Advised by Walter to act coolly uninterested, Connie succeeds only in hurting her beau's feelings. Next she tries a different stance—making a follow-up date with Mr. Boynton, intending to turn the tables by leaving him waiting.

The plot of this episode somewhat recalls the series pilot—once again Connie is foolishly taking romantic advice from Walter Denton. Walter tells Connie that his friends at the malt shop are mystified by her interest in Mr. Boynton—"How you get such a large charge out of such a shy guy."

15. *The Hurricane* (January 16, 1953). Left in charge at Madison High while Mr. Conklin awaits the delivery of some new furniture at home, Connie hears a weather report on Walter's homemade radio concerning an approaching hurricane. After dismissing classes for the day, Connie and her friends gather at the Conklins' house, where his new bamboo furniture seems just the thing to board up the windows for the storm. Too bad the station broadcasting the weather alert happens to be in downtown Bombay, India.

16. *Old Marblehead* (January 23, 1953). Mr. Conklin has ordered a bust in his own likeness, to be placed in the school library. In order to finance this piece of art, he has instituted the "Conklin Carelessness Code," in which he fines students and faculty for minor rule infractions. Connie, who's racked up so many fines that she can't afford lunch in the school cafeteria, finds a unique way to settle the score.

Remake of a 1949 radio episode.

17. *Monsieur LeBlanche* (January 30, 1953). While Mr. Boynton is away at a biologists' convention, Connie decides to encourage the attentions of Madison High's French teacher, Maurice LeBlanche, who seems to fancy her. Thanks to some sloppy translation by Walter Denton,

Connie believes the perfume-scented note Mr. LeBlanche sent her is a *billet-doux*. Actually, he's hoping to borrow $50 from Connie to buy a used car from Mr. Conklin.

This episode introduces Maurice Marsac in his recurring role as Madison High faculty member Maurice LeBlanche. He takes the place of a similar character from the radio series, Jacques Monet, played by Gerald Mohr. Inside joke? When Connie sends Mr. LeBlanche home after realizing he didn't want a date, she mutters, "Goodbye, my fancy." (Eve Arden was featured in a 1951 film by this title.) Remake of a 1949 radio episode.

18. *Cure That Habit* (February 6, 1953). *Cast:* Parley Baer (*Mr. Chambers*). Practical-joking Walter Denton forges Mr. Conklin's signature to a request for literature on alcoholism from an organization called "Cure That Habit, Inc." Mr. Chambers, head of the organization and father of a teenage son who attends Madison High, alerts school board chair Mr. Stone. Thanks to a series of coincidences involving Mr. Conklin's recurring case of hiccups, some stray animals let loose in his office by Stretch Snodgrass, and the principal's broken eyeglasses, Mr. Stone is convinced that Madison's principal is indeed a stumbling, hiccupping, delusional drunk.

This is the first television appearance of the recurring character of Stretch Snodgrass, dopey student athlete of Madison High, played by Leonard Smith. The (unseen) character of Minerva, Mrs. Davis' cat, is also introduced. Remake of a 1950 radio episode.

19. *The Model Teacher* (February 13, 1953). Connie is chosen as Model Teacher of the Year by *Snap* magazine. As a result of the honor, she is followed around for an entire day by the magazine's pretty layout editor, Stephanie Forrest, who proceeds to take an all-too-frank set of photos. When Miss Forrest not only butters up Walter and Mr. Conklin, but also finds Mr. Boynton intriguing, Connie decides she no longer wants to be Teacher of the Year.

Remake of a 1948 radio episode.

20. *Wake-Up Plan* (February 20, 1953). *Cast:* Lou Merrill (*Mr. Gleason*), Charles Evans (*Mr. Stone*). Connie is in hot water when she accidentally takes some of Mrs. Davis's sleeping pills, making her late to school. But the combination of the pills, plus Mr. Conklin's new early-morning calisthenics program for faculty, has almost everyone at Madison a little drowsy when Mr. Stone pays a visit.

21. *The Cafeteria Strike* (February 27, 1953). Thanks to the new chef in Madison High's cafeteria (who happens to be Mr. Conklin's brother-in-law), the food is so awful that Walter Denton is organizing a boycott. When a visiting journalist overhears Connie say that the cafeteria cuisine is "putrid," he plans an exposé in his newspaper. With her job in jeopardy (again), Connie devises a plan to save the day, using Mr. Boynton's family recipe for meatballs.

Remake of a 1949 radio episode.

22. *Mr. Casey's Will* (March 6, 1953). Mrs. Davis's sister Angela has appointed Connie executrix of her late cat's will. Among those due to inherit something are Mr. Conklin, Mr. Boynton, and Walter, none of whom actually remembers meeting "Mister Casey." Connie bets Mrs. Davis that her friends are too honest to take advantage of the situation, but she is destined to be disillusioned.

23. *Conklin's Love Nest* (March 13, 1953). *Cast:* Maurice Marsac (*Mr. LeBlanche*). Mr. Conklin has an apartment available to rent, and all of Connie's friends think it would be perfect for her and Mr. Boynton. Walter decides that Mr. LeBlanche is the right person to suggest to Mr. Boynton that it's time he gives up the lonely life of a bachelor. Before the day is over, Connie receives a marriage proposal—but not from the right man; Mr. Conklin rents his apartment; and Mr. Boynton has a new, French-speaking roommate to keep him company.

According to this episode, Connie pays Mrs. Davis $40 a month in rent. Once again, a misunderstanding results from the fact that only Harriet Conklin really understands Mr. LeBlanche's French.

24. *The Honest Burglar* (March 20, 1953). Connie is awakened in the middle of the night by a strange man in Mrs. Davis's kitchen. After learning that the unemployed man, Joe Phillips, broke into the house in search of food, Connie arranges for him to fill in as Madison High's custodian. But when valuables begin to disappear around school, she fears that her trust in Mr. Phillips was misplaced.

Connie (to burglar): "Well, if you're looking for money, I can save us both a lot of trouble. I'm a schoolteacher."

Remake of a 1950 radio episode.

25. *Fisher's Pawn Shop* (March 27, 1953). *Cast:* Frank Nelson (*Mr. Fisher*). Looking forward to attending the opening game of Madison High's baseball season with Mr. Boynton, Connie is disappointed to learn that the game has been canceled because the team can't afford uniforms. In order to raise money to rent uniforms, Connie and her friends all try to transact business at the nearby pawn shop with items they have borrowed from one another.

Actor Frank Nelson (1911–1986), well-remembered for his many appearances with Jack Benny, appears here as pawn shop owner Mr. Fisher. And, no, he doesn't greet each new customer by turning around and saying, "Yeeeeeessssss?" Remake of a 1950 radio episode.

26. *Lulu, the Pin-Up Boat* (April 3, 1953). *Cast:* Joseph Kearns (*Mr. Michaels*). Insisting on propriety at Madison High, Mr. Conklin not only decrees conservative dress for students and faculty, but also conducts a search of student lockers, confiscating Walter Denton's pinup photos. Walter's photo of Betty Grable finds its way to Mr. Conklin's desk drawer, but he tells Connie it's a picture of his motorboat, *Lulu*. When straitlaced Assistant Superintendent Michaels pays a visit, he's shocked by the photo, and somehow Connie's explanations about *Lulu* don't seem to help.

Actor Joseph Kearns, who will later settle into a recurring role as Superintendent Stone, plays Mr. Michaels here.

27. *The Yodar Kritch Award* (April 10, 1953). *Cast:* Eddie Ryder (*Bones Snodgrass*). It's time to present the school's annual Yodar Kritch Award, given to a student for "unique achievement in English literature." Connie is looking forward to attending an after-school barbecue held at the home of Winston "Bones" Snodgrass, Stretch's equally dimwitted brother, because Walter and his friends have planned a romantic meeting for her there with Mr. Boynton. But when Bones's father, upset about his grades, decrees that his son's barbecue will be canceled unless Bones wins the Kritch Award, Connie takes on the formidable challenge of tutoring the hapless student.

Though Mr. Boynton plays a part in the plot of this episode, Robert Rockwell does not appear. The idea that Madison High was founded by Yodar Kritch was first introduced on TV in #26, "Fisher's Pawn Shop."

28. *Madame Brooks DuBarry* (April 17, 1953). *Cast:* Maurice Marsac (*Mr. LeBlanche*). Mr. Conklin's belief that Connie is a bad influence on his daughter Harriet is only increased when Miss Brooks and Mr. Boynton run out of gas on the way home from a dance, and are forced to spend the night stranded on a deserted highway. Harriet invites her father to observe Connie spending a quiet evening with Mr. Boynton, so as to disprove his suspicions, but unfortunately they're just in time to witness yet another fervent attempt by Mr. LeBlanche to make Mr. Boynton jealous.

29. *Marinated Hearing* (April 24, 1953). *Cast:* Charles Evans (*Mr. Stone*). It's "Board of Education Day" at Madison High, and Mr. Conklin has planned an elaborate ceremony to curry the favor of board chair Mr. Stone. Mischievous Walter arranges for the old school cannon to be fired right alongside Mr. Conklin during the ceremony. Rendered temporarily deaf, Mr. Conklin assigns Connie to read the fawning speech he wrote, unaware that it's inadvertently been torn up and pieced back together with chunks of an essay about baboons that Bones Snodgrass wrote for biology class.

Remake of a 1950 radio episode.

30. *The Festival* (May 1, 1953). Armed with a chic new dress, Connie is looking forward to her date with Mr. Boynton at the school festival. But the softhearted schoolteacher is distressed to realize that school staff members Gus Geary and his lady friend, Katie, can't afford to take part in the event. Despite Mrs. Davis's admonition that "charity begins at home," Connie and Philip find themselves sacrificing their own interests—and new wardrobes—to help Gus and Katie.

Burt Mustin reprises his role from #9 as Gus. Actress Elvia Allman (1904–1992), perhaps best-remembered as Selma Plout on *Petticoat Junction,* plays Katie. Just a few months prior to this appearance, she played the forewoman of Kramer's Kandy Kitchen on the classic "Job Switching" episode of Desilu's *I Love Lucy.*

31. ***Suzy Prentiss*** **(May 8, 1953).** *Cast:* Eddie Ryder (*Bones Snodgrass*), Pattee Chapman (*Suzy Prentiss*). Bones Snodgrass's academic performance is even worse than usual lately, thanks to his having fallen in love. The object of his affection is a transfer student named Suzy Prentiss, who is even more stupid than Bones himself. Connie decides the two numbskulls would make a perfect couple, if only they had suitable formal wear to attend the school board banquet.

The plot of this episode so closely resembles #30 that it's surprising the writers and production staff chose to have them air back-to-back. This time, it's the Conklins who own evening clothes that someone else needs to borrow. Remake of a 1950 radio episode.

32. ***Conklin Plays Detective*** **(May 15, 1953).** *Cast:* Eddie Ryder (*Bones Snodgrass*). Mr. Conklin is determined to find the culprit who stole his typewriter and made an expensive long-distance call on his office telephone. When Connie, Walter, and Bones come to the conclusion that Mr. Boynton was the guilty party, they resort to desperate measures in order to protect their friend.

33. ***Public Property on Parade*** **(May 22, 1953).** *Cast:* Eddie Ryder (*Bones Snodgrass*), Leo Curley (*Mayor*). Connie ghostwrites a stirring speech on respecting public property that Mr. Conklin is to deliver at the City Hall banquet, and then incinerates the script when she thinks that he doesn't like it. Faced with a short deadline for rewriting, and the recent shutoff of electricity at Mrs. Davis's house, Connie sets up shop on the sidewalk to do some fast typing. With only the best of intentions, Mr. Boynton, Walter, and Bones Snodgrass temporarily liberate various pieces of public property so that Connie will have the tools she needs to finish her work.

34. ***Mrs. Davis Reads Tea Leaves*** **(May 29, 1953).** Using tea leaves to predict Connie's future, Mrs. Davis tells her that she will come into unexpected money, be treated more kindly by Mr. Conklin, and, most importantly, become Mr. Boynton's June bride. When she not only receives a tax refund check, but is also told that Mr. Boynton has an important question to ask her, Connie starts to believe her fortune is coming true. Little does she know that Mr. Boynton wants to operate a summer camp for children, and hopes she will agree to invest in the business, and serve as his partner.

35. ***The Stolen Wardrobe*** **(June 5, 1953).** *Cast:* Herb Vigran (*Mr. Smith*), Peter Leeds (*Jerry Jones*). Two crooks who robbed Sherry's Department Store duck into Connie's classroom to evade capture. Loaded down with furs and gowns they have liberated, they tell the perpetually impoverished teacher they are salesmen who want her to model the clothes for the other women of Madison High, as a promotional gimmick. After learning of the robbery, Connie's friends try to return the clothes to the store, but are mistaken for the thieves. With their detailed descriptions broadcast over the radio, Mr. Conklin, Mr. Boynton, and Walter disguise themselves with the only costumes available—Connie's newfound finery.

36. ***Aunt Mattie Boynton*** **(June 12, 1953).** *Cast:* Mary Jane Croft (*Daisy Enright*). Mr. Boynton tells Connie and her rival, Miss Enright, that he would get married if he could find a woman as industrious as his Aunt Mattie, who not only taught school but raised a large family. When

Mr. Conklin announces that he wants a teacher to introduce a business administration course at Madison, both ladies seek the assignment in order to impress Mr. Boynton. Lacking the business administration coursework that Miss Enright boasts, Connie tries another tack to show her financial savvy—arranging to get the fuel oil Mr. Conklin needs for his house at a bargain price.

Mary Jane Croft makes her TV debut as Miss Enright. A busy and successful radio actress, she made her mark on television as well, seen in recurring roles as Clara Randolph on *The Adventures of Ozzie and Harriet* (1952–1966) and as Lucy's pal Mary Jane on *The Lucy Show* (1962–1968) and *Here's Lucy* (1968–1974).

37. *Capistrano's Revenge* **(June 19, 1953).** *Cast:* Eddie Ryder (*Bones Snodgrass*). Connie, looking after a bird with a broken wing, entrusts his care to Mr. Boynton. When the biology teacher wrongly believes the bird has died, neither he, Mr. Conklin, nor Walter Denton has the heart to tell Miss Brooks. Bones Snodgrass brings the bird back from his father's pet store just as the others try bringing in substitute sparrows.

This episode features a rare display of warmth between Connie and her principal, whom she twice kisses on the cheek to thank for his kindness.

38. *June Bride* **(June 26, 1953).** *Cast:* Maurice Marsac (*Mr. LeBlanche*), Jerry Hausner (*Messenger*). Mr. LeBlanche asks Connie to serve as stand-in for his French bride. When Walter overhears the pair discussing the ceremony, and obtaining a license, he jumps to the wrong conclusion. Connie's friends, believing she has despaired of ever marrying Mr. Boynton, turn up at the ceremony in hopes of convincing her to avoid a "spite marriage."

SECOND SEASON (1953–54)

39. *Clay City Chaperone* **(October 2, 1953).** *Cast:* Mary Jane Croft (*Daisy Enright*). Both Connie and Miss Enright strive to be named female chaperone for an out-of-town football game and dance, so as to spend time with fellow chaperone Mr. Boynton. At first Connie, believing Miss Enright has won the competition, talks Mr. Boynton out of attending. Then, once she is named chaperone, it's up to her to change his mind.

This season opener shows that the set for Mr. Conklin's office has been rearranged since last season, with his desk more prominently downstage.

40. *Bones, Son of Cyrano* **(October 9, 1953).** Walter is jealous because an anonymous admirer has been sending love poetry to Harriet Conklin. When Connie advises him to fight fire with fire, Walter uses an excerpt from *Cyrano de Bergerac*, written out for him by Mr. Boynton. The romantic poem in the handwriting of the shy biology teacher takes turns passing into the wrong hands, leading to multiple complications.

41. *Spare That Rod* **(October 16, 1953).** When Walter finds an old letter from the Board of Education chiding the principal of Madison High for his "flagrantly dictatorial" methods, he leads Mr. Conklin to believe it was addressed to him. Wanting to protect his job, Mr. Conklin not only develops a more genial persona, but encourages Connie and her friends to prepare a list of his faults. Unfortunately for them, Mr. Conklin notices the 1944 postmark on the letter just before they arrive with their list.

Stretch Snodgrass returns, taking the place of his brother. No smarter than his brother, Stretch obliges when Walter tells him to "listen to this letter," bending down to put his ear to the paper. Remake of a 1950 radio episode.

42. *Faculty Band* **(October 23, 1953).** Mr. Boynton has lined up 11 teachers to play in the faculty band he's conducting. Naturally Connie wants to add herself to the ensemble, despite her distinctly limited experience playing either the piano or the violin. She's forced to think fast when it develops that Mr. Conklin also covets the last open slot in the band.

43. *The Little Visitor* (October 30, 1953). *Cast:* Joseph Kearns (*Mr. Stone*), Jerry Hausner (*Salesman*). When Connie hears from Mrs. Conklin that her family is expecting a "little visitor," the conclusion-jumping schoolteacher congratulates her principal and shops for a bassinet. In fact, the expected visitor is a pet monkey that belongs to Mrs. Conklin's sister. The resulting confusion causes board chair Mr. Stone to reconsider his decision to offer Mr. Conklin a promotion.

Joseph Kearns makes his debut in the recurring role of Mr. Stone. Desilu favorite Jerry Hausner plays the salesman at Sherry's Department Store.

44. *Trial by Jury* (November 6, 1953). Connie wants to keep her traffic ticket a secret from Mr. Conklin. But even after Mr. Boynton, Walter, and Bones do their best to help her get out of school for her day in court, the jury proves to have an oddly familiar face.

45. *Phone Book Follies* (November 13, 1953). The phone company is issuing new directories, but requires that the old ones be returned in exchange. When both Connie's and Mr. Conklin's phone books turn up missing, each suspects the other of having committed some petty pilfering.

46. *Thanksgiving Show* (November 20, 1953). *Cast:* Paula Winslowe (*Martha Conklin*). Unable to afford anything more than a measly squab for Thanksgiving dinner, Mrs. Davis suggests that Connie wangle an invitation to eat at a friend's house. But Connie's best efforts to share a holiday meal with Walter, Mr. Boynton, and the Conklins only result in more mouths to feed at her own house.

This episode introduces Paula Winslowe as Mrs. Conklin, replacing Virginia Gordon. Remake of a 1949 radio episode.

47. *Vitamin E-4* (November 27, 1953). *Cast:* Joseph Kearns (*Mr. Stone*), Barney Phillips (*Police Lieutenant*). Learning that her sister Doris is expecting a baby, Connie feels pressed to help with expenses. Offered a job by the mysterious Professor Anderson, who manufactures Vitamin E-4, Connie resolves to get herself fired from Madison so that she can accept the more lucrative opportunity.

Reprising a line previously heard in the series pilot, Connie has another argument with Mr. Boynton in which she retorts, "Wanna make something of it, Frog-Boy?" The climactic scene, in which Connie, Boynton, and Conklin try their hands at manufacturing Vitamin E-4, is reminiscent of *I Love Lucy*'s "Job Switching" episode. We also learn here that Mr. Boynton has a younger brother named Bob.

48. *Swap Week* (December 11, 1953). *Cast:* Robert Ellis (*Larry Clayton*). Connie's new student, Larry Clayton, institutes a fad for swapping at Madison High. Among the unexpectedly hot tickets for trading are ownership stakes in Walter's dilapidated jalopy, which Mr. Boynton hopes to use to keep an important appointment with Mr. Stone.

49. *Golden Slippers* (December 18, 1953). *Cast:* Dan Tobin (*T.J. McFadden*), Joe Forte (*Mr. Hilman*). A modern-day Cinderella story begins when Connie tries on shoes in a local store. The mysterious salesman lends her a pair of golden slippers to wear to Madison High's dance, telling her they must be returned by midnight. A gown, flowers, and transportation by coach make the schoolteacher's evening quite memorable, but an explanation for the odd happenings doesn't come until she and Mrs. Davis hear a late-night radio broadcast.

This episode features an interesting guest player—actor Joe Forte (1893–1967), who originated the role of Osgood Conklin on radio.

50. *Christmas Show* (December 25, 1953). *Cast:* Sammy Ogg (*Boy*). Left alone for a dull Christmas Eve with only Mrs. Davis's cat for company, Connie dozes off and dreams of a magic holiday tree that seems to have an effect on anyone who touches it. She wakes just in time to receive an unexpected visit by the Conklins, Mr. Boynton, and Walter Denton.

Mrs. Davis's cat, Minerva, who's frequently mentioned in the show's scripts, makes a rare on-camera appearance here. An offstage human provides a not-terribly-convincing meow for the feline. Note that the four-legged performer cast as Minerva doesn't seem terribly happy to be held and snuggled by Eve Arden, nearly giving her a back-legged kick at one point. Sheldon Leonard is credited here as camera director.

51. *Hospital Capers* (January 8, 1954). *Cast:* Frank Nelson (*Mr. Glint*). After a bad fall lands Mr. Boynton in the hospital, an ambulance-chasing lawyer persuades him he should sue the owner of the property where the accident took place. That owner happens to be Mr. Conklin, whose insurance policy renewal Connie forgot to mail.

This is the first episode to credit Arthur Alsberg as a writer, along with Lewis and Quillan. Visiting Mr. Boynton, Connie brings three books chosen "at random" for him to read while he convalesces—*Marriage Made Easy, No Woman of His Own; Or, My Bachelorhood Drove Me Insane*, and a work of poetry titled *Honeymoons Are Lots of Fun, Two Can Live as Cheap as One*.

52. *Postage Due* (January 15, 1954). *Cast:* Junius Matthews (*Mr. Bagley*), Jerry Hausner (*Barber*), Gail Bonney (*Landlady*), Barney Phillips (*Detective*), Peter Leeds (*Greengrocer*). Feeling guilty because she owes him 20 cents for an insufficiently stamped letter, Connie tries to locate elderly postman Mr. Bagley. When she learns that he abruptly quit his job the day before, Connie fears that the kindly old man has met with foul play.

This episode, chock full of frequently seen *Brooks* players, features a *Dragnet* parody.

53. *Do It Yourself* (January 22, 1954). Convinced by Walter that she can build a piece of furniture she needs for her bedroom, Connie asks Mr. Conklin for the loan of some tools from shop class. Thanks to Walter, Mr. Conklin believes that his English teacher is perfectly competent to use woodworking tools—and to build him a new garage.

54. *Bobbsey Twins in Stir* (January 29, 1954). *Cast:* Earle Ross (*Mr. Fairchild*), Eddie Ryder (*Bones*), Joseph Kearns (*Mr. Stone*), Frank Gerstle (*Officer Ross*), Douglas Evans (*Mr. Brady*). "Love Your Neighbor Week" finds everyone at Madison High striving to raise money for charity. When a con man persuades Mrs. Davis to sell phony tickets to the Policeman's Ball, Connie unwittingly makes matters worse by not only selling tickets, but printing more in the school print shop.

55. *The Jockey* (February 12, 1954). *Cast:* Pat Goldin (*Billy Bunker*). Mr. Boynton asks Connie and Mrs. Davis to take in two temporary house guests—his friend Billy Bunker, a jockey, and his horse, Margie Girl. When Billy turns up at school, Connie and Mr. Boynton try to convince Mr. Conklin that the diminutive, middle-aged jockey is a transfer student he's forgotten.

56. *Brooks' New Car* (February 19, 1954). *Cast:* Paula Winslowe (*Mrs. Conklin*). Proud owner of a new used car, Connie dents its fender trying to back out of a tight parking space. After taking her car to the repair shop, she learns that the same shop is currently repairing Mr. Conklin's vehicle, which was damaged in the same incident.

A running joke revived from #44, "Trial by Jury," concerns a slippery slope outside the Madison Theater, where both Connie and Mr. Conklin have now had accidents. Did one of the writers actually plunge down a hill and crash into a fruit stand, as both characters have now done?

57. *The Hobo Jungle* (February 26, 1954). *Cast:* Sid Melton (*Mr. Poole*). Connie learns that her honor student Larry Brent is homeless, living with his father and two friends in a "hobo jungle." Intending to report the situation so that Larry can be found a proper home, she instead finds herself attempting to keep his secret from Mr. Conklin.

58. *The Wild Goose* (March 12, 1954). Mischievous Walter Denton plays an April Fool's joke on Mr. Conklin, tricking him into believing he won a television set on a radio quiz program called *Lucky Goldmine*. But when Mr. Conklin dispatches Connie to Sherry's Department Store to pick up his set, she, Mr. Boynton, and Stretch Snodgrass innocently steal merchandise under the watchful eye of the store detective.

Jane Morgan does not appear as Mrs. Davis in this episode. Instead, a typical breakfast scene

Mr. Conklin (Gale Gordon) foolishly thinks *Our Miss Brooks* (Eve) can build him a new garage, in the 1954 episode "Do It Yourself."

is played with her sister Angela Devon, played by Jesslyn Fax. After suffering a stroke, Morgan will be absent from the series for the next several weeks. Remake of a 1950 radio episode.

59. *Hello, Mr. Chips* (March 19, 1954). *Cast:* Gil Frye (*Mr. Philpot*). Since Mr. Boynton has been overheard to say he may not get married until he's older, Connie and Walter embark on a scheme to convince the biology teacher he's aging rapidly. When Mr. Conklin assigns Connie to play host to a visiting British schoolmaster, she decides that the handsome visitor might help arouse a spark in her usual suitor.

60. *Parlor Game* (March 26, 1954). *Cast:* Paula Winslowe (*Mrs. Conklin*). Disgusted by the burgeoning romance between his daughter, Harriet, and Walter Denton, Mr. Conklin wants Connie to set a good example for the girl. Recruited to spend a boring evening at the Conklins,' Connie tries to cut it short by annoying her boss with a ridiculously convoluted parlor game she invented.

In this episode's funniest scene, Connie takes lessons from Harriet on how to get a man to put his arm around you, and rouse his passions with music.

61. *A Dry Scalp Is Better Than None* (April 9, 1954). Mrs. Davis's hypochondriac sister, Angela, makes a bid for sympathy by claiming her doctor has given her only one month to live. Connie and her friends decide to grant Angela's last wish by throwing an off-season Christmas party.

62. *The English Test* (April 16, 1954). Connie's latest English test results in flunking grades for most of her students. As a result, Mr. Conklin demands that she tutor Harriet privately, interrupting Connie's planned date with Mr. Boynton. Trying to impress the biology teacher, she takes on the task of teaching not only Harriet but Walter and numbskulled classmate Nora.

Once again, reference is made to Mr. Boynton's ideal woman, his beloved Aunt Mattie, whose accomplishments Connie can never quite match. Louis A. Nicoletti appears as Nora's father.

63. *Second-Hand First Aid* (April 23, 1954). *Cast:* Mary Jane Croft (*Daisy Enright*). When Miss Enright takes a leave of absence from Madison High, Mr. Conklin drafts Connie to take over the night class in first aid that her rival had been teaching. Mr. Conklin invites himself and Miss Enright over to Connie's house to assess the new instructor's first-aid skills, giving Connie a golden opportunity to get the best of both her principal and her longtime rival.

Remake of a 1951 radio episode.

64. *The Egg* (April 30, 1954). Mrs. Davis gives Connie an egg that she feels sure is due to hatch shortly. When Connie takes the egg to school, amateur photographer Mr. Conklin decides that the birth of a baby chick would be just the subject to help him win a magazine's photo contest.

65. *The Bakery* (May 14, 1954). *Cast:* Mary Jane Croft (*Daisy Enright*). Connie springs into action when she hears that one of Mr. Boynton's old flames is in town.

66. *Old Age Plan* (May 21, 1954). Angela's women's group is selling old-age annuities. Promised a commission if she can sign up faculty at Madison High for the plan, Connie finds her sales pitch succeeds only in making her friends develop psychosomatic symptoms of their advancing years.

67. *The Hawkins Travel Agency* (May 28, 1954). *Cast:* Joseph Kearns (*Superintendent Stone*). Connie is promised a discounted deal on her summer vacation by the Hawkins Travel Agency if she can sign up some of her friends as clients. Little does she know that both Mr. Boynton and Mr. Conklin have been offered a similar deal, leading to a last-ditch effort by all three to make a sales pitch to Mr. Stone.

68. *The Bicycle Thief* (June 11, 1954). Mr. Conklin posts a notice on the school bulletin board offering a reward for recovering his stolen bicycle. Connie and Mr. Boynton, who find out that the bicycle was borrowed temporarily by a student whose family is having financial problems, try to keep the boy from facing the principal's wrath.

69. *Just Remember the Red River Valley* (June 18, 1954). *Cast:* Frank Nelson (*Matthew Jones*), Joseph Kearns (*Superintendent Stone*). Since Connie is short of money as usual, Mrs. Davis suggests that she take a summer job with Deacon Jones's traveling square-dance troupe. A case of mistaken identity causes Connie and her friends to audition their hillbilly act for a school official investigating Madison High's poor test scores.

THIRD SEASON (1954–55)

70. *The Miserable Caballeros* **(October 1, 1954).** *Cast:* Ricky Vera (*Ricky Velasco*), Hy Averback (*Uncle Roberto*), Rico Alaniz (*Uncle Alberto*). A 10-year-old Mexican boy turns up in Connie's classroom, saying he ran away from his cruel uncle and wishes to enroll in Madison High. Charmed, Connie and her friends try to find a way to help the boy, unaware that there's more to his story than meets the eye.

The recurring character of Ricky Velasco, played by child actor Ricky Vera, is introduced here. Vera will come back as a different character in Season 4.

71. *Blood, Sweat, and Laughs* **(October 15, 1954).** *Cast:* Leo Curley (*Mr. Hennessey*). The school board is sponsoring a costume ball, which Connie and Mr. Conklin will be attending. When Connie picks up their costumes, however, she winds up with the wrong set of clothes.

72. *Life Can Be Bones* **(October 22, 1954).** Connie isn't pleased to see that the new teacher in Madison's biology department is an attractive woman. With the help of Walter Denton, Connie leads Mr. Boynton to believe that there are ancient fossils buried in Mrs. Davis's backyard, which will hopefully distract him from the newcomer.

73. *Two-Way Stretch Snodgrass* **(October 29, 1954).** *Cast:* Ray Teal (*Jasper Flint*). Mr. Conklin's rival at neighboring Hamilton High School tries to convince Madison's star athlete, Stretch Snodgrass, to transfer schools. When Hamilton's new coach sets out to obtain permission from Stretch's parents for the transfer, he finds himself contending with impostors in the form of Mr. Conklin, Connie, and Walter.

Richard Crenna does a very funny impersonation of Leonard Smith playing Stretch Snodgrass.

74. *Angela's Wedding* **(November 5, 1954).** *Cast:* Sam Hearn (*Gregory Farnsworth*), Ben Gage (*Coach*). Mrs. Davis's sister is planning to marry her pen pal whom she met through the Why-Be-Lonely Club, even though she's never laid eyes on the man. A case of mistaken identity has her thinking that Madison High's new coach is her intended.

75. *Van Gogh, Man, Gogh* **(November 12, 1954).** A newspaper article reveals that a prominent art dealer is touring high schools, hoping to discover a gifted new artist. While Connie paints a self-portrait, and Mr. Boynton creates a likeness of his frog, MacDougall, it's Walter's depiction of his favorite teacher that unexpectedly causes a sensation.

76. *Jewel Robbery* **(November 26, 1954).** Connie sees Mr. Boynton outside Frank's Jewelry Store just after it's been robbed, and deduces that a recent blow to his head has given him criminal tendencies. The policeman investigating the case comes to Madison High only to find at least three people ready to confess to the crime.

When Connie, alluding to the crime she thinks Mr. Boynton committed, tells Mrs. Davis, "Mr. Boynton *did* something last night!" the unflappable landlady, thinking he was on a date with Connie, retorts, "It's about time!"

77. *Space, Who Needs It?* **(December 3, 1954).** Infatuated with his new homemade telescope, Mr. Conklin proudly announces he has discovered a new planet, which he dubs Conklin, Junior. Little does he know that he's the victim of yet another Walter Denton practical joke.

78. *The Novelist* **(December 10, 1954).** *Cast:* John Smith (*Terence Layton*). Terence Layton, a student at Madison High seven years ago, is now a successful author. His newest manuscript, a memoir of his high school years, quotes Connie as calling Mr. Conklin "the nation's most unprincipled principal."

Actor John Smith (1931–1995) was later the star of TV's *Laramie*.

79. *Four Leaf Clover* **(December 17, 1954).** *Cast:* Sid Melton (*Sammy Clark*), Eddie Garr (*Officer Harvey Fletcher*), Hy Averback (*Paul Morrell*). When she finds a four-leaf clover on her way to school, Connie feels assured that it will be her lucky day. But after a run-in with the police, car trouble, and a quarrel with Mr. Boynton, she's forced to rethink her position.

80. *The Citizen's League* (January 7, 1955). *Cast:* Marjorie Bennett (*Mrs. Duffy*), Paula Winslowe (*Mrs. Conklin*). Connie's reading from a patriotic pamphlet causes her, Mr. Boynton, and Mr. Conklin to reflect on their darkest secrets. As it turns out, all three are thinking back to the Fourth of July, when they collectively caused a lady pianist to miss her chance at playing at the governor's wedding.

81. *Buddy* (January 14, 1955). A letter delivered to Connie by mistake causes both Mr. Conklin and Mr. Boynton to fear that their lives have been threatened by an aggressive bully whom they encountered in the park a few days earlier. Meanwhile, Ricky Velasco pays a return visit to Madison High.

Ricky Vera makes his second appearance as Ricky Velasco.

82. *Noodnick, Daughter of Medic* (January 21, 1955). *Cast:* Dan Tobin (*Dr. Keller*), Joseph Kearns (*Mr. Stone*). Connie is finally set to be named head of Madison's English department, provided she can pass a physical exam with a somewhat distracted doctor. Meanwhile, Mr. Conklin, having heard that his English teacher is to be promoted, jumps to the wrong conclusion and thinks his own tenure at Madison is coming to an end.

Remake of a 1949 radio episode.

83. *The Stuffed Gopher* (January 28, 1955). When Madison High is vandalized, Mr. Conklin blames Connie, who supposedly left a door unlocked after working late. But when the real culprit turns out to be a student whose intentions were better than his brains, Connie and friends scheme to set things right without charges being pressed.

84. *Safari O'Toole* (February 4, 1955). *Cast:* Burt Mustin (*Safari O'Toole*), Frank Nelson (*Mr. Fisher*). Mrs. Davis's gentleman caller, Safari O'Toole, thrills her with his stories of jungle escapades, until Connie and Mr. Boynton realize he's a phony. Mrs. Davis's birthday party that evening demonstrates that Safari isn't the only one with a secret or two up his sleeve.

85. *The Weighing Machine* (February 11, 1955). After losing a penny in a sidewalk vending machine, Connie is persuaded by Mrs. Davis and Mr. Boynton not to let the matter drop. When Walter brings the offending machine to school, Connie finds herself making some fast explanations to its owner.

86. *Public Speaker's Nightmare* (February 18, 1955). *Cast:* Gail Bonney (*Mrs. Ferguson*), Earle Ross (*Mr. Fogarty*). Just before important visitors are due to arrive at Madison, Connie innocently lends Mr. Conklin a book that renders him terrified of speaking in public. With help from Walter Denton, Connie and Mr. Boynton devise a plan to pre-record their principal's speech.

87. *The Auction* (February 25, 1955). Mr. Conklin puts Connie in charge of obtaining merchandise for the school's charity auction. Thanks to the brain power of one Stretch Snodgrass, Mr. Conklin's own new furniture ends up being auctioned off for a song.

Remake of a 1950 radio episode.

88. *The Mambo* (March 4, 1955). *Cast:* Ivan Kirov (*Orville Mason*), Jerry Hausner (*Elmer*). Mr. Conklin thinks a dance craze at the local malt shop is distracting Madison's students from completing their homework assignments.

89. *The Dream* (March 11, 1955). Is Connie finally marrying her longtime beloved Mr. Boynton? No, it's all just a dream, and even the dream comes with a rude awakening.

90. *The Return of Red Smith* (March 25, 1955). *Cast:* Ian Wolfe (*Mr. Smith*). Mrs. Davis is expecting a visit from her long-ago boyfriend, Red Smith, whose snobbish family forbade them to marry when they were teenagers. Since Mrs. Davis has led Smith to believe that she is socially prominent and wealthy, Connie and Mr. Boynton try to help her put on a false front for his visit.

Hearing that Mrs. Davis's furniture may be repossessed, Mr. Boynton offers to lend some items from his apartment, saying, "I've got a loveseat I never use." Connie retorts, "You're telling me!"

91. *Le Chien Chaud et Le Mouton Noir* **(April 1, 1955).** *Cast:* Joseph Kearns (*Mr. Stone*), Philip Van Zandt (*Mr. Dishong*). In financial straits as usual, Connie applies for a night job at what turns out to be a hot-dog stand owned by Mr. Conklin. Unluckily for both teacher and principal, their moonlighting attracts the attention of Mr. Stone, who's on a crusade against faculty holding second jobs.

92. *Kritch Cave* **(April 15, 1955).** *Cast:* Parley Baer (*Mr. Maynard*). When Mr. Conklin learns that some land adjoining Madison High is to be sold for $100 an acre, he puts Connie in charge of obtaining a higher price. Connie manages to do exactly that—unfortunately, the land she sold turns out to be that on which the school itself sits.

93. *Fargo's Whiskers* **(April 22, 1955).** Advised by Harriet to change her look in order to revive Mr. Boynton's interest, Connie is frustrated when not only a new hairstyle, but wigs and costumes from the school's drama department, fail to attract his attention. Unluckily for Connie, new school inspector Mr. Fargo arrives for a visit just as her behavior is growing exceedingly outlandish.

94. *The Great Baseball Slide* **(April 29, 1955).** Anticipating the visit of a baseball scout, Walter Denton appoints himself Stretch Snodgrass's manager, and sells Connie, Mr. Boynton, and Mr. Conklin shares in the student athlete's future prospects. But when the scout for the White Sox turns up, it seems that there's another Madison High stalwart who's captured his interest.

95. *Turnabout Day* **(May 6, 1955).** *Cast:* Joseph Kearns (*Mr. Stone*). Walter Denton's suggestion that students and teachers at Madison change places for the day is grudgingly approved by Mr. Conklin, because he thinks his boss, Mr. Stone, favored the idea. But when Mr. Stone turns up and declares himself unaware of the entire scheme, Connie and Mr. Conklin have some fast explaining to do.

Gale Gordon earns one of the episode's biggest laughs when he makes his entrance as "student" Osgood Conklin, riding a bicycle and sporting a beanie and Mickey Mouse T-shirt. But he's arguably topped by Leonard Smith as Stretch Snodgrass in drag, wearing a ballerina dress.

96. *Here Is Your Past* **(May 13, 1955).** *Cast:* Hy Averback (*Mr. Clary*), Philip Van Zandt (*Mr. Jason*), John Hiestand (*Jeff Cartwright*). For the past couple of days, Connie has been disturbed by a strange man who seems to be following her and watching her every move. She finally learns that she's being profiled by a *This Is Your Life*–style TV show, but her friends and colleagues are in no mood to cooperate.

97. *Madison Mascot* **(May 20, 1955).** *Cast:* Jack Kruschen (*Dan Beck*), William Newell (*Mike Beck*). When his rival at another school finds a bear cub to serve as the school mascot, Mr. Conklin decides Madison needs something similar. Thanks to a message conveyed by Stretch Snodgrass, Connie thinks her boss has assigned her the task of purchasing an elephant.

Remake of a 1949 radio episode.

98. *The Big Jump* **(May 27, 1955).** *Cast:* Jerry Hausner (*Mr. Faylen*). Publicity-loving Mr. Conklin volunteers to jump from the school roof into a safety net to demonstrate a civil-defense exercise. But when the time comes to carry out his stunt, he looks among his faculty for someone to take his place.

99. *Home-Cooked Meal* **(June 3, 1955).** *Cast:* Mary Jane Croft (*Daisy Enright*). Competing once again with Miss Enright for the attentions of Mr. Boynton, Connie offers to cook his first meal on the new stove in his apartment. She unwittingly fills his kitchen with gas just before Mr. Conklin arrives on the scene.

Fourth Season (1955–56)

100. *The Blind Date* (October 7, 1955). After Connie and Mr. Boynton have a quarrel, Walter tricks them into accepting a blind date with each other. Meanwhile, Mr. Conklin is unnerved to hear that his old flame Lulu Mae is in town for a visit.

This is the final episode to feature the established supporting cast and storyline.

101. *Transition Show* (October 14, 1955). *Cast:* Gail Bonney (*Miss Hannibal*). With Madison High scheduled to be demolished in favor of a new highway, both Connie and Mr. Conklin lose their jobs. After sending out applications, Connie is pleased to be hired as instructor of English and dramatics at Mrs. Nestor's private elementary school. Thinking she has finally escaped the clutches of Mr. Conklin, whom she has told off, Connie is dismayed to learn he, too, has been hired at the same school.

This episode introduces Nana Bryant as Winona Nestor, Bob Sweeney as her amiable brother, vice-principal Oliver Munsey, and William Ching as gym instructor Clint Albright. According to this script, Mr. Boynton (not seen) has accepted a transfer to Monroe High School.

102. *Who's Who* (October 21, 1955). When Connie is late to work for the second time, Mrs. Nestor informs her of the school rule that faculty must live within five miles of campus. Connie reluctantly arranges to move out of Mrs. Davis's place, and rent a room with Angela. Lonely, Connie makes friends with one of her students, who's missing the teacher she replaced.

This episode introduces Ricky Vera as Benny Romero. Jesslyn Fax returns as Angela. Nana Bryant makes her final appearance as Mrs. Nestor; the actress died on December 24, 1955.

103. *Burnt Picnic Basket* (October 28, 1955). Killjoy Mr. Conklin replaces Mr. Munsey as director of the school's annual picnic, and promptly proceeds to take all the fun out of the event. When Connie accidentally incinerates all but one of the picnic baskets, she and Mr. Munsey try to keep their principal none the wiser.

104. *Big Ears* (November 4, 1955). Connie scoffs at Angela's fortunetelling, until some of the events she predicted seem to be coming true.

This episode introduces Isabel Randolph as Ruth Nestor. One passing remark by Connie in the opening scene explains that the original Mrs. Nestor has been succeeded as head of the school by her sister Ruth. The two characters are virtually indistinguishable.

105. *Have Bed—Will Travel* (November 11, 1955). *Cast:* Sandra Gould (*Miss Dooley*). Hearing that Mrs. Davis is lonely without her, Connie plots to have her former landlady move in with her and Angela. When Mrs. Davis proves reluctant to make the change, Mr. Munsey suggests that Connie tell her she's needed because Angela is ill.

Veteran character actress Sandra Gould, seen here as a nurse, was the wife of producer Larry Berns. She is best known for her role as Gladys Kravitz in the color episodes of *Bewitched*.

106. *Protest Meeting* (November 18, 1955). *Cast:* Don Beddoe (*Mr. Hobart*). Mr. Conklin posts a new set of rules for faculty behavior that are so stringent that the entire faculty plans a revolt. But when the teachers are unable to return from their offsite organizational meeting in time, Connie and Mr. Munsey employ mannequins from the school drama department to convince near sighted Mrs. Nestor that all is as it should be in the hallowed halls.

107. *The King and Miss Brooks* (November 25, 1955). *Cast:* Hy Averback (*Maharajah*). Connie's latest student is an Indian boy whose father is the Maharajah of Boongaddy. Because she has been so helpful to the boy, his widowed father offers the humble schoolteacher a chance to relocate to India with them as a member of the royal family.

Desi Arnaz makes a cameo appearance in the dream sequence that comprises most of the show's second act. Actor Hy Averback will return to the series later this season in the recurring role of Benny Romero's father.

108. *Mad Man Munsey* (December 2, 1955). *Cast:* Burt Mustin (*Grandfather*). After a couple of low-key dates with Mr. Munsey, Connie is startled when two beautiful women show up to demand she leave their man alone. Mr. Munsey explains that he would obtain a controlling interest in the school if he were to remarry, and his sister Mrs. Nestor is desperate to prevent this. Taking advantage of Mr. Conklin's latest tactic, an intercom that allows him to listen in on any room in the building, Connie and Oliver decide to give their tricky bosses the good scare they deserve.

109. *Connie and Bonnie* **(December 9, 1955).** When Connie is unwittingly caught in a raid on a gambling den, she fears that the article in the next day's newspaper will cost her her job. Mr. Munsey comes to the rescue when he offers to alter a photograph, making it look as if Connie has a twin sister. Naturally, Mr. Conklin insists on meeting Connie's disreputable, former burlesque queen sibling in person.

110. *Music Box Revue* **(December 23, 1955).** Connie buys her friends and co-workers music boxes as Christmas gifts, from a boy selling them door-to-door. The boxes play "Jingle Bells," but only for those who have the proper holiday spirit. When Connie learns that Benny Romero is spending Christmas Eve alone in the school dorm, she forgets about her own problems.

111. *The New Gym Instructor* **(December 30, 1955).** *Cast:* Peter Leeds (*Laundry Man*). Since Connie is becoming the school's most popular teacher, Mrs. Nestor and Mr. Conklin want to keep her happy. Knowing that she disliked being pursued by former gym instructor Mr. Allbright, they allow Connie to choose his replacement from between two candidates—one who's well-qualified, and one who's quite handsome.

Gene Barry joins the cast as Gene Talbot. He receives more prominent billing in the show's closing credits than any other featured actor has had in the past. Gale Gordon is similarly upgraded.

112. *Skeleton in the Closet* **(January 6, 1956).** *Cast:* Herb Vigran (*Phil Watley*), Larry Blake (*Charlie Davenport*). Connie is being blackmailed by an old acquaintance who knows about a mild run-in she had with the law during her college days. When the man shows up on school grounds, determined to either collect his money or tell Mr. Conklin about Connie's past, she and Mr. Munsey take drastic steps to silence him.

This episode, which opens with Mrs. Davis and her sister Angela avidly enjoying a violent TV show, features references to numerous real-life police and detective programs popular in the 1950s, among them *Racket Squad* and Desilu's own *The Lineup*.

113. *Amalgamation* **(January 13, 1956).** *Cast:* Eleanor Audley (*Mrs. Pryor*), Danny Richards, Jr. (*Billy*). Mrs. Nestor signs an agreement to share faculty resources with an adjoining school that specializes in spoiled Hollywood children. After one unpleasant meeting with principal Mrs. Pryor, who believes in letting her students have "free expression" no matter what, Connie and her fellow faculty members are determined to halt the amalgamation of the two institutions.

114. *Reunion* **(January 20, 1956).** *Cast:* Doris Singleton (*Ellie Norton*), Jeanne Tatum (*Gladys Simpkins*). Reunited with two old friends with whom she served in the WACs, Connie is the only one of the trio who's still single. Advised by her friends that she should take up a job where she will have a better chance of meeting eligible men, Connie announces her plans to leave Mrs. Nestor's school. The men in her life determine to show her that she should stay put.

115. *Twins at School* **(January 27, 1956).** *Cast:* Peter Leeds (*Charlie*). Unable to resist buying a new car, Connie knows she will need a moonlighting job to pay for it. Since second jobs are against the rules at Mrs. Nestor's School, she revives her imaginary twin sister, "Bonnie," as an alibi. Though Mr. Conklin isn't fooled by Connie's disguise, he, too, has bought a new car, and decides two (or four) can play at the twin game.

116. *Mrs. Nestor's Boyfriend* **(February 3, 1956).** *Cast:* Will Wright (*Henry Finley*). Connie and her fellow teachers are frustrated by Mrs. Nestor's strict new no-fraternizing rule. Speculating that Mrs. Nestor wouldn't be so severe if she had a little romance in her own life, Connie decides that the pesky florist who's been chasing an uninterested Mrs. Davis will fill the bill nicely.

117. *Acting Director* (February 10, 1956). *Cast:* Herb Vigran (*Garson Felix*), Peter Leeds (*Grady*), Nancy Kulp (*Miss Hannibal*). Left in charge during Mrs. Nestor's absence, Connie unwittingly approves a school visit by a talent scout for Warner Bros. who's been told the school faculty is bursting with untapped movie stars. While Connie tries to keep the situation under control, Mr. Conklin, Mr. Munsey, and Mr. Talbot don a series of costumes from past school plays to match the roles they believe are being cast.

Nancy Kulp (1921–1991), who assumes the recurring role of Mrs. Nestor's secretary with this installment, is best-remembered as Jane Hathaway on *The Beverly Hillbillies* (1962–1971).

118. *Mr. Boynton's Return* (February 17, 1956). *Cast:* Frank Nelson (*Ticket Agent*), Veola Vonn (*Girl*). Connie is elated to learn that Mr. Boynton will be passing through town on the way to visit his parents. Unfortunately, circumstances conspire to prevent her from spending time with him, causing her to resort to drastic action as he prepares to catch his departing plane.

Veteran character actor Frank Nelson, often seen on *Our Miss Brooks* and other Desilu shows, appears here alongside his real-life wife, actress Veola Vonn.

119. *White Lies* (February 24, 1956). *Cast:* Elliott Reid. When Mrs. Davis's old boyfriend pays a visit, she persuades Connie to pose as her, so he will believe she is still youthful. Confusion between the ex-boyfriend and his nephew, a school supply salesman, further muddies the waters before Mrs. Davis and her long-ago love are finally reunited.

120. *The Great Land Purchase* (March 2, 1956). *Cast:* Byron Foulger (*Irving Fisher*), Charles Williams (*Mr. Peterson*), Dick Ryan (*Army Colonel*). Mrs. Davis is interested in purchasing her sister Angela's house, but they are quibbling over the sale price. Trying to bluff Angela into lowering her price, Connie conspires to make her believe that Mrs. Davis will buy another house instead. The plan goes awry when the ladies accidentally agree to purchase Mr. Conklin's old house, which now sits next door to an all-night bowling alley.

121. *Raffle Ticket* (March 9, 1956). *Cast:* Frank Nelson (*Mr. Kilgallen*). Connie, who's won $1,000 in a raffle, is determined to claim her prize without running afoul of her boss, who tells her that gambling is against school rules. Too bad Mr. Conklin happens to be a member of the same organization that's awarding the prize.

122. *Library Quiz* (March 16, 1956). *Cast:* Danny Richards, Jr., Cheryl Callaway (*Students*). A millionaire intends to donate his private library to either Mrs. Nestor's Elementary School or another nearby one. Connie and Mr. Conklin find themselves competing against two exceptionally bright children in a quiz to determine which school will prevail.

Isabel Randolph makes her final appearance as Ruth Nestor. The character will remain off-screen for subsequent episodes.

123. *A Mother for Benny* (March 23, 1956). *Cast:* Hy Averback (*Roberto Romero*), Doris Singleton (*Louise March*). Benny Romero tries to play Cupid for his widowed father and Connie. When Connie realizes that one of the girls in her class is fatherless, she concocts the idea of pairing up Roberto Romero with the girl's mother.

Doris Singleton and Hy Averback previously played husband and wife Caroline and Charley Appleby on *I Love Lucy*. Averback is making his second *Brooks* appearance as father to one of Connie's students.

124. *Connie and Frankie* (March 30, 1956). *Cast:* Peggie Castle (*Frankie Chapman*), Nancy Kulp (*Miss Hannibal*), Paula Winslowe (*Mrs. Conklin*). Connie is thrilled when Mr. Boynton, whose school in Arizona is now defunct, applies for work at Mrs. Nestor's Elementary School. Unfortunately, he's accompanied by his former colleague, beautiful and blonde Frankie Chapman, who charms Mr. Conklin into hiring her as well. Pulling out the big guns, Connie enlists the help of Mrs. Conklin to handle this latest threat to her happiness.

Nancy Kulp reprises her role as Miss Hannibal, whose first name we learn here to be Lucretia. She's now romantically involved with Oliver Munsey. This is the first episode in quite some time to feature Martha Conklin onscreen. According to this script, Gene Talbot has left the school. Actor Gene Barry's name has been dropped from the closing crawl, and Robert Rockwell's restored, billed after Gale Gordon.

125. *Top Hat, White Tie, and Bindle* (April 6, 1956). *Cast:* Hy Averback (*Roberto Romero*). The relationship between Roberto Romero and Louise March has progressed to the point where it looks as if Benny will soon have the mother he's long wanted. But when Louise's daughter Karen insists on having the wedding right away, before Louise can return from a business trip, Connie is called upon to serve as a proxy bride.

Doris Singleton's character of Louise March is discussed but not seen in this segment. The script makes reference to the fact that Connie has been asked to serve as a proxy bride before, as seen in the first-season episode "June Bride."

126. *24 Hours* (April 13, 1956). *Cast:* Nancy Kulp (*Miss Hannibal*), Peter Leeds (*Bob Lansing*), Sandra Gould (*Grace Lansing*). Love is in the air—Mr. Munsey and Miss Hannibal are billing and cooing, as are Mr. Conklin and his wife. Encouraged by these examples, Mr. Boynton agrees to reconsider his stance on marriage—if 24 hours pass without his seeing some example of marital discord.

127. *Geraldine* (April 20, 1956). *Cast:* Earle Ross (*Harvey Wheaton*), George Chandler (*Mr. Simpson*). At the urging of Benny, Connie buys a worn-out old nag named Geraldine from the milkman. When the dairy owner tries to reclaim the horse, who happens to be expecting a blessed event, Connie and her friends conspire to give Geraldine a happy ending.

128. *The $350,000 Question* (April 27, 1956). A TV quiz show uses a question sent in by Connie, leading her to believe she has won a boatload of prizes. All her friends promptly cozy up to her in the hopes that she will share the wealth.

According to this episode, Mr. Munsey and Miss Hannibal (who doesn't appear) are now engaged to be married.

129. *Principal for a Day* (May 4, 1956). *Cast:* Hy Averback (*Roberto Romero*). Hearing that the school is due to be sold, Connie and her friends fear for their jobs. When Benny's father agrees to buy it, Connie finds herself appointed principal, but the promotion doesn't last long.

130. *Travel Crazy* (May 11, 1956). Connie and friends agree they will each contribute $300 toward a travel fund, with the winner of a spelling bee to be awarded all the cash. Confident her knowledge of the English language will guarantee her a victory, Connie prepares for a series of increasingly lavish trips as the prize money accumulates.

The Eve Arden Show

Eve Arden (*Liza Hammond*), Allyn Joslyn (*George Howell*), Frances Bavier (*Nora Martin*), Gail Stone (*Jenny Hammond*), Karen Green (*Mary Hammond*), Willard Waterman (*Carl Foster*)
Producers: Edmund L. Hartmann, Al Lewis, Robert Sparks. *Writers:* Peggy Chantler, William Cowley, Edmund L. Hartmann, Sherman Marks, Sol Saks. Based on Emily Kimbrough's novel *It Gives Me Great Pleasure*. *Directors:* Sheldon Leonard, John Rich, William D. Russell. *Associate Producer:* Brooks West. *Director of Photography:* Robert deGrasse. *Production Manager:* W. Argyle Nelson. *Editorial Supervisor:* Dann Cahn. *Film Editor:* Bernie Cooper. *Art Director:* Claudio Guzman. *Set Decorator:* Ted Offenbecker. *Property Master:* Ernest Graber. *Rerecording Editor:* Robert Reeve. *Camera Coordinator:* James Niver. *Costumer:* Marjorie W. Henderson. *Makeup:* Lee Greenway. *Hair Stylist:* Gertrude Wheeler. *Sound Recorder:* David Forrest. *Sound:* Glen Glenn Sound. Westhaven Productions; filmed by Desilu.

Aired Tuesdays at 8:30 P.M. on CBS-TV. First aired September 17, 1957; last aired March 25, 1958.

1. *It Gives Me Great Pleasure* (September 17, 1957). Successful novelist Liza Hammond, author of *Summer's End*, is offered a lecture tour that would bring in needed money, but must overcome a severe case of stage fright if she is to be a successful lecturer.

2. *Housework* (September 24, 1957). Liza has been telling listeners on her lecture circuit that women need their own creative outlets, and shouldn't be tied down to housework. Yet when a magazine photographer arrives at Liza's door in New York, she's doing exactly the kind of work she deplored.

3. *Cover Girl* (October 1, 1957). Liza attracts some unwanted male attention after her publisher issues a paperback edition of *Summer's End* with a phony glamour shot of its author. Goaded into it by George, Liza accepts a blind date with her publisher's old Army buddy, David Ferris, who is expecting the woman he saw on the book jacket.

4. *The French View* (October 8, 1957). A visiting Frenchwoman who has written a book about love and romance upsets life in the Hammond household while making lots of friends in the neighborhood. Her houseguest's popularity causes Liza to develop an inferiority complex.

5. *The New Liza Hammond* (October 15, 1957). *Cast:* Lloyd Corrigan. George decides that Liza's lack of self-confidence merits professional attention, but he doesn't much like the results when a psychologist convinces her to "think big—be big."

6. *Local Girl* (October 22, 1957). Liza discovers that her writing has made her persona non grata in her hometown when she returns to fulfill a speaking engagement.

The premise of this episode recalls the real-life publicity surrounding first-time author Grace Metalious, and her book *Peyton Place*, widely believed to have made her a pariah in the small New England town where she and her family lived.

7. *White Elephant Sale* (October 29, 1957). *Cast:* Marguerite Chapman (*Mrs. Kenyon*). Liza's daughters are quite impressed with their friend Joyce's mother, the shining light of the local PTA. Competing for the attention of her own daughters, Liza is determined to make an impression at the PTA's white elephant sale.

8. *Liza and the Bombshell* (November 5, 1957). *Cast:* Mary Beth Hughes. Liza accepts an assignment ghostwriting the memoirs of a notorious striptease artist. Hoping she will win an award from a mothers' organization, Liza is reluctant to be seen visiting the theater where the burlesque queen performs.

9. *Liza Among the Courtwrights* (November 19, 1957). *Cast:* Herbert Anderson, Donald Foster. A well-heeled young man who's infatuated with Liza follows her throughout her lecture tour of New England, but he isn't the only member of his family to appreciate her charms.

10. *Jenny's Unrequited Love* (November 26, 1957). Liza tries to help Jenny cope with a crush that isn't returned, while Mary takes up football.

11. *Liza Hammond Enterprises* (December 3, 1957). *Cast:* Keith Andes (*Chuck Miller*). Liza hires handsome Chuck Miller, an old friend, to help keep her family on a budget.

12. *The Montana Date* (December 10, 1957). George books Liza for a speaking date in a remote Montana town, where she finds a well-to-do rancher her only listener.

In a very topical line for 1957 TV, Eve, as Liza, finds herself romantically pursued by her rancher fan and says, "I've heard of adult westerns, but this is getting out of hand!"

13. *Mary's First Date* (December 17, 1957). Concerned that Mary is developing into a tomboy, Liza resolves to help her daughter explore new interests. A school dance seems to provide the perfect opportunity, provided Liza's daughter can find an appropriate date.

14. *The Christmas Angel* (December 24, 1957). *Cast:* Dennis Holmes. An unexpected houseguest, a rambunctious seven-year-old boy, wreaks havoc with the family's traditional holiday activities.

15. *A Hotel Is Not a Home* (December 31, 1957). *Cast:* Vera Vague. Liza's latest stint on the lecture circuit, and the many social events it entails, leave her longing for some downtime and privacy. Instead, she finds herself pursued by three socially prominent women who all want to claim her as a houseguest.

Barbara Jo Allen, known professionally as Vera Vague (a scatterbrained character she established on radio), was a longtime friend of Eve's.

16. *Safari* **(January 7, 1958).** Liza, trying to prove to George that she's overcoming her reticent nature, accepts an invitation to accompany an African explorer on a safari. Confident she can keep pace, she finds that a camping trip gives her reason to reconsider.

17. *The New Tenant* **(January 14, 1958).** *Cast:* Bill Goodwin (*Ed Weston*), Willard Waterman (*Carl Foster*), Danny Richards, Jr. (*Melvin*), Joan Taber. While staying temporarily in a different apartment, Liza encounters a man who aggressively pursues her romantically.

18. *Liza's Reunion Dance* **(January 21, 1958).** *Cast:* Craig Stevens (*Himself*). Liza's family springs into action to help out when she seems unable to find a date for her college reunion dance.

19. *Mary's Report Card* **(January 28, 1958).** The girls' report cards demonstrate that twins don't necessarily share the same academic gifts. Mary's poor grades cause Liza to rethink her TV speech on successfully combining motherhood and a career.

20. *The Hollywood Offer* **(February 4, 1958).** Liza receives a phone call from a Hollywood producer interested in adapting her work for the screen.

21. *The Rivals* **(February 11, 1958).** Jenny and Mary compete for the affections of a boy, the son of one of George's clients.

22. *Liza's Nightmare* **(February 18, 1958).** *Cast:* Willard Waterman (*Carl Foster*). Liza is torn between traveling to Washington to earn a much-needed lecture fee, or staying home with Jenny, who's in bed with a cold. Persuaded to keep her professional engagement, a guilt-ridden Liza can find no solace even when she's asleep.

23. *Liza Meets Young Korea* **(March 4, 1958).** *Cast:* Philip Ahn. George's latest publicity gimmick has Liza's apartment overrun with Korean children.

24. *Ed Weston Returns* **(March 11, 1958).** *Cast:* Bill Goodwin (*Ed Weston*), Willard Waterman (*Carl Foster*), Danny Richards, Jr. (*Melvin*). Cheapskate Mr. Foster isn't pleased by his cousin's burgeoning romance with Liza, believing that Ed has come into money. Mr. Foster, his nephew Melvin, and the equally disapproving George conspire to put the romantic fire out.

25. *Full Time Mother* **(March 18, 1958).** *Cast:* Willard Waterman (*Carl Foster*). Feeling that the girls need more of her attention, Liza decides to take a hiatus from her career to spend more time with them. While Nora takes a vacation, Liza assumes command at home, despite George's skepticism.

26. *Liza and the Harvard Man* **(March 25, 1958).** An old flame from college days reenters Liza's life. Their reminiscences about the good times they enjoyed result in a marriage proposal for Liza.

The Mothers-in-Law

Eve Arden (*Eve Hubbard*), Kaye Ballard (*Kaye Buell*), Roger C. Carmel (*Roger Buell*, season 1), Richard Deacon (*Roger Buell*, season 2), Herbert Rudley (*Herb Buell*), Jerry Fogel (*Jerry Buell*), Deborah Walley (*Suzie Hubbard Buell*)

Executive Producer: Desi Arnaz. *Producers:* Al Lewis, Elliott Lewis. *Creators/Script Consultants:* Bob Carroll, Jr., Madelyn Davis. *Director of Photography:* Henry Freulich. *Music Composer/Conductor:* Wilbur Hatch. *Art Directors:* Pato Guzman, Howard Hollander. *Assistant Directors:* Val Raset, Charles R. Shyer. *Camera Coordinator:* Robert Sousa. *Set Decorators:* Carl Biddiscombe, Arthur Jeph Parker, Dorcy W. Howard. *Property Master:* Everett Israelson. *Music Editor:* Ed Norton. *Post-Production Supervisor:* Douglas Hines. *Costumes:* Marjorie M. Henderson. *Sound Engineer:* E.E. Campbell. *Makeup Artist:* Lee Greenway. *Hair*

Stylist: Beth Langston. *Titles:* Format Productions. Desi Arnaz Productions for United Artists Television; filmed by Desilu.

Aired Sundays at 8:30 P.M. on NBC-TV. First telecast, September 10, 1967; last aired September 7, 1969.

1. *On Again, Off Again Lohengrin* (September 10, 1967). *Writers:* Madelyn Davis, Bob Carroll, Jr. *Director:* Desi Arnaz. Eve and Herb Hubbard have an unfortunately timed quarrel with their neighbors the Buells, just in time for Suzie Hubbard to announce that she's engaged to marry the Buells' son Jerry. The soon-to-be mothers-in-law Eve and Kaye do their best to get along while planning their children's wedding, but chaos erupts when rainclouds appear on the morning of the outdoor ceremony.

2. *Everybody Goes on a Honeymoon* (September 17, 1967). *Writers:* Madelyn Davis, Bob Carroll, Jr. *Director:* Desi Arnaz. *Cast:* Carl Reindel (*Golf Starter*), Bart Greene (*Room Clerk*). While Suzie and Jerry set off for a honeymoon at Lake Arrowhead, Eve and Herb decide to spend a relaxing weekend at Palm Springs, only to find Roger and Kaye registered at the same hotel. When the kids change their plans, and show up in Palm Springs, they aren't able to get a room, so Eve, Kaye, and their husbands find themselves bunking together during a very restless night.

3. *All Fall Down* (September 24, 1967). *Writers:* Hugh Wedlock, Allan Manings. *Director:* Desi Arnaz. The Buells' ski weekend is cut short when Kaye takes a fall in the hotel lobby and breaks her leg. During a reenactment of the accident, Eve suffers the same injury. Staying together overnight while their husbands are away, the ladies watch a scary movie on TV, and let their imaginations run wild when they hear noises downstairs.

4. *A Night to Forget* (October 1, 1967). *Writers:* Madelyn Davis, Bob Carroll, Jr. *Director:* Maury Thompson. *Cast:* Desi Arnaz (*Raphael del Gado*), Lou Krugman (*Tony Roma*). While using the pay phone in a department store, Eve and Kaye are locked in for the night. With their last dime, they try to call home for help, only to misdial and contact a bullfighter in Barcelona.

This episode introduces Desi in his recurring role as Raphael del Gado. Since he is acting in the segment, Desi turns over directorial duties to his longtime colleague Maury Thompson, who had most recently been house director on *The Lucy Show*.

5. *The Newlyweds Move In* (October 8, 1967). *Writers:* Madelyn Davis, Bob Carroll, Jr. *Director:* Desi Arnaz. *Cast:* Judy Franklin (*Cynthia*), Larry Bishop (*Grocery Boy*), Jan Hirsch (*Peggy*), David Galligan (*Paul*), Rick Bentley (*John*). Disliking the shabby apartment Jerry and Suzie planned to rent, Eve and Kaye persuade them to move into the Hubbards' garage apartment instead. The mothers-in-law are doing their best to keep their distance from the newlyweds, but can't resist checking up on the kids when they have their first dinner party.

Eve Arden and Kaye Ballard do a nifty physical comedy bit, caught clinging to the garage door when it's unexpectedly raised.

6. *The Career Girls* (October 15, 1967). *Writers:* Fred S. Fox, Seaman Jacobs. *Director:* Desi Arnaz. *Cast:* Rob Reiner (*The Director*), Paula Bowser (*Girl Dancer*). Wanting to prevent Eve and Kaye from smothering the newlyweds with attention, Herb and Roger suggest their wives get part-time jobs. The ladies decide to seek employment in show business, and work up an act that gets them hired for the cast of a musical revue.

Desi Arnaz, Jr. (born 1953) can be spotted briefly as a drummer. Rob Reiner (born 1947) makes an early television appearance, more than three years prior to being cast as Mike Stivic on *All in the Family* (1971–1979).

7. *Who's Afraid of Elizabeth Taylor?* (October 22, 1967). *Writers:* Madelyn Davis, Bob Carroll, Jr. *Director:* Desi Arnaz. Eve and Kaye take offense when their husbands admit that, given the chance, they would enjoy having a dinner date with Elizabeth Taylor. Before long, both the wives and the husbands realize their squabble was silly, and try to find a way to make up without losing face.

According to co-star Kaye Ballard, this was one of three episodes that derived from a story idea she suggested, and was based on an argument that her brother had with his wife.

8. *My Son, the Actor* (October 29, 1967). *Writers:* Madelyn Davis, Bob Carroll, Jr. *Director:* Desi Arnaz. A school aptitude test suggests that Jerry might have a bent for the performing arts. He decides to audition for the school musical with an original work written by his father, and is joined onstage by his wife, parents, and in-laws.

9. *How Do You Moonlight a Meatball?* (November 5, 1967). *Writers:* Fred S. Fox, Seaman Jacobs. *Director:* Desi Arnaz. *Cast:* Percy Helton (*Dean Roberts*), Florence MacMichael (*Maid*), Judy Howard (*First Woman*), Emlen Davies (*Second Woman*). When Jerry loses his job, leaving the newlyweds in financial trouble, Eve and Kaye come to the rescue by helping them establish a business delivering Italian food to campus. The mothers-in-law have just made a delivery to a fancy campus event when Suzie calls to say that her engagement ring is baked into one of the meatballs.

Actress Florence MacMichael, best-known for her featured role as Winnie Kirkwood on TV's *Mister Ed* but also a veteran of Eve's West Coast *Auntie Mame* company, makes her first of several appearances on *The Mothers-in-Law*. Unfortunately, her name will almost invariably be misspelled in the credits (as MacMichaels) when she appears on this show.

10. *I Thought He'd Never Leave* (November 12, 1967). *Writers:* Sydney Zelinka, Ronald Axe. *Director:* Elliott Lewis. *Cast:* Larry Storch (*Robber*), Robert Anderson (*Policeman*). An escaping bank robber takes Eve hostage in her own house. Naturally, the tense twosome is quickly joined by Kaye, Roger, and Herb as the crook plots his getaway.

Guest star Storch was the star of his own recently canceled sitcom, ABC's *F Troop* (1965–1967).

11. *The Great Bicycle Race* (November 19, 1967). *Writers:* Madelyn Davis, Bob Carroll, Jr. *Director:* Elliott Lewis. *Cast:* Paul Napier (*George*). Afraid she and her friends are growing lazy and out of shape, Eve persuades the others to join Suzie and Jerry's bicycle club. Taking a wrong turn, the foursome ends up lost and stranded overnight.

12. *Through the Looking Glass* (November 26, 1967). *Writer:* Howard Ostroff. *Director:* Desi Arnaz. *Cast:* Alan Reed, Sr. (*Police Sergeant*), Jay Novello (*The Bum*), Stafford Repp (*Patrolman Carver*). Eve and Kaye are wearing silly costumes because they're performing in a play at the children's hospital. Roger is dressed like the central character in his newest script, while Herb has donned the ceremonial garb of his lodge. All four, plus Suzie and Jerry, end up in the local precinct trying to explain their circumstances to a frustrated desk sergeant.

This episode benefits from the strong performances of two fine character actors—Alan Reed (the voice of Fred Flintstone) as the policeman, and Desilu favorite Jay Novello (Mr. Merriweather in the classic *I Love Lucy* segment "The Séance") as an inebriated inmate.

13. *Divorce Mother-in-Law Style* (December 3, 1967). *Writers:* Bill Idelson, Harvey Miller. *Director:* Elliott Lewis. *Cast:* Roger Ewing (*Carter Case*), Adrienne Hayes (*Anna Maria*). When Suzie's wealthy ex-boyfriend Carter comes to town, Eve is in no particular hurry to tell him that she's married. Offended, Kaye retaliates by digging up Jerry's high school girlfriend, and the newlyweds decide to teach them both a lesson by pretending they're getting a divorce.

14. *The Not Cold Enough War* (December 10, 1967). *Writer:* William O'Halloren. *Director:* Desi Arnaz. *Cast:* Herb Edelman (*Sgt. Crump*), Bobs Watson (*Officer Bailey*), Adam Keefe (*Whip Larson*), Judy Franklin (*Cynthia*). Eve and Herb get a new refrigerator, and sell their old one to Roger and Kaye. But when the old refrigerator breaks down shortly after the Buells install it, they want their money back.

This episode uses a premise similar to that of the *I Love Lucy* episode "Never Do Business with Friends."

15. *You Challenge Me to a What?* (December 17, 1967). *Writers:* Madelyn Davis, Bob Carroll, Jr. *Director:* Desi Arnaz. *Cast:* Benjie Bancroft (*First Policeman*), Gary C. Smith (*Second Policeman*). The latest Hubbard-Buell argument, which takes place during a backyard barbecue, inspires Herb and Roger to challenge each other to a duel. As it turns out, both men have exaggerated their fencing expertise, and their wives plot to call off the duel while allowing their husbands to save face.

16. *Everybody Wants to Be a Writer* (December 31, 1967). *Writer:* William O'Hallaren. *Directors:* Elliott Lewis, Desi Arnaz. *Cast:* Peter Whitney (*Terrence Archibald*), Lee Millar (*Assistant Director*), Jim Begg (*Mail Room Boy*), Vonda Barra (*Script Girl*). Urged once again by their husbands to find outside interests, Eve and Kaye decide to take up TV scriptwriting. Meanwhile, Herb's latest client is TV writer/director Terrance Archibald, who's pursuing a plagiarism suit. Thanks to a misunderstanding, Roger mails one of Archibald's own scripts, with Eve's and Kaye's names attached.

Character actor Jim Begg (1938–2008) will make multiple appearances in small roles in this series.

17. *The Kids Move Out* (January 7, 1968). *Writers:* Madelyn Davis, Bob Carroll, Jr. *Director:* Elliott Lewis. *Cast:* Jerry Hausner (*Janitor*), Paul Napier (*Phone Man*), Larry Mancine (*Moving Man*). Feeling a loss of privacy, Jerry and Suzie decide to move from the garage apartment into an apartment that some friends are subletting. Three days later, the kids are having second thoughts about their impulsive move, and their parents can't resist sneaking into the new apartment to check up on them.

This episode features a strong performance by actor Jerry Hausner (1909–1993), best-known as Ricky Ricardo's agent Jerry on *I Love Lucy*.

18. *The Hombre Who Came to Dinner (Part I)* (January 14, 1968). *Writers:* Madelyn Davis, Bob Carroll, Jr. *Directors:* Elliott Lewis, Desi Arnaz. *Cast:* Desi Arnaz (*Señor Raphael del Gado*), Miguel Landa (*Umberto*), Pepin Betancourt (*Fernando*), Pat Stich (*Car-Hop*). Señor Raphael del Gado, the famed Mexican bullfighter whom Eve and Kaye met thanks to a telephone mix-up (see episode #4), is in town and Eve insists that he stay at the Hubbards' house. A few days later, the constant stream of visitors, late-night parties, and general mayhem leads Eve and her friends to rue their hospitality.

19. *The Hombre Who Came to Dinner (Part II)* (January 21, 1968). *Writers:* Madelyn Davis, Bob Carroll, Jr. *Directors:* Desi Arnaz, Elliott Lewis. *Cast:* Desi Arnaz (*Señor Raphael del Gado*), Desi Arnaz, Jr. (*Tommy*). Señor del Gado is injured in a freak accident just as he's finally ready to leave the Hubbards' house. Distressed that his injury will prevent him from starring in a benefit show in Mexico City, the bullfighter arranges for his friends the Hubbards and the Buells to join the cast.

The 14-year-old Desi Arnaz, Jr., in his first significant role in the series, plays grocery story delivery boy Tommy, providing an opportunity to show off his drumming skills.

20. *Don't Give Up the Sloop* (January 28, 1968). *Writers:* Bill Idelson, Harvey Miller. *Director:* Elliott Lewis. Eve and Kaye both lay claim to the sailboat given as a prize for Kaye's correct answer to a TV quiz show. The Hubbards and the Buells finally agree to share the sloop and its expenses, but have a falling-out when they can't agree on who should serve as captain, and when each couple will have use of the craft.

21. *I'd Tell You I Love You, But We're Not Speaking* (February 4, 1968). *Writers:* Madelyn Davis, Bob Carroll, Jr., Robert Daniels, Mark Howard. *Director:* Desi Arnaz. *Cast:* Brooks West (*Prof. Hutton*). Jerry and Suzie's first fight causes an estrangement among the Hubbards and the

Buells. Jerry arranges for his college psychology instructor, Professor Hutton, to lead the two families in a group sensitivity session to work out their issues.

Eve's real-life husband, actor Brooks West, is the guest star in this episode. The segment's comic highlight comes when Eve and Kaye, during the sensitivity session, mimic each other.

22. *Herb's Little Helpers* (February 11, 1968). *Writers:* Madelyn Davis, Bob Carroll, Jr., William O'Hallaren. *Director:* Elliott Lewis. *Cast:* Jerome Cowan (*Mr. Hedges*), Donna Loren (*Cindy*), Jimmy Boyd (*Harold*), Herbert Vigran (*Judge*), Jeff Donnell (*Elaine*). Eve and Kaye serve as temporary secretaries to Herb and his important new client, jobs for which they are ill-equipped. Sent to the courthouse to deliver legal papers, the ladies stumble on an impromptu wedding, unaware that the bride-to-be is the daughter of Herb's client.

23. *Bye, Bye Blackmailer* (February 25, 1968). *Writers:* Madelyn Davis, Bob Carroll, Jr., William O'Hallaren. *Director:* Elliott Lewis. To help Roger repay the money he owes Herb, Eve secretly borrows $100 from their emergency fund. When Herb finds the money missing, and Eve refuses to explain, he and Roger jump to the conclusion that Eve is being blackmailed.

24. *The Wig Story* (March 3, 1968). *Writers:* Michael Morris, Madelyn Davis, Bob Carroll, Jr. *Director:* Elliott Lewis. When Kaye tries on Eve's blonde wig, it arouses sparks of passion in Roger. At first delighted by her husband's newfound attentiveness, Kaye goes into a funk when she concludes that he's really fantasizing about another woman.

The second of three episodes based on an idea submitted by Kaye Ballard. Michael Morris, who co-scripted this segment, also wrote *All in the Family*'s 1973 segment "Black is the Color of My True Love's Wig," which focuses on a similar situation between Mike and Gloria.

25. *It's Only Money* (March 10, 1968). *Writer:* Sydney Zelinka. *Director:* Elliott Lewis. *Cast:* Benny Rubin (*Waiter*), Romo Vincent (*Maitre d'*). Herb is angry when Roger doesn't pay his fair share of a $44 dinner check. Instead of talking things out, Herb tries to regain the money he lost by betting Roger in games of golf and gin rummy, but to no avail.

26. *I Haven't Got a Secret* (March 17, 1968). *Writers:* Peggy Chantler Dick, Douglas Dick. *Director:* Desi Arnaz. Roger's about to close a lucrative deal for his own TV soap opera, but cautions Kaye not to tell anyone until the contract is signed. Naturally, she spills the beans to Eve, who worries what will happen if the Buells become millionaires.

27. *Jerry's Night Out with the Boys* (March 24, 1968). *Writers:* Madelyn Davis, Bob Carroll, Jr., William O'Hallaren. *Directors:* Desi Arnaz, Elliott Lewis. *Cast:* Jim Begg (*Man*). Jerry wants a night out to play poker with the boys, and Suzie doesn't mind—until Eve and Kaye convince her she should. Before long, it's the women at the Hubbards' house, and the men at the Buells,' and all are having an equally dull time.

This script resembles Davis and Carroll's script for the *I Love Lucy* episode "Vacation from Marriage."

28. *The Long, Long Weekend* (March 31, 1968). *Writers:* Madelyn Davis, Bob Carroll, Jr. *Director:* Elliott Lewis. When the kids drop out of a family weekend at Lake Arrowhead, Eve and Herb decide they don't want to go either. The Hubbards' made-up excuse to avoid spending another weekend with the Buells works fine, until both couples show up at the cabin.

29. *Jealousy Makes the Heart Grow Fonder* (April 7, 1968). *Writer:* Sydney Zelinka. *Cast:* Beverly Garland (*Audrey Fleming*). Eve isn't the least bit jealous of Herb's glamorous ex-girlfriend Audrey—until she overhears them discussing an upcoming trip to Acapulco. Wrongly concluding that her marriage is in danger, Eve goes along with Kaye's crazy plan to make her husband jealous.

30. *How Not to Manage a Rock Group* (April 28, 1968). *Writer:* Don Nelson. *Director:* Desi Arnaz. *Cast:* The Seeds (*The Warts*), Joe Besser (*Bandleader*), John Myhers (*Studio Engineer*). Suzie and Jerry persuade their parents to invest in an up-and-coming rock group, the Warts.

After sinking $500 into a recording session, the Hubbards and the Buells decide to revamp the group, causing the band members to rebel.

The Seeds were a Los Angeles–based rock group active between the mid-1960s and the early 1970s. They are seen here singing their hit song, "Pushin' Too Hard," which made the *Billboard* charts.

SECOND SEASON (1968–69)

31. *Here Comes the Bride, Again* **(September 15, 1968).** *Writers:* Madelyn Davis, Bob Carroll, Jr. *Director:* Desi Arnaz. *Cast:* Jeanette Nolan (*Gabriella Balotta*), William Lanteau (*Mark Redfield*), Judy Franklin (*Cynthia*), Jan Allyson (*Peggy*). Because Kaye was reluctant to tell her traditional Italian grandmother that Jerry and Suzie eloped, the 84-year-old shows up a year later expecting to attend an elaborate wedding ceremony. Eve and Kaye manage to persuade their husbands to take part in a staged wedding, but their plans go awry when a TV host shows up to interview Jerry and Suzie about their first year of married life.

This episode features a strong character performance by the veteran actress Jeanette Nolan (1911–1998), heavily made up to play the elderly Mrs. Balotta. She will return as a different character in #47, "Nanny, Go Home." Introduced in the show's closing moments is a story thread that will become important throughout the season, when Suzie announces she is pregnant. Richard Deacon makes his first appearance here as Roger. According to Kaye Ballard, this episode was also based on a story idea she provided.

32. *The Match Game* **(September 22, 1968).** *Writers:* Madelyn Davis, Bob Carroll, Jr. *Director:* Elliott Lewis. *Cast:* Paul Lynde (*Mr. Logan*). Jerry is in danger of losing his part-time job at a computer dating service because business is so slow. Wanting to help, Eve, Kaye, and their husbands all pose as clients, but are in for a surprise when the computer finds them matches.

Paul Lynde (1926–1982) is billed in the opening titles for his guest appearance as Jerry's boss, "Love Bug" Logan.

33. *A Little Pregnancy Goes a Long Way* **(September 29, 1968).** *Writers:* Madelyn Davis, Bob Carroll, Jr. *Director:* Elliott Lewis. *Cast:* Shirley Mitchell (*Margaret Cornell*), Harry Hickox (*Vic Cornell*), June Whitley (*Betty Trumbull*), Bruce Kirby (*Bill Trumbull*), Jim Begg (*Steward*). Jerry solicits the help of Herb and Roger after the mothers-in-law talk Suzie into suffering from morning sickness and cravings. Herb suggests they take their wives away for a weekend in a mountain cabin, but the ladies think they're being invited on a cruise to Hawaii.

Shirley Mitchell (born 1919), well remembered for her recurring role as Marion Strong on *I Love Lucy,* appears here as the female half of the frequently mentioned, but rarely seen, Cornells.

34. *Love Thy Neighbor—If You Can Get Him to Move* **(October 6, 1968).** *Writers:* Fred S. Fox, Seaman Jacobs. *Director:* Elliott Lewis. The Hubbards and the Buells reminisce about their experiences when they first became neighbors, before Jerry and Suzie were born. Welcoming at first to the new arrivals, young Eve and Herb soon realize that the Buells could give lessons in being presumptuous.

The flashback scenes that comprise most of this episode find Richard Deacon (as Roger) sporting a toupee, Eve wearing a blonde wig and a youthful ensemble, and, best of all, a bewigged Kaye Ballard resembling a mid-1940s Joan Crawford.

35. *I Didn't Raise Myself to Be a Grandmother* **(October 13, 1968).** *Writers:* Madelyn Davis, Bob Carroll, Jr. *Director:* Elliott Lewis. *Cast:* Bruce Kirby (*Bill Turnbull*). As the reality of impending grandparenthood sinks in, Eve, Kaye, and their husbands begin to feel old. An indoor jogging routine designed to improve their physical fitness instead leaves the foursome in poor shape for their song-and-dance routine at the Garden Club benefit.

36. *Even Mothers-in-Law Have Mothers-in-Law* **(October 20, 1968).** *Writers:* Fred S. Fox, Seaman Jacobs. *Director:* Elliott Lewis. *Cast:* Doris Packer (*Clarita Hubbard*), Barbara Morrison

(*Francis* [sic] *Buell*). Fed up with Eve and Kaye's interference, Jerry and Suzie decide to "fight mothers-in-law with mothers-in-law." Invited to come for a visit, Herb and Roger's mothers occupy all their daughters-in-law's time with sightseeing until Eve and Kaye devise a plan to send them home.

37. *The Matador Makes a Movie* (October 27, 1968). *Writers:* Madelyn Davis, Bob Carroll, Jr. *Director:* Desi Arnaz. *Cast:* Desi Arnaz (*Señor Raphael del Gado*), Desi Arnaz, Jr. (*Stagehand*), Joseph Mell (*Chuck*), Jim Begg (*Delivery Boy*), John Myhers (*Studio Head*). Learning that their old friend Señor Raphael del Gado is in Hollywood to produce a film in which he will star, Eve and Kaye invite him to dinner so as to score jobs. Though del Gado willingly gives small roles in *The Sheik of Araby* to all the Hubbards and the Buells, he lives to regret his generosity when they unwittingly make a shambles of the production.

Desi Arnaz, Jr., who had recently begun his featured role as Craig Carter in *Here's Lucy*, cameos here as the stagehand who operates the clapper on the movie set. Desi, Sr. makes his final on-camera appearance here.

38. *It's a Dog's Life* (November 10, 1968). *Writers:* Robert Fisher, Arthur Marx. *Director:* Elliott Lewis. *Cast:* John Byner (*Arnold Lacy*). Jerry and Suzie want a dog, so naturally Eve and Kaye each buy them one. Meanwhile, Herb and Roger, who want their wives to have eye exams after receiving a traffic ticket, employ a trick to make their point.

39. *The First Anniversary Is the Hardest* (November 24, 1968). *Writers:* Madelyn Davis, Bob Carroll, Jr. *Director:* Desi Arnaz. *Cast:* Joe Besser (*Tramp*), Stafford Repp (*Policeman*), Jerry Pyne (*Man*), Stephanie Adamick (*Girl*). Jerry and Suzie can't afford to enjoy dinner out on their first anniversary. Knowing Jerry is too proud to accept a handout, the parents plant some cash for him to find in his old sports jacket. When Suzie gives the jacket away to charity, Eve and Kaye go on a mad hunt to retrieve the cash.

40. *The Birth of Everything but the Blues* (December 1, 1968). *Writer:* Elaine Di Bello Bradish. *Director:* Elliott Lewis. *Cast:* Herbert Voland (*Dr. Burton*), Del Moore (*First Man*), Frank Inn (*Second Man*), Mel Blanc (*David, the Mynah Bird*). To raise extra money, Suzie advertises her services as a pet sitter. But when she falls ill, it's Eve and Kaye who wind up babysitting a menagerie of creatures, several of whom are expectant mothers.

Famed animal trainer Frank Inn (1916–2002), known for his work with animal stars such as Benji, Arnold the Pig (*Green Acres*), and Cleo (*The People's Choice*), makes a rare on-camera appearance in the tag scene of this episode, leading a bear on a leash.

41. *Nome, Schnome, I'd Rather Have It at Home* (December 8, 1968). *Writer:* Henry Garson. *Director:* Desi Arnaz. Jerry and Suzie announce that he's taking a job in Alaska, and will be moving there after graduation. Though Eve and Kaye claim they have accepted the kids' decision, their nightmares tell a different story.

Dialogue in the opening scene between Eve and Kaye includes references to actor Richard Crenna, Eve's co-star in *Our Miss Brooks*.

42. *Hail, Hail, The Gang's Still Here* (December 15, 1968). *Writers:* Madelyn Davis, Bob Carroll, Jr. *Director:* Elliott Lewis. *Cast:* Shirley Mitchell (*Margaret Cornell*), Harry Hickox (*Vic Cornell*), June Whitley (*Betty Trumbull*), Bruce Kirby (*Bill Trumbull*). Wanting an evening alone, Eve and Herb tell the Buells they're going out to dinner and the theater. Thinking they'll have the house to themselves, Eve and Herb are forced to hide in their own home when Kaye and Roger come over to watch *Green Valley, U.S.A.*, the prime-time soap opera he writes.

This episode is reminiscent of the series pilot, with Kaye and Roger helping themselves to the Hubbards' TV and food while they're supposedly not home.

43. *Didn't You Used to Be Ossie Snick?* (December 22, 1968). *Writers:* Fred S. Fox, Seaman Jacobs. *Director:* Desi Arnaz. Cast: Ozzie Nelson (*Ossie Snick*). Herb's new client, Owen Sinclair, is a TV producer who went by the name Ossie Snick during his prior career as a bandleader.

When the Hubbards reunite Ossie with Kaye, the onetime girl singer with his orchestra, she gets an opportunity to perform on his TV special — if she can overcome her stage fright.

Ozzie Nelson composed an original song called "North Dakota Moon" that figures into the plot of this segment.

44. *Make Room for Baby* **(January 5, 1969).** *Writers:* Madelyn Davis, Bob Carroll, Jr. *Director:* Elliott Lewis. With all the gifts Eve and Kaye have bought for the new baby, Suzie and Jerry's apartment is bursting at the seams. Herb and Roger allow their wives to persuade them to build an addition, but they soon regret it.

45. *Haven't You Had That Baby Yet?* **(January 12, 1969).** *Writers:* Madelyn Davis, Bob Carroll, Jr. *Director:* Elliott Lewis. *Cast:* Herbert Voland (*Dr. Butler*), Vonda Barra (*Charlotte*). Suzie is a week past her expected due date, and still hasn't given birth. Not allowed to attend her college graduation, Suzie stays home to watch the televised ceremony, going into labor just as Jerry is giving his commencement speech.

46. *And Baby Makes Four* **(January 19, 1969).** *Writers:* Madelyn Davis, Bob Carroll, Jr. *Director:* Elliott Lewis. *Cast:* Alice Ghostley (*Mrs. Wiley*), Herbert Voland (*Dr. Butler*), Avery Schreiber (*Mr. Crawford*), Vonda Barra (*Charlotte*), Florence MacMichael (*Woman*), Judy Howard (*Nurse*). Left to their own devices in the hospital waiting room, Eve and Kaye try the patience of a nurse who won't admit them to the maternity ward. After months of arguing over whether Suzie will give them a grandson or a granddaughter, the mothers-in-law are thrilled when she presents them with twins Joey and Hildy.

Actress Florence MacMichael, seen briefly here as a maternity patient, once again suffers the indignity of having her name misspelled in the closing credits.

47. *Nanny Go Home* **(January 26, 1969).** *Writers:* Elaine di Bello Bradish, Madelyn Davis, Bob Carroll, Jr. *Director:* Elliott Lewis. *Cast:* Jeanette Nolan (*Annie McTaggert*), Jerry Hausner (*Laundry Man*). To keep Eve and Kaye from interfering with the babies, Herb and Roger hire a strict nanny who keeps visiting hours at a minimum. But when even Suzie tires of Nanny McTaggert's strict rules, the mothers-in-law devise a plot to set things right again.

48. *Double Trouble in the Nursery* **(February 2, 1969).** *Writer:* Bruce Howard. *Director:* Elliott Lewis. Exhausted, Jerry and Suzie take off for a weekend at Lake Arrowhead. Eve and Kaye throw themselves wholeheartedly into the job of babysitters for the twins, but Herb and Roger are feeling neglected.

49. *Void Where Prohibited by In-Laws* **(February 9, 1969).** *Writer:* Skip Webster. *Director:* Elliott Lewis. *Cast:* Benny Rubin (*Mr. Pratt*), Flip Mark (*Felix*). Eager to win college scholarships for their grandchildren, Eve and Kaye enter a contest to guess how many pieces of Blimpos cereal are contained in a large barrel. To simplify their calculations, the ladies buy their own barrel and supply of cereal, hoping to make an accurate count while their husbands are busy with a golf game.

50. *Guess Who's Coming Forever* **(February 23, 1969).** *Writers:* Arthur Marx, Robert Fisher. *Director:* Elliott Lewis. *Cast:* Scoey Mitchlll (*Solomon Elkins*), Skip Battyn (*Haggard J. Haggard*). Since Jerry and Suzie are house-hunting, Eve and Kaye reluctantly agree to rent the garage apartment. Young lawyer Solomon Elkins puts down six months' rent in advance, but when the kids' plans change, the new tenant refuses to give up the apartment, believing the mothers-in-law don't want him there because he is black.

Actor-comedian Scoey Mitchlll (and, yes, that is how he spells his last name) went on to star in his own TV sitcom, the short-lived *Barefoot in the Park* (ABC, 1970–71).

51. *Every In-Law Wants to Get In on the Act* **(March 2, 1969).** *Writer:* Bruce Howard. *Director:* Elliott Lewis. *Cast:* Jimmy Durante (*Himself*), Herbie Faye (*Manny Winters*), Del Moore (*Fred Cooper*), Florence MacMichael (*Ruth Cooper*). Jerry's relatives think his jokes and impersonations are good enough to give him a chance at a show business career. With help from Herb's client, who operates a nightclub, Jerry is scheduled to make his professional debut, until a sudden attack of flu sidelines him—allowing Eve, Kaye, and their husbands an irresistible opportunity.

Desi Arnaz's dear friend Jimmy Durante (1893–1980), billed as "Our Very Special Guest Star," turns up in the closing moments of this segment, while the Hubbards and the Buells are performing their version of his "Inka Dinka Doo" number.

52. *Two on the Aisle* (March 16, 1969). *Writer:* Sydney Zelinka. *Director:* Elliott Lewis. *Cast:* Terry [sic] Garr (*Usher*), Joe Besser (*Joe*), Vanda Barra (*Mrs. Smith*), Paul Napier (*Mrs. Smith*). When the Hubbards receive two theater tickets anonymously in the mail, Kaye and Roger convince them it's a burglar's ruse to ensure an empty house. But after the Buells take the tickets, Eve and Roger learn a friend sent the tickets, and the two couples fight over who will get to see the show.

53. *Take Her, He's Mine* (March 23, 1969). *Writers:* Madelyn Davis, Bob Carroll, Jr. *Director:* Elliott Lewis. *Cast:* Joi Lansing (*Barbara*). On deadline with a movie script, Roger hires a secretary whose beauty makes Kaye very nervous. Soon, both Roger and Herb are employing Barbara's secretarial skills, and their wives mistakenly think the new employee is a threat to their happiness.

This was one of the last television appearances of buxom blonde Joi Lansing (1929–1972), who played recurring roles in *The Bob Cummings Show* (1955–1959) and *The Beverly Hillbillies* (1962–1971).

Kaye and Eve (right) have had a rough day at work in the *Mothers-in-Law* segment "The Charge of the Wife Brigade." Glowering over them is Herbert Rudley.

54. *Show Business Is No Business* (March 30, 1969). *Writers:* Robert Fisher, Arthur Marx. *Director:* Elliott Lewis. *Cast:* Don Rickles (*Himself*). Comedian Don Rickles agrees to emcee a show for the lodge to which he, Herb, and Roger belong. But Herb's plan to repay the favor with a home-cooked meal turns disastrous when Eve and Kaye learn Rickles needs a woman to appear in his act.

55. *The Charge of the Wife Brigade* (April 6, 1969). *Writers:* Arthur Marx, Robert Fisher. *Director:* Elliott Lewis. *Cast:* Roy Stuart (*Mr. Finch*), Monty Margetts (*Mrs. Crutcher*). Angered by their wives' spending habits, Herb and Roger cut off Eve and Kaye's credit cards, and challenge them to hold jobs for a month. Eve and Kaye are hired as saleladies at their favorite department store, but after being fired they pawn their fur coats so as to have enough money to look as if they're earning paychecks.

Character actress Monty Margetts (1912–1997), seen here as a department store customer, was among the candidates considered to play the housekeeper on *The Brady Bunch*. Roy Stuart (1927–2005), cast as the mothers-in-law's excitable boss, was best known for his recurring role as Sergeant Boyle on *Gomer Pyle, U.S.M.C.*

56. *The Not-So-Grand Opera* (April 13, 1969). *Writers:* Elaine di Bello Bradish, Madelyn Davis, Bob Carroll, Jr. *Director:* Elliott Lewis. *Cast:* Marni Nixon (*Herself*), Mary Jane Croft (*Carol Yates*), John Myhers (*Bob Simpson*), Marjorie Bennett (*Lucille*), Donna Hall (*Horse Trainer*), Mary Dean, Clare Gordon, Jeannine Wagner, Gloria Grace Prosper, Maurita Phillips, Brenda Fairaday (*Valkyries*)

Eve and Kaye both hope to play the lead in a local production of a Wagnerian opera, but they can't compete with professional singer Marni Nixon, who's just moved into the community. Cast in supporting roles that find them riding a white horse onstage, the ladies struggle with an uncooperative equine on opening night.

Actress Mary Jane Croft (1916–1999), who worked frequently with Eve on *Our Miss Brooks*, makes her only *Mothers-in-Law* appearance here. Mary Jane was the wife of series producer/director Elliott Lewis.

Guest Appearances

A regular and welcome presence on television from the late 1940s through the 1980s (and since, thanks to filmed reruns), Eve not only starred in three weekly series but also turned up frequently as a guest star on other programs.

Her lively, warm personality and quick wit made her a favorite celebrity panelist on game shows such as *The Hollywood Squares, The Name's the Same, It's Your Bet, What's My Line?, Password, Personality,* and others. As a commercial spokeswoman, Eve endorsed products including Imperial margarine. She was a welcome guest on the talk shows of Mike Douglas, David Frost, Dick Cavett, Toni Tennille, and others.

Listed here are some 70 of Eve's most noteworthy TV guest performances, ranging from 1948 to 1987, and comprising some of the most popular, widely seen shows from the first 40 years of broadcast television.

The Texaco Star Theater. NBC, September 7, 1948. Although it would gain fame as the home of comedian Milton Berle, this early variety show wasn't his exclusively from the start. In this segment, comic Jack Carter was the host, and his guests were Eve, Herb Shriner, Jack Pearl, dancer Betty Bruce, and the Fredarrys, a bicycling act. According to *Variety*, the result "slipped into mediocrity." Eve appeared in a comedy sketch that the reviewer reported "was so sad that her embarrassment upon taking the curtain bow was visible on the TV screen" (September 15, 1948).

The Ed Wynn Show. CBS, November 17, 1949. This live, West Coast-based variety show was a favorite haunt of film actors giving TV a tentative try. A few weeks after Eve appears, Wynn will play host to Lucille Ball and Desi Arnaz.

Starlight Theatre. "Julie." CBS, February 8, 1951. *Cast:* Eve Arden, Philip Bourneuf, Leo Penn, Betsy Von Furstenberg. This live dramatic anthology series featured romantically tinged stories. According to a listing in the *Long Beach* (CA) *Independent*, Eve played "a mature stage actress who realizes that she is about to ruin a young actress' career because of her own blighted romance" (February 22, 1951). *Billboard* called it "a half hour of diverting drama," and added, "Miss Arden was unusually good as the star" (February 17, 1951).

Stars in the Eye. CBS, November 15, 1952. *Producer/Director:* Ralph Levy. Eve and her *Our Miss Brooks* co-star Gale Gordon are among the many Hollywood-based CBS stars seen in an hour-long celebration of the opening of the network's Television City complex. Other shows represented include *Amos 'n' Andy, I Love Lucy, The Jack Benny Program, My Friend Irma,* and *The George Burns and Gracie Allen Show.*

What's My Line? CBS, January 2, 1955. *Cast:* John Daly, Eve Arden, Bennett Cerf, Betty Furness, Dorothy Kilgallen, Sam Levenson. Mystery guest Eve answers questions with a horn (once for yes, twice for no) to avoid using that distinctive voice, but Miss Kilgallen guesses her identity anyway.

Toast of the Town. CBS, January 30, 1955. Host Ed Sullivan presents "A Cavalcade of Radio, 1920–1955," a retrospective of great moments from the medium that is rapidly being replaced by television. Eve, recreating a bit from *Our Miss Brooks,* appears alongside Jack Benny, Edgar Bergen, Art Linkletter, Rudy Vallee, Ed Wynn, and many others.

I Love Lucy. "Hollywood at Last." CBS, February 7, 1955. *Cast:* Lucille Ball (*Lucy Ricardo*), Desi Arnaz (*Ricky Ricardo*), Vivian Vance (*Ethel Mertz*), William Frawley (*Fred Mertz*), William Holden (*Himself*), Eve Arden (*Herself*), Harry Bartell (*Waiter*), Dayton Lummis (*Mr. Sherman*), Dani Sue Nolan (*Secretary*), Bobby Jellison (*Bobby*)

In this iconic *Lucy* segment, Lucy and the Mertzes are newly arrived in Hollywood, and enjoy lunch at the Hollywood Brown Derby, where they hope to see movie stars in person. Checking out the restaurant's famous framed caricatures of celebrities, Lucy and Ethel can't decide whether one particular picture depicts Judy Holliday or Shelley Winters. Tapping the woman in the next booth, Ethel asks her—Holliday or Winters? Turning to face the camera, Eve says, "Neither. That's Eve Arden." She gets up and exits to hearty studio applause. Mortified, Ethel gasps, "What she must think of me!"

Climax! "The Louella Parsons Story." CBS, March 8, 1956. *Director:* John Frankenheimer. Eve is one of 28 celebrities making cameo appearances in this program dramatizing "the true story of a young girl whose ambition to be a writer carried her from a small town in Illinois to wealth and fame in Hollywood...." Teresa Wright plays the famed columnist.

The Ed Sullivan Show. CBS, April 29, 1956. Eve is guest host, while Ed is on a talent-scouting trip to Japan. Performers include comedienne Jean Carroll and singer Kate Smith, who's saluted on her 25th anniversary in broadcasting.

The Dinah Shore Chevy Show. NBC, April 13, 1958. Dinah's guests are Eve, Eddie Bracken, and the Mary Kaye Trio. Eve joins Dinah in what the syndicated *TV Key* column described as "a satire on cosmeticians and their valuable oils."

The Dinah Shore Chevy Show. NBC, January 11, 1959. In her second visit with Dinah, "special guest" Eve participates in a series of musical and dance numbers tied to a theme about visiting Rio de Janeiro. During the course of the 60-minute live broadcast, the two ladies duet on "Sentimental Journey," as well as an original number called "The Orango-Tango." Solo, Eve sings "South America, Take It Away." In a jungle sketch, Dinah makes a joking reference to her sponsor when Eve hears animal noises and says, "Maybe it's a Jaguar!" Dinah cracks, "Not on this show!" Also seen are comedian Dick Shawn, musician Red Norvo, and an Indian dance team, Sujata and Asoka.

The Perry Como Show. NBC, March 7, 1959. The crooner's guests are Eve, Ronnie Burns, and comedian Max Bygraves. *Variety* commented, "Miss Arden discussed her early Hollywood days and reprised a tongue-twisting tune from a musical she appeared in with Danny Kaye [*Let's Face It*]. Hers was an arresting routine" (March 11, 1959).

The Perry Como Show. NBC, May 3, 1959. The popular singer welcomes Eve, Tennessee Ernie Ford, and Bob and Ray. Eve duets with Como on "Drop That Name."

The Red Skelton Show. "Appleby's Bird Woman." CBS, October 13, 1959. When George finds a bird in his wife's bed, he believes it is his wife, and acts accordingly.

The George Gobel Show. CBS, December 6, 1959. "Romance suffers an attack of insomnia when Eve Arden plays Sleeping Beauty to George Gobel's Prince Charming.... Eve and George give their impression of what happened to Beauty and her Prince a few years after the famous eye-opening kiss that wound up the fairy tale" (*Lima* [OH] *News*).

Startime. "Meet Cyd Charisse." NBC, December 29, 1959. *Executive Producer:* Hubbell Robinson. Eve, singer Tony Martin (Charisse's husband) and dancer James Mitchell are the guests in the actress/dancer's first television special. UPI's Fred Danzig credited Eve with the "two flashes of wit and airiness" found in a program he otherwise thought disappointing. "One was the dance performed by Miss Charisse and Miss Arden to 'Baubles, Bangles, and Beads.' The other was Miss Arden's ferocious flapper dancing, which was tossed into the midst of an otherwise amateurishly conceived beatnik sketch" (December 30, 1959).

The Perry Como Show. NBC, April 4, 1960. *Cast:* Eve Arden, Marty Allen & Steve Rossi, Sarah Vaughan, the Piero Brothers. Eve sings a specialty number in this baseball-themed segment. In the closing sketch, "At the Moving Picture Ball," Eve plays the gossip columnist who hosts the event.

The Ford Show. NBC, October 13, 1960. *Cast:* Tennessee Ernie Ford, Eve Arden. "Comedienne Eve Arden, tonight's guest, makes a visit to Piney Flat, Tenn., and who does she run into but ol' Ern, a hotel proprietor with ideas about giving his guest the royal treatment." (*Pasadena Star-News*)

Checkmate. "Death by Design." CBS, May 20, 1961. *Writer:* Bob Duncan. *Cast:* Anthony George (*Don Corey*), Doug McClure (*Jed Sills*), Sebastian Cabot (*Dr. Carl Hyatt*), Eve Arden (*Georgia Golden*), Larry Gates (*Harry Winters*), Patric Knowles (*Bill Pearson*), Barney Phillips (*Lt. Brand*), Barbara Wilson (*Francine*), Janet Lake (*Sheila*)

Georgia Golden, partner in a financially troubled fashion design business, hires the men of Checkmate, Inc. to investigate threats against her life. Among the suspects are her business partner, a rival designer who's also her ex-boyfriend, and her sister. Eve would be cast once again as a fashion designer in her 1979 guest appearance on *Vega$*.

I've Got a Secret. CBS, August 30, 1961. Host Garry Moore and Eve use a variety of radio sound-effects devices to create aural scenarios, with panelists Bill Cullen, Henry Morgan, Bess Myerson, and Betsy Palmer invited to supply funny captions. Example: the sound of a cash register ringing, followed by a door slamming. Eve reads the caption: "That's the last time I ever accept a dinner invitation from Jack Benny!"

The Red Skelton Show. CBS, October 3, 1961. George Appleby sees a chance for freedom when he learns that he may not be legally married to shrewish Clara, played once again by Eve.

My Three Sons. "A Holiday for Tramp." ABC, March 8, 1962. *Executive Producer:* Don Fedderson. *Producer:* George Tibbles. *Writer:* Dorothy Cooper Foote. *Director:* Richard Whorf. *Cast:* Fred MacMurray (*Steve Douglas*), William Frawley ("*Bub*" *O'Casey*), Tim Considine (*Mike Douglas*), Don Grady (*Robbie Douglas*), Stanley Livingston (*Chip Douglas*), Eve Arden (*Marissa Montaigne*), Maudie Prickett (*Brownie*), Reta Shaw (*Mrs. Bradshaw*), Lois January (*Mrs. Nichols*), Charles Seel (*Conductor*)

Greeting their father at the railroad station as he returns from a business trip, the members of the Douglas clan don't notice that their dog, Tramp, has jumped aboard the departing train. On board, Tramp makes friends with glamorous, cynical, but basically soft-hearted actress Marissa Montaigne, who grows surprisingly attached to the mutt she nicknames "Whiskers" before he's returned to his rightful owners. Eve, reunited with her co-star from *Cocoanut Grove* (1938), is billed as Special Guest Star.

The Red Skelton Hour. CBS, January 8, 1963. *Cast:* Red Skelton, Eve Arden (*Clara Appleby*). In the skit "Where There's a Will, There's a Wife," meek George Appleby tries to win his wife's respect by leading her to believe he stands to inherit a substantial sum of money. According to critic Leonard Hoffman in the *Tucson Daily Citizen*, Eve "plays the aggressive Clara almost well enough to be believable, then lets it explode in farcical fashion" (January 8, 1963).

Vacation Playhouse. "He's All Yours." CBS, July 20, 1964. *Executive Producer:* Harry Ackerman. *Producer:* Walter Shenson. *Writers:* Sy Gomberg, Al Lewis. *Director:* Don Taylor. *Cast:* Eve Arden

(*Claudia Cooper*), Cindy Carol (*Marsha Cooper*), Howard Smith (*J.T. Gittings*), Jeremy Lloyd (*Bertie Barrington*), Ambrosine Phillpotts (*Lady Matilda Barrington*), Nicholas Parsons (*Squifft*), Derek Bond (*George Andrews*)

This unsold sitcom pilot, also known at various stages as *The Eve Arden Show* or *Take Him, He's Yours,* aired as an episode of *Vacation Playhouse,* the summer replacement series for *The Lucy Show.* Eve plays Claudia Cooper, a widow with a teenaged daughter who arrives in London to take up a job managing the International Travel Agency. The travel agency is but one of many companies owned by wealthy tycoon J.T. Gittings, whose sister Tillie (now Lady Matilda Barrington) has saddled him with his incompetent nephew Bertie as an employee. Having made a complete botch of every job he's previously held, Bertie now wants to serve as manager of the travel agency, and hapless Mrs. Cooper is assigned to keep things under control, while nominally serving as his assistant. Bertie immediately proclaims that he has "already got a million top-notch ideas." The first one he puts into place involves a promotion for an exotic vacation to a remote tropical island, for which Bertie attracts attention by dressing the staff in native costume, filling the agency with dancing girls, a monkey, and a pig rescued from a luau, and serving a rum-based drink that results in office bedlam. Claudia saves the day, and her job, and manages to prevent Bertie from being "sacked" as well.

This comedy pilot teamed Eve with actor/writer Jeremy Lloyd, later to be known as co-creator (with David Croft) of the popular British sitcom *Are You Being Served?* Actor Howard Smith, perhaps best-remembered as the overbearing businessman Harvey Griffin on *Hazel,* plays a similar role here as J.T. Gittings.

The syndicated *TV Key* column rated this "strictly for Eve Arden fans." The pilot episode was shot on location in England. According to Eve's autobiography, the network and potential sponsors would consider a weekly series only if production was returned stateside, which she thought would undermine the comedy.

The Red Skelton Hour. CBS, January 12, 1965. Guest Eve plays the proprietor of a charm school that promises to make a gentleman out of anyone in seven days or less. She hadn't reckoned with the likes of Clem Kadiddlehopper.

Laredo. "Which Way Did They Go?" NBC, November 18, 1965. *Executive Producers:* Richard Irving, Howard Christie. *Producer:* Frederick Shorr. *Writer:* Gerry Day. *Director:* Leon Benson. *Cast:* Neville Brand (*Reese Bennett*), Peter Brown (*Chad Cooper*), William Smith (*Joe Riley*), Philip Carey (*Capt. Ed Parmalee*), Eve Arden (*Emma Bristow*), Myron Healey (*Bolt*), Lyle Talbot (*Sheriff*), Rita D'Amico (*Carlotta*), Doodles Weaver (*The Man*), Grandon Rhodes (*Wentworth*), Lane Bradford (*Amos Slaughter*)

Texas Rangers Reese, Chad, and Joe capture a gang of bank robbers and lock them up, along with their loot, in the town of San Saba. While there, Reese is smitten with lady lecturer Emma Bristow, who's having a hard time selling the local denizens tickets to her high-toned program. With the help of Reese and a pretty dancing girl named Carlotta, Emma's lecture is a sellout—providing just the distraction needed for her own gang to rob the bank. Billed as "Special Guest Star," Eve plays most of her scenes as the larcenous Emma opposite Neville Brand as the rough-hewn, froggy-voiced Ranger who's enamored of her.

Bewitched. "And Then There Were Three." ABC, January 13, 1966. *Executive Producer:* Harry Ackerman. *Producer:* Jerry Davis. *Writer:* Bernard Slade. *Director:* William Asher. *Cast:* Elizabeth Montgomery (*Samantha Stephens/Serena*), Dick York (*Darrin Stephens*), Agnes Moorehead (*Endora*), Eve Arden (*Nurse Kelton*), Gene Blakely (*Dave*), Bobby Byles (*Fred Potter*), Joseph Mell (*Manager*), Mason Curry (*Dr. Anton*), Celeste Yarnall (*Student Nurse*)

Tabitha Stephens (here, spelled Tabatha) is born, and Samantha's cousin Serena is introduced, in this episode guest starring Eve. Back in the maternity ward roughly a quarter-century after her role in *A Child Is Born* (1940), she's the officious hospital nurse who tries in vain to maintain order in Samantha's room. Before the day is over, Nurse Kelton finds Darrin dressed in full Indian headdress and costume, is briefly turned into a frog by Serena, and clashes with Endora, who purrs, "When did *you* get out of charm school?" This guest appearance reunites Eve with some of the off-camera principals responsible for the success of *Our Miss Brooks*, including executive producer Harry Ackerman and director William Asher.

Run for Your Life. "Who's Watching the Fleshpot?" NBC, March 7, 1966. *Writer:* Roy Huggins. *Director:* Leslie H. Martinson. *Cast:* Ben Gazzara (*Paul*), Eve Arden (*Mame Huston*), Bobby Darin (*Mark Shepherd*), Davey Davison (*Marcia Huston*), Jeff Corey (*Abe Lincoln*), Maurice Marsac (*Delgado*), Nicholas Colasanto (*Benno Capalupo*), Thordis Brandt (*Else Brandy*), Jocelyn Lane (*Brigitte Lemaire*), Nadia Sanders (*Poucette Clement*)

Terminally ill lawyer Paul Bryan, visiting the French Riviera, is reunited with his old friend Mark, a beachcomber who earns a living showing tourists the sights. Mark enlists Paul's help entertaining well-to-do Mame Huston and her teenage daughter. This was an unsold pilot for a spinoff series starring actor/singer Bobby Darin.

The Man from U.N.C.L.E. "The Minus-X Affair." NBC, April 8, 1966. *Cast:* Robert Vaughn (*Napoleon Solo*), David McCallum (*Illya Kuryakin*), Leo G. Carroll (*Alexander Waverly*), Eve Arden (*Dr. Lillian Stimmler*), Theo Marcuse, Sharon Farrell (*Leslie*). Eve plays a research scientist, Dr. Stimmler, whose "Plus X" serum is stolen from her lab.

Neville Brand played the Texas Ranger enamored of Eve's Emma Bristow in her 1965 guest appearance on *Laredo*.

The Red Skelton Hour. "Absence Makes the Hate Grow Fonder." CBS, January 24, 1967. *Cast:* Eve Arden, Marilyn Michaels. The social director of a resort hotel tries to help George and Clara Appleby enjoy their stay.

The Red Skelton Hour. CBS, September 5, 1967. Skelton's 15th season opener features Eve once again playing his wife, Clara Appleby, with guest star Robert Stack (*The Untouchables*) as a bad guy who holds the quarrelsome couple hostage.

The Danny Thomas Hour. "The Royal Follies of 1933." NBC, December 10, 1967. *Executive Producer:* Danny Thomas. *Producers:* Alan Handley, Bob Wynn. *Director:* Alan Handley. *Writer:* Sheldon Keller. *Cast:* Danny Thomas (*Prince Wolfgang*), Eve Arden (*Thelda Cunningham*), Hans Conried (*Von Plinkle*), Shirley Jones (*Peggy Ruby*), Gale Gordon (*Anthony Baxter*), Kurt Kasznar (*Hansie*), Ken Berry (*Skip Thompson*), Jackie Joseph (*Suzie Evans*). Prince Wolfgang, heir to the throne of the tiny and impoverished country of Delgravia, plans to marry rich heiress Thelda Cunningham for the benefit of his people. At the eleventh hour, he runs away instead, and joins the cast of a Broadway revue, where he falls in love with a chorus girl. Advance publicity described the show as "a spoof of those Thirties film musicals with bizarre plots and lavish dance numbers."

Rowan & Martin's Laugh-In. NBC, September 23, 1968. *Executive Producer:* George Schlatter. *Producer:* Paul W. Keyes. *Co-Producer:* Carolyn Raskin. *Director:* Gordon Wiles. *Writers:* Chris Beard, Jim Carlson, Dave Cox, Phil Hahn, Jack Hanrahan, Coslough Johnson, Paul W. Keyes,

Marc London, Allan Manings, Jack Mendelsohn, Jim Mulligan, David Panich, Hugh Wedlock, Jr. *Cast:* Dan Rowan, Dick Martin, Chelsea Brown, Ruth Buzzi, Judy Carne, Henry Gibson, Goldie Hawn, Arte Johnson, Dave Madden, Pigmeat Markham, Alan Sues, Eve Arden, Arlene Dahl, Zsa Zsa Gabor, George Kirby, Jack Lemmon, Sonny Tufts, John Wayne, Patrick Wayne. Eve is the principal guest star in this second-season episode of the popular variety show. In various blackouts, she dresses as Whistler's mother, delivers a plug for *The Mothers-in-Law* ("You know,

"Absence Makes the Hate Grow Fonder" for the Applebys, George and Clara, played by Red Skelton and Eve on *The Red Skelton Hour*.

Danny Thomas (left) was joined by guest players Hans Conried, Kurt Kasznar, and Eve in "The Royal Follies of 1933" on *The Danny Thomas Hour.*

I always seem to be working when that's on—but I hear it's fantastic"), and postulates on Burbank's "proud history" of vacant lots. In one skit, Eve revives her Russian accent from *The Doughgirls* as a classical actress, Countess Olga, turned striptease artist. In a segment saluting the telephone, Eve heads the female cast in a song-and-dance number as "Mother Bell and Her Ding-a-Lings." This episode aired opposite the CBS premiere of Lucille Ball's third sitcom, *Here's Lucy.*

What's It All About, World? ABC, April 10, 1969. *Producers:* Ernest Chambers, Saul Ilson. This limited-run variety show hosted by Dean Jones was described by TV historians Tim Brooks and Earle Marsh as "a satirical revue that made fun of contemporary mores and hallowed institutions in a light, relatively inoffensive way." Eve was seen singing and dancing to Jacques Brel's "Madeleine" in a routine that also featured Lorene Yarnell of Shields and Yarnell.

The Liberace Show. CBS, August 19, 1969. Eve guest stars on this summer replacement show spotlighting the popular pianist, along with singers Mary Hopkins and Matt Monro, as well as ventriloquist Ray Alan. Eve, along with the Jack Parnell orchestra and the Irving Davies dancers, performs a musical number, "Typically English," and joins the ensemble in singing "Those Were the Days."

In Name Only. ABC, November 25, 1969. *Executive Producer:* Harry Ackerman. *Producer/Director:* E.W. Swackhamer. *Writer:* Bernard Slade. *Cast:* Michael Callan (*Steve Braden*), Ann Prentiss (*Jill Willis*), Eve Arden (*Aunt Theda*), Ruth Buzzi (*Ruth Clayton*), Christopher Connelly (*Tony Caruso*), Bill Daily (*Peter Garrity*), Elinor Donahue (*Ethel Garrity*), Herb Edelman (*Bert Clayton*), Paul Ford (*Elwy Pertwhistle*), Elsa Lanchester (*Mrs. Caruso*), Alan Reed (*Phil Haskell*), Herbert Voland (*Sgt. Mulligan*), Heather Young (*Debbie Caruso*), Barbara Bostock (*Agnes*)

Marriage counselors Steve and Jill unwittingly used a phony minister to unite some of their clients in matrimony. Now they must inform three couples that their unions are legally invalid. This ABC *Movie of the Week* was also an unsold series pilot from Screen Gems. It uses the same basic premise as Eve's 1952 film *We're Not Married!*

The Game Game. Syndicated, February 1970. *Producer:* Ira Barmak. Jim McKrell hosts, with celebrity guests Eve, Pat Boone, Peter Lawford, and Vera Miles. A lesser-known credit of game show maven Chuck Barris (*The Newlywed Game, The Gong Show*), this syndicated daily entry challenged panelists to match the answers given by a team of psychiatric professionals.

Love, American Style. "Love and the New Roommate." ABC, February 12, 1971. *Director:* Richard Michaels. *Cast:* Eve Arden, Christopher Connelly, Kelly Jean Peters, Elaine Shore, Debbie Watson. Two college students who have recently married decide to keep the union a secret from their parents, who are paying for their education.

The Movie Game. Syndicated, January 1971. Celebrities, playing on behalf of audience members, displayed their knowledge of Hollywood trivia in this syndicated daytime game show hosted by Larry Blyden. Eve is a celebrity panelist along with Charlie Callas, Leslie Nielsen, Carl Reiner, Brenda Vaccaro, and Dennis Weaver.

Love, American Style. "Love and the Contact Lens." ABC, December 31, 1971. *Writers:* R.S. Allen, Harvey Bullock. *Cast:* Eve Arden, Michele Lee (*April*), Hal Buckley (*Bud*). While awaiting the arrival of her boyfriend, a young woman realizes she has lost her contact lens. Her mother, played by Eve, tries to help her keep her imperfect vision a secret from the man she loves.

This Is Your Life. Syndicated, February 1972. Eve and Gale Gordon are among the guests surprising their *Our Miss Brooks* co-star Richard Crenna with his life story.

A Very Missing Person. ABC, March 4, 1972. *Producer:* Edward J. Montagne. *Writer:* Phillip H. Reisman, Jr., based on the novel *Hildegarde Withers Makes the Scene* by Stuart Palmer, Fletcher Flora. *Director:* Russell Mayberry. *Cast:* Eve Arden (*Hildegarde Withers*), James Gregory (*Oscar Piper*), Julie Newmar (*Aletha Westering*), Ray Danton (*Capt. Westering*), Skye Aubrey (*Lenore Gregory/Isobel*), Dennis Rucker (*Aloysius "Al" Fister*), Robert Easton (*Onofre*), Woodrow Parfrey (*Eberhardt*), Bob Hastings (*James Malloy*), Pat Morita (*Delmar Faulkenstein*), Ezra Stone (*Judge*), Udana Power (*Mariette*), Savannah Bentley (*Mrs. Singer*), Arthur Malet (*Higgins*)

Retired schoolteacher-turned-detective Hildegarde Withers is hired to locate missing San Francisco heiress Lenore Gregory. In New York, where the young woman was last seen, Hildegarde enlists the help of her sometimes-reluctant ally Sergeant Piper, as well as a motorcycle-riding young assistant, Al. Indefatigable Miss Withers tracks Lenore to the yacht where the members of a strange cult called "The Karma" live—just in time to defend the young heiress from a murder charge.

This 90-minute TV-movie also served as a pilot for a series, one of a trio that Universal Television packaged as "Great Detectives." (The other two entries cast Stewart Granger as Sherlock Holmes and Robert Conrad as Nick Carter). The Hildegarde Withers mysteries of author Stuart

Palmer originated in the 1930s, and had previously been the basis for a B-movie series starring Edna May Oliver. The syndicated *TV Scout* column termed this "A bit talky, but witty and stylish" (March 4, 1972). The Associated Press's Cynthia Lowry commented, "It was a busy story built around dropouts and con men and really didn't make much sense.... There was constant reference to Miss Withers' advanced age—and Miss Arden did not look in the least like a little old spinster lady" (March 4, 1972). The *Los Angeles Times*'s Kevin Thomas liked the movie and thought Eve's "way with a wisecrack and a batted eye is just as much fun as ever" (March 6, 1972).

The Dean Martin Show. NBC, September 28, 1972. *Executive Producer:* Greg Garrison. *Cast:* Eve Arden, Lynn Anderson, Fess Parker. Eve appears in a sketch about the private life of a schoolteacher, and a western skit in which she portrays a saloon girl. Dean and Eve sing "Almost Like Being in Love."

All My Darling Daughters. ABC, November 22, 1972. *Executive Producer:* David Victor. *Producer:* David J. O'Connell. *Teleplay:* John Gay. *Story:* Robert Presnell, Jr., Stan Dreben. *Director:* David Lowell Rich. *Cast:* Robert Young (*Judge Charles A. Raleigh*), Raymond Massey (*Matthew Cunningham*), Eve Arden (*Miss Freeling*), Darleen Carr (*Susan Raleigh*), Judy Strangis (*Robin Raleigh*), Fawne Harriman (*Charlotte Raleigh*), Darrell Larson (*Andy O'Brien*), Jerry Fogel (*Jerry Greene*), Colby Chester (*Bradley Coombs*), Michael Richardson (*Biff Brynner*), Bruno Kirby (*Anthony Stephanelli*), William Kerwin (*Lester*), John Lupton (*Prosecuting Attorney*), Ben Wright (*Mr. Carter*), Richard Roat (*Defense Attorney*), Virginia Gregg (*Witness*), Ilka Windish (*Mrs. Stephanelli*), Dale Johnson (*Court Clerk*), Ann Loos (*Miss Markham*), Kathi Sawyer (*Maid of Honor*)

Judge Charles Raleigh, widowed father of four adult daughters, is trying to resolve a scheduling conflict between the wedding plans of Charlotte and Susan, both of whom need to say "I do" before the end of the month. His suggestion that they hold a double wedding seems to work—until daughter Susan's boyfriend takes a job out of town and insists that they be married immediately. Just as a triple wedding seems to be the answer for all concerned, youngest daughter Robin confesses to her grandfather that she, too, is in love, but fears her father will be lonely if she leaves home.

Eve, basically a guest star, plays a few quick scenes as Miss Freeling, the harried wedding consultant who is thrown for a loop every time her plans have to be adjusted to accommodate another bride and groom. At the ceremony itself, when Judge Raleigh learns that the justice of the peace has been delayed, he tells Miss Freeling, not for the first time, that there's been a slight change of plans—to which Eve responds, "My God, you don't have *another* daughter?" *All My Darling Daughters* reunited Eve with actor Jerry Fogel, who played her son-in-law on *The Mothers-in-Law*, though they don't share any scenes here. This *ABC Movie of the Week* was sufficiently popular to generate a sequel, *My Darling Daughters' Anniversary,* which doesn't feature Eve.

The Girl with Something Extra. "The Greening of Aunt Fran." NBC, January 18, 1974. *Writer:* Stan Cutler. *Director:* Richard Kinon. *Cast:* Sally Field (*Sally Burton*), John Davidson (*John Burton*), Zohra Lampert (*Anne*), Stephanie Edwards (*Angela*), Eve Arden (*Aunt Fran*), William Windom (*Stuart Kline*)

This short-lived sitcom cast Sally Field as a young wife whose extrasensory perception caused comic difficulties, and John Davidson as her husband, an attorney. "When Aunt Fran ... reveals she needs some legal counsel regarding an inheritance matter, John (John Davidson) arranges for Stuart Kline ... of his law office to represent her. Complications set in when an overdue tab from Las Vegas is uncovered" (*Warren* [PA] *Times Observer,* January 18, 1974).

The ABC Afternoon Playbreak. "Mother of the Bride." ABC, January 9, 1974. *Writers:* Lila Garrett, Sandy Krinski. *Director:* Burt Brinckerhoff. *Cast:* Eve Arden (*Millie Owens*), Don Porter (*George Owens*), Jennifer Salt (*Jody Owens*), Elizabeth Allen (*Amy Whitman*), Kip Niven (*Steve Whitman*), Elliott Reid (*Gary Whitman*), Philip Sterling (*Harry Prosnick*)

In the midst of making lavish plans for her daughter's impending wedding, Millie Owens learns that the ceremony must now take place in six days, rather than six weeks as originally

Eve (center) is the overwhelmed "Mother of the Bride" in her Emmy-nominated performance on *The ABC Afternoon Playbreak*. Also pictured are Don Porter and Jennifer Salt.

scheduled. Under the gun, Millie is nonetheless determined to see that Jody has the dream wedding she's always wanted. The *New York Times*'s Howard Thompson described this as "an archly comic television exercise running 90 long minutes" which left Eve "broadly paddling upstream" (January 9, 1974). Nonetheless, Eve was nominated for a Daytime Emmy as Best Actress for her performance.

Owen Marshall, Counselor at Law. "The Sterilization of Judy Simpson." ABC, February 16, 1974. *Cast:* Arthur Hill (*Owen Marshall*), David Soul (*Ted Warrick*), Eve Arden (*Dr. Lucille Barras*), Dwan Smith (*Judy Simpson*), Clarice Taylor (*Mrs. Simpson*). Attorney Owen Marshall takes the case of a mildly retarded 18-year-old girl rebelling against a doctor's recommendation that she be sterilized, for which the teenager's mother has signed her consent.

According to an ABC press release, "Eve Arden guest stars as 'Dr. Lucille,' who has devoted her life to a clinic which serves a depressed area, and is deeply concerned about the poverty and deprivation of the people living there. Thus, she has taken it upon herself to perform numerous sterilization operations on young women in order to spare them and their families from what she considers even more hopeless conditions. She convinces Judy's mother that the operation should be performed, especially since Judy had undergone an abortion following a sexual assault on her."

The Tony Awards. ABC, April 20, 1975. *Producer:* Alexander H. Cohen. *Writer:* Hildy Parks. *Director:* Clark Jones. Eve is among the presenters (along with Fred Astaire, Milton Berle, Angela Lansbury, Jack Lemmon, Walter Matthau, Rosalind Russell, and many others) in this mostly live broadcast that also features some pre-taped inserts. The show's sketches and musical numbers are devoted to revisiting shows staged throughout the history of the Winter Garden Theatre, from which the broadcast originates. Both of Eve's *Ziegfeld Follies* (1934 and 1936) are so commemorated, and her duet with Bob Hope from the latter show ("I Can't Get Started with You") is recreated with younger performers. Eve herself appears in a taped segment to announce the nominees for Best Supporting Actor in a Musical. Paying tribute to the function of the supporting player, Eve says, "As long as Mr. Ziegfeld was alive, no one was ever billed above the title in the *Ziegfeld Follies*, not even the star of the show. The words *Ziegfeld Follies* brought them into the theater, and then it was up to the actors to keep them there."

Harry and Maggie. CBS, April 25, 1975. *Creator:* Joseph Goodson. *Writers/Producers:* Arnold Margolin, James Parker. *Director:* Jay Sandrich. *Cast:* Don Knotts (*Harry Kellogg*), Eve Arden (*Maggie Sturdivant*), Tom Poston (*Arlo Wilson*), Lucille Benson (*Thelma*), Kathy Davis (*Clovis Kellogg*), Eddie Quillan (*Max Lovechild*). Widower Harry Kellogg, raising a teenaged daughter on his own in a small town, balks at his sister-in-law's efforts to horn in. Maggie, divorced five times, decides Harry needs her help and moves in against his wishes. Harry tries to get her out of his house by

Eve co-starred with Don Knotts in *Harry and Maggie*, an unsold pilot for a CBS comedy series.

fixing her up with an eligible bachelor. A CBS press release described this unsold series pilot as "a comedy about the clashing lifestyles of a grumpy Iowa widower and his aggressive, flamboyant, and sophisticated sister-in-law." It aired as a "Friday Comedy Special" in April, and was rerun in July.

Ellery Queen. "The Adventure of Miss Aggie's Farewell Performance." NBC, October 19, 1975. *Executive Producers:* Richard Levinson, William Link. *Producers:* Peter S. Fischer, Michael Rhodes. *Writers:* Peter Fischer, Richard Levinson, William Link. *Director:* James Sheldon. *Cast:* Jim Hutton (*Ellery Queen*), David Wayne (*Inspector Richard Queen*), Eve Arden (*Vera Bethune*), Betty White (*Louise Demery*), John Hillerman (*Simon Brimmer*), Nan Martin (*Olivia Burns*), John McGiver (*Mr. Pearl*), Bert Parks (*Lawrence Denver*), Paul Shenar (*Wendell Warren*), Beatrice Colen (*Mary Lou Gumm*). Actress Vera Bethune plays the starring role of Miss Aggie, wise and loving small-town high school principal, in the popular radio soap opera *Every Day's Journey*. During a live broadcast, Vera collapses, apparently due to poison in the water pitcher kept in the studio. The hospitalized star entrusts Ellery Queen with the task of solving the mystery, but she is finished off by a late-night shooting before he can do so. Interviewing such suspects as her co-stars, her agent, the program's organist, announcer, and writers, Ellery must deduce who wanted Vera Bethune dead.

Her character killed by a fatal gunshot midway through the program, Eve has a relatively small number of scenes here, but makes them count. Her character is an amusingly acerbic type who remarks to a young actress, "Anita dear.... Try to speak a little softer today, will you...? Not that I think you're overdoing it, but you know how the network people are." This short-lived TV adaptation of the popular Ellery Queen mystery stories is done by several of the same people who will later enjoy greater success with *Murder, She Wrote*.

Dean Martin Celebrity Roast. NBC, February 3, 1977. Eve is among the guests roasting *Police Woman* star Angie Dickinson, along with James Stewart, Orson Welles, Cindy Williams, and Rex Reed.

Maude. "Maude's Aunt." CBS, March 7, 1977. *Writer:* Bill Davenport. *Director:* Hal Cooper. *Cast:* Beatrice Arthur (*Maude Findlay*), Bill Macy (*Walter Findlay*), Conrad Bain (*Dr. Arthur Harmon*), Rue McClanahan (*Vivian Cavender Harmon*), Hermione Baddeley (*Nell Naugatuck*), J. Pat O'Malley (*Bert Beasley*), Eve Arden (*Lola Ashburn*)

Maude's beloved, saucy Aunt Lola, whose niece calls her "fascinating ... years ahead of her time," pays a visit to Tuckahoe. Not so enamored of Lola are Walter, who describes her as "rude and offensive," and Mrs. Naugatuck, who happens to be out of town. In her absence, Lola stirs up a fuss by accompanying Mrs. Naugatuck's husband, Bert, to a lodge meeting. Later, called upon to explain herself, Lola confesses to Maude that she's a lonely woman who has to take her fun where she can find it. Says Eve, as Lola, of her larger-than-life persona, "I guess that's why they call me a living legend."

CBS: On the Air. CBS, March 31, 1978. *Producer:* Lee Miller. *Writer:* Hildy Parks. *Director:* Clark Jones. This multi-part special, airing over seven consecutive nights, celebrates the 50th anniversary of CBS. Co-host of the Friday night segment, Eve joins Richard Crenna, Bonnie Franklin, Linda Lavin, and Jim Nabors in a song, "Person to Person." Popular CBS shows that were Friday night staples, among them *Our Miss Brooks*, are saluted.

Grease Day U.S.A. Syndicated, June 1978. Eve, along with John Travolta and Olivia Newton-John, is among the stars appearing in this special celebrating the Hollywood premiere of their film *Grease*. A "post-premiere prom," taped on the set used in the film, follows.

A Guide for the Married Woman. ABC, October 13, 1978. *Producer:* Lee Miller. *Teleplay:* Frank Tarloff. *Story:* Frank Tarloff, Jewel Jaffe, Jerry Rannow. *Director:* Hy Averback. *Cast:* Cybill Shepherd (*Julie Walker*), Charles Frank (*Jerry Walker*), Barbara Feldon (*Maggie*), Eve Arden (*Employment Lady*), John Beradino (*Doctor*), John Byner (*Elevator Man*), Mary Frances Crosby (*Eloise*), Bill Dana (*Ed Small*), Bonnie Franklin (*Shirley*), George Gobel (*Hallway Man*), John Hillerman (*Marvin*), Elaine Joyce (*Helen*), Bernie Kopell (*Bill*), Peter Marshall (*Fred Hurley*), Tom Poston (*Marty Gibson*), Sarah Purcell (*Marsha*), Bob Seagren (*Chuck*), Chuck Woolery (*Tennis Pro*), Allison Balson (*Debby Walker*), Steven Mond (*Arnold Walker*)

After nine of years of marriage and two children, the romance has gone out of the Walkers' relationship. Bored and unfulfilled as a housewife, Julie considers going back to work, but is advised instead by her friends to spice up her existence with an extramarital affair.

Eve, one of several name actors seen in "Special Appearance" cameos here, appears briefly as an employment counselor who tries to help Julie find part-time work. Because Julie spends so much time taking care of her children, Debby and Arnold, as well as running household errands, Eve's character finally says, "Why don't you come back when Debby and Arnold are in college?" Eve is directed here by her longtime friend and colleague Hy Averback, who as an actor in the 1950s was seen frequently on *Our Miss Brooks*.

Flying High. "It Was Just One of Those Days." CBS, October 20, 1978. *Executive Producer:* Mark Carliner. *Producer:* Robert Van Scoyk. *Director:* Alan Myerson. *Cast:* Pat Klous (*Marcy Bowers*), Connie Sellecca (*Lisa Benton*), Kathryn Witt (*Pam Bellagio*), Howard Platt (*Capt. Doug March*), Ken Olfson (*Raymond Strickman*), Eve Arden (*Clarissa "Wedgie" Wedge*), Charles Knox Robinson (*Anatole*), Marc Gilpin (*Bobby*), Jackie Mason (*Rabbi Goldman*), Rick Jason (*Captain Stacy*)

Eve was among the guest stars in this short-lived series about the adventures of three fun-loving stewardesses, a cross between two ABC hits, *Charlie's Angels* and *The Love Boat*. She played, according to *TV Guide*, a "hard-boiled senior flight attendant on her last pre-retirement run."

Bobby Vinton's Rock 'n Rollers. CBS, November 17, 1978. *Producers:* Sid and Marty Krofft. According to a network press release, "Bobby Vinton stars in his first network music-variety special, a fast-moving trip into the nostalgia of rock 'n' roll, dancing and roller skating." Guests included Eve, Gale Gordon, Fabian, Penny Marshall, Erik Estrada, and Stockard Channing.

Vega$. "Design for Death." ABC, October 31, 1979. *Executive Producers:* Aaron Spelling, Douglas S. Cramer. *Supervising Producer:* E. Duke Vincent. *Producers:* Phil Fehrle, Larry Forrester. *Writer:* Ken Pettus. *Director:* Phil Bondelli. *Cast:* Robert Urich (*Dan Tanna*), Greg Morris (*Lt. David Nelson*), Bart Braverman (*Binzer*), Phyllis Davis (*Bea Travis*), Eve Arden (*Sarah Bancroft*), Barbi Benton (*Holly*), Gary Crosby (*Tom Bancroft*), Cliff Osmond (*Henry Gates*), Paul Mantee (*Roy*), Frank Marth (*George Crowley*), Linda Thompson (*Rita Mason*), Pepper Davis (*Manny*). The Desert Inn Hotel is set to play host to a fashion show introducing designer Sarah Bancroft's new line of Sun Goddess swimwear. Detective Dan Tanna is called in to investigate when a series of accidents befalling the swimsuit models threatens to stop the show. The murder of a model with whom Dan was romantically involved makes him more determined than ever to get to the bottom of the mystery.

"Special Guest Star" Eve has a sizable role in this segment, as the stylishly dressed (by Nolan Miller) couturier who manages to make a few wry comments amidst the mayhem. When one of Sarah's models apologizes for almost missing a shoot, explaining she was caught in traffic, Eve responds, "Models are supposed to stop traffic, Holly, not be stopped by it." Surrounded by bikini-clad young ladies, Eve explains to her fashion show audience, "Incidentally, these suits are marvelous for travel. They fit into your coin purse." Initially uncertain about young Mr. Tanna's professional skills, Eve's character nevertheless gives him a once-over, noting as he walks away, "Oh, my, he *is* a charmer."

This is Eve's first guest appearance in one of super-producer Aaron Spelling's popular ABC shows. Roles on *The Love Boat* and *Hart to Hart* will follow.

Alice. "Alice in TV Land." CBS, January 13, 1980. *Executive Producers:* Bob Carroll, Jr., Madelyn Davis. *Writers:* Bob Fisher, Arthur Marx. *Director:* Norman Abbott. Cast: Linda Lavin (*Alice Hyatt*), Vic Tayback (*Mel Sharples*), Polly Holliday (*Flo Castleberry*), Beth Howland (*Vera Gorman*), Philip McKeon (*Tommy Hyatt*), Dave Madden (*Earl Hicks*), Eve Arden (*Martha MacIntire*), Christian Juttner (*Billy*), Ed Kenney (*Announcer*). Eve plays a talk-show host whose program gives a forum to teenagers and their problems. Alice and her friends from Mel's Diner are delighted by Tommy's appearance on the show, until he begins being too honest for their comfort, causing them to demand equal time for rebuttal.

The Love Boat. ABC, January 19, 1980. *Executive Producers:* Douglas S. Cramer, Aaron Spelling. *Producer:* Henry Colman, Gordon Farr, Lynne Farr. *Writer:* Lee Aronsohn. *Director:* Roger Duchowny. *Cast:* Gavin MacLeod (*Capt. Merrill Stubing*), Bernie Kopell (*Dr. Adam Bricker*), Lauren Tewes (*Julie McCoy*), Fred Grandy (*Burl "Gopher" Smith*), Ted Lange (*Isaac Washington*), Jill Whelan (*Vicki Stubing*), Loni Anderson (*Kitty Fields*), Eve Arden (*Verna Wasser*), Randall Carver (*Elmer Fargas*), Pam Grier (*Cynthia Wilbur*), Robert Guillaume (*Frank Belloque*), Rich Little (*Steve Sorrell*), Suzy Mandel (*Trina*), Denise Nicholas (*Maura Belloque*), Donny Osmond (*Danny Fields*), Richard Paul (*Mr. Shoenfield*), Slim Pickens (*Grandpa Shoenfield*), Marion Ross (*Emily Hayward*), Richard Roundtree (*Dave Williams*). This two-hour segment centers on an aspiring singer's plight when his hillbilly family accompanies him on a cruise. In the "Moonlight and Moonshine" segment, Eve plays an author who tries to get closer to the grandfather of the rural clan so that she can gather material for her next book.

B.J. and the Bear. "The Girls of Hollywood High." NBC, February 23, 1980. *Executive Producers:* Glen A. Larson, Michael Sloan. *Producer:* Robert F. O'Neill. *Writer:* Glen A. Larson. *Director:* Bruce Bilson. *Cast:* Greg Evigan (*B.J. McKay*), Eve Arden (*Helen Jarvis*), Rebecca Reynolds (*Heather Fern*), Heather Thomas (*Caroline Capote*), Lloyd Bochner (*Marty Franks*), Michael Pataki (*Det. Rizzo*), Burr DeBenning (*Garrett Logan*), Craig Stevens (*Hank Rogers*), Stuart Pankin (*Harvey Kreppler*), Vito Scotti (*Warehouse Man*), Helena Carroll (*Doris*). Trucker

Eve guest starred on *Alice* as talk show host Martha MacIntyre, who elicits some frank statements from her guest Tommy (Philip McKeon).

B.J. McKay hires Texas International, a detective agency run by Helen Jarvis, to locate his missing sister, who vanished after attending an upscale party in Hollywood. This was producer Glen A. Larson's second pilot for an *Eyes of Texas* series; in the first, the owner of the detective agency was played by Eve's former *Mothers-in-Law* co-star Roger C. Carmel.

Hart to Hart. "Does She or Doesn't She?" ABC, March 18, 1980. *Executive Producers:* Leonard Goldberg, Aaron Spelling. *Producer:* Mart Crowley. *Creator:* Sidney Sheldon. *Writers:* Jeff Myrow, Donna Myrow. *Director:* George W. Brooks. *Cast:* Robert Wagner (*Jonathan Hart*), Stefanie Powers (*Jennifer Hart*), Lionel Stander (*Max*), Stephen Parr (*Barry Saxon*), Eve Arden (*Sophie Green*), Frank Marth (*Harold Micklin*), Susan Bartells (*Sally Hutchins*), Jack Ramage (*Martin Hutchins*), Tandy Cronyn (*Gail Davis*), Jo McDonnell (*Elise*), Jon Cutler (*Lt. Montgomery*), Tony Brafa (*Alfredo Carbona*). Jennifer Hart's hairdresser, owner of Barry's Hotheads, narrowly escapes being shot by an angry woman customer. At the behest of Barry's longtime receptionist, Sophie, the Harts investigate a case involving a loan shark who bugs Barry's salons in order to blackmail his wealthy clients. Eve receives "Special Guest Star" billing for her smallish role as Sophie. She has an amusing moment on the telephone in which she reacts to an outburst by an unseen celebrity client, saying indignantly, "I understood that, Zsa Zsa! My first husband was Hungarian."

The Dream Merchants. Syndicated, May 1980. *Executive Producer:* Milton Sperling. *Producer:* Hugh Benson. *Teleplay:* Chester Krumholtz, Laurence Richards. *Director:* Vincent Sherman. *Cast:*

Mark Harmon (*Johnny Edge*), Vincent Gardenia (*Peter Kessler*), Morgan Fairchild (*Dulcie Warren*), Brianne Leary (*Doris Kessler*), Robert Picardo (*Mark Kessler*), Kaye Ballard (*Esther Kessler*), Eve Arden (*Coralee*), Morgan Brittany (*Astrid James*), Red Buttons (*Bruce Benson*), Robert Culp (*Henry Farnum*), Howard Duff (*Charles Slade*), José Ferrer (*George Pappas*), Robert Goulet (*Craig Warren*), David Groh (*Rocco Salvatore*), Carolyn Jones (*Vera*), Fernando Lamas (*Conrad Stillman*), Ray Milland (*Lawrence Radford*). This four-hour miniseries, based on Harold Robbins's 1949 novel, tells the story of filmmaker Johnny Edge (loosely based on Universal founder Carl Laemmle), and the Hollywood studio he establishes, Magnum Pictures. The story begins in 1912, as a young Johnny is fascinated by early, primitive moving pictures, and continues through the silent era and into the 1930s. Eve, a "Special Guest Star" along with a dozen other familiar movie and TV faces, is seen briefly as a Hedda Hopper-type gossip columnist, Coralee, who reports on the on- and offscreen dramas of Magnum and its stars. In one scene, she pursues the story of a director's clandestine romance with his leading lady; later, she discusses the coming advent of motion pictures with sound. Each of her three key scenes finds her accompanied by a different, handsome young man, who is introduced as "my new secretary." Eve's *Mothers-in-Law* co-star Kaye Ballard has a more substantial featured role as the matriarch of the Kessler clan. This was one of the last directorial credits of Vincent Sherman, well-suited to this assignment with his background helming Golden Age Hollywood dramas starring Joan Crawford and Bette Davis, among others.

The Tony Awards. CBS, June 8, 1980. *Executive Producer:* Alexander H. Cohen. *Producer/Writer:* Hildy Parks. *Director:* Clark Jones. Eve is among the presenters seen during the two-hour live broadcast, hosted by Mary Tyler Moore and Jason Robards. The show is centered around the theme of understudies. Carol Channing tells the audience about understudying Eve "many, many years ago" in *Let's Face It,* and being fired because she did not perform the musical routine as written. Eve herself then comes onstage, and in turn recalls being understudy to Fanny Brice in both *Ziegfeld Follies* shows. Presenting the Best Scenic Design award, Eve rips open the envelope, and reads the name of John Lee Beatty (*Talley's Folly*). As he bounds toward the stage, she cries out, "Wait! Wait! It's a tie!" adding the name of David Mitchell (*Barnum*). Having navigated that tricky patch, she remarks, "The scenery may be lovely, but if you can't see it, you can't vote for it," and announces David Hersey (*Evita*) as the winner for Outstanding Lighting Design. Eve and the entire company are onstage again at the finale to sing "I Love New York."

Nuts and Bolts. ABC, August 24, 1981. *Producer:* David Gerber. *Cast:* Rich Little (*Miles Fenton*), Eve Arden (*Martha Fenton*), Tammy Lauren (*Lucy Fenton*), Justin Dana (*Alex Fenton*), Jo Ann Pflug (*Karen Prescott*), Mitchell Young Evans (*Robot Primo*), Douglas V. Fowley (*Voice of Primo*), Tommy McLoughlin (*Robot Victor*), Garnett Smith (*Victor's Voice*), William Daniels (*Warren Berlinger*)

This unsold sitcom pilot, aired as an "ABC Monday Comedy Special," starred impressionist Rich Little as a widowed computer engineer who uses robots to raise his children. Eve played Little's mother.

A Gift of Music. Syndicated, Fall 1981. *Writer:* Harry Crane. *Director:* Jeff Margolis. Eve is among the hosts (along with Greer Garson, Lorne Greene, Donald O'Connor, Twiggy, and Dionne Warwick) for this two-hour "musical celebration of Hollywood's contribution to music" from the 1920s through the 1980s.

Faerie Tale Theater. "Cinderella." Showtime, September 11, 1982. *Executive Producer:* Shelley Duvall. *Producers:* Frederic S. Fuchs, Bridget Terry. *Writers:* Rod Ash, Mark Curtiss. *Director:* Mark Cullingham. *Cast:* Jennifer Beals (*Cinderella*), Matthew Broderick (*Prince Henry*), Jean Stapleton (*Fairy Godmother*), Eve Arden (*Wicked Stepmother*), James Noble (*King Rupert III*), Tim Thomerson (*Royal Adviser*), Jane Alden (*Arlene*), Edie McClurg (*Bertha*), Mark Blankfield (*Edgar*), David McCharen (*Alfred*), Charlie Dell (*Arturo*), Lise Lang (*Young Lady at Ball*), Nancy Lenehan (*Maiden at Ball*), Ty Crowley (*Gentleman at Ball*), Monroe Sheppard (*Coachman*), Nancy Omi, Pat Ast (*Slipper Contestants*), Shelley Duvall (*Host*), Joseph Maher (*Narrator*)

Eve is cast as the Wicked Stepmother in this retelling of the classic fairy tale. Displaying just a touch of favoritism toward her own daughters, she decrees that Cinderella's household chores will comprise "cooking ... waxing ... sweeping, polishing, cleaning, scouring, dishes, trash, gardening, bed making, and various miscellaneous chores, including laundry and everything else," while her siblings are assigned tasks such as "bathing yourself, brushing your own hair, and maintaining an attractive appearance." With the help of her Southern-accented Fairy Godmother, Cinderella is allowed to attend the royal ball, where she quickly captures the heart of the handsome prince. Joseph Maher, Eve's leading man from *Under the Rainbow*, narrates the hour-long program.

Great Performances. "Alice in Wonderland." PBS, October 3, 1983. *Executive Producer:* Jac Venza. *Producer:* Ann Blumenthal. *Writer:* Lewis Carroll. *Director:* Kirk Browning. *Cast:* Eve Arden (*Queen of Hearts*), Kaye Ballard (*Duchess*), Kate Burton (*Alice*), Richard Burton (*White Knight*), James Coco (*King of Hearts*), Tony Cummings (*Knave of Hearts*), André De Shields (*Tweedledum*), Colleen Dewhurst (*Red Queen*), André Gregory (*Mad Hatter*), Geoffrey Holder (*Cheshire Cat*), Zeljko Ivanek (*March Hare*), Nathan Lane (*Mouse*), Donald O'Connor (*Mock Turtle*), Austin Pendleton (*White Rabbit*), Maureen Stapleton (*White Queen*), Swen Swenson (*Gryphon*), Fritz Weaver (*Caterpillar*), Alan Weeks (*Tweedledee*), Richard Woods (*Humpty-Dumpty*)

A star-studded cast brings Lewis Carroll's classic to life in this videotaped performance of the production that ran briefly on Broadway in December 1982 and January 1983. Kate Burton stars as Alice alongside her famous father, Richard, as the White Knight. Top-billed in the alphabetical cast list, Eve plays the imperious Queen of Hearts, alongside James Coco as her weak-willed king. She's reunited here with several actors with whom she'd worked before, notably her co-star from *The Mothers-in-Law*, Kaye Ballard, and Donald O'Connor, with whom Eve had worked onstage and in film (*Curtain Call at Cactus Creek*). The Broadway show, which featured a largely different cast aside from the Burtons, was conceived by Eva Le Gallienne and Florida Friebus, and had its original production in 1932. As Eve noted in her autobiography, when offered this role, she thought, "Who could resist that cast?"

Masquerade. "Diamonds." ABC, December 22, 1983. *Executive Producers:* Glen A. Larson, Renee Valente. *Producers:* Andrew Schneider, Mark Rodgers. *Writer:* William Read Woodfield. *Director:* Peter Crane. *Cast:* Rod Taylor (*Lavender*), Kirstie Alley (*Casey Collins*), Greg Evigan (*Danny Doyle*), Morgan Brittany (*Buffy Huntington*), Eve Arden (*Mrs. Woodman*), David Hemmings (*Marlos*), Dick Gautier (*Mr. Gordon*), Jeff East (*Tim*), Rick Lenz (*Norman Webber*), Yuliis Ruval (*Hildy*)

Described by a United Press International reporter as a cross between *Mission: Impossible* and *The Love Boat*, this lighthearted spy show used a succession of weekly guest stars to play ordinary citizens recruited for temporary espionage assignments with the National Intelligence Agency. Eve was a guest star in the second aired episode, in which Lavender's team of amateurs must prevent the sale of secret NATO missile codes to East German intelligence. As Mrs. Woodman, an expert dog trainer, she issues commands in Dutch to call off two guard dogs standing watch over a heavily secured vault. Eve and David Hemmings receive "Special Guest Star" billing.

Hour Magazine. Syndicated, 1985. *Cast:* Gary Collins, Eve Arden, Richard Crenna. Eve and Richard reminisce about *Our Miss Brooks*. Crenna shows that he can still summon the voice of Walter Denton, while Eve disputes Collins's statement that Miss Brooks was man-hungry—"I was Boynton-hungry." She mentions that she is finishing her autobiography, as yet untitled.

The Bugs Bunny/Looney Tunes All-Star 50th Anniversary. CBS, January 14, 1986. *Executive Producer:* Lorne Michaels. *Producers:* Mary Salter, Tom Gammill, Max Pross. *Writers:* Tom Gammill, Max Pross, Greg Ford. *Director:* Gary Weis. Eve is among the live-action guest stars (along with George Burns, Cher, Steve Martin, Bill Murray, and others) reminiscing about the great cartoon players. She appears in the segment devoted to Porky Pig, reflecting on the rivalry with Daffy Duck that caused him to leave the studio ("I tried to persuade him to stay..."), and also remembers the brief career of Petunia Pig ("Such a nice girl. She tried so hard. I don't think she could handle the pressure.")

Steven Spielberg's Amazing Stories. "Secret Cinema." NBC, April 6, 1986. *Executive Producer:* Steven Spielberg. *Producer:* David E. Vogel. *Writer/Director:* Paul Bartel. *Cast:* Penny Peyser (*Jane Fitzpatrick*), Griffin Dunne (*Dick/Rick*), Eve Arden (*Jane's Mother*), Paul Bartel (*Dr. Shreck*), Mary Woronov (*Nurse*), Richard Paul (*Mr. Krupp*), Alix Elias (*Lady Customer*), Barry Dennen (*News Dealer*), Gary Goodrow (*Doorman*)

Hapless Jane, dumped by her boyfriend on the eve of their wedding, is unaware that her entire life is being filmed with secret cameras for a comedy serial called *The Adventures of Jane*. Eve plays Jane's mother, who drops one of the first hints about the Secret Cinema when she asks her daughter to autograph photos of herself for the ladies in her bridge club. Eve heads the list of alphabetically ordered stars in this segment, written and directed by Paul Bartel, who also plays Jane's *faux* therapist whose office wall is decorated with poster art of Olivia de Havilland in *The Snake Pit*.

The American Film Institute Salute to Barbara Stanwyck. ABC, May 23, 1987. *Director:* Dwight Hemion. Eve is among the colleagues, along with Fred MacMurray, John Huston, Billy Wilder, Linda Evans and others, paying tribute to Stanwyck as she receives the AFI's Life Achievement Award. Jane Fonda hosts the television broadcast of the presentation, taped in early April.

Falcon Crest. "Manhunt." CBS, November 20, 1987. *Executive Producer/Creator:* Earl Hamner. *Writer:* James Fritzhand. *Director:* Michael A. Hoey. Cast: Jane Wyman (*Angela Channing*), David Selby (*Richard Channing*), Susan Sullivan (*Maggie Gioberti*), Lorenzo Lamas (*Lance Cumson*), Ana-Alicia (*Melissa Agretti*), Eddie Albert (*Carlton Travis*), Eve Arden (*Lillian Nash Darlington*)

Eve is reunited with Jane Wyman, her co-star from *The Doughgirls* and *The Lady Takes a Sailor*, in a guest appearance on this popular prime-time soap opera. Eve plays a socially prominent woman in Washington, D.C., wife of a Supreme Court judge, who helps Angela Channing fight back against her enemy Carlton Travis.

IV

Broadway Performances

Ziegfeld Follies of 1934 (1934)

Producers: Lee Shubert, Mrs. Florenz Ziegfeld, Jr. *Director*: Bobby Connolly. *Writers*: Fred Allen, H.I. Philips, Harry Turgend. *Musical Director*: John McManus. *Stage Manager*: Dan Brennan. *Choreographer*: Robert Alton. Opened January 4, 1934 at the Winter Garden Theatre; closed June 9, 1934. 182 performances.

Cast: Fanny Brice, Eugene Howard, Willie Howard, Buddy Ebsen, Vilma Ebsen, John Adair, Eve Arden, Judith Barron, Patricia Bowman, Dorothy Buckley, Joseph Carey, Jack Coogan, Hope Dare, Loretta Dennison, Brice Hutchins [Bob Cummings], Vivian Janis, Ruth Kane, James Kitson, Victor Morley, Jack Ross, Caroline Ryan, Marie Stevens, Oliver Wakefield, Betty Worth.

Parade (1935)

Director: Philip Loeb. *Music/Dance Director*: Robert Alton. *Orchestral Direction*: Max Meth. *Writers*: Alan Baxter, Michael Blankfort, Kyle Crichton, Frank Gabrielson, David Lesan, Paul Peters, George Sklar. *Scenic Design*: Lee Simonson. *Costume Design*: Constance Ripley, Irene Sharaff, Billi Livingston, Lee Simonson. Opened May 20, 1935, at the Guild Theatre; closed June 22, 1935. 40 performances.

Cast: Avis Andrews, Eve Arden, Ethel Axel, Charles D. Brown, Leon Janney, David Lawrence, Lois Leng, J. Elliott Leonard, David Lesan, Roger Logan, Earl Oxford, Ralph Riggs, Polly Rose, Jimmy Savo, Ezra Stone, Jerome Thor, Jean Travers, Marguerite White.

Ziegfeld Follies of 1936 (1936)

Book: David Freeman. *Director*: John Murray Anderson. *Producers*: Billie Burke Ziegfeld, J.J. Shubert, Lee Shubert. *Music*: Vernon Duke. *Lyrics*: Ira Gershwin. *Musical Director*: John McManus. *Ballet Director*: George Balanchine. Opened January 30, 1936, at the Winter Garden Theatre; closed May 9, 1936. 115 performances.

Cast: Fanny Brice, Bob Hope, Gertrude Niesen, Eve Arden, Judy Canova, Josephine Baker, June Preisser, the Nicholas Brothers, Roger Davis, Gene Ashley, Vicki Belling, Herman Belmonte, Prescott Brown, Florine Callahan, George Church, Mary Alice Moore, Eileen O'Driscoll, Jessica Pepper, Peggy Quinn, Marlyn Stuart, Peggy Thomas, Ethel Thorsen.

Very Warm for May (1939-40)

A musical in two acts by Jerome Kern and Oscar Hammerstein II. *Producer*: Max Gordon. *Musical Director*: Robert Emmett Dolan. *Dances*: Albertina Rasch. *Stage Manager*: Frank Hall. Opened November 17, 1939, at the Alvin Theatre; closed January 6, 1940. 59 performances.

Cast: Grace McDonald (*May Graham*), Donald Brian (*William Graham*), Jack Whiting (*Johnny Graham*),

Eve Arden (*Winnie Spofford*), Richard Quine (*Sonny Spofford*), Frances Mercer (*Liz Spofford*), Max Showalter (*Lowell Pennyfeather*), Hiram Sherman (*Ogdon Quiler*), William Torpey (*Jethro Hancock*), Avon Long (*Jackson*), Ray Mayer (*Kenny*), Len Mence (*Beamish*), Seldon Bennett (*Schlessinger*), Bruce Evans (*Electrician*)

Two for the Show (1940)

Book: Nancy Hamilton, Richard Haydn. *Music*: Morgan Lewis. *Producers*: Gertrude Macy, Stanley Gilkey. *Directors*: John Murray Anderson, Joshua Logan. *Musical Director*: Robert Alton. *Stage Manager*: Kurt Steinbart. Opened February 8, 1940 at the Booth Theatre; closed May 25, 1940. 124 performances.

Cast: William Archibald, Eve Arden, Virginia Bolen, Frances Comstock, Norton Dean, Alfred Drake, Brenda Forbes, Nadine Gae, Willard Gary, Richard Haydn, Eunice Healy, Betty Hutton, Kathryn Kimber, Austine McDonnell, Dean Norton, Richard Smart, Robert Smith, Tommy Wonder, Keenan Wynn.

Let's Face It! (1941–43)

A musical comedy in two acts. *Book*: Herbert and Dorothy Fields, based on *The Cradle Snatchers*. *Music and Lyrics*: Cole Porter. *Director*: Edgar MacGregor. *Dances and Ensembles*: Charles Walters. *Musical Director*: Max Meth. *Settings*: Harry Horner. Costumes: John Harkrider. Opened October 29, 1941, at the Imperial Theatre. 263 performances.

Cast: Danny Kaye (*Jerry Walker*), Eve Arden (*Maggie Watson*), Benny Baker (*Frankie Burns*), Mary Jane Walsh (*Winnie Potter*), Vivian Vance (*Nancy Collister*), Jack Williams (*Eddie Hilliard*), Edith Meiser (*Cornelia Abigail Pigeon*), Joseph Macaulay (*Julian Watson*), James Todd (*George Collister*), Fred Irving Lewis (*Judge Henry Clay Pigeon*), Marguerite Benton (*Madge Hall/Vocalist*), Helene Bliss (*Helen Marcy/Vocalist*), Helen Devlin (*Dorothy Crowthers*), Lois Bolton (*Mrs. Fink*), Margie Evans (*Mrs. Wigglesworth*), Marion Harvey (*Molly Wincor*), Beverly Whitney (*Margaret Howard*), Jane Ball (*Ann Todd*), Sunnie O'Dea (*Muriel McGillicuddy*), Nanette Fabray (*Jean Blanchard*), Houston Richards (*Lt. Wiggins*), Betty Moran (*Gloria Gunther*), Miriam Franklin (*Sigana Earle*), William Lilling (*Master of Ceremonies*), Fred Nay (*Pvt. Walsh*), Kalita Humphreys (*Mrs. Wiggins/Anna*), Sally Bond (*Maid*), Henry Austin (*Phillip/Royal Guard*), Tony Caridi (*Jules/Royal Guard*), Mary Parker, Billy Daniel (*Dance Team*), Tommy Gleason, Ollie West, Roy Russell, Ricki Tanzi (*Royal Guards*), Janice Joyce, Beverly Whitney, Lisa Rutherford, Frances Williams (*Vocalists*), Billie Dee, Mary Ann Parker, Peggy Carroll, Sondra Barrett, Jean Scott, Jean Trybom, Marilynn Randels, Peggy Littlejohn, Pat Likely, Zynaid Spencer, Renee Russell, Pamela Clifford, Edith Turgell (*Guests*), Garry Davis, George Florence, Fred Deming, Dale Priest, Mickey Moore, Jack Riley, Joel Friend, Frank Ghegan, Randolph Hughes (*Selectees*)

Moose Murders (1983)

Writer: Arthur Bicknell. *Director*: John Roach. *Associate Producer*: Ricka Kanter Fisher. *Stage Manager*: Clifford Schwartz. *Costume Design*: John Carver Sullivan. *Scenic Design*: Marjorie Bradley Kellogg. Opened February 22, 1983, at the Eugene O'Neill Theatre; closed February 22, 1983. 1 performance.

Cast: Eve Arden* (*Hedda Holloway*), Mara Hobel (*Gay Holloway*), Dennis Florzak (*Sidney Holloway*), June Gable (*Snooks Keene*), Nicholas Hormann (*Nelson Fay*), Lisa McMillan (*Nurse Dagmar*), Don Potter (*Howie Keene*), Scott Evans (*Stinky Holloway*), Lillie Robertson (*Lauraine Holloway Fay*)

* *Replaced during previews by Holland Taylor.*

Bibliography

Books

Arden, Eve. *Three Phases of Eve: An Autobiography.* New York: St. Martin's, 1985.
Banfield, Stephen. *Jerome Kern.* New Haven: Yale University Press, 2006.
Barrios, Richard. *A Song in the Dark: The Birth of the Musical Film.* 2d ed. New York: Oxford University Press, 2010.
Bernds, Edward. *Mr. Bernds Goes to Hollywood: My Early Life and Career in Sound Recording at Columbia with Frank Capra and Others.* Lanham, MD: Scarecrow, 1999.
Billips, Connie, and Arthur Pierce. *Lux Presents Hollywood: A Show-by-Show History of the* Lux Radio Theatre *and the* Lux Video Theatre, *1934–1957.* Jefferson, NC: McFarland, 1995.
Bordman, Gerald. *Jerome Kern: His Life and Music.* New York: Oxford University Press, 1980.
Brooks, Tim, and Earle Marsh. *The Complete Directory to Prime Time Network and Cable TV Shows, 1946–Present.* 9th ed. New York: Ballantine, 2007.
Cain, James M. *The Postman Always Rings Twice, Double Indemnity, Mildred Pierce, and Selected Stories.* New York: Knopf, 2003.
Caspary, Vera. *The Secrets of Grown-Ups.* New York: Dodd, Mead, 1979.
Cox, Jim. *The Great Radio Sitcoms.* Jefferson, NC: McFarland, 2007.
Davis, Madelyn Pugh, with Bob Carroll, Jr. *Laughing with Lucy: My Life with America's Leading Lady of Comedy.* Cincinnati: Emmis, 2005.
Dunning, John. *Tune in Yesterday: The Ultimate Encyclopedia of Old-Time Radio, 1925–1976.* Englewood Cliffs, NJ: Prentice-Hall, 1976.
Erickson, Hal. *Syndicated Television: The First Forty Years, 1947–1987.* Jefferson, NC: McFarland, 1989.
Fidelman, Geoffrey Mark. *The Lucy Book: A Complete Guide to Her Five Decades on Television.* Los Angeles: Renaissance, 1999.
Garnett, Tay, with Fredda Dudley Balling. *Light Your Torches and Pull Up Your Tights.* New Rochelle, NY: Arlington House, 1973.
Goldberg, Lee. *Unsold TV Pilots, 1955 through 1988.* Jefferson, NC: McFarland, 1990.
Goldman, Herbert G. *Fanny Brice: The Original Funny Girl.* New York: Oxford University Press, 1992.
Gordon, Eric A. *Mark the Music: The Life and Work of Marc Blitzstein.* New York: St. Martin's, 1989.
Gordon, Max. *Max Gordon Presents.* New York: Bernard Geis, 1963.
Gordon, Ruth. *Over Twenty-One: A Comedy.* New York: Random House, 1944.
Gottfried, Martin. *Nobody's Fool: The Lives of Danny Kaye.* New York: Simon & Schuster, 1994.
Grossman, Barbara W. *Funny Woman: The Life and Times of Fanny Brice.* Bloomington: Indiana University Press, 1991.
Hadleigh, Boze. *Hollywood Gays.* New York: Barricade, 1996.
Hayter-Menzies, Grant. *Mrs. Ziegfeld: The Public and Private Lives of Billie Burke.* Jefferson, NC: McFarland, 2009.

Hyatt, Wesley. *A Critical History of Television's* The Red Skelton Show, *1951–1971*. Jefferson, NC: McFarland, 2004.
Inman, David M. *Performers' Television Credits, 1948–2000*. Jefferson, NC: McFarland, 2001.
_____. *Television Variety Shows: Histories and Episode Guides to 57 Programs*. Jefferson, NC: McFarland, 2006.
Jordan, Richard Tyler. *But Darling, I'm Your Auntie Mame! The Amazing History of the World's Favorite Madcap Aunt*. Santa Barbara, CA: Capra, 1998.
Kear, Lynn. *Kay Francis: A Passionate Life and Career*. Jefferson, NC: McFarland, 2006.
Kimbrough, Emily. *It Gives Me Great Pleasure*. New York: Dodd, Mead, 1948.
Kulzer, Dina-Marie. *Television Series Regulars of the Fifties and Sixties in Interview*. Jefferson, NC: McFarland, 1992.
Lax, Eric. *Conversations with Woody Allen: His Films, the Movies, and Moviemaking*. New York: Knopf, 2007.
Leonard, Sheldon. *And the Show Goes On: Broadway and Hollywood Adventures*. New York: Limelight, 1995.
LoMonaco, Martha Schmoyer. *Summer Stock: An American Theatrical Phenomenon*. New York: Palgrave Macmillan, 2004.
Lucas, Eddie. *Close-Ups: Conversations with Our TV Favorites*. Albany, GA: BearManor Media, 2007.
MacDougall, Ranald, edited with an introduction by Albert J. LaValley. *Mildred Pierce*. Madison: University of Wisconsin Press, 1980.
Maltin, Leonard, ed. *Leonard Maltin's Movie Encyclopedia*. New York: Plume, 1995.
McCaffrey, Donald W. *Bound and Gagged in Hollywood: Edmund L. Hartmann, Screenwriter and Producer*. Lanham, MD: Scarecrow, 2006.
Mordden, Ethan. *Sing for Your Supper: The Broadway Musical in the 1930s*. New York: Palgrave Macmillan, 2005.
Murray, Ken. *Life on a Pogo Stick: Autobiography of a Comedian*. Philadelphia: Holt, Rinehart & Winston, 1960.
Nachman, Gerald. *Right Here on Our Stage Tonight!: Ed Sullivan's America*. Berkeley: University of California Press, 2009.
Nadel, Norman. *A Pictorial History of the Theatre Guild*. New York: Crown, 1969.
Oppenheimer, George. *Here Today: A Comedy in Three Acts*. New York: Samuel French, 1940.
Parish, James Robert, and T. Allan Taylor. *Good Dames: Virtue in the Cinema*. South Brunswick, NJ: A.S. Barnes, 1974.
Sanders, Coyne Steven, and Tom Gilbert. *Desilu: The Story of Lucille Ball and Desi Arnaz*. New York: Morrow, 1993.
Santopietro, Tom. *Considering Doris Day*. New York: St. Martin's, 2007.
Sennett, Ted. *Warner Brothers Presents: The Most Exciting Years, from* The Jazz Singer *to* White Heat. New Rochelle, NY: Arlington House, 1971.
Sillman, Leonard. *Here Lies Leonard Sillman, Straightened Out at Last: An Autobiography*. New York: Citadel, 1959.
Strait, Raymond. *Bob Hope: A Tribute*. New York: Pinnacle, 2003.
Terrace, Vincent. *Fifty Years of Television: A Guide to Series and Pilots, 1937–1988*. New York: Cornwall, 1991.
Tucker, David C. *Shirley Booth: A Biography and Career Record*. Jefferson, NC: McFarland, 2008.
_____. *The Women Who Made Television Funny: Ten Stars of 1950s Sitcoms*. Jefferson, NC: McFarland, 2007.
Ware, Susan, ed. *Notable American Women: A Biographical Dictionary Completing the Twentieth Century*. Cambridge, MA: Belknap, 2004.
Wells, Jeff. *Jeff Chandler: Film, Record, Radio, Television and Theater Performances*. Jefferson, NC: McFarland, 2005.
Winer, Deborah Grace. *On the Sunny Side of the Street: The Life and Lyrics of Dorothy Fields*. New York: Schirmer, 1997.
Yanizyn, James Elliot. "The Mothers-in-Law: Historical Analysis of a Television Series." Thesis (M.S.) — San Diego State University, 1974.

Articles

Adams, Val. "A Recruit Discourses on TV Acting." *New York Times*, September 14, 1952.
_____. "She Likes School." *New York Times*, September 4, 1949.

Arden, Eve. "I'll Always Remember: The Audience That Sobbed." *Long Beach* (CA) *Independent Press-Telegram*, July 28, 1957.
_____. "People Appreciate Comedy." *Las Cruces* (NM) *Sun-News*, August 4, 1968.
Bawden, Jim. "Our Miss Arden." *Toronto Star*, February 2, 1991.
Belser, Emily. "'Lucy' and Murrow Win TV Emmys." *Cedar Rapids* (IA) *Gazette*, February 12, 1954.
"Blonde Avoids Dictates of Film Studio Contracts." *Los Angeles Times*, July 24, 1938.
Brady, Thomas F. "Hollywood Labor: Actors' and Directors' Guilds Caution TV Union Not to Transgress—Other Items." *New York Times*, March 26, 1950.
Campbell, Genie. "Not Easy to Outdo 'Papa's Picture.'" *Chicago Herald*, April 30, 1976.
"'Child Is Born' Cast All Wear Wedding Rings." *Panama City* (FL) *News-Herald*, January 29, 1940.
Coe, Richard L. "Dry-Voiced Arden Finally Gets Man." *Washington Post*, June 29, 1950.
Colander, Pat. "Eve Creates the Legends and Laughs." *Chicago Tribune*, February 14, 1975.
Colton, Helen. "All About Eve." *New York Times*, February 4, 1951.
Cone, Theresa Loeb. "Eve Arden Is Not Real 'Aunt Mame.'" *Oakland Tribune*, October 17, 1958.
Coons, Robbin. "Virginia Van Upp Is Proud." *Beatrice* (NE) *Daily Sun*, May 11, 1944.
Crosby, John. "Seeing Radio in Review." *Portsmouth* (OH) *Times*, October 28, 1947.
Daniels, Mary. "No Typecasting for 'Our Miss Brooks.'" *Chicago Tribune*, July 24, 1970.
"Divorce Won by Eve Arden." *Los Angeles Times*, July 27, 1947.
Dutton, Walt. "Eve Arden: Son-in-Law's Best Friend." *Los Angeles Times*, October 29, 1967.
Evans, Harry. "This Is 'Our Miss Brooks'—and Family." *Family Circle*, December 1953.
"Eve Arden Cavorts in a New Show." *TV Guide*, November 30, 1957.
"Eve Arden Out of Rut in New Warner Film." *Hayward* (CA) *Daily Review*, August 11, 1960.
Fessier, Michael, Jr. "Mrs. West of the Zucchini Patch." *TV Guide*, December 9, 1967.
Goldberg, Hyman. "Our Favorite Schoolmarm: Eve Arden." *Cosmopolitan*, June 1953.
Graham, Jefferson. "Classy Arden, TV's Model Working Woman." *USA Today*, November 13, 1990.
"Guest Stars: Proud Parents." *Syracuse Herald-Journal*, July 21, 1965.
Gwynn, Edith. "Cary Grant Turned Down 'Oscar' Role." *Wisconsin State Journal*, March 31, 1948.
Hopper, Hedda. "All About Eve." *Chicago Tribune Magazine*, February 21, 1960.
_____. "The Arden of Eve." *Chicago Tribune*, September 19, 1948.
Humphrey, Hal. "Eve Arden Holds Own Post-Mortem." *Oakland Tribune*, February 13, 1958.
Johnson, Erskine. "In Hollywood." *Gastonia* (NC) *Gazette*, April 21, 1950.
Johnson, Hazel. "Eve Arden Stays Busy Although Show Dropped." *Nevada State Journal*, September 23, 1958.
Kahn, Alexander. "Hollywood Film Shop." *Dunkirk* (NY) *Evening Observer*, December 18, 1940.
Knapp, Dan. "Eve Arden Knows Where Happiness Is At." *Los Angeles Times*, May 17, 1970.
Korman, Seymour. "Man Chaser Reforms!" *Chicago Tribune*, December 28, 1957.
Krebs, Albin. "Eve Arden, Actress, Is Dead at 83; Starred in TV's 'Our Miss Brooks.'" *New York Times*, November 13, 1990.
Lane, Lydia. "The Smooth-Sailing Eve Arden." *Los Angeles Times*, May 21, 1978.
Leonard, William. "Eve Arden Receives a Ringing Greeting, Warm 'Hello, Dolly!'" *Chicago Tribune*, June 14, 1966.
MacPherson, Virginia. "Eve Arden's Caustic Humor Pops Out Only in Her Films." *Long Beach* (CA) *Press-Telegram*, November 4, 1950.
Mantle, Burns. "Jerome Kern's Tunes Destined to Be Popular." *Chicago Tribune*, November 26, 1939.
Morris, Gary. "Forgotten Master: Gregory La Cava." *Bright Lights Film Journal*, #44, May 2004.
"Movie Rehearsal Latest Technique." *Cumberland* (MD) *Times*, July 10, 1960.
Nachman, Gerald. "Have Yourself a Merry Little Movie." *San Francisco Chronicle*, December 23, 1990.
Nadel, Norman. "A Producer Looks Back—and Ahead." *Frederick* (MD) *News-Post*, March 20, 1980.
"Noted Star to Open at Dufwin in Favorite." *Oakland Tribune*, January 26, 1929.
Page, Eleanor. "And the Stars Came Out." *Chicago Tribune*, January 14, 1968.
Reed, Rex. "Two Hot Mamas in Hot Water." *New York Times*, September 10, 1967.
Rickey, Carrie. "The Many Talents of Eve Arden." *Philadelphia Inquirer*, November 13, 1990.
Robertson, Campbell. "A Broadway Flop Again Raises Its Antlers." *New York Times*, April 21, 2008.
Scheuer, Philip K. "Eve Arden Wins 'Hover Girl' Title." *Los Angeles Times*, March 31, 1946.
_____. "Sillman's 'New Faces' Now Famous." *Los Angeles Times*, May 1, 1943.
Scott, Vernon. "Actress Won't Lose Her Identity." *Zanesville* (OH) *Times Recorder*, July 3, 1974.

_____. "Desi's Show: It's Corny, But Successful." *Long Beach* (CA) *Independent Press-Telegram*, February 4, 1968.
_____. "Eve Arden Finds Few People Understand." *Redlands* (CA) *Daily Facts*, November 26, 1960.
Shaffer, Rosalind. "Eenie, Meenie, Minie Mo—Here's Oscar." *Salt Lake Tribune*, March 3, 1946.
Shales, Tom. "TV Selling It Like It Is." *Los Angeles Times*, October 14, 1975.
Sharbutt, Jay. "Our Miss Brooks on Broadway." *Stars and Stripes*, February 4, 1983.
"She's a One-Man Woman." *TV Guide*, April 2, 1954.
Simpson, Peg. "Supporting Player Shares Honors in *Our Miss Brooks*." *Syracuse* (NY) *Post-Standard*, December 19, 1952.
Smith, Cecil. "Eve Arden Rated as Best Bet to Wear Lucille Ball's Abdicated Comedy Crown." *Los Angeles Times*, August 18, 1957.
_____. "Mame's Due! Life Begins!" *Los Angeles Times*, August 10, 1958.
Strauss, Theodore. "Easy Did It, For a Nice Change: The Career of *Let's Face It* Was Almost Casual From the Idea to the Subsequent Hit." *New York Times*, November 16, 1941.
"Teachers' Pet." *TV Guide*, May 1, 1953.
"The Theater: Stagestruck." *Time*, August 8, 1949.
Thomas, Bob. "Eve Arden Bids Farewell to Movies, Prefers Video." *Bakersfield Californian*, August 9, 1952.
_____. "The Fourth Phase of Eve Arden." *Paris* (TX) *News*, June 26, 1985.
_____. "Fred Allen Levels Blast at Favorite Target—Veeps." *Panama City* (FL) *News-Herald*, January 6, 1952.
Torre, Marie. "Eve Arden Plans to Quit *Our Miss Brooks* Role." *Oakland Tribune*, March 12, 1956.
Turner, Marjorie. "'Eve' Comes Naturally to Arden." *Syracuse* (NY) *Herald-Journal*, September 15, 1949.
Vadeboncoeur, Joan F. "June Gable's Serving Grits in 'Pump Boys.'" *Syracuse Herald-Journal*, April 26, 1984.
Von Blon, Katherine T. "Entente Seen as Beneficial." *Los Angeles Times*, August 9, 1931.
Warga, Wayne. "Three Roles for Eve Arden." *Los Angeles Times*, February 15, 1978.
West, Alice Pardoe. "Behind the Scenes." *Ogden* (UT) *Standard-Examiner*, April 22, 1951.
Wilson, Elizabeth. "Teachers' Pet." *Liberty*, February 1950.
Wolters, Larry. "Our Miss Brooks at Home." *Chicago Tribune Magazine*, October 18, 1953.
Zolotow, Sam. "'Brecht' Returns to Off Broadway; 'Unlimited Engagement' Set with Low Admission Scale; Eve Arden Wooed; Strasberg Explains." *New York Times*, June 27, 1963.

Websites

http://www.findagrave.com
http://www.imdb.com
http://www.newspaperarchive.com

Index

Numbers in *bold italics* indicate pages with photographs.

Abbott, Bud 113
ABC Afternoon Playbreak 175
The ABC Movie of the Week 175
Abel, Walter *93*, 95
Abrahams, Maurice 39
Absurd Person Singular 35
Academy Awards 13, 46, 82, 91
Ace, Goodman 12
Ackerman, Harry 171
Action in the North Atlantic 106
Adam's Rib 60
Adamson, Harold 79
The Addams Family 135
The Adventures of Marco Polo 53
The Adventures of Ozzie and Harriet 45, 145
The Adventures of Superman 80
Airplane! 136
Airplane II 137
Alan, Ray 174
Alda, Robert 19
Alice 35, 179
"Alice in Wonderland" 182
All in the Family 159, 162
All My Children 117
All My Darling Daughters 175
"All the Things You Are" 10
Allen, Fred 120–121
Allen, Woody 37, 103
Allgood, Sara 104
Allman, Elvia 144
Alsburg, Arthur 147
"Amateur Night" 6
The American Film Institute Salute to Barbara Stanwyck 183
American International Pictures 128
The Amos 'n' Andy Show 79, 167
Amsterdam, Morey 32
Anatomy of a Murder 29, 124–126
Anderson, Warner 92
The Andy Griffith Show 26, 106–107
Applause 35

Ardley Productions 29
Are You Being Served? 170
Arkin, Adam 135
Armster, Ann 22
Armster, Stanley 22
Arnaz, Desi 26, 31, 33–34, 35, 86, 102, 153, 159, 164, 166, 167
Arnaz, Desi, Jr. 159, 161, 164
The Arnelo Affair 43, 96–98
Arthur, Jean 33
Asher, William 171
Astaire, Fred 41
Astor, Mary 41
At the Circus 55, 56
Ates, Roscoe 69
Aumont, Jean-Pierre 99
Auntie Mame 28, 160
Avalon, Frankie 128
Averback, Hy 153, 155, 178
Ayckbourn, Alan 35–36
Azzara, Candy 136

"Babalu" 86
"Baby Snooks Goes Hollywood" 6
Bacon, Irving 61
Bacon, Lloyd 57
Baker, Belle 29
Baker, Benny 74
Baker, Jack 129
Ball, Lucille 9, 21, 24, 33, 47, 102, 167, 173
Ballard, Kaye 32–35, 136, 160, 162, 163, *166*, 181, 182
Bandbox Repertory Theatre 4, 90
Banks, Joan 119
Barefoot in the Park (play) 36
Barefoot in the Park (TV) 165
Barney Miller 131
Barrios, Richard 40
Barris, Chuck 174
Barry, Gene 25, 154, 156
Barrymore, John 13

Bartel, Paul 183
Bartlett, Sy 46
Barty, Billy 135
Basie, Count 78
Bates, Florence 141
Bedtime Story 64, 75–76, 94
Beekman Place 35
Begg, Jim 161
Benavente, Jacinto 5
Benchley, Robert 76, 85–86
Benedict, Billy 69
Bennett, Constance 50
Bennett, Joan 12, 69
Benny, Jack 95, 168, 169
Bergen, Edgar 9, 48, *49*, 168
Bergen, Edward (Ned) 9, 14, 15, 48, *95*, 100
Bergen, Liza 14
Berjer, Barbara 30
Berle, Milton 167
Berman, Pandro S. 68
Bernds, Edward 39
Berns, Larry 153
Best, Willie 59, 135
The Beverly Hillbillies 102, 155, 166
Bewitched (film) 97
Bewitched (TV) 107, 112, 153, 170–171
Bicknell, Arthur 36–37
Big Town 16
Big Town Czar 51–52, 72
Billingsley, Barbara 123
Biography 14
Birch, Patricia 137
B.J. and the Bear 179–180
Blair, June 124
Blitzstein, Marc 6
Blondell, Joan 133
Blue, Ben 44–46
Blyden, Larry 174
Blyth, Ann 13, *90*
Bob and Ray 168
The Bob Cummings Show 166

191

Bob Hope: A Tribute (Strait) 6
Bobby Vinton's Rock 'n' Rollers 179
Bogart, Humphrey 106
Bonanza 33
Bond, Ward 72
Bondi, Beulah 12, 15
Booth, Shirley 16, 119
Bordman, Gerald 10
Bound and Gagged in Hollywood (McCaffrey) 27
Bow, Clara 66
Bowman, Lee 108
Bracken, Eddie 168
The Brady Bunch 166
Brand, Neville 170, *171*
Brel, Jacques 173
Brennan, Eileen 136
Brennan, Walter 113
Brice, Fanny 6, 7, 181
Broadway Highlights 7, 138
Broderick, Helen 64
Brooke, Hillary 123
Brooks, Albert 87
Brophy, Edward 82
Brown, Gilmor 5
Brown, Vanessa *116*, 117
Bruce, Betty 167
Bryant, Nana 25, 153
Buchanan, Alice 4
The Bugs Bunny–Looney Tunes All-Star 50th Anniversary 182–183
Burke, Billie 5, 54
Burnett, Carol 111
Burns, George 182
Burton, Kate 182
Burton, Richard 182
Butterflies Are Free 35
Buttram, Pat 129
Buzzell, Eddie 56
Bygraves, Max 168
Byington, Spring 56
Byrnes, Edd 133

Cactus Flower 35
Cady, Frank 110, 117
Caesar, Sid *132*, 137
Cahn, Dann 34
Cahn, Sammy 94
Cain, James M. 90
Callahan, Mushy 107
Canova, Judy 6
Cantor, Eddie 12, 13
Carmel, Roger C. 34, 180
The Carol Burnett Show 111
The Carol Channing Show 31
Carr, Allan 132
Carrie 136
Carrillo, Leo 4
Carroll, Bob, Jr. 32, 34
Carroll, Earl 86
Carroll, Jean 168
Carroll, Joan 77
Carroll, Lewis 182
Carroll, Madeleine 119
Carson, Jack 14–*15*, 43, 47, 84, *108*
Carter, Ann 74
Carter, Jack 167

Casablanca 71
Caspary, Vera 117
Catlett, Walter 72
Caulfield, Maxwell 137
Cavett, Dick 167
CBS: On the Air 178
Champion, Gower 30
Chandler, Jeff 17, *18*, 23
Chaney, Lon, Jr. 70
Change of Heart 79
Channing, Carol 30, 180
Channing, Stockard 35, 179
Checkmate 169
Cher 182
A Child Is Born 56–58, 106, 170
Ching, William 25, 99, 153
Christie, Audrey 102
"Cinderella" 181–182
Citizen Kane 77
Claire, Ina 14
Clark, Dane 91, *106*
Clark, Fred 110, *129*
Climax! 168
Coca, Imogene 24
Cochran, Steve 94, 95
Cocoanut Grove 44–46, 169
Colby, Anita 82
Cole, Kay 32
The Colgate Comedy Hour 24
Colgate-Palmolive-Peet, Inc. 17
Collins, Ray 111, 112
"The Colonel's Lady" 29
Command Performance 13
Compton, Joyce 72, 76
The Computer Wore Tennis Shoes 131
Comrade X 62–63, 99
Conklin, Peggy *47*
Conn, Didi 137
Connelly, Joe 35
Conover, Harry 82
Conrad, Robert 174
Conried, Hans *173*
Considering Doris Day (Santopietro) 109
Conversations with Woody Allen (Lax) 37, 103
Conway, Tom *104*, 105
Cook, Mary Lou 70
Coppin, Grace 11
Corday, Mara 123
Corey, Wendell 15
The Corn Is Green 13
Costello, Lou 113
Cover Girl 80–82
Cowan, Lester 104
Cowl, Jane 15
CPO Sharkey 135
The Cradle Snatchers 11, 80
Crawford, Broderick 54
Crawford, Joan 2, 12, 14, 40–41, 46, 70, 85, 91, *118*, 119, 127, 181
Crenna, Richard (Dick) 17, *21*, 22–23, 25, 124, 150, 164, 174, 178, 182
Croft, Mary Jane 19, 22, 145, 167
Crosby, Bing 8
Cullen, Bill 169

"Cupid and Psyche" 5
The Curse of the Cat People 74
Curtain Call at Cactus Creek 88, 112–114, 182
Curtiz, Michael 96, 108

da Costa, Morton 28
Daigneau, Kenneth 4
Dana, Vic 30
Dancing Lady 5, 40–41
Dandridge, Dorothy 78
Daniels, Marc 102
The Danny Kaye Show 12–13, 94
The Danny Thomas Hour 171
Darin, Bobby 171
The Dark at the Top of the Stairs 29, 126–128
Dark Shadows 30
da Silva, Howard *116*, 117
Davenport, Harry *65*
Davidson, John 175
Davis, Bette 57, 181
Davis, Joan 13, 50
Davis, Madelyn 32, 33, 34
Davis, Rufe *45*
Davis, Stanley 14
Day, Doris 91, 107, 108, 109, *114*
Days of Our Lives 43
Deacon, Richard 34, 163
The Deadly Claw 123
Dean Martin Celebrity Roast 178
The Dean Martin Show 175
Deathtrap 102
De Carlo, Yvonne 80, 99
Dee, Frances 89
de Liagre, Alfred, Jr. 102
Demarest, William 122–123
DeMille, Cecil B. 9
Dennis, Patrick 36
Denny, Reginald 41
Desi Arnaz Productions 31
Desilu Productions 22, 31, 49
"Destry Has Ridden Again" 11
De Wolfe, Billy *114*
Dickinson, Angie 178
Dietrich, Marlene 11, 72
Dilson, John 50
The Dinah Shore Chevy Show 168
Donahue, Elinor 115
Double Indemnity 90
The Doughgirls 12, 82–84, 106, 112, 173, 183
Douglas, Melvyn *65*
Douglas, Mike 167
Douglas, Paul *120*
Douglas, Robert 110
Dracula's Daughter 57
Dragnet 147
Dragon, Carmen 82
Drake, Alfred 11
The Dream Merchants 100, 180–181
Drew, Ellen 46
Duffy, Henry 4
Duffy's Tavern 16
Dulcy 4
Dumont, Margaret 56
Dunning, John 17

Dunnock, Mildred 57
Durante, Jimmy 166
Dynasty II: The Colbys 137

Earhart, Amelia 50
Earl Carroll Sketchbook 87
Earl Carroll Vanities 74, 86–87
Ebsen, Buddy 6
Ebsen, Vilma 6
The Ed Sullivan Show 33, 168
The Ed Wynn Show 167
Eddie 135
Edwards, Cliff *61*
The Egg and I 103
Elinson, Jack 14
Ellerbe, Harry 14, 19
Ellery Queen 177–178
Ellington, Duke 125
Elliot, Laura 112
Elliott, Dick 69
Emerson, Hope 123
Emmy Awards 24, 27, 176
"Endlessly" 87
Estrada, Erik 179
Eternally Yours 54
Ettlinger, Don 16
The Eve Arden Show 1, 26–28, 76, 115, 156–158
"The Eve Arden Show" (1964 pilot) 30, 170
"The Eve Arden Show" (1965 pilot) 29
"The Eyes of Texas" 180

F Troop 160
Fabian 179
Fabray, Nanette 57
Faerie Tale Theater 181–182
Falcon Crest 37, 183
Falkenburg, Jinx 74, 82
Farnum, William 74
Farrell, Charles 95
Farrow, John 50
Father Knows Best 115
Fax, Jesslyn 148, 153
Faye, Alice 50
The FBI 33
Feld, Fritz 56
Ferber, Edna 44
Ferrer, Mel 103
Fidelman, Geoffrey Mark 34
Field, Betty 102
Field, Mary 123
Field, Sally 175
Fields, Joseph 83
Fields, W.C. 8
Fighting the Racketeers 52
Finkleman, Ken 137
Fisher, Carrie 135
Fitzgerald, Geraldine 57
Five 97
Flavin, James 104, 105
Flying High 178
Flynn, Joe 130, 131
Fogel, Jerry 175
Ford, Francis 74
Ford, Tennessee Ernie 168, 169
The Ford Show 169

The Forgotten Woman 52–54
Forte, Joe 16, 146
Foster, Donald 20
Foster, Preston 12
Foulger, Byron 121
Fowley, Douglas *59*
Francis, Arlene 30, 83
Francis, Kay 50
Frank, Louisa 3
Franken, Steve 29
Franklin, Bonnie 178
Frawley, William 110
Frazee, Jane 70
The Fredarrys 167
Freedley, Vincent 11
Freeman, Kathleen 139
Freleng, Friz 108
Freund, Karl 49
Friday the 13th 136
Friebus, Florida 182
Froman, Jane 6
Frost, David 167
Fulmer, Ray 28
Funicello, Annette 128

Gable, Clark 41, *62*, 127
Gable, June 37
Gabor, Zsa Zsa 22, 35, 121
Gallagher, Helen 64
The Game Game 174
Gardner, Ava 104
Garfield, John 47
Garland, Judy 134
Garnett, Tay 54, 59, 60
Garson, Greer 181
Gazzara, Ben 125
General Foods 22
Gentleman's Agreement 103
George, Gladys 57, 94
The George Burns and Gracie Allen Show (radio) 16
The George Burns and Gracie Allen Show (TV) 129, 167
The George Gobel Show 168
Gershe, Leonard 35
Gifford, Frances 43, *97*, 98
A Gift of Music 181
The Girl with Something Extra 175
"A Girl's Best Friend Is Wall Street" 68
Gobel, George 27, 168
Goldberg, Whoopi 135
Goldsmith, I.G. 117
Goldwyn, Samuel 12, 53–54, 80, 94
Gomer Pyle, U.S.M.C. 166
Goodbye Charlie 29
Goodbye, My Fancy 100, 117–119
Goodman, Dody 30, 133, 137
Goodner, Carol 12
Goodwin, Bill 115
Gordon, Eric A. 6
Gordon, Gale 16, *18*, 22, 24, 25, 129, *148*, 152, 154, 156, 167, 174, 179
Gordon, Max 9, 10
Gordon, Ruth 19, 20

Gordon, Virginia 16, 46
Gould, Sandra 153
Granger, Stewart 174
Grant, Cary 96
Grease 1, 36, 132–133, 178
Grease Day U.S.A. 178
Grease II 36, 136–138
"Great Detectives" 174
The Great Gildersleeve 16
Great Performances 182
Green, Karen 26
Green Acres 117, 129, 164
Greene, Lorne 181
Greer, Jane 85
Gregory, James 131
Grey, Virginia 71
Grey, Zane 74
Group Theatre 6
A Guide for the Married Woman 178
Gurie, Sigrid 53–54

Hairston, Jester 121
Haley, Jack 13
Hall, Thurston 69
Hamilton, Nancy 11
Hammerstein, Oscar, II 9, 10, 11
"Harlem Sandman" 78
Harry and Maggie 35, 177
Hart to Hart 35, 95, 180
Hartmann, Edmund L. 27
Hatch, Wilbur 32
Hausner, Jerry 117, 146, 161
Having Wonderful Time 9, 46–47
Hawaiian Eye 137
Haydn, Richard 11
Hayes, John Michael 20
Hayward, Susan 78, 79
Hayworth, Rita
Hazel 170
Heaven Can Wait 66
Heckart, Eileen 102, 127
Hellman, Sam 83
Hello, Dolly! 30–31
Hemmings, David 182
Henry Duffy Players, Inc. 4, 40
Hepburn, Katharine 9
Here Lies Leonard Sillman: Straightened Out at Last (Sillman) 5
Here Today 19, 21–22
Here's Lucy 145, 164, 173
"He's All Yours" 30, 169
Hey, Landlord! 33
Hi Jinx 74
Hilliard, Harriet *45*, 74
Hit Parade of 1943 78–79, 86, 102
Hoffman, Charles 102
Holden, Gloria 57
Holden, William 21
"Hollywood at Last" 168
Hollywood Life 138
Hollywood Music Box Theatre 5
The Hollywood Squares 167
Holm, Celeste 103
Hope, Bob 6, 13, 80, 177
Hopkins, Mary 174
Horton, Edward Everett 8, 42
Hour Magazine 182

Howard, Eugene 6
Howard, Shemp 70
Howard, Willie 6
Howe, Dorothy 45
Humphreys, Kalita 12
Hunter, Tab 136, 137
Hussey, Ruth 119, *122*
Hutton, Betty 11, 80

I Dream of Jeannie 52
I Love Lucy 22, 24, 26, 32, 49, 61, 84, 110, 117, 141, 144, 146, 155, 160, 161, 162, 167, 168
I Married a Monster from Outer Space 121
I Walked with a Zombie 89
In Name Only 174
Inge, William 29, 126
Inn, Frank 164
Irene 64
Isacksen, Peter 135
It Gives Me Great Pleasure (Kimbrough) 26
It's a Great Life 26
I've Got a Secret 169

The Jack Benny Program 167
James, Harry 12
Jerome Kern: His Life and Music (Bordman) 10
Joanie's Tea Room 13
Johnson, Nunnally 120
Johnson, Rita 68
The Johnson Wax Show with Fibber McGee and Molly 16
Jones, Dean 173
Joslyn, Allyn 26, 76, 110
"Julie" 167
Junior Miss 83

Kane, Carol 136
Kanin, Fay 119
Kanin, Garson
Karloff, Boris 80
Karnes, Robert *116*
Kasznar, Kurt *173*
Kaufman, George S. 44, 83
Kaye, Benjamin M. 60
Kaye, Danny 11, 12-13, 80, *93-95*, 168
Kearns, Joseph 124, 125, 140, 143, 146
Keaton, Buster *129*
Keeler, Ruby 64
Kelly, Patsy 64
Kendall, Kay 33
Kenton, Erle C. 39-40
Kern, James V. 83, 84
Kern, Jerome 9, 10
The Kid from Brooklyn 93-95
Kilgallen, Dorothy 168
Kimbrough, Emily 26
King, Freeman 135
Kiss Me Again 66
Klein, Larry 14
Knight, Shirley 127
Knotts, Don 35, *177*
Kober, Arthur 47

Kohner, Frederick 89
Kolb, Clarence 76, 94-95
Korman, Harvey 111
Kruger, Otto 81
Kullmann, Charles 99
Kulp, Nancy 155
Kulzer, Dina-Marie 16
Kurnitz, Harry 105

La Cava, Gregory 8, *43*, 44
The Lady Takes a Sailor 76, 109-110
The Lady Wants Mink 87, 121-123
Laemmle, Carl 181
La Jolla Playhouse 14, 15, 19
Lamarr, Hedy 63
Lamont, Charles 113
Lander, David L. 136
Land's End 31
Lane, Charles 46
Lanfield, Sidney 80
Lansbury, Angela 13, 127
Lansing, Joi 166
Lanza, Mario 126
Laramie 150
Laredo 170
Lassie 123
Last of the Duanes 72-74
Laugh with Ken Murray 7-8
Laurence, Paula 104
LaValley, Albert J. 90-91
Laverne & Shirley 136
Lavin, Linda 178
Lawrence, Gertrude 11
Lawrence, Vicki 111
Lax, Eric 37, 103
Leave It to Beaver 123
Lee, Billy *45*
Lee, Pinky *87*
Leeds, Andrea 44, 48
Le Gallienne, Eva 182
Leisen, Mitchell 29
Lemmon, Jack 110
Leonard, Robert Z. 68
Leonard, Sheldon 47, 147
Let's Face It (film) 79-80
Let's Face It (play) 11-12, 78, 80, 94, 168, 181, 186
The Letter 98
Letter of Introduction 9, 47-49, 108
A Letter to Three Wives 117
Lever Brothers 26
Lewis, Al 24, 147
Lewis, Cathy 24
Lewis, Elliott 21, 33, 167
Lewis, Jerry 112, 139
The Liberace Show 174
The Life and Legend of Wyatt Earp 27
Life Begins 57
Life on a Pogo Stick (Murray) 8
Light Your Torches and Pull Up Your Tights (Garnett) 60
Lights Out 97
The Lineup 154
Linkletter, Art 168
Little, Rich 181

Little Me 36, 88
Lloyd, Harold 94
Lloyd, Jeremy 170
Lloyd, Norman 15
Lockhart, Gene 123
Lombard, Carole 33
Lombardi, Ltd. 4
The Lone Star Ranger 74
Long, Audrey *85*
Lorring, Joan 13
"The Louella Parsons Story" 168
Love, American Style 174
"Love and the Contact Lens" 174
"Love and the New Roommate" 174
The Love Boat 35, 179
Low and Behold 5
Lubin, Arthur 52
Lubitsch, Ernst 66
Luce, Henry 119
The Lucy Book (Fidelman) 34
The Lucy Show 145, 159, 170
Lumet, Sidney 102
Lux Presents Hollywood (Billips) 9
The Lux Radio Theatre 9, 12, 44, 69, 119
Lynde, Paul 163
Lynn, Diana 103, 111
Lynn, Jeffrey 106
Lytess, Natasha 63

MacDougall, Ranald 91
Mack, Dick 12
MacLane, Barton 51-52, 72
MacMahon, Aline 57
MacMichael, Florence 28, 160, 165
MacMurray, Fred 45, 169, 183
Maher, Joseph 135, 182
Main, Marjorie 103
Maltin, Leonard 1, 37
The Man from U.N.C.L.E. 171
Mann, Delbert 127, 128
Manning, Irene *83*
Manpower 52, 72
The Many Loves of Dobie Gillis 29
Marbury, Elisabeth (Bessie) 10
March, Fredric *75*, 76
Margetts, Monty 166
Margie 127
Maricle, Marijane 35
Mark the Music: The Life and Work of Marc Blitzstein (Gordon) 6
Marks, Sherman 26
Marriage-Go-Round 28, 35
The Marriage of Kitty 4
Marsac, Maurice 142
Marshall, Penny 179
Martin, Dean 112, 175
Martin, Freddy 78
Martin, Mary 104
Martin, Steve 182
Martin, Tony 169
Marty 127, 128
Marx, Groucho *55*, 56
Marx, Harpo 56
Mary Hartman, Mary Hartman 136

The Mary Kaye Trio 168
Masquerade 182
Maude 35, 178
Max Gordon Presents (Gordon) 10
Maxwell, Roberta 35
Mayehoff, Eddie 30
Mayo, Virginia 94
McCaffrey, Donald W. 27
McCarthy, Joseph 125
McCarty, Mary 30
McCrary, Tex 74, 82
McCrea, Joel 89
McDonald, Grace 9
McGuire, Dorothy 126, 127
McHale's Navy 131
McKeon, Philip **180**
McKrell, Jim 174
McMartin, John 35
McMichael, Joe 70
McMichael, Judd 70
McMichael, Ted 70
McMillan, Gloria 17, *21*, 22, 25, 124
McQueen, Butterfly 90
"Meet Cyd Charisse" 169
Meet Me at Parky's 87
Meiser, Edith 80
Menjou, Adolphe 48, 108
Mercer, Frances 9
Merman, Ethel 10, 77
Merrick, David 35
The Merry Macs 70
Meyer, Torben 64
Mildred Pierce 1, 4, 12, 14, 40, 70, 85, 89–91, 103, 108, 111
The Milky Way 94
Miller, Ann 9, 35, 47
Miller, Nolan 179
Miller, Sidney 29
Minnelli, Vincente 10
The Miracle of Morgan's Creek 80
"Miss Grant Takes Richmond" 21
Mr. Bernds Goes to Hollywood (Bernds) 39
Mister Ed 160
Mitchell, James 169
Mitchell, Scoey 165
Mitchell, Shirley 163
Mohr, Gerald 142
Moltke, Alexandra 30
Mommie Dearest 14
Mona McCluskey 32
Monro, Matt 174
Monroe, Marilyn 63
Montez, Maria 99
Montgomery, George 74
Moore, Constance 87
Moore, Florence 60
Moore, Garry 169
Moose Murders 36–37, 186
The More the Merrier 84
Morgan, Dennis **109**
Morgan, Henry 169
Morgan, Jane 17, 22, 147
Morgan, Russ 7
Morris, Michael 162
Morris, Wayne 101

"Mother of the Bride" 175–176
The Mothers-in-Law 1, 21, 31–35, 129, 158–167, 172, 175
The Mothers-in-Law: Historical Analysis of a Television Series (Yanizyn) 32
The Movie Game 174
Murder, She Wrote 178
Murray, Bill 182
Murray, Ken 7, *8*
Mustin, Burt 140, 144
My Darling Daughters' Anniversary 175
My Dream Is Yours 19, 107–109
My Favorite Husband 16
My Friend Irma 24, 167
My Little Margie 76, 95, 113, 123
My Reputation 84, 91–93
My Sister Eileen 83
My Three Sons 84, 169
Myerson, Bess 169

Nabors, Jim 178
Nagel, Conrad 119
Naked City 52
Natural Ingredients 35
Neagle, Anna 64
Neill, Noel 80
Nelson, David 124
Nelson, Frank 143, 155
Nelson, Harriet *see* Hilliard, Harriet
Nelson, Ozzie 45, 165
Neumann, E. Jack 30
New Faces 5
Newton-John, Olivia 132, 137, 178
Nicoletti, Louis A. 149
Nicolosi, Joseph 104
Niesen, Gertrude 6
Night and Day 95–96
Ninotchka 63, 66
Niven, David 54
Nixon, Marni 167
No, No, Nanette 63–65, 115
Nolan, Jeanette 163
Norton, Jack 69, 82
Norvo, Red 168
Novello, Jay 160
Now You See Him, Now You Don't 131
Nurse Edith Cavell 64
Nuts and Bolts 181

O. Henry's Full House 121
Obliging Young Lady 69, 76–78
Oboler, Arch 97–98
O'Brien, Pat *59*
O'Connell, Arthur 125
O'Connor, Donald 24, 36, 88, 112, 113, 114, 136, 181, 182
Off the Air 138
Oh, Doctor 8, 41–42, 138
O'Keefe, Dennis 87, *122*, 123
Oliver, Edna May 175
Olsen, Moroni 90
One for the Book 103
One Touch of Venus 19, 103–105

O'Neil, Nance 5
Oppenheim, George 19
Our Miss Brooks (film) 25, 123–124
Our Miss Brooks (radio) 13, 16–19, 20, 22, 25–26, 105, 168
Our Miss Brooks (TV) 22–26, 28, 49, 99, 113, 121, 123, 124, 125, 126, 139–156, 164, 167, 171, 174, 178, 182
Ouspenskaya, Maria 136
Over Twenty-One 19
Overton, Frank **127**
Owen Marshall, Counselor at Law 176

Packard, Elon 14
Page, Gale 56
Paid in Full 103, 111–112
Paige, Robert 70
Paley, William 31
Palmer, Betsy 169
Palmer, Stuart 174–175
Panama Hattie 77
Pan-Americana 14, 69, 84–86, 91
Pandemonium 36, 88, 135–136
Parade 6, 185
Parke, Harry 87
Parker, Eleanor **101**, 102
Parker, Penney 127
Parkyakarkus 87
Pasadena Playhouse 5, 23
The Passion Flower 4
Password 167
Patrick, Gail 9, 79
Patrick, Lee 90
Patrick the Great 88–89, 91, 113
Pearl, Jack 167
Peary, Harold 12
Peck, Gregory 14
The People's Choice 164
The Perry Como Show 168, 169
Perry Mason 125
Petticoat Junction 45, 144
Peyton Place 112
Pfeiffer, Michelle 137
The Phil Harris–Alice Faye Show 16
The Philadelphia Story 66
Philips, Mary 57
Phyllis 140
Pickford, Mary 75
The Picture of Dorian Gray 13
Pierce, Arthur 9
The Pink Jungle 28
Pinocchio 61
Pitts, ZaSu 54, 64, 80, 115
Poltergeist 135
Porter, Cole 96
Porter, Don 124, *176*
Povah, Phyllis 80
Powell, Dick 107
Power, Tyrone 5
Preminger, Otto 29, 125
Presnell, F.G. 58
Pressman, Lawrence 35
Preston, Robert 126, 127
Previn, André 70

Previn, Charles 70
Price, Vincent 112
Prickett, Maudie 106–107
The Private Practice of Dr. Dana 17
Private Secretary 124
Procter & Gamble 32
Pryor, Roger 60–*61*
The Purple Rose of Cairo 37
"Pushin' Too Hard" 163

Quedens, Charles Peter 3
Quedens, Lucille Frank 3, 8
Quillan, Joe 147
Quine, Richard 9

Racket Squad 154
Radio Hall of Fame 17
A Rainy Day in Newark 30
Randolph, Isabel 25, 123, 140, 153, 155
Rash, Steve 135
Reagan, Ronald 101, 102
The Real McCoys 113
Red Channels 117
The Red Skelton Hour 169, 170, 171
The Red Skelton Show 168, 169
Reed, Alan 160
Reed, Rex 178
Regan, Phil 7
Reichard, Loise 47
Reid, Frances 43–44
Reiner, Rob 159
Reinhold, Judge 136
Reisch, Walter 99
Remick, Lee 125
Rettig, Tommy 123
Reubens, Paul 136
Revere, Anne 13, 91, 103
Rich, Frank 37
Ridgely, John 84, 92
Rimsky-Korsakov, Nikolai 98–99
The Road to Rome 15
Roberts, Florence 4
Roberts, Lynne 74
Roberts, Stanley 29
Robertson, Stuart 64
Rockwell, Robert 17, 23, 25, 156
Rogers, Buddy 74–75
Rogers, Ginger 9, 30, 120–121
Rogers, Kasey 112
Romero, Cesar 14, 131
Rosenbloom, "Slapsie" Maxie 50
Rowan & Martin's Laugh-In 171-173
"The Royal Follies of 1933" 171
Rubinstein, Zelda 135
Rudley, Herbert *31*, 32, *166*
Ruggles, Charlie 84
Run for Your Life 171
Ruskin, Shimen 47
Russell, Kurt 130, 131
Russell, Rosalind 2, 9, 28, 33, 119
Rutherford, Ann 71
Ryan, Peggy 88

Sahara Hotel, 29–30
Sakall, S.Z. 115
Saks, Sol 26
Salt, Jennifer *176*
San Antonio Rose 69–70, 113
Santley, Joseph 87
Santopietro, Tom 109
Savo, Jimmy 6
Scary Movie 136
Scott, Debralee 136
Scott, George C. 125
Scott, Lizabeth 2, 91, 111
Scott, Zachary *90*, 106
The Sealtest Village Store 13–15
"Secret Cinema" 183
The Seeds 163
Seiter, William A. 105
Send Another Coffin 60
"Send for the Militia" 6
Sentell, Alfred 46
Sergeant Deadhead 30, 128–129
77 Sunset Strip 127, 133
Shawn, Dick 168
She Couldn't Say No 60–62
She Knew All the Answers 68–69
"She Knew All the Answers" (radio) 12
Sheridan, Ann *83*
Sherman, Hiram 9, 10
Sherman, Ransom 107
Sherman, Vincent 100, 181
Sherwood, Robert E. 15
Shore, Dinah 24, 74
Shore, Pauly 135
"The Show-Off" 12
Shriner, Herb 167
Shubert, Lee 5
Shulton Company 26
Silla, Felix 135
Sillman, Leonard 5
Silvers, Phil 131
Sing for Your Supper 74–75
A Single Indiscretion 37
Singleton, Doris 12, 155, 156
Skelton, Red 47, 71, *172*
Slightly Honorable 58–60, 85
Smith, Alexis 61, *83*–84, 106
Smith, Howard 170
Smith, John 150
Smith, Kate 168
Smith, Leonard 17, 22, 124, 142, 150, 152
Smothers, Tom 136
The Smothers Brothers Comedy Hour 136
Son-in-Law 135
Son of Dracula 70
Sondheim, Stephen 10
A Song in the Dark: The Birth of the Musical Film (Barrios) 40
The Song of Love 4, 39–40
Song of Scheherazade 80, 98–99
Sothern, Ann 61
Spelling, Aaron 179
Stack, Robert 171
Stage Door 8–9, 42–44, 47, 79
"Stage Door" (radio) 9, 44
Stander, Lionel 12, 95

Stanwyck, Barbara 2, 91, *92*–93, 119, 183
Starlight Theatre 167
Stars in the Eye 167
Startime 169
"The Sterilization of Judy Simpson" 176
Steven Spielberg's Amazing Stories 183
Stevens, Connie 137
Stevens, Craig 84, 110
Stewart, Donald Ogden 66
Stewart, James 125, 178
Stewart, Nick 79, 102
Stigwood, Robert 132
Stoloff, Morris 82
Stone, Gail 26
Storch, Larry 160
Storm, Gale *113*
Strait, Raymond 6
Strangers on a Train 112
The Strongest Man in the World 35
Strudwick, Shepperd *116*
Stuart, Roy 166
Styne, Jule 79, 94
Sullavan, Margaret 102
Sullivan, Barry 14
Sullivan, Ed 51, 56, 168
Suspense 20–21
Sutton, Grady 69
Sweeney, Bob 25, 153

Tail Spin 50
"Take Him, He's Yours" 170
Talbott, Gloria 121
Tarantula 123
Taylor, Holland 37
Tea for Two 108, 114–115
Teasdale, Verree 94
Teatro Leo Carrillo 5
Ted Healy and His Stooges 41
Teichmann, Howard 30
Television Series Regulars of the Fifties and Sixties in Interview (Kulzer) 16
Temple, Shirley 102, 112
Tennille, Toni 167
Terry, Phillip 14, 69, 85
The Texaco Star Theater 22, 167
That Hagen Girl 102
That Uncertain Feeling 65–66, 99
That's My Man 126
This Is Your Life 174
Thomas, Danny *173*
Thompson, Kay 5
Thompson, Maury 34, 159
Thorn, Bert 20
Three Husbands 77, 115–117
Three Phases of Eve (Arden) 2, 37
Thuna, Lee 35
Tibbles, George 35
Titanic 99
"To a Skylark" 11
The Toast of the Town 168
Tone, Franchot 12, 69
The Tony Awards 176–177, 180
Topper 123
Traver, Robert 125

Travolta, John 137, 178
Treen, Mary 79
Trouble in Paradise 66
Truex, Ernest 71, 85
Tugend, Harry 80
Tully, Tom 110
Tune In Yesterday (Dunning) 17
Turner, Lana 67
Turney, Catherine 4, 90–91
Twenty Million Sweethearts 107
Two and a Half Men 37
Two for the Show 11, 186

Under Papa's Picture 35
Under the Rainbow 133–135
The Unfaithful 98, 100
The Untouchables 171
Up in Arms 12

Vacation Playhouse 30, 169
Vague, Vera 158
Valdes, Miguelito 86
Vallee, Rudy 7, 8, 13, 168
Valley Music Theater 30
Vance, Vivian 102
Van Druten, John 102
Van Patten, Dick 130
Van Upp, Virginia 81
Vega$ 169, 179
Veidt, Conrad 71
Venuta, Benay 28
Vera, Ricky 25, 150, 151, 153
Vera-Ellen 94
A Very Missing Person 174–175
Very Warm for May 9–11, 185–186
Voelker, John D. 126

The Voice of the Turtle 100–103, 127
Vonn, Veola 155

Walburn, Raymond 80
Wallace, Richard 69
Walley, Deborah 32, 129
Wallis, Hal B. 112
Walters, Charles 5
Walton, Francis 50
Wanamaker, Sam 119
Warner, Jack 2, 12, 102
Warner Bros. 12, 50, 82, 83, 92, 119, 127
Warrick, Ruth 77, *116*, 117
Warwick, Dionne 181
Weinrib, Lennie 30
Welch, Joseph N. 125
"The Well-Dressed Corpse" 20–21
Welles, Orson 178
We're Not Married! 119–121, 174
West, Brooks 2, 19–20, 21–22, 24, *28*, 29, 35, 37, 125–126, 162
West, Connie 15, 30
West, Douglas Brooks 24
West, Duncan Paris 24
Westley, Helen 76
What's It All About, World? 173
What's My Line? 83, 167
When a Stranger Calls 136
Whiplash 105–107
The Whistler 16
Whistling in Brooklyn 71
Whistling in Dixie 71
Whistling in the Dark 70–71
Wilcox, Frank 102
Wilcox, Herbert 64

Williams, Cindy 178
Williams, Emlyn *116*
Wilson, Don 95
Wilson, Marie 24
Wingo 27
Wings 74
Winslowe, Paula 146
Winston, Harry Leon 41
Winter, Dale 4
Wish You Were Here 47
The Wizard of Oz 134
The Wolf Man 70, 136
A Woman's Face 71
The Women 80
Women in the Wind 49–50
Women's Christian Temperance Union 3
Wonderful Town 30
Wright, Teresa 168
Wyman, Jane 2, 37, *83*–84, 91, 102, *109*, 183
Wynn, Ed 168
Wynn, Keenan 11

Yanizyn, James Elliot 32, 33
Yarnell, Lorene 173
Young, Loretta 24, 54, 57, *75*, 76
Young, Roland 64
Your Show of Shows 133

Ziegfeld, Florenz 66, 177
Ziegfeld Follies of 1934 5–6, 68, 176, 181, 185
Ziegfeld Follies of 1936 6–7, 68, 176–177, 181, 185
Ziegfeld Girl 40, 66–68, 125
Zimbalist, Efrem, Jr. 127

www.ingramcontent.com/pod-product-compliance
Ingram Content Group UK Ltd.
Pitfield, Milton Keynes, MK11 3LW, UK
UKHW050525150426
5217IPUK00026B/1803